THE DEVELOPMENT OF THE PAPACY

THE DEVELOPMENT OF THE PAPACY

by

H. BURN-MURDOCH

LL.D. Cantab.

FABER & FABER LIMITED
24 Russell Square
London

First published in mcmliv
by Faber and Faber Limited
24 Russell Square, London, W.C.1
Printed in Great Britain by
Western Printing Services Limited, Bristol

Domine Jesu Christe, qui dixisti Apostolis tuis Pacem relinquo vobis, pacem meam do vobis; ne respicias peccata mea, sed fidem Ecclesiae tuae: eamque secundum voluntatem tuam pacificare et coadunare digneris: Qui vivis et regnas Deus per omnia saecula saeculorum. Amen.

Preface

Some excuse is needed for adding another volume to the hundreds that have been written to support or oppose the Doctrine of the Papacy. *A priori* reasoning is often used, but historical proof has been appealed to chiefly. The great *Dogmatic Constitution on the Church*, declared at the Vatican Council in 1870, is expressly based on its appeal to 'the ancient and constant faith of the Church'. This book attempts to follow out that appeal by examining the evidence of the words and actions of the leaders of the Church, century by century, stage by stage. We cannot interrogate the Fathers and hear their answers to questions that we should dearly like to ask, but we may gain from their writings some knowledge of what their answers would have been.

Many devout and able men have been ranged on each side of the controversy. This is an attempt to set the opposing views and arguments side by side, in a method not so much controversial as (to coin a word) ambiversial. A whole-hearted pursuit of truth calls for the scrutiny of every fact, and the weighing of every serious argument, opposed to the opinion towards which the searcher inclines.[1] The book is offered to the searcher; it is not its purpose to disturb the belief of anyone who is fully assured that he has already found the truth.

The literature and records of the centuries are a vast quarry. For this book, the choice of matter is predetermined. As far as possible, every event or writing relied upon by advocates for either side must be set out, at least in summary. (I would here acknowledge indebtedness to Mr C. F. B. Allnatt's *Cathedra Petri* for its valuable collection of quotations from the Fathers.) In appeals to the teaching of the Fathers, however, different selections of quotations are often made from their writings to accompany the different arguments advanced.

[1] 'We are not sure we are right until we have made the best case possible for those who are wrong.' (Lord Acton, *Letters*, p. 154.)

Here I have sought to combine and complete the relevant quotations from each Father in order to gain a true understanding of his mind.

The arguments on each side must be stated separately from the facts; I have tried to present the views and arguments advanced by the best writers, often quoting their own words. Where a fact or event is likewise in dispute, the conflicting versions of it must be stated.

The history of the Church throughout the centuries is crowded with event. In this study of the development of the Papacy, century by century, there must be frugality of treatment; matters that do not affect the central inquiry must be left out, however interesting in themselves. One great question is central and vital, and the reader will have it always in mind: Are the distinctive doctrines defined in the *Dogmatic Constitution* part of the divinely-revealed truth which every Christian is bound to accept and believe? Many able and sincere writers have confidently answered that question in the affirmative, many others in the negative. The letters A and N are used in this book to distinguish conveniently the views and arguments on the Affirmative side (the Ayes) from those on the Negative (the Noes). (They may be weighed against each other as if they were set in parallel columns.) This somewhat academic approach will not conceal from the understanding reader the gravity of the question in issue.

It is here attempted to present the whole inquiry intelligibly before the English reader of ordinary education, who claims no special historical knowledge, and who cannot devote years to libraries of history and controversy.

'So long as it was a question of affirming or denying that St Peter occupied the same position in the Apostolic Church as a mediaeval or modern Pope in a vastly different ecclesiastical system, rational discussion was ruled out and controversialists were reduced to blind affirmations of faith in their contradictory interpretations of the same texts. Once it is seen that the question at issue is rather whether the Vatican Decrees are a true growth or a deviation from whatever Petrine primacy can be discerned in the New Testament, the dispute becomes worth while. It is too much to expect immediate agreement; but we can at least look forward to an argument in which the protagonists are fighting on the same plane.'[1] It might even be discovered more exactly where Christian beliefs divide. As between two men, or groups of men, both of whom hold firmly to the Catholic Creeds, at what

[1] Rev. T. M. Parker in *Laudate* for December, 1945 (vol. xxiii, No. 80, at pp. 68–9), in an article on 'The Papal Question Today', being a review of Dr Jalland's *The Church and the Papacy*.

exact point begins the cleavage of belief regarding the Doctrine of the Papacy? Where does the path of understanding bifurcate and lead some to Rome, others away from it? Is it perhaps a divergence as to what is meant by 'Tradition' (see chapter LXXII(ii), or as to the title, the Vicar of Christ, and its implications (see chapter VI)? Ought we to acknowledge the terse logic of Duns Scotus—*Potuit, decuit, ergo fecit*, 'God is all-powerful, it was meet and necessary that this should be ordained, therefore He did so ordain'?

The best justification for this book is its new method of approach. To follow out that method through all the wilderness of history and the welter of debate has been a difficult task, but one that has cried out to be undertaken. Someone better qualified than I may, perhaps, adopt the method and do better with it. Ideally, the statements of fact ought to be drawn up by a joint committee of scholars representing opposite views; they would divide into groups to formulate their arguments.

I have tried to state all facts accurately and to set out fairly the strongest arguments on each side. As was once said by an able and candid scholar[1] of great charm, 'I have done my best to be careful and fair, I dare say with imperfect success'. But I cannot be too grateful for help that has been given me. I am greatly indebted, in the first place, to the Rev. R. Cant of Cambridge, formerly Vice-Principal of St Chad's College, Durham, for a critical reading of the whole typescript, and to the Rev. T. M. Parker of Oxford, for valuable constructive criticisms and suggestions. Then, being particularly anxious for a fair and forcible presentation of the 'Affirmative' position, I am extremely grateful for generous help from that side, and in particular from one who stands high both in the Church and in scholarship. It has enabled me to correct some errors, to re-word many statements and phrases, and to amplify and strengthen the arguments on the 'A' side. But the whole responsibility for the book rests on me.

With the kind permission of the Right Rev. Abbot of Downside, Messrs Longmans, Green and Co., and Messrs Sheed and Ward, I have included Abbot Chapman's exposition from Scripture of the pre-eminence of St Peter, and also some of his translations of passages from St Chrysostom. Passages from Eusebius' *Ecclesiastical History* are quoted in the translation of Dr H. J. Lawlor and Dr J. E. L. Oulton by kind permission of the S.P.C.K.

A source-book, *Documents Illustrating Papal Authority A.D. 96–454*, has now been published by S.P.C.K. since this book was written, and will be found very useful.

[1] Abbot John Chapman, O.S.B., *Studies on the Early Papacy*, p. 185.

Contents

PART I

INTRODUCTORY

PART II

THE FIRST TWO CENTURIES

PART III

THE THIRD CENTURY

PART IV

THE FOURTH CENTURY

PART VI

THE EAST UNTIL SEPARATION FROM THE WEST

PART VII

THE WEST UNTIL SEPARATION OF THE EAST, A.D. 1054

CONTENTS

PART VIII

THE PAPACY AFTER SEPARATION OF THE EAST

PART IX

THE NINETEENTH, THE CENTURY OF DEFINITION

CONTENTS

PART VIII

THE PAPACY AFTER SEPARATION OF THE EAST

PART IX

THE NINETEENTH, THE CENTURY OF DEFINITION

Abbreviated References used in the Notes

Acta Trid.	Acta authentica Concilli Tridentini, ed. Augustin Theiner, Zagrabiae Croatiae, 1874
Acton, *Letters*	Lord Acton, *Letters to Mary, daughter of the Rt Hon. W. Gladstone*, 1913
„ *Correspondence*	Lord Acton, *Selections from the correspondence of the first Lord Acton*, 1917
„ *Hist. Freedom*	Lord Acton, *The History of Freedom and other Essays*, 1907
Allnatt	C. F. B. Allnatt, *Cathedra Petri*, 3rd ed. 1883
Aquinas, *Summa*	St Thomas Aquinas, *Summa Theologica*, Paris, 1652
„ *Opuscula*	St Thomas Aquinas, *Opuscula omnia*, Paris, 1656
„ *Opp.*	St Thomas Aquinas, *Omnia opera*, Venice, 1775
Athan., St	St Athanasius, *Opera*, Benedictine ed., Paris, 1698
Augustine, St	*Opera*, Benedictine ed., Paris, 1679–1700; also *PL* xxxii–xlvi
Bardenhewer	Prof. Otto Bardenhewer, *Patrology*, auth. E.T., T. J. Shahan, D. D. Frieburg im Breislau, 1908
Barnes, *CR*	Mgr A. S. Barnes, *Christianity at Rome in the Apostolic Age*, 1938
„ *Mon.*	Mgr A. S. Barnes, *The Early Church in the Light of the Monuments*, 1913
Baronius	Cardinal Caesar Baronius (1538–1607), *Annales Ecclesiastici*, Antwerp, 1612–29
Barraclough	Geoffrey Barraclough, *Papal Provisions*, 1935

ABBREVIATED REFERENCES USED IN NOTES

Basil, St	St Basil the Great, *Opera*, Benedictine ed., Paris, 1721–30
Batiffol, *PC*	Mgr Pierre Batiffol, Litt.D., *Primitive Catholicism*, auth. E.T., 1911
,, *C.&P.*	Mgr Pierre Batiffol, Litt.D., *Catholicism and Papacy; some Anglican and Russian Difficulties*, auth. E.T., 1925
Belloc	Hilaire Belloc, *How the Reformation Happened*, 1928
Benson	Abp E. W. Benson, *Cyprian: his Life: his Times: his Work*, 1897
Bettenson	Henry Bettenson, *Documents of the Christian Church*, Oxford, 1943
Bévenot	Maurice Bévenot, S.J., *St Cyprian's De Unitate*, 1938
Bingham	Rev. Joseph Bingham (1668–1723), *Origines Ecclesiasticae* or *The Antiquities of the Christian Church*, ed. 1840
Bottalla	Paulo Bottalla, S.J., *The Pope and the Church*, 1868
Bright	Canon William Bright, D.D., *Chapters of Early English Church History*, 3rd ed., Oxford, 1897
Brodrick	James Brodrick, S.J., *Robert Bellarmine, 1542–1621*, 1950
Butler	Abbot Cuthbert Butler, O.S.B., *The Vatican Council*, 1930
Cano	Bp F. Melchior Cano (1509–60) *De Locis theologicis*, *Opera*, Cologne, 1605
Cath. Enc.	*The Catholic Encyclopaedia*, 16 vols., New York, 1907–14
Chapman, *GCC*	Abbot John Chapman, O.S.B., *Bishop Gore and the Catholic Claims*, 1905
,, *FEGC*	Abbot John Chapman, O.S.B., *The First Eight General Councils and Papal Infallibility*, 1906
,, *Honorius*	Abbot John Chapman, O.S.B., *The Condemnation of Pope Honorius*, 1907
,, *Studies*	Abbot John Chapman, O.S.B., *Studies on the Early Papacy*, 1928

ABBREVIATED REFERENCES USED IN NOTES

Chrysostom, St	St John Chrysostom, *Opera*, Benedictine Ed., Paris, 1718
Clarke	W. K. Lowther Clarke, D.D., *The First Epistle of Clement to the Corinthians*, 1937
CMH	Cambridge Mediaeval History
Codex J.C.	*Codex Juris Canonici*, Rome, 1934
Coll. Avell.	*Collectio Avellana; Epistolae imperatorum etc.*, ed. Otto Günther, Vienna, 1895–8
Conway	Bertrand L. Conway, C.S.P., *The Question Box*, 2nd ed., New York, 1929
Corpus J.C.	*Corpus Juris Civilis Romani*, ed. Krüger, vols. I and II, Berlin, 1877, vol. III (Novellae), ed. Schöll, Berlin, 1895
Creighton	Bp M. Creighton, *History of the Popes*, ed., 1897
Cyril, St	St Cyril of Alexandria, *Opera*, ed. Aubert, Paris, 1638
Davenport	E. H. Davenport, *The False Decretals*, Oxford, 1914
DCB	W. Smith, D.D. and Henry Wace, D.D., *Dictionary of Christian Biography*, 1877
Denny	Rev. Edward Denny, *Papalism: a treatise on the Claims of the Papacy as set forth in the Encyclical Satis Cognitum*, 1912
Denzinger	Henricus Denzinger, *Enchiridion symbolarum et definitionum*, ed. 18–20, Freiburg, 1932
Dogm. Const.	'Pastor aeternus', the *First Dogmatic Constitution on the Church of Christ*, declared by Pope Pius IX at the Vatican Council, 1870 (Latin and English in Butler, vol. II, tr. in *The Decrees of the Vatican Council*, by Fr V. McNabb, O.P., 1907, also in *Rome and Reunion*, by Fr E. C. Messenger, 1934)
Döllinger, *FA*	J. J. I. von Döllinger, D.D., *The First Age of Christianity and the Church*, E.T. 3rd ed., 1877
,, *Hist.*	J. J. I. von Döllinger, D.D., *A History of the Church*, E.T., E. Cox, D.D., 1840

Duchesne, *CS*	Mgr Louis Duchesne, Litt.D., *The Churches Separated from Rome* (Paris, 1896), auth. E.T., 1907
„ *EH*	Mgr Louis Duchesne, Litt.D., *Early History of the Christian Church to the end of the Third Century*, E.T., 1909
„ *CW*	Mgr Louis Duchesne, Litt.D., *Christian Worship*, E.T., 5th ed., 1919, tr. from the 4th ed.
„ *BTS*	Mgr Louis Duchesne, Litt.D., *The Beginnings of the Temporal Sovereignty of the Popes*, A.D. 754–1073, auth. E.T., 1908
Dvornik	Francis Dvornik, D.D., *The Photian Schism, History and Legend*, 1948
Enc. Brit.	*Encyclopaedia Britannica*, 11th ed., London, 1910, new ed., Chicago, 1948
Euseb.	Eusebius Pamphili, Bp of Caesarea (*c.* 260–340), *Ecclesiastical History*, ed. E. Burton, Oxford, 1838, E.T., Lawlor and Oulton
Evagrius	Evagrius Scholasticus (*c.* 537–594), *Ecclesiastical History*, E.T., Bohn, 1854
Every	George Every, S.S.M., *The Byzantine Patriarchate*, 451–1204, 1947
Fessler	Bp Joseph Fessler, *The True and the False Infallibility of the Popes*, 1875
Fleury	Abbot Claude Fleury (1640–1723), *Histoire Ecclésiastique*, Paris, 1752–61
Fortescue, *OEC*	Adrian Fortescue, Ph.D., D.D., *The Orthodox Eastern Church*, 1907
„ *UEC*	Adrian Fortescue, Ph.D., D.D., *The Uniate Eastern Churches*, 1923
Funk	Prof. F. X. Funk, *A Manual of Church History*, E.T. by W. H. Kent, O.S.C., 1914
Gibbon	Edward Gibbon, *Decline and Fall of the Roman Empire*, ed. J. B. Bury, 1909
Gratian	*Decretum Gratiani*, ed. Turin, 1620.
Gregory Naz., St	St Gregory Nazianzen, *Opera*, Benedictine ed., Paris, 1609
Hardouin	Jean Hardouin, S.J. (1646–1729) *Acta Conciliorum, etc., usque ad* 1714, Paris, 1715

ABBREVIATED REFERENCES USED IN NOTES

Hefele	Bp K. J. Hefele, *History of the Christian Councils*, E.T., 1871–96
Henderson	E. F. Henderson, Ph.D., *Select Historical Documents of the Middle Ages*, 1892
Hergenröther	Cardinal Hergenröther, *Anti-Janus*, E.T., Dublin, 1870
Hinschius	Paul Hinschius, *Decretales Pseudo-Isidorianae*, Lipsiae, 1863
Hughes	Rev. P. Hughes, L.S.H., *A History of the Church*, 1934–47
Hull	Robert Hull, S.J., *Medieval Theories of the Papacy*, 1934
Humphrey	William Humphrey, S.J., *The Divine Teacher*, 5th ed., 1885
Iren., St	St Irenaeus of Lyons, *Treatise Against the Heresies*, Cambridge, 1857, E.T., A. Roberts, D.D., Clark's Ante-Nicene Lib.
Jalland, *Leo*	T. G. Jalland, D.D., *The Life and Times of St Leo the Great*, 1941
,, *CP*	T. G. Jalland, D.D., *The Church and the Papacy*, 1944
James	M. R. James, Litt.D., *The Apocryphal New Testament*, 1924
Johnson	Mgr Vernon Johnson, *One Lord, One Faith*, 1929
Kidd, *CR*	B. J. Kidd, D.D., *The Counter-Reformation 1550–1600*, 1933
,, *RP*	B. J. Kidd, D.D., *The Roman Primacy to A.D.* 461, 1936
,, *DI*	B. J. Kidd, D.D., *Documents Illustrative of the History of the Church*, 1938–41
Labbe	P. Labbe and G. Cossart, *Sacrosancta concilia ad an* 1664, Paris, 1672
Lawlor and Oulton	H. J. Lawlor, D.D. and J. E. L. Oulton, B.D., *Ecclesiastical History of Eusebius*, tr. and notes, 1927–8
Lebreton and Zeiller	Julius Lebreton, S.J. and Jacques Zeiller, *The History of the Primitive Church*, auth. E.T., 1942–7
Liber Pont.	*Liber Pontificalis*, ed. L. Duchesne, Paris, 1886–92

Lightfoot, *Clem.*	Bp J. B. Lightfoot, *The Apostolic Fathers*, Pt. I, 1890
,, *Ign.*	Bp J. B. Lightfoot, *The Apostolic Fathers*, Pt. II, 1889
,, *Diss.*	Bp J. B. Lightfoot, *Dissertation on the Christian Ministry* in Comm. on *Galatians*, 2nd ed. rev. 1866
McNabb	Vincent McNabb, O.P., *Infallibility*, 1927
Maistre	Count J. de Maistre, *The Pope* (1817), E.T., 1850
Mann	Mgr Horace Mann, *Lives of the Popes: in the Early Middle Ages*, 1902–32
Manning, *OCI*	Cardinal H. E. Manning, *The Oecumenical Council and the Infallibility of the Roman Pontiff*, 1869
,, *VCD*	Cardinal H. E. Manning, *The Vatican Council and its Definitions*, 1870 (Both reprinted as *Petri Privilegium*, 1871)
,, *TMHG*	Cardinal H. E. Manning, *The Temporal Mission of the Holy Ghost*, 4th ed., 1892
Mansi	Abp J. D. Mansi (1692–1769), *Sacrorum conciliorum collectio* (Florence and Venice), 1759–98; facsim. reprint and contin. to 1870 ed. Martin and Petit, Paris, 1901–27
Maritain	Jacques Maritain, *The Things that are not Caesar's*, 1930
Martin	E. J. Martin, D.D., *A History of the Iconoclastic Controversy*, 1930
Maycock	A. L. Maycock, M.A., *The Inquisition*, 1926
MBVP	*Maxima Bibliotheca Veterum Patrum*, Lugduni, 1677
Messenger	Rev. E. C. Messenger, Ph.D., *Rome and Reunion*, 1934
Milman	H. H. Milman, D.D., *History of Latin Christianity*, 4th ed., 1867
Mirbt	D. Carl Mirbt, *Quellen zur Geschichte des Papsttums und des romische Katholizismus*, 4th ed., Tübingen, 1924
Newman, *Arians*	Cardinal J. H. Newman, *The Arians of the Fourth Century*, 4th ed., 1876

ABBREVIATED REFERENCES USED IN NOTES

Newman, *Development*	Cardinal J. H. Newman, *Essay on the Development of Christian Doctrine*, 1st ed., 1845, new ed., 1878
Nicephorus	Callistus Xantopulus Nicephorus (fl. 1320–30), *Historia Ecclesiae*, Paris, 1630
Nielsen	Bp Fredrik Nielsen, *The History of the Papacy in the XIXth Century*, E.T., 1906
Origen	Origenis, *Opera Omnia*, Paris, 1733–59
Pastor	Dr Ludwig Pastor, *The History of the Popes* (1305–1732), tr. by F. I. Antrobus, 1891–8
Pears	Sir Edwin Pears, *The Destruction of the Greek Empire and the Capture of Constantinople by the Turks*, 1903
Perrone	Giovanni Perrone, S.J., *Praelectiones Theologicae*, 1841
PG	J. P. Migne, *Patrologia Graeca*, 166 vols, Paris, 1857–66
PBLPB	J. R. Palanque, G. Bardy, P. de Labriolle, G. du Plinval and Louis Brehier, *The Church in the Roman Empire*, tr. E. C. Messenger, Ph.D., vol. I, 1948, vol. II, 1952 (paging continuous)
PL	J. P. Migne, *Patrologia Latina*, 221 vols, Paris, 1844–64
Puller	F. W. Puller, S.S.J.E., *The Primitive Saints and the See of Rome*, 3rd ed., 1914
Pusey	Rev. E. B. Pusey, D.D., *Eirenicon, Part II* ('First Letter to Newman'), 1869
Ramsay	Sir W. M. Ramsay, *St Paul the Traveller and the Roman Citizen*
Ranke	Leopold von Ranke, *The History of the Popes during the Last Four Centuries*, E.T., 1908
Raynaldus	Odoricus Raynaldus, *Annales Ecclesiastici* (1198–1534), Lucca, 1748
Rivington, *PC*	Rev. Luke Rivington, D.D., *The Primitive Church and the See of Peter*, 1894
„ *Auth.*	Rev. Luke Rivington, D.D., *Authority*, 1888
„ *Dust.*	Rev. Luke Rivington, D.D., *Dust, a letter to the Rev. C. Gore*, 1888

ABBREVIATED REFERENCES USED IN NOTES

Rivington, *RP*	Rev. Luke Rivington, D.D., *The Roman Primacy, A.D.* 430–451, 1899
Robertson	A. Robertson, D.D., *Regnum Dei* (Bampton Lectures), 1901
Roy	Jules Roy, *Saint Nicholas I*, auth. tr. M. Maitland, 1901
Ryder	Rev. H. I. D. Ryder, *Catholic Controversy*, 3rd ed., 1882
Salembier	L. Salembier, *The Great Schism of the West*, auth. tr. 1907
Salmon	Rev. George Salmon, D.D., *The Infallibility of the Church* (1888), 2nd ed., 1923
Satis cogn.	Pope Leo XIII, Encyclical 'Satis cognitum', 29 June 1896, auth. tr. in *Companion to the Encyc. Satis Cogn.*, by Rev. S. J. Smith, S.J. (C.T.S., 1896)
Sheehan	Abp M. Sheehan, D.D., *Apologetics and Catholic Doctrine*, 4th rev. ed., Dublin, 1949
Shotwell and Loomis	J. T. Shotwell, LL.D. and Louise R. Loomis, *The See of Peter*, New York, 1927
Socrates	Socrates Scholasticus (5th cent.), *Ecclesiastical History*, A.D. 323–439
Sozomen	Hermias Sozomen (5th cent.), *Ecclesiastical History* (together, Greek and Latin, Cambridge, 1720)
Symonds	H. E. Symonds, C.R., D.D., *The Church Universal and the See of Rome*, 1939
Tellenbach	Gerd Tellenbach, *Church, State, and Christian Society at the time of the Investiture Contest*, E.T., Oxford, 1940
Tertullian	*Opera Basileae*, 1539; *PL*, vols i–iii
Theodoret	Theodoret, Bp of Cyrrhus (*c.* 393—457), *Ecclesiastical History*, *PG*, lxxx–lxxxiv, E.T., Bohn, 1854 and Sel. Lib. Nic. Frs., 2nd ser., vol. III
Tillemont	L. de Tillemont (1637–98), *Memoires pour Servir a l'Histoire Ecclésiastique des Six premiers Siècles*, Paris, 1712
Turner, *CA*	Prof. C. H. Turner, Litt.D., *Catholic and Apostolic*, 1931

ABBREVIATED REFERENCES USED IN NOTES

Turner, *Studies*	Prof. C. H. Turner, Litt.D., *Studies in Early Church History*, 1912
Ullmann, *GS*	Walter Ullmann, J.U.D., *The Origins of the Great Schism*, 1948
,, *MP*	Walter Ullmann, J.U.D., *Medieval Papalism*, 1949
Vacandard	Abbé E. Vacandard, *The Inquisition*, tr. Bernard L. Conway, C.S.P., 1908
Vincent, St	S. Vincentius Lirinensis, *Commonitorium* (A.D. 434), Oxford, 1886
Wadding	Lucas Wadding, *Πρεσβεία, sive Legatio Philippi III et IV Cath. Regum Hispaniarum ad SS. DD. NN. Paulum PP V. et Gregorium XV, De definienda Controv. Immac. concept. B. V. Mariae.* Lovanii, 1624
Waterworth	Rev. J. Waterworth, *Canons and Decrees of the Council of Trent*, 1888
Whitney	Prof. J. P. Whitney, D.D., *Hildebrandine Essays*, 1932
Wilhelm and Scannnell	Joseph Wilhelm, D.D. and Th. B. Scannell, *Manual of Catholic Theology*, 1890

PART ONE

INTRODUCTORY

CHAPTER I

The Doctrine of the Papacy

The Doctrine of the Papacy, which separates from communion with the Holy Roman Church all Christians who do not accept it, is defined in the *First Dogmatic Constitution on the Church.* This was declared and promulgated by His Holiness Pope Pius IX, for the belief and acceptance of all the faithful, during the fourth session of the Vatican Council of 1870, after full deliberation, 'the Sacred Council approving'. (Other decrees had been pronounced at an earlier session, defining Catholic doctrine concerning God the Creator, Revelation, Faith, and Reason. They are all commonly referred to as decrees of the Vatican Council, or 'Vatican Decrees'.)

The Dogmatic Constitution defines 'in accordance with the ancient and universal faith of the universal Church', the primacy, supreme jurisdiction, and sovereign power of St Peter, and of the bishops or pontiffs of Rome in succession to him, and it further declares, 'faithfully adhering to the tradition received from the beginning of the Christian faith', that the teaching of the Roman pontiff (under certain carefully defined conditions) is divinely endowed with infallibility.

Between the Church of Rome and various Protestant communions there are, unhappily, other serious doctrinal differences; but for vast numbers of Christians of the Orthodox Churches of the East, the Old Catholic Churches, and Churches of the Anglican Communion, the distinctive doctrines now defined in the *Dogmatic Constitution* are the great and formidable barrier from communion with the Roman see. These other Churches hold firmly to the Nicene Creed (as it was redeclared by the Fathers at Constantinople and Chalcedon). They hold that our Lord founded a visible Church, and endowed it with a continuing ministry of apostolic authority; but they do not accept the Doctrine of the Papacy. The following summary of its teaching is condensed from its actual wording:

I. Our Lord Jesus Christ appointed Blessed Peter the prince of all the Apostles and visible head of the whole Church Militant, and conferred on him a primacy of true and proper jurisdiction. II. Blessed Peter, the foundation of the Catholic Church, received the keys of the kingdom from our Lord. He lives, presides, and judges to this day always in his successors the Bishops of the Holy See of Rome. III. The Roman Pontiff is the successor of Blessed Peter, and is true Vicar of Christ, Head of the whole Church, Father and Teacher of all Christians. Our Lord has given him full power to rule and govern the universal Church. By the appointment of our Lord the Roman Church possesses a sovereignty of ordinary power over all other Churches, and all, both pastors and faithful, are bound to submit to the jurisdiction of the Roman Pontiff (not only in faith and morals but also in the discipline and government of the Church), so that the Church of Christ may be one flock under one supreme Pastor. He is the supreme judge of the faithful. This is the Teaching of Catholic truth, from which no one can deviate without loss of faith and of salvation.

IV. It is a dogma divinely revealed that the Roman Pontiff, when he speaks *ex cathedra* as Pastor and Teacher of all Christians, and defines a doctrine concerning faith or morals, to be held by the whole Church, is divinely endowed with the infallibility promised by the Divine Redeemer; such definitions are irreformable of themselves and not from consent of the Church. If any one contradict this, let him be anathema.

This doctrine of infallibility is the subject of the last chapter of this book,[1] where the full definition will be found quoted; from inattention to its precise terms it has sometimes been misunderstood.

The *Dogmatic Constitution* declares that the doctrines it defines are binding on the belief of all Christians as 'the teaching of Catholic truth from which no one can deviate without loss of faith and of salvation', and this is emphasized by the anathemas pronounced against anyone who gainsays them. More than six centuries ago, an earlier pope pronounced and defined that 'for every human creature it is altogether necessary to salvation that he be subject to the Roman Pontiff'.[2] Pope Pius XI, in his Encyclical 'Mortalium animos' of 1928, declared that all true Christians must believe the infallibility of the Roman pontiff (as defined in 1870) 'with the same faith as they believe the incarnation of our Lord', so that these doctrines are to be believed by Christians as fully and implicitly as if they were expressed in the Nicene Creed. The

[1] Ch. lxxiv.

[2] Pope Boniface VIII, Bull 'Unam sanctam', A.D. 1302, Denzinger, 469, Mirbt no. 372, p. 210; outside the one (Roman) Church 'there is neither salvation nor remission of sins'. Similarly in the Bull 'Cantate Domino' of Pope Eugenius IV. None outside 'whether pagans, Jews, heretics or schismatics, can partake of eternal life, but they shall go into eternal fire', Denzinger 714, and an Encyclical of 10 August 1864 of Pope Pius IX. But modern Roman theologians hold that a Protestant *in good faith* may be saved.

present pope, His Holiness Pope Pius XII, declares that 'Christ and His Vicar constitute only one Head'.[1]

The vital and essential importance of the doctrines that are now defined in the *Dogmatic Constitution* is manifest. It is constantly emphasized, as when Cardinal Vaughan teaches that each pope is a 'living Divine Teacher';[2] and when a theologian of less authority declares that 'The Sovereign Pontiff is the necessary, the only, the exclusive basis of Christianity'. His supremacy is 'the capital dogma, without which Christianity cannot subsist, . . . everything else is merely accessory',[3] he is following a canonized doctor of the Church, Cardinal Bellarmine, who declared that the primacy of the pontiff is 'the highest matter of Christianity'.[4] It is impossible to exaggerate its importance. No thoughtful Christian, therefore, can dare to treat lightly the question of belief and acceptance. If it is true, he must not delay, at his soul's peril, to seek admission into the Holy Roman Church, notwithstanding any Protestant prejudices that he may have against its ways.

If, on the other hand, after prayerful thought, and such study as is within his power, a man remain unconvinced of its truth, and unable to accept the Doctrine of the Papacy as verily part of the Catholic Faith, he must not profess to accept it, no matter how greatly he may feel attracted to the Holy Roman Church and to Roman piety—to 'the massiveness, the awful reality of the spiritual life within the Roman Catholic Church'[5]—'its world-wide extension, and the quality of its world-wideness, its powers to draw members of different races together in the bond of brotherhood, the rock-like firmness of its witness to the Faith, the extraordinary competence, within their own range, of its theologians, the naturalness with which different ranks and classes worship before one altar, and the completeness of self-devotion which it expects and receives'.[6]

How then is a Christian to answer for himself the momentous question, whether or not the Doctrine of the Papacy is part of the Catholic Faith, which he must acknowledge and believe? For however unwilling he may be to trust his own judgement in so vital a decision (and he must pray for grace to judge aright), he cannot altogether avoid doing

[1] Encyclical 'Mystici Corporis Christi', 29 June 1943, following Boniface VIII in 'Unam sanctam'.

[2] Rivington, *PC*, pp. xi, xii, xv.

[3] De Maistre, pp. 320–1.

[4] Etenim de quare agitur, cum de primatu Pontificis agitur? Brevissime dicam, de summa rei Christianae, *De summo pontifice*, *Opp.* (Cologne, 1620), i, 498.

[5] F. von Hügel, *Letters to a Niece*, p. 68.

[6] A. G. Hebert, S.S.M., *The Form of the Church*, 1944, p. 101.

so. If he decides on acceptance, he 'does, in truth, exercise private judgement, once for all, in his decision to submit to the teaching of the Church'.[1] 'The recognition that an authority is such that I ought to submit to it without question, is no less the result of an act of private judgement than the recognition that I must receive nothing without direct proof.'[2] If we decide that the whole teaching of the Roman Church is infallibly true, we shall thenceforward take on trust from her all our religious faith. 'But it is clear that our certainty, that any of the things she teaches us is right, cannot be greater than whatever certainty we have that our private judgement has decided the question rightly whether we ought to submit unreservedly to her teaching.'[3] 'If they [Roman Catholics] use their private judgement on no other question, they must use it on the question, Are we bound to submit implicitly to the authority of the Church of Rome?'[4]

Acceptance of the Doctrine of the Papacy is urged upon Christians in five different ways. (i) It is often said to be self-evidently true to any Christian. (ii) Its truth is said to be proved by results, i.e., the results of acceptance or rejection. (iii) It is to be accepted as an act of pure faith. (iv) Above all, it is said to have been the settled faith of the whole Church from the beginning, 'the ancient and constant faith of the universal Church'. (v) Yet again, even if it should seem to have been known or understood at first only in embryo, or as a germ, it is said to have reached maturity by a development that has been natural, logical, and inevitable.

Something must be said about terminology. The *Holy Roman Church* has been an official and liturgical title ever since the Council of Trent.[5] The fuller title is the *Holy*, *Catholic*, *Apostolic*, *Roman Church*.[6] According to the Doctrine of the Papacy, none of these four adjectives rightly belongs to any other Christian body; it follows that any one of them is distinctive in itself, and 'Catholic' is frequently used alone. That implies, and is meant to imply, that no other Church is Catholic. But there are other Churches which hold the faith of the Catholic Creeds and which

[1] Salmon, p. 49. [2] Ryder, p. 173. [3] Salmon, p. 48. [4] Ibid., p. 53.

[5] So also in the *Codex Juris Canonici*, 1919, which opens with the *Professio Catholicae Fidei*.

[6] Pope Pius IX, *Dogmatic Constitution on Catholic Faith*, 3 April 1870, cap. i, Denzinger, 1782. For three or four centuries 'the Church of the Romans' or 'the Roman Church' was a usual and sufficient name, but by the fourth century there were Novatian and Donatist bishops of Rome (Duchesne, *EH*, ii, 366). The Roman clergy called Pope Zosimus (A.D. 418) 'pope of the catholic Church of the Roman city' (Coll. Avell. 63). Afterwards under the Barbarian kings there were Arian bishops of Rome. It became necessary to distinguish 'the bishop of the Catholic Church of Rome' (Hughes, ii, 71).

(rightly or wrongly) claim to be Catholic Churches. The expression 'Roman Catholic'[1] is often objected to. The question of terminology seems to be settled, however, by the official declaration issued from the Vatican in 1930, that the term *Roman* is 'precisely the expression which distinguishes the Catholic religion from all other Christian confessions', and that to suppress the word *Roman* 'could only disgust and offend Catholics'.[2] *Roman*[3] or *Holy Roman* must therefore be used here in abbreviation of the full-length *Holy Catholic Apostolic Roman.*

[1] Employed by Pope Pius XI in his Encyclical on Education in 1929.
[2] Official Correspondence with the Holy See, White Paper Cmd. 3588, 1930, p. 48.
[3] The Index of Prohibited Books refers to 'the Roman Church'.

CHAPTER II

Proofs of the Doctrine of the Papacy

(i) *Self-evident truth, or* a priori *reasoning*

Sometimes it is claimed as self-evident to any open-minded Christian that the bishop of Rome, the pope, is the true Vicar of Christ on Earth, with authority to speak and govern in His Name (for if there *must* be such an office, there is no other for whom it is claimed). Thus Cardinal Newman wrote: 'The absolute need of a spiritual supremacy is at present the strongest of arguments in favour of the fact of its supply.'[1] 'Christianity . . . must, humanly speaking, have an infallible expounder.'[2] Cardinal Vaughan wrote: 'If the Church is visible at all, it must have a visible Head, at least as visible as the body itself.'[3] But this assertion does not carry conviction to everyone; to some it seems like the logic of Arius.[4] Holy Scripture describes Christ Himself, and no other, as Head of the Church;[5] this was the constant teaching of St Augustine.[6] 'The paradox, if paradox it be, of a visible body with an invisible head, belongs to the Old Testament as to the New.'[7]

Similarly Pope Leo XIII declared, in 1896, that 'Since Christ willed that His Kingdom should be visible, He *was obliged*, when He ascended

[1] *Development*, 1878 ed., p. 89. [2] Ibid., p. 90.

[3] Rivington, *PC*, p. vii, *Auth.* 5: cp. St Thomas Aquinas, 'to talk of a body without a head in the same order of life as the rest of the body is to use words without meaning', *Contra Errores Graecorum*, Prolog. II, *Opuscula*, p. 10.

[4] A human father's existence precedes the existence of his son. Arius argued, with anthropomorphic reasoning, that the divine Son was therefore a created being, even though 'created before all time'.

[5] Eph. v, 23; Col. i, 18. In Roman doctrine, Christ is the true Head, but the Pope as His representative on earth is also visible Head, subordinately to Him (Cardinal Gasparri, *Catechism for Adults*, Q. 128). 'Christ and His Vicar constitute only one Head' (Pope Pius XII).

[6] Infra, ch. xxxvii (i).

[7] Dr H. L. Goudge in *Anglo-Russian Symposium*, ed. E. L. Mascall, 1934, p. 39. He cites Judges viii, 22, 23; 1 Sam. xii, 12; Isa. xxxiii, 22.

into Heaven, to designate a vice-gerent on earth. . . . Because He was about to withdraw His visible presence from the Church, *it was necessary* that He should appoint some one in His place, to have the charge of the universal Church.'[1] Pope Pius XII also has declared that 'Such was His wisdom that He could in no wise leave the social body of His Church without a visible head'.[2] For anyone to whom these propositions seem self-evidently true, no further argument is needed in support of the claims of the Roman bishop, because no other bishop has made claim to be the vicegerent of Christ. But there are many who do not feel that man is empowered to judge what was 'necessary' for God, or what He was 'obliged' to do. For them the question must be, *did* our Lord appoint St Peter, and after him each bishop of Rome, to be His vicar on earth?

To some minds, the Roman doctrine seems to be evidently true for another reason, namely the great number of saints who have held it, and the outstanding holiness that has graced many of them: these are looked on as the especial fruits of the distinctive doctrine of the *Dogmatic Constitution* rather than only of what is expressed in the Faith of Nicaea. Thus one convert to the Roman Faith was persuaded by the autobiography of St Thérèse of Lisieux, and by visiting the scenes of her life there. To him it seemed that the certainty and unity of belief of St Thérèse and others was theirs 'because they all believe in a definite authority which they know to be supernatural and Divine, to which they gave unhesitating and loving obedience. . . . To St Thérèse Faith was belief in certain truths because they had been revealed to and taught by a teacher outside her who had Divine authority and therefore the right to claim her absolute obedience.'[3]

But there are other Christians who recognize a profusion of saints and saintliness outside the communion of the Roman see, who attribute it to the Faith that is shared by all alike, rather than to belief in a Vicar of Christ and a living divine teacher. For them, the truth of the Doctrine of the Papacy is not proved by a distinctive type of Roman saintliness, any more than it is disproved by past or present blemishes within the Roman Church. To some people, indeed, those dark periods in the annals of the past when the papal chair itself was a centre of corruption and vice seem to render the claims of Rome 'evidently' untrue.

This book can have little interest or usefulness for any to whom either the truth or the untruth of the *Dogmatic Constitution* is 'self-evident'. It is not written for them, nor is it designed to shake the belief

[1] Encyclical 'Satis Cognitum' (italics mine).
[2] Encyclical 'Mystici Corporis', 29 June 1943.
[3] Johnson, pp. 41, 42.

of anyone whose belief is clear and firm. It is written in the view that the true solution of this great religious problem cannot be regarded as self-evident; that each side of the question can claim numbers of learned, able, and devout Christians, and that it is a Christian's duty to seek it with what understanding and discernment God has given him, and to follow willingly the truth as it may be revealed to him.

(ii) *The argument from results*

The argument from what is regarded as self-evident truth may be called the *a priori* argument. The controversy is often approached from the opposite end, that is to say, in an argument based on the consequences of acceptance or rejection of the Papal Doctrine. It may be called the argument *a posteriori.* Here we are on delicate ground, because this aspect of the question is coloured by the spectacles through which it is looked at, and is affected by our likes and dislikes, by our prejudice in either direction. The comparison of the saintliness to be found within or without the Roman allegiance has been mentioned already. Another notable *a posteriori* argument is often based upon the activities of the Holy Office, the Inquisition, which have aroused detestation. Various other examples will probably come to the reader's mind. To dilate upon them here would run counter to the present theme; the quest of truth, as far as it is humanly possible, should be disencumbered of prejudice, of preconceived likes and dislikes.

There is, however, one branch of this argument that seriously involves a most important principal, that of the unity of the Church. According to the Doctrine of the Papacy the whole matter is plain and simple; the unity prayed for by our Lord, *that they may be one*, does exist and has always existed; it consists in communion with the bishop of Rome. Any Christian who is not in this communion is outside the Church. There is thus no disunity of the Church; there can be no actual disunity. The unity of the Roman Church within its wide borders is indeed its most magnetic attraction for many Christians, at present outside it, who yearn for unity. Yet there is a contrary view; the Church is indeed one, notwithstanding that the outward unity it ought to maintain is at present broken (just as a family remains one family even in dissension). On each side of the controversy the argument is presented simply and forcibly.

A. The Church is one and united. Unity exists within the Church acknowledging the governance of the Vicar of Christ, which is the Catholic Church and the whole Catholic Church. Those who have broken away from that unity into schism have proceeded to disintegrate into innumerable heresies and sects, thus proving the true nature of schism by its fruits. 'By this disintegration and by their disunity in so many questions of faith, they have frequently shown that unwillingness to accept papal claims cannot be the only, nor the main, cause of their disunity.'

N. The erroneous claims of sovereign jurisdiction (as distinguished from primacy and presidency) that were gradually and progressively put forward for the Roman see (sometimes by ambitious and domineering popes, sometimes in all good faith by saintly popes), resulted not in maintaining the former unity of the Church, but in actual divisions. Faults on the other side also there certainly were, but it was the untrue, unscriptural, and unprimitive sovereignty asserted by Rome that was the fundamental cause of division and the evils that have followed. Within the Roman allegiance itself, an artificial unity is maintained by enforced acceptance of claims (defined by Pope Pius IX in 1870) that are untrue, that were unheard of in the primitive Church of the first three centuries at least, and that are irreconcilable with what the Fathers of the early centuries said and did.

It is the aim of this book to state the various heads of controversy as they are seen from opposite sides, not to offer a judgement between them. To many persons on each side of the question this argument from results seems to be sufficient and decisive. For them it is therefore hardly necessary to read on. The book is not for them.

(iii) *Acceptance as an act of pure faith*

'Faith is a supernatural virtue, whereby, inspired and assisted by the grace of God, we believe that the things which He has revealed are true; not because the intrinsic truth of the things is plainly perceived by the natural light of reason, but because of the authority of God Himself, who reveals them, and who can neither be deceived nor deceive. For faith, as the apostle testifies, is "the substance of things hoped for, the conviction of things that appear not".'[1] It 'is itself a gift of God'[2]. And 'although faith is above reason, there can never be any real discrepancy between faith and reason; since the same God who reveals mysteries

[1] Heb. xi, 1.
[2] Pope Pius IX, *Dogmatic Constitution on the Catholic Faith*, 24 April 1870, cap. iii; Denzinger, 1791.

and infuses faith has bestowed the light of reason on the human mind, and God cannot deny Himself, nor can truth ever contradict truth'.[1]

More shortly, 'faith is a supernatural gift of God which enables us to believe without doubting whatever God has revealed'.[2]

These definitions of faith may, perhaps, be accepted by Christians of all communions. Yet the reason why so many feel unable to accept the Doctrine of the Papacy is precisely that they have not recognized it as part of the truth revealed by God.

(iv) *Claimed to be primitive, constant, and universal*

'The Church is a living witness to a revelation which is final, from which nothing can be taken away, and to which nothing can be added. This is the fundamental principle.'[3] 'Revelation was given in its entirety by Our Lord and His Apostles. After the death of the last of the twelve, it could receive no increment.'[4] 'The dignity and perfection of Christian Revelation require that no further public Revelation is to be made.'[5] 'We believe that no new doctrine can be introduced into the Church, but that every doctrine which we hold has existed and been taught since the time of the Apostles, having been handed down by them to their successors.'[6]

In statements such as these the theologians of the Roman Church unanimously declare the finality of revelation and 'the faith which was once for all delivered to the saints',[7] and they repudiate any addition to it. The principle was asserted by St Vincent of Lerins in his famous *Commonitorium*, written in A.D. 434, which has always been acknowledged as a sound exposition of Catholic principle:

> Within the Catholic Church itself we are greatly to consider, that we hold that which hath been believed every where, always and of all men (*quod ubique, quod semper, quod ab omnibus creditum est*): for that is truly and properly Catholic (as the very force and nature of the word doth declare, which comprehendeth all things in general after an universal manner). And that we shall do if we follow Universality, Antiquity, Consent. Universality we shall follow thus, if we profess that one faith to be true which the whole Church throughout the world acknowledgeth and confesseth. Antiquity shall we follow if we part not any whit from those senses which it is plain that our holy elders and Fathers made known. Consent likewise if in this very antiquity we follow the definitions and

[1] *Dogmatic Constitution on the Catholic Faith*, cap. iv; Denzinger, 1796.
[2] *Catechism of Christian Doctrine*, ch. ii, p. 9.
[3] Chapman, *GCC*, p. 25. See ch. lxxii (ii) infra.
[4] G. H. Joyce, S.J., in *Cath. Enc*, xiii, 4. [5] Wilhelm and Scannell, i, 14.
[6] Cardinal Wiseman, *Moorfield Lectures* (1847), i, 60. [7] Jude 3.

opinions of all, or at any rate almost all, the priests and doctors alike.[1]

St Vincent emphasizes this same principle over and over again,[2] saying, for example:

> The Church of Christ, a careful and diligent keeper of doctrines committed to her charge, never changeth anything in them, diminisheth nothing, addeth nothing.[3]

On this principle Pope Pius IX himself expressly founded the definitions of the *Dogmatic Constitution*, declaring that he propounded them 'in accordance with the ancient and constant faith of the universal Church', and 'faithfully adhering to the tradition received from the beginning of the Christian faith'.[4] His successor, Pope Leo XIII, issued the Encyclical 'Satis cognitum' in 1896 as a reasoned support of the *Dogmatic Constitution*. In it he wrote that 'as to the nature and authority of the Roman Pontiff, no newly conceived opinion is set forth, but the venerable and constant belief of every age'. 'The consent of antiquity ever acknowledged, without the slightest doubt or hesitation, the Bishops of Rome, and revered them as the legitimate successors of St Peter.'

It is claimed that the Doctrine of the Papacy has been firmly held from the very beginning, and that it is proved thus to be an essential part of the true Catholic Faith: that, in substance, there is nothing proclaimed that is new, that has not been firmly believed by the universal Church from its earliest days. It is right to say 'in substance', because the *Dogmatic Constitution* was deliberately worded as a restatement; but what is claimed is, that it states in careful definition only what has always been believed in substance.

Faithful members of the Holy Roman Church must not only accept the definition as binding on their belief, but they must also accept the declaration that it has been the faith of the Church from the beginning; it is unnecessary for them to verify this by reading for themselves the records and history of the earliest centuries of the Church. Cardinal Manning wrote that 'All appeals to Scripture alone, or to Scripture and antiquity, whether by individuals or by local Churches, are no more than appeals from the Divine voice of the living Church, and are therefore essentially rationalistic'.[5] 'The appeal to antiquity is both a treason and a heresy.'[6] Abbot Chapman explains that this saying refers only

[1] Cap. ii.

[2] Cap. ix, xiv, xxi, xxviii, xxix. He excludes not only what is *contra* the original deposit, but what is *praeter*, beside it, xx, xxii.

[3] Cap. xxiii. [4] Preface, and cap. iv. [5] Manning, *TMHG*, p. 29.

[6] Ibid., p. 241.

to 'appeal behind the present teaching of the Roman Church'.[1] It may seem reasonable to think that 'the venerable and constant belief' of the Church in the early centuries cannot be verified without an actual study of that belief, as shown in the Church's own history and its doctrinal writings; to attempt an objective study is the first aim of this book. The reader must be warned, however, of a doctrine according to which there is no occasion for any study of the kind.[2]

(v) *The theory of development*

Did St Peter occupy, or lay claim to, a position of supreme authority that can fittingly now be described as 'Vicar of Christ'? Was an individual office of this tremendous jurisdiction and supreme authority known to the Apostolic Church, or actually accorded to St Peter in the word or conduct of his fellow apostles and the Church? Holy Scripture does not seem to affirm this explicitly.

Moreover, the records of the first two centuries at least, although they are fairly copious, do not yield us a clear statement that a bishop of Rome is, individually, and more than other bishops, the successor of St Peter. Although all the bishops of the Church have always been the recognized successors and representatives of the twelve apostles, and particular sees, such as Rome and Ephesus, claimed individual apostles as their founders, the early records do not seem to claim that the bishop of Rome represented St Peter individually in any sense of unique significance. St Peter and St Paul were venerated there as joint founders of the local Church; St Paul imparted no individual Pauline office to its bishop, and the earliest records do not seem to notice the imparting of a special Petrine office, that office which according to the Doctrine of the Papacy is so tremendous and so unique.

These considerations lead to a line of thought that is associated with the name of Cardinal Newman. For some years before he was received into the Church of Rome, he had felt irresistibly drawn to it,[3] yet troubled by historical difficulties such as these. During that time he wrote his well-known *Essay on the Development of Christian Doctrine*, and he published it immediately after his reception. Its purpose was 'to explain certain difficulties in its history'.[4] The theory was 'undoubtedly an hypothesis to account for a difficulty'.[5] 'While Apostles

[1] *GCC*, p. 39.
[2] Infra, ch. lxxii (ii).
[3] Conviction had come to him six years before, *Life*, by W. Ward, 1927 ed., pp. 68–9; John Morley, *Life of Gladstone*, i, 311.
[4] Newman, *Development*, 1878 ed., preface, p. vii.
[5] Op cit., 1st ed. 1845, p. 27; 1878 ed., p. 30.

were on earth, there was the need neither of Bishop nor Pope; their power was dormant, or exercised by Apostles. In course of time, first the power of the Bishop awoke, and then the power of the Pope.'[1] Both were of divine institution. 'The Papal power might be divinely bestowed, yet in the first instances more or less dormant.'[2] 'First local disturbances gave rise to Bishops, and next oecumenical disturbances gave rise to Popes.'[3] 'Christianity developed . . . into the form, first of a Catholic, then of a Papal Church.'[4] The great texts concerning the Rock and the Keys 'are not precepts merely, but prophecies and promises . . . to be fulfilled according to the need, and to be interpreted by the event.'[5] 'The *regalia Petri* might sleep, . . . not as obsolete, for they had never been carried into effect, but as a mysterious privilege, which was not understood; as an unfulfilled prophecy.'[6]

But Newman argued that in the earliest Fathers there is found scarcely more explicit evidence for Catholic truths, such as the doctrine of the Holy Trinity, or of original sin,[7] than there is for the papacy. If the rule of *Quod semper* were applied with equal strictness, it would rule out the former as much as the latter. Therefore this 'dictum of Vincentius . . . is hardly available now, or effective of any satisfactory result'.[8]

In place of the Vincentian Canon, Newman relies on a process of true 'development of an idea'. This is 'the germination and maturation of some truth on a large mental field'.[9] It is distinguished from its converse, 'corruption', by various tests. In an extensive survey of ecclesiastical history, the doctrines of the papacy are presented as the *logical issue* of the original teaching of the Church,[10] 'developments faithfully drawn from the ideas to which they profess to belong',[11] and in no way a corruption.

Newman's expanded theory was thought by many to be inconsistent with Catholic theological teaching on the finality of Revelation, and it met with severe criticism from different sides. There is a certain difficulty in reconciling it with the declarations of the *Dogmatic Constitution* itself, and with Pope Leo XIII's Encyclical claim, 'the venerable and constant belief of every age'. Consequently it is not always given prominence in writings for the defence and establishment

[1] Op. cit., 1845, p. 165; 1878, sim., p. 149. [2] Op. cit., 1845, p. 169; 1878, p. 153.
[3] Op. cit., 1845, p. 167; 1878, sim., p. 151. [4] Op. cit., 1845, p. 169; 1878, p. 153.
[5] Op. cit., 1845, p. 172; 1878, p. 156.
[6] Op. cit., 1878, p. 150; 1845, sim., p. 166.
[7] But cp. Origen, *De Princip.* I, pref. 2, 4, Opp. I. 2, 3; Puller, p. 429.
[8] Op. cit., 1845, p. 24; 1878, p. 27 [9] Op. cit., 1845, p. 38; 1878, p. 37.
[10] Op. cit., 1878, p. 195. [11] Op. cit., 1845, p. 86.

of the Doctrine of the Papacy; thus the great *Catholic Encyclopaedia* has no article on Development.[1]

Nevertheless there is a principle of development which, in a carefully limited sense, cannot be wisely or rightly left out of account, and which is in fact often invoked. Thus Mgr Batiffol says, 'the identity of the Papacy throughout the centuries ought to be understood as functioning in accordance with the law of development'.[2] Although the revelation of doctrine was final, its meaning, and sometimes its application, may come in time to be seen more clearly under the continuing guidance of the Holy Spirit. The Fathers at Nicaea kept the ancient faith unchanged, yet they declared it anew in order to correct errors and misunderstandings that had arisen.

So Abbot Chapman explains that the words 'in accordance with the ancient and constant faith of the universal Church' in the *Dogmatic Constitution* 'are to be understood in the sense in which they are true of every dogma of the faith. It is not meant that the belief in every part of the Church in every century as to every detail of the Vatican definition can be demonstrated by historical proof. This could hardly be done with regard to the unity of God or the Catholicity of the Church. It is sufficient for the proof of the antiquity of a dogma if we can trace its germ in early ages, and follow its necessary logical development.'[3]

St Vincent of Lerins himself has a passage in his *Commonitorium* that is referred to as supporting the principle of development:

> But perhaps someone will say, 'Will there then be no progress of religion in the Church of Christ?' There will indeed, the greatest progress. For who is so full of hate to men, so hated by God, as to attempt to deny this? But in such wise, however, that it should be a true progress of faith, and not a change. Now it belongs to progress that each thing should be increased into its own self; it belongs, on the contrary, to change, that one thing should be turned into another. Therefore the intelligence, knowledge, wisdom, both of a single man and of the whole Church, must grow, and make great and enormous progress by the advance of ages and centuries, but only within their own nature, that is to say, in the same dogma, the same sense, and the same meaning.[4]

St Vincent then explains this more precisely by the analogy of the child and the man. 'The limbs of infants be small, of young men great,

[1] There is a reference to it at the end of the article on Revelation, vol. xiii, p. 4. But it enters into many theological works under the head of 'Evolution of *Dogma*' or 'Tradition' (see below ch. lxxii (ii)).

[2] Batiffol, *C & P*, p. 74.

[3] *GCC*, p. 62 n. 1.

[4] Cap. xxiii; sed in suo duntaxat genere, in eodem scilicet dogmate, eodem sensu, eademque sententia.

yet not divers but the same.' In the human form, if any member be added, or taken from it, the body becomes either monstrous or weakened. Christian doctrine likewise 'must with time become more ample', yet 'admit no further change, no variety in definition'.[1] Referring to St Paul's teaching, he emphasizes that 'whosoever preacheth a new dogma is to be accursed'.[2]

He also says that the wheaten seed of true doctrine sowed by our forefathers gives us rich crops of pure doctrine, but we must take heed not to reap 'the spurious error of cockle'.

An argument for 'logical development' is often fortified by resort to a different metaphor, not used by St Vincent, that of the acorn and the oak. The developed Doctrine of the Papacy is likened to an oak whose originating 'acorn' may be found in the earliest age, and even in Holy Scripture. Like all metaphors, this must be used with caution. An acorn can grow into nothing but an oak, but an 'acorn' of religious truth may grow wrongly into an untruth. In this way heresies have begun; the great Arian heresy affords an example. The 'acorn' was the truth that our Lord is the Son of God. It grew awry into the false doctrine (which all but prevailed) that the Second Person of the Blessed Trinity was not 'in the beginning', and is thus inferior to the Godhead.

Dr Rivington denies that Newman was 'striking out a new theory'.[3] As he says, 'No one who appeals to the primitive Church professes to find in her actual life a literal transcript of his own position.... What, then, do we ourselves mean when we say that the papal *régime* was in existence in the earliest beginnings of Christianity? The question really is as to whether the alleged counterpart in the early Church differs from its successor in the present, in substance, in principle, in essential features.'[4] Dr Rivington adopts the metaphor of the acorn and the oak. In one respect only his presentation of the problem may need qualification; that is when he proposes to seek for the 'acorn' throughout 'the first *four* centuries of the Christian era'.[5] For no Father before the third century seems to associate the office of the Roman bishop expressly with St Peter or a Petrine office, and in the fourth century there were

[1] Commonitorium, cap. xxiii.

[2] Ibid., cap. ix; si quis novum dogma adnunciaverit anathematizetur, Gal, i, 8. A dogma might be either traditional and true, or new and false, as when the Sixth General Council anathematized the 'impious dogmas' of Sergius and others—the Monothelite heresy (Mansi, xi, 991; Hardouin iii, 1332). But in modern Roman use, 'dogma' is confined to doctrine which has been declared to be a *truth of Revelation*; cp. Codex J.C. canon 1325.

[3] *PC*, p. xx. [4] *PC*, p. xix. [5] Ibid.

marked developments in its position and authority. The 'ancient and constant faith' and tradition 'from the beginning of the Christian faith' should first be looked for in the earliest centuries.

Having in view then (1) The authoritative definition of Pope Pius IX, which he based on its 'accordance with the ancient and constant faith of the universal Church': (2) The authoritative exposition by Pope Leo XIII, that 'no newly conceived opinion is set forth, but the venerable and constant belief of every age': and (3) The absence of any equally authoritative approval of a doctrine of development, going beyond the limits proposed by St Vincent, we are bound to use that doctrine with great care, and we should not strain it beyond these limits.

In proceeding to the study of Holy Scripture and the early Christian writings it must, however, be recognized that the *wording* of the definitions of Pope Pius IX need not be expected there. We shall find there no later expressions such as the 'Vicar of Christ', or the 'living Divine Voice'. The actuality is to be sought for, not the phraseology. As Dr Rivington well says, it is 'the substance, the principle, the essential features' of the papacy that are to be looked for. We must look, therefore, for evidence of the earliest recognition in the Church of (1) an individual and supreme jurisdiction, first of St Peter, and then of the bishop of Rome for the time being, and (2) a Petrine office in the occupant of the Roman see as an individual guarantor of infallible truth. These things are the substance of which the *Dogmatic Constitution* claims to be only a new and careful definition. It is that unmistakable substance that we shall look for, century by century.

CHAPTER III

Holy Scripture

The passages of Scripture that throw light upon the position and authority of St Peter fall into three groups:

1. His pre-eminence among the apostles is clearly shown by a large number of texts.

2. On three notable Petrine texts, of which the most important is that concerning 'the Rock', especial reliance is placed as establishing the Doctrine of the Papacy.

3. Some other texts have been thought to show that St Peter's pre-eminence did not carry with it an individual jurisdiction over the other apostles and the Church.

(i) *The pre-eminence of St Peter*

In the Gospels and the Acts, 'St Peter's name is mentioned on over one hundred and ninety occasions, while the number of occasions on which the name of St John, who comes next, is mentioned is only twenty-nine'.[1]

He was the first of the twelve to be chosen.[2] The passages in the following series were collected by Abbot Chapman[3] to show the 'firstness' or primacy of St Peter:

> The Bible and the Fathers teach quite plainly the primacy of St Peter. The most casual reader of Scripture must notice how incomparably more often St Peter is mentioned in the Gospels than is any other of the disciples. Everyone must remark his eager and impulsive character. He seems always to be putting himself forward.
>
> It is Peter who asks leave to walk on the water.[4] It is Peter who takes our Lord and rebukes Him, when he hears the prophecy of the Passion.[5] It is Peter who cries out at a miracle, 'Depart from me, for I am a sinful

[1] Johnson, p. 116. [2] Matt. iv, 18; x, 2; Mark i, 16; iii, 16; Luke vi, 14.
[3] *GCC*, pp. 45–6. [4] Matt. xiv, 28. [5] Matt. xvi, 22; Mark viii, 32.

man, O Lord'.[1] It is Peter who exclaims, 'Thou shalt never wash my feet', and then, changed in an instant, urges a contrary prayer.[2] It is Peter who vehemently proclaims, 'Though all should be offended, yet will not I',[3] and who asks, 'Why cannot I follow Thee now?'[4] and it is Peter who takes one of the two swords, and makes a clumsy dash at the high priest's servant,[5] and who, in spite of the danger, follows his Master 'afar off' to the palace of the high priest, and in his excitement thrice denies his Master with cursing and swearing.[6]

The same eagerness makes him the spokesman of the Apostles. Peter asks our Lord to explain a parable.[7] Peter asks how often must one forgive a brother.[8] Peter calls attention to the dead fig tree.[9] Peter says, 'Lord, sayest Thou this to us, or also to all'.[10] Peter says, 'Behold, we have left all and have followed Thee. What shall we have for this'[11] Peter says, 'Lord, to whom shall we go? Thou hast the words of eternal life.'[12] Peter, answering a question addressed to all, cries, 'Thou art the Christ, the Son of the living God'.[13]

But is it only his natural vivacity which makes him the spokesman of the Apostles? Is it not also his position among the Apostles? To begin with, he is one of the three who are chosen above the twelve, who are mentioned first in the lists of the Apostles.[14] These three speak to our Lord apart, that He may tell them what He might have left unsaid in the presence of the rest.[15] He chooses them to be the witnesses of the raising of the dead,[16] of His Transfiguration,[17] and of His Agony.[18] But even among these three it is Peter who is the spokesman. He proposes to remain on Tabor: 'It is good for us to be here.' And our Lord Himself recognizes this leadership. 'He saith to Peter: Could ye not watch?' He speaks as to the leader of the three. 'He saith to Simon, Sleepest thou? Watch ye and pray.'[19]

In the same vein the evangelist speaks of the three as 'Peter and they that were with him',[20] and the same expression stands for the disciples.[21] After the Resurrection, the angel bids the women, 'Go tell His disciples and Peter';[22] and we find the same distinction of Peter from the rest in the Acts: 'Peter with the eleven', 'Peter and the Apostles'.[23] So also in St Paul's account of the witnesses of the Resurrection: 'He was seen by Cephas, then by the twelve.'[24]

But St Peter is not only mentioned first, he is actually called 'the first',

[1] Luke v, 8. [2] John xiii, 9. [3] Matt. xxvi, 33, 35; Mark xiv, 29; Luke xxii, 34.
[4] John xiii, 37. [5] John xviii, 10.
[6] Matt. xxvi, 58, 69–75; Mark xiv, 54, 66–72; Luke xxii, 54–62; John xviii, 15, 25–7.
[7] Matt. xv, 15. [8] Matt. xviii, 21. [9] Mark xi, 21.
[10] Luke xii, 41. [11] Matt. xix, 27; Mark x, 28; Luke xviii, 28.
[12] John vi, 69 [13] Matt. xvi, 16
[14] Mark iii, 16; Luke vi, 14; Acts i, 13; Andrew, however, is put next to Peter by Matt. x, 2, as his brother.
[15] Mark xiii, 3. [16] Mark v, 37; Luke viii, 51.
[17] Matt. xvii, 1; Mark ix, 2; Luke ix, 28. [18] Matt. xxvi, 37; Mark xiv, 33.
[19] Matt. xxvi, 40–1; Mark xiv, 37, 38. [20] Luke ix, 32. [21] Luke viii, 45.
[22] Mark xvi, 7. [23] Acts ii, 14; v, 29; Cp. St Ignatius, *Smyrn.*, iii, 2.
[24] 1 Cor. xv, 5.

ὁ πρῶτος, in St Matthew's list of Apostles.[1] In consequence he is often called 'first' by the Fathers, and they constantly mention his firstness or 'primacy'. Continually they repeat that he is 'the first of the disciples'.

But merely to recognize a firstness or primacy in St Peter falls altogether short of the Doctrine of the Papacy, and in the *Dogmatic Constitution* Pope Pius IX pronounced an express anathema on anyone who says that St Peter received a primacy of honour only, and not of true and proper jurisdiction.[2]

A. The pre-eminence of St Peter is shown by Scripture beyond any possibility of dispute. To deny that he received from our Lord a real primacy of jurisdiction implies that he received a mere primacy of honour, and 'the conception of an empty primacy of honour being established by our Lord among His Apostles is so revoltingly anti-Christian as to be nothing less than blasphemous'.[3]

N. The fallacy in the argument above lies in its false alternative. St Peter's firstness was certainly no empty pre-eminence. The Acts of the Apostles record his outstanding part in the foundation of the Church during the first twenty years or so after Pentecost,[4] although there is no indication that it continued. But the alternative to the sovereignty of a Supreme Pontiff and Vicar of Christ is not a 'primacy of empty honour', but a real firstness, an initiative and leadership in act and speech among apostles of equal 'rank', a primacy *inter pares*.

(ii) *The three great Petrine texts*[5]

1. '*Thou art Peter*' (*the Rock and the Keys*) (Matt. xvi, 15–19)

Jesus saith to them: But whom do you say that I am? Simon Peter answered and said: Thou art Christ the Son of the living God. And Jesus answering, said to him: Blessed art thou Simon Bar-Jona: because flesh and blood hath not revealed it to thee, but my Father who is in heaven. And I say to thee: That thou art Peter; and upon this rock I will build my church, and the gates of hell shall not prevail against it. And I will give to thee the keys of the kingdom of heaven. And whatsoever thou shalt bind upon earth, it shall be bound also in heaven: and whatsoever thou shalt loose on earth, it shall be loosed also in heaven.

2. '*Feed My lambs, feed My sheep*' (John xxi, 15–17)

When therefore they had dined, Jesus saith to Simon Peter: Simon, son of John, lovest thou me more than these? He saith to him: Yea, Lord,

[1] x, 2. [2] Cap. i. [3] Chapman, *Studies*, p. 103.
[4] Chs, i–vi, viii–xii, and xv.
[5] The Rheims version, translated from the Vulgate, is here followed.

thou knowest that I love thee. He saith to him: Feed my lambs. He saith to him again: Simon, son of John, lovest thou me? He saith to him: Yes, Lord, thou knowest that I love thee. He saith to him: Feed my lambs. He saith to him the third time: Simon, son of John, lovest thou me? Peter was grieved, because he had said to him the third time, Lovest thou me? And he said to him: Lord, thou knowest that I love thee. He said to him, Feed my sheep.

3. '*Confirm thy brethren*' (Luke xxii, 31, 32)

And the Lord said: Simon, Simon, behold Satan hath desired to have you that he may sift you as wheat. But I have prayed for thee, that thy faith fail not: and thou being once converted, confirm thy brethren.

These three Scripture passages, and especially the first of them, constitute the Scriptural foundation of the papacy. They have been called 'the Charter texts', 'the charter of investiture of the papacy'.[1] What should be understood as their true meaning has been discussed by commentators ever since the early centuries, and is ever in dispute between those Christians who hold the Doctrine of the Papacy and those others who reject it.

It is generally agreed that in questions of interpretation of the Scriptures it is of prime importance to consult the Christian Fathers, as the early Catholic writers on theology are called. Their exposition was formerly held to be so decisive that the Creed of Pope Pius IV in 1564[2] seems to exclude any interpretation of Holy Scripture '*otherwise than according to* the unanimous consent of the Fathers'; but this was modified by Pope Pius IX at the Vatican Council in 1870[3] so as only to forbid any interpretation *contrary to* the unanimous consent of the Fathers. In regard to these important passages, there is much diversity of expression amongst the Fathers; in fact, the Fathers are copiously quoted on both sides and what has been written in discussion of their opinions would fill many volumes.

Individual Fathers will be mentioned later, in the order of their times, with quotation from such of their writings as seem to have a bearing upon the Doctrine of the Papacy. In the mean time, however, an attempt must be made to indicate how these passages have been variously understood, and the principal arguments advanced in support of the different views.

[1] Freppel, *St Cyprian*, cit., Benson, p. 277.

[2] Bull, 'Injunctum nobis', 13 November 1564; Denzinger, 995, Mirbt no. 480, p. 338. Nec eam (sacram scripturam) nisi iuxta unanimem consensum patrum accipiam et interpretabor.

[3] Session iii, Dogmatic Constitution on the Catholic Faith, cap. ii; Denzinger, 1788.

'UPON THIS ROCK'

(1)

A. The true meaning is plain. St Peter is the Rock on which our Lord says that He will build His Church, and the earliest Fathers so understood it. Other interpretations are all collateral and indirect. 'The literal interpretation which refers the rock to St Peter, so far from excluding the other interpretations, is perfectly consistent with them. . . . Peter is the rock because he represents, and in a manner embodies, the principle of faith in Christ. On this account some of the Fathers, whilst taking the rock in its literal sense, at the same time say also that faith in Christ, or public confession of this faith, is the rock of the Church. These interpretations, far from being incompatible, rather are naturally implied in each other, and serve to bring out the full import of the words of Christ.'[1]

N. The Fathers interpret this in very different ways. Seventeen understand the rock as St Peter himself, but forty-four understand it as the faith confessed by him,[2] eight as meaning all the apostles, and sixteen as meaning Christ Himself.[3] Some Fathers suggest two or more different interpretations, not apparently considering the question thus left open to have a bearing upon 'the principal matter of Christianity'. Thus St Augustine at one time took St Peter to be 'the rock', but latterly thought otherwise, and in his *Retractiones* he ends, 'of these two meanings let the reader choose the more probable'.[4] A Confession of Faith could be, symbolically, a foundation, but it could not be a visible Head of the Church. Those Fathers who interpreted the Rock as the Confession cannot have discerned the papacy in this text.

(2)

A. 'From this text it is clear that by the will and command of God, the Church rests upon St Peter just as a building rests on its foundation. Now the proper nature of a foundation is to be a principle of cohesion for the various parts of the building. It must be the necessary condition of stability and strength. Remove it and the whole building falls. It is

[1] Bottalla, i, 36–8, Allnatt, pp. 16–18.

[2] So also the Roman Missal (Collect for Vigil of SS. Peter and Paul), 'God, who hast established us on the rock of the apostolic confession'.

[3] 'For other foundation no man can lay, but that which is laid; which is Jesus Christ.' 1 Cor. iii, 11.

[4] *Retract.*, lib. i, cxxi; *PL*, xxxiii, 618.

consequently the office of St Peter to support the Church, and to guard it in all its strength and indestructible unity. How could he fulfil this office without the power of commanding, forbidding, and judging, which is properly called *jurisdiction*?'[1]

N. A foundation is not 'a principle of cohesion'; but whatever be the exact sense, it is metaphorical. In a sense in which St Peter, like the other apostles, was a 'foundation' (Eph. ii, 19, 20), his conspicuous work of founding was performed and completed. Thus some Fathers, like Tertullian,[2] think that the promise was fulfilled by St Peter's having taken the lead in founding the Church on the day of Pentecost.

'The Lord's promise is fulfilled: the primacy is completed: the foundations are laid on the rock, whether of Peter's confession or of Peter's courage or of Peter's steadfastness. From this time forward the work passes into other hands.... Paul completes what Peter had begun. The silence of the later apostolic history is not less significant than the eloquence of the earlier as to the meaning of Peter's primacy. In the first part he is everything; in the subsequent record he is nowhere at all. He is only once again mentioned in the Acts,[3] and even here he does not bear the chief part. Where the Church at large, as an expansive missionary Church, is concerned, Paul, not Peter, is the prominent personage: where the Church of Jerusalem appears as the visible centre of unity, James, not Peter, is the chief agent.[4] Peter retains the first place as missionary evangelist to the Hebrew Christians, but nothing more.'[5]

(3)

A. 'Peter was thus established by our Lord as the means of imparting to the Church indefectibility and unity, and of permanently securing these properties to her. Peter was invested with supreme spiritual authority to legislate for the whole Church: to teach, to inspect, to judge, to proscribe erroneous doctrine, or whatever would tend to the the destruction of the Church; to appoint to offices or remove therefrom, or limit or extend the jurisdiction thereof, as the safety or welfare of the Church would require: in one word, to exercise as supreme head and ruler and teacher and pastor all spiritual functions whatever that are necessary for the well-being or existence of the Church.'[6]

[1] Pope Leo XIII in 'Satis cogn.' [2] *De Pudicit.*, xxi. [3] xv, 7.
[4] Acts xii, 17; xv, 13; xxi, 18; Gal. ii, 9, 12. [5] Lightfoot, *Clem.*, ii, 489–90.
[6] Professor P. A. Murray, *Irish Annual Miscellany*, iii, 300.

N. 'If our Lord meant all this, we may ask, why did He not say it? Who found out that He meant it? The apostles did not at the time; for up to the night before His death the dispute went on, which should be the greatest. When James and John petitioned that in His kingdom they might sit with Him, one on each hand, they do not seem to have suspected, and their Master gave them no hint, that the chief place in His kingdom had already been given away. There is . . . no other indication in the New Testament that the Apostolic Church so understood our Lord's words recorded by St Matthew.'[1] The conception of the Roman bishop as Head of the Church was still unknown to St Augustine.[2]

(4)

A. 'It was necessary that a government of this kind, since it belongs to the constitution and formation of the Church as its principal element—that is, as the principle of unity and the foundation of stability—should in no wise come to an end with St Peter, but should pass to his successors from one to another. . . . For this reason the Pontiffs who succeed Peter in the Roman Episcopate receive the supreme power in the Church *jure divino*.'[3]

N. A foundation is laid once for all, and in the sense in which St Peter was truly a foundation (as were all the apostles, Eph. ii, 19, 20) it is false metaphor to speak of its constant replacement and renewal. A foundation can have no successor.

In his individual eminence, as distinct from the apostolic office that St Peter shared equally with the other apostles, he could have no successor.

'The great Greek commentators (and the early Latin commentators too) in annotating Matthew xvi and John xxi do not make any reference to the successors of St Peter; they simply speak of his own primacy. . . . As a rule, it is only the popes themselves who directly cite these passages as the grounds of their own jurisdiction.'[4]

The earliest evidence for the putting forward of a claim by a Roman bishop to the primacy of St Peter is found in A.D. 256.[5]

[1] Salmon, p. 334.
[2] *Infra*, ch. xxxvii (i).
[3] Satis cogn.
[4] Chapman, *GCC*, p. 92.
[5] St Cyprian, Ep. lxxxv, 18 (from Firmilian); infra, ch. xx. A sarcasm of Tertullian, half a century earlier, is thought to be aimed at what he considered pretentiousness in a Roman bishop; but there is no mention of a primacy or of St Peter. See below, ch. xvi.,

'THE KEYS OF THE KINGDOM OF HEAVEN'

It is well recognized that in Holy Scripture 'the keys' are an emblem of stewardship and authority. Thus when Shebna was deposed from being steward of the palace, 'the key of the house of David' was to be laid on the shoulder of Eliakim.[1] In this promise, 'The Church is typified not only as an edifice but as a kingdom, and everyone knows that the keys constitute the usual sign of governing authority'.[2] Yet the remaining part of our Lord's promise to St Peter in Matt. xvi, 19, regarding binding and loosing, is also a promise of governing authority, and this was made equally to all the apostles.[3] 'This metaphorical expression of binding and loosing indicates the power of making laws and of judging and of punishing; and the power is said to be of such amplitude and force that God will ratify whatever is decreed by it.'[4]

The symbol of the keys in the promise to St Peter is so striking an expression that all the Fathers associate it particularly with him. So it is urged on the one hand (A) that no promise or gift to the others of the twelve is recorded in the same words. It is said nevertheless (N) that the same authority was conferred on all the apostles; the support of the Fathers is claimed for this view. Thus, for example, St Augustine says, 'Did Peter receive the keys and Paul not? Did Peter receive them and did not John and James receive them? But when in signification Peter represented the person of the Church, that which was given to him alone was given to the Church.'[5] And similarly St Jerome says: 'But you say that the Church is founded on Peter, although the same thing is done in another place upon all the Apostles, and all receive the keys of the kingdom of heaven, and the solidity of the Church is established equally upon all.'[6] St Cyprian had taught the same doctrine.[7]

'FEED MY LAMBS'

Just as the promise of Matt. xvi is understood as having been made to St Peter alone, so this passage is claimed also as its fulfilment to St Peter alone. 'Laying upon him [St Peter]', says the 'Satis cognitum', 'the injunction, Feed My lambs—Feed My sheep. That is, He confides to him without exception all those who were to belong to His fold....

[1] Isa. xxii, 22; cp. also Rev. i, 18; iii, 7.
[2] Satis cogn.
[3] Matt. xviii, 18; John xx, 22–3.
[4] Satis cogn.
[5] Sermo cxlix, cap. 7; *PL*, xxxviii, 802; sim. Sermo ccxcv, cap. 2; *PL*, xxxviii, 1349.
[6] Adv. Jovin., i, cap. xxvi; *PL*, xxiii, 247.
[7] Infra, ch. xix (ii).

As Shepherd of the Christian flock he has received the power of governing all men for whose salvation Jesus Christ shed His blood.'[1]

Many Fathers regard the thrice-repeated question and reply, and the triple injunction, as blotting out St Peter's triple denial and restoring him to his apostleship.[2]

Because of this striking passage, St Peter, in commentaries and sermons too numerous to quote, and in Christian art, is always looked upon as the typical pastor.

In one view, however, in support of which the teaching of the Fathers is claimed, St Peter was honoured again as the representative of all others on whom the injunction was equally laid. Thus St Augustine says: 'His pastoral office He hath imparted to His members also: for both Peter is shepherd, and Paul is shepherd, and the other Apostles are shepherds, and good bishops shepherds.'[3] 'For not he [St Peter] alone amongst the disciples merited to feed the Lord's sheep; but when Christ speaks to one, unity is commended, and to Peter primarily, because amongst the Apostles Peter is the first.'[4]

'CONFIRM THY BRETHREN'

'Our Lord's words very strongly bring out a special gift to St Peter: "Satan hath desired to have *you*. . . . But I have prayed for *thee*."'[5]

A. 'Since all Christians must be clearly united in the communion of one immutable faith, Christ the Lord, in virtue of His prayers, obtained for Peter that in the fulfilment of his office he should never fall away from the Faith—But I have asked for thee that thy faith fail not (Luke xxii, 32); and He furthermore commanded him to impart light and strength to his brethren as often as the need should arise, "Confirm thy brethren" (ibid.). He willed then that he whom He had designated as the foundation of the Church should be the defence of its faith.'[6]

[1] Satis cogn.

[2] St Ambrose, Apol. David, c. ix, 50; *PL*, xix, 871; St Cyril Alex., *in S. Joann.*, lib. xii, cap. i; 'Jesus received him, and by the triple questioning and confession He healed the triple denial', St Gregory Nazian., *Orat.*, xxxix, 18; St Chrysostom, *De Poenitentia*, Hom. v, 2, opp. ii, 311; *In Joann.*, Hom. lxxxviii, 1, opp. viii, 525.

[3] St Augustine, *in Joann. Evan.*, tract. xlvii; *PL*, xxxv, 1734.

[4] St Augustine, Sermo ccxcv *in Natal. Apost. Pet. et Paul*, n. 2, 4 (Allnatt, p. 36), sim. in Sermo ccxvi, cap. iv, *PL*, xxxviii, 1354.

[5] Salmon, p. 342; Luke xxii, 31.

[6] Satis cogn.

N. In the most famous and most usual interpretation which forty-four of the most ancient and subsequent Fathers and doctors declare, this passage had reference to St Peter's fall.[1]

To confirm or strengthen the brethren is no peculiar prerogative of St Peter according to the New Testament. 'The same word *sterizein* is used in three or four places in the Acts (xiv, 21; xv, 32, 41; xviii, 23) of St Paul's confirming the Churches of Syria and Cilicia, of Judas and Silas confirming the Thessalonian Church. And most remarkable of all, Paul when purposing to visit Rome, which is said to have been Peter's peculiar charge, expects that it is by *his* instrumentality this benefit will be conferred on the Roman Church' (Rom. i, 11): the same word *sterizein* is used here.[2]

The interpretation given in 'Satis cognitum' was unknown in the first six centuries of the history of the Church. The earliest instance of the use of the text as referring to the bishops of Rome is that made by Pope Agatho in A.D. 680.[3]

(iii) *New Testament passages which, it is said, are inconsistent with the Roman interpretation of the three Petrine texts*

(a) *Suggesting that the same power and authority was conferred by our Lord on all the apostles*

You also shall sit on twelve seats, judging the twelve tribes of Israel. Matt. xix. 28.

And I dispose to you, as my Father hath disposed to me, a kingdom; That you may eat and drink at my table in my kingdom: and may sit upon twelve thrones, judging the twelve tribes of Israel. Luke xxii, 29, 30.

Amen I say to you, whatsoever you shall bind upon earth, shall be bound also in heaven: and whatsoever you shall loose upon earth shall be loosed also in heaven. Matt. xviii, 19.

He breathed on them; and he said to them: Receive ye the Holy Ghost: Whose sins you shall forgive, they are forgiven them: and whose sins you shall retain, they are retained. John xx, 22, 23.

You are fellow citizens with the saints, and the domestics of God, built upon the foundation of the apostles and prophets, Jesus Christ himself being the chief corner stone. Eph. ii. 19, 20.

And the wall of the city had twelve foundations, and in them, the twelve names of the twelve Apostles of the Lamb. Rev. xxi, 14.

[1] Friedrich, *Documenta ad illustrandum Concilium Vaticanum*, i, 5.
[2] Salmon, p. 343.
[3] Mansi, xi, 242; Denny, sects. 149, 157.

(b) *Suggesting that the other apostles were unaware that St Peter had jurisdiction over them*

In the way they had disputed among themselves which of them should be the greatest. Mark ix, 33, 34.

And there entered a thought into them, which of them should be the greater. Luke ix, 46.

And James and John the sons of Zebedee, come to him, saying . . . Grant to us, that we may sit, one on thy right hand, and the other on thy left hand, in thy glory. Mark x, 35, 37.

And there was also a strife among them, which of them should seem to be the greater. [At the Last Supper]. Luke xxii, 24.

A. St Peter's primatial authority was at first only promised ('on this Rock', etc.) and was not conferred until after the Resurrection.

N. Even so, the apostles cannot have understood a promise of jurisdiction over them, and they show no sign of attaching such a meaning to it afterwards, even in the light of what they were told after the Resurrection.

(c) *Suggesting that the Holy Ghost alone is Vicar of Christ; that if our Lord appointed any human Vicar, He would have said so*

John xiv–xvii (our Lord to His disciples at the Last Supper), especially xiv, 16, 17, 26; xv, 7, 13.

A. The office is implied in our Lord's command to St Peter, 'Feed My lambs', etc.

N. The early Fathers perceived no such implication and knew of no such human office. Thus Sts Gregory Nazianzen, Ambrose, John Chrysostom, and Cyril interpret the thrice-repeated question and reply, and the triple injunction, as blotting out St Peter's triple denial, and restoring him to apostleship.

(d) *Suggesting that the early Apostolic Church was unaware of a supreme authority in St Peter*

Then he saith to them: But whom do you say that I am? Peter answering said to him: Thou art the Christ. And he strictly charged them that they should not tell any man of him. Mark viii. 29, 30; similarly Luke ix, 20, 21. (These evangelists seem to omit the promise to St Peter as if it were of minor importance and unessential to the Gospel.)

Now when the apostles, who were in Jerusalem, had heard that Samaria had received the word of God, they sent unto them Peter and John. Acts viii, 14.

And when Peter was come up to Jerusalem, they that were of the circumcision contended with him, saying: Why didst thou go in to men uncircumcised, and didst eat with them? Acts xi, 2, 3.

(At the Council of Jerusalem.) And the apostles and ancients assembled to consider this matter. And when there had been much disputing, Peter rising up said to them . . . And all the multitude held their peace: and they heard Barnabas and Paul. . . . And after they had held their peace, James answered, saying . . . For which cause I judge . . . Acts xv, 6–19 ('ἐγὸ κρίνω, Vulgate *ego judico*).

A. St Peter, as Supreme Head over the other apostles and the whole Church, presided at the council. 'The idea that James had *arche* (rule) over Peter is, of course, ludicrous.'[1] St James only meant 'I think' or 'I am of opinion'.

N. That is asserted because, in the A view, St Peter *must* have presided. But the Scripture not only fails to support the assertion, it plainly contradicts it. St Peter was neither the first nor the last to address the council. St James the Just (bishop of Jerusalem in fact, though not then in name) presided,[2] and pronounced judgement as president or at least summed up as chairman—*ego judico*.

St Peter's testimony was indeed momentous. It gave the council the startling proof that Gentiles might enter Christ's Church. When the Holy Ghost fell on Cornelius and those with him, St Peter had been the chosen minister, and he was now the witness. There was a true sense in which Christ's *world-wide* Church had indeed been 'built' on St Peter; he had actually been a great stone in its 'foundation'. In the earlier chapters of the Acts, St Peter occupies the leading position, which Scripture does not show him as occupying afterwards. His glorious destiny was already accomplished.

(e) *Suggesting the equal authority of St Peter and the other apostles*

But of them who seemed to be something (what they were some time, it is nothing to me, God accepteth not the person of man), for to me, they that seemed to be something added nothing. But contrariwise, when they had seen that to me was committed the gospel of the uncircumcision, as to Peter was that of the circumcision: (For he that wrought in Peter to the apostleship of the circumcision, wrought in me also among the gentiles.) And when they had known the grace that was given to me, *James and Cephas and John, who seemed to be pillars*, gave to me and Barnabas the right hands of fellowship: that we should go unto the gentiles, and they unto the circumcision: Only that we should be mindful of the poor: which same thing also I was careful to do.

But when Cephas was come to Antioch, I withstood him to the face,

[1] Chapman, *Studies*, p. 90.

[2] Jalland, *CP*, p. 62; St John Chrysostom says that St James 'was invested with the chief rule'. See below ch. xxxiii (ii).

because he was to be blamed. For before that some came from James, he did eat with the gentiles: but when they were come, he withdrew and separated himself, fearing those who were of the circumcision. And to his dissimulation the rest of the Jews consented, so that Barnabas also was led by them into that dissimulation. But when I saw that they walked not uprightly unto the truth of the gospel, I said to Cephas before them all: if thou, being a Jew, livest after the manner of the gentiles, and not as the Jews do, how dost thou compel the gentiles to live as do the Jews? Gal. ii, 6–14.

For I reckon that I am not a whit behind the very chiefest apostles. 2 Cor. xi, 5. (R.V., from the original Greek).[1]

I have in no way come short of them that are above measure apostles. 2 Cor. xii, 11.

The burden I [St Paul, not St Peter] carry every day, my anxious care for all the churches. 2 Cor. xi, 28.

(f) *Suggesting that St Peter did not claim to have been given an individaul authority or jurisdiction*

There is no indication of any claim of this kind in either of St Peter's Epistles, or in the Gospel according to St Mark (which, according to the earliest Fathers, was written down by St Mark from the teaching of St Peter himself),[2] nor indeed anywhere in the New Testament.

A. St Paul records that 'I went up to Jerusalem to visit Cephas, and tarried with him fifteen days',[3] clearly implying St Peter's primacy.

'Even if it can be proved that St Peter never exercised his authority over the other apostles, this would not prove he did not possess it.'

N. According to Holy Scripture, the 'firstness' or primacy of St Peter was manifested in his initiative, leadership, and spokesmanship, but carried with it no sovereignty or jurisdiction over the other apostles. Nor is there any indication that his teaching was endowed with infallibility beyond the teaching of St Paul and the others.

Of St Paul's visit to St Peter, St John Chrysostom says: 'wanting nothing of Peter, not even his assent, but being of equal dignity with him, he comes to him as a greater and older'.[4]

[1] *Λογίζομαι γὰρ μηδὲν ὑστερηκέναι τῶν ὑπερλίαν ἀγποστόλων.* In the Rheims version, not translated from the original Greek: 'For I suppose that I have done nothing less than the great apostles.'

[2] Papias, apud. Euseb., II, xv; VI, xxv, 5; III, xxxix, 15; St Iren., III, i, 1; Tertullian, *adv. Marcion.*, IV, 5; also Origen and St Clement Alex.

[3] Gal. i, 18.

[4] *In Gal.*, i, 18; Opp. x, 677–8; Infra, ch. xxxiii.

PART TWO

THE FIRST TWO CENTURIES

CHAPTER IV

St Peter and Rome

(i) *St Peter's presence, and martyrdom, at Rome*

It appears beyond reasonable doubt that both St Peter and St Paul died as martyrs at Rome, although Holy Scripture does not record it.

The first epistle of St Peter seems to have been written from 'Babylon', a well-known mystical name for Rome.[1] St Clement of Rome, writing *circa* A.D. 96, takes St Peter and St Paul as examples of 'champions' of the Faith; he calls them 'the good apostles', perhaps suggesting 'an affectionate remembrance of those whom he had known personally'.[2] Probably the oldest statement that one of the apostles was executed by Nero is found in a curious apocalyptic tract, the *Testament of Hezekiah*, 'one of the twelve shall be delivered into his hands'. Its date is thought to lie between 75 and 100.[3] St Ignatius, writing to the Romans *circa* A.D. 110, says: 'I do not enjoin you as Peter and Paul did.'[4] St Dionysius, Bishop of Corinth, writing *circa* A.D. 170 to the Romans, from whom a letter had recently come, said:

> Ye also, by such instructions, have united the trees of the Romans and Corinthians, planted by Peter and Paul. For both alike came to our Corinth and taught us; likewise they came together to Italy, and having taught there, suffered martyrdom at the same time.[5]

St Irenaeus, Bishop of Lyons, writing *circa* A.D. 185, said that St Matthew published a gospel in Hebrew 'while Peter and Paul were

[1] 1 Pet. v, 13; Lightfoot, *Clem.*, ii, 492; Euseb., II, xv, 2. Yet he may have written from the actual Babylon, where was a large Jewish settlement; cp. Acts ii, 9, and 1 Pet. i, 1.

[2] Lightfoot, *Clem.*, ii, 25. Yet he seems to distinguish from them those of the elect who 'set a brave example among ourselves', caps. 5, 6.

[3] Shotwell and Loomis, pp. 69–71. [4] *Rom.*, 4.

[5] Euseb., II, xxv, 8; Lightfoot, *Clem.*, ii, 494.

preaching and founding the Church in Rome'.[1] St Clement of Alexandria, about A.D. 190, wrote that St Peter preached at Rome and St Mark in his gospel recorded what was said.[2] Tertullian of Carthage, a little later, wrote:

> We read in the lives of the Caesars, Nero was the first to stain the rising faith with blood. Then Peter is girt by another (an allusion to John xxi, 18), when he is bound to the cross; then Paul obtains his birth-right of Roman citizenship, when he is born again there by the nobility of martyrdom.[3]

And he says of 'the Romans' that they were those 'to whom Peter and Paul conjointly left the gospel sealed with their own blood'.[4] A Roman document of about the same time, attributed to Gaius, a Roman presbyter,[5] says: 'I can point out the trophies of the apostles. For if thou wilt go to the Vatican, or the Ostian Way, thou shalt find the trophies of those who founded this church'. Origen of Alexandria (186–255) says that:

> Peter, it seems, preached in Pontus and Galatia and Bithinia, in Cappadocia and Asia, to those Jews who were of the Dispersion. He came also to Rome at last[6] and was crucified head-downwards; for he requested that he might suffer thus. What need to speak of Paul, who from Jerusalem even unto Illyricum has fully preached the gospel of Christ, and afterwards was martyred at Rome under Nero?[7]

All this evidence is fragmentary, but nothing is known to discredit it. It is strongly supported by the 'argument from silence'. This form of argument depends upon the degree of likelihood that some particular fact would have been mentioned if it had been known. In view of the pride taken in 'apostolic foundation', and the custody of the relics of the martyrs, by every Church that could claim this distinction, it is significant that no other Church ever claimed to be the place of martyrdom of the two glorious apostles, or the shrine of their relics. If any other Church could have made that claim, it is unlikely that it would have omitted to make it.

(ii) *Was St Peter 'bishop' of Rome?*

For an intelligent approach to this question, it is necessary to distinguish between the name or title of 'bishop' and the office or order of

[1] II, i, 1. [2] Euseb., VI, xiv, 6. [3] *Scorpiace*, p. 15.
[4] *Adv. Marcion*, III, iii, 2, 3; similarly in *De praescr. haereticorum*, xxxvi.
[5] Euseb., II, xxv, 7; but see Lightfoot, *Clem.*, ii, 377–88.
[6] *καὶ ἐπὶ τέλει ἐν Ῥώμῃ γενόμενος* [7] *Comm. on Genesis*, iii, in Euseb., III, i, 1.

ministry to which that name came ultimately to be applied. 'Bishop' originally meant only 'overseer', and it was a word in ordinary use before the Christian era. It did not have the great and dignified associations that have since gathered round it. In the first century, in Gentile churches which had no resident apostle, the local presbyters were *de facto* overseers, and were often so described.[1] We do not find the presbyters called overseers at Jerusalem, where St James presided.

On the other hand, the New Testament never gives the name of 'bishop' either to the original apostles, or St Paul, or their numerous colleagues in the chief pastorate who are also called 'apostles', such as St James of Jerusalem and the other 'brethren' of the Lord,[2] Andronicus, Junias or Junianus,[3] Barnabas,[4] Silvanus, and Timothy.[5]

The position held by apostolic delegates such as Timothy in Ephesus and Titus in Crete, although their local presidency was only temporary, 'nevertheless fairly represents the functions of the bishop early in the second century. They were in fact the link between the Apostle whose superintendence was occasional and general, and the bishop who exercised a permanent supervision over an individual congregation';[6] but they were not called bishops. St. Paul appointed Timothy to 'the work of an evangelist'.[7] Eusebius calls 'evangelists' those who 'occupied the first step in the succession from the apostles'.[8] That may have been a usual description for these secondary or intermediate apostles,[9] but they did not receive the title of 'overseer'. Nor did St James of Jerusalem, who presided over the Church there in a position indistinguishable from that of the later 'diocesan' bishop; in the New Testament, he is simply 'James', although later generations always accounted him as having been the bishop. It might have seemed unfitting to describe an apostle, or a secondary apostle, as a mere overseer. The letters of St Ignatius show that throughout Asia Minor, by the beginning of the second century, the style of 'the bishop' had become attached in each Church to a resident minister of the higher, apostolic, order. But when the Roman Church wrote to Corinth about A.D. 96, the Scriptural des-

[1] Phil. i, 1 (Philippi); Tit. i, 7 (Crete); Acts xx, 17; 1 Tim. v, 17; Tit. i, 5; 1 Pet. v, 1 (Asia Minor).

[2] Gal. i, 19; 1 Cor. ix, 5; xv, 7; see Lightfoot, *Apostle*, p. 92; F. J. A. Hort, *The Christian Ecclesia*, p. 77.

[3] Rom. xvi, 7; see Lightfoot, *Apostle*, p. 96.

[4] 1 Cor. ix, 5, 6,; Lightfoot, *Apostle*, p. 96; Acts xiii, 2, 3; xiv, 4, 14.

[5] 1 Thess. i, 1. [6] Lightfoot, *Diss.*, p. 99. [7] 2 Tim. iv, 5. [8] iii, 37.

[9] G. Salmon, D.D., in *Expositor*, 1887, vi, 26; Turner, *Studies*, p. 28; cp. Calvin Inst., IV, iii, 4; T. M. Lindsay, *Church and Ministry in Early Centuries*, 4th ed. 1902, p. 80 n.

cription of 'bishops' was still applied to presbyters there.[1] Apparently St Clement, who was then the chief pastor of Rome, and who wrote the letter, was not yet called 'bishop' in the language of the time,[2] even if 'bishop' in the nature of his office; it was after his day that his successors were so called. It is probably a verbal anachronism to call St Peter or any other of the first apostles 'bishop'.[3]

But the actual relationship of an apostle to a church in which he had come to reside did not depend on titles. Any one of the twelve, or St Paul, an apostle 'not from men, neither through man', must have taken a presidential place in any local church where he happened to be. If St John's position at Ephesus was not exactly that of bishop, it was only because it was even greater; and the greater includes the less. 'The Episcopate slept in the Apostolate.'[4] St Peter and St Paul, resident at Rome, could not be less than its chief pastors. The whole evidence preserved to us from the first two centuries points to their having both been there, and having suffered martyrdom at about the same time. These early records agree, as has been seen, in regarding the two great apostles equally as founders of the Roman Church. Seeing that mon-episcopacy—which does not admit of more than one bishop of one diocese—was a later development, a joint presidency of St Peter and St Paul is not ruled out of possibility; Epiphanius, writing in A.D. 375, gives a list of Roman bishops beginning with 'first Peter *and* Paul, apostles and bishops'.[5] For the same reason it is quite possible that St Clement was ordained to the apostolic ministry of the chief pastorate by St Peter, as Tertullian says,[6] although he did not succeed to the actual presidency of Rome until some twenty-five years later, after Linus and Anencletus.

Whether or not St Peter is rightly included in the list of *bishops* of Rome has been much disputed, and the numbering of the early bishops is relied on in argument. The earliest list is that written by St Irenaeus, *circa* A.D. 185. About the same time a Christian Jew named Hegesippus, while residing in Rome, made another list, which has not survived. St Irenaeus refers to the very great and most ancient church 'founded and established by two most glorious apostles, Peter and Paul':[7]

> The blessed apostles, then, having founded and builded the church,

[1] Clem., *ad Cor.*, pp. 44, 47, 54.

[2] Similarly, the style of 'pope', in early use at Alexandria and Carthage, was not adopted at Rome until the fourth century; Battifol, *PC*, p. 290.

[3] Barnes, *CR*, p. 37.

[4] Döllinger, *FA*, ii, 130; cp. Newman, passages quoted supra, ch. ii (v).

[5] *Haeres*, xxvii, 6; Lightfoot, *Clem.*, i, 169, 329.

[6] *De praescr. heret.*, cap. xxxii.

[7] III, iii, 2.

committed the ministry of the episcopate to Linus . . . and his successor is Anencletus: and after him in the third place from the apostles the episcopate is allotted to Clement. . . . To this Clement again, Evaristus succeeds, and to Evaristus Alexander: then Xystus in like manner is appointed, sixth from the apostles: and after him Telesphorus, who also was a glorious martyr: afterwards Hyginus, then Pius, and after him Anicetus. Anicetus having been succeeded by Soter, now, in the twelfth place from the apostles, Eleutherius holds the office.[1]

Some later Roman lists contain variations that are now recognized as mistaken (thus Anencletus is sometimes 'Cletus' and is sometimes counted twice; some put Clement next after Linus); but the list given by St Irenaeus from Linus to Eleutherius is accepted as historically correct. It is convenient to tabulate here these names, together with their approximate dates:

1. Linus	67–79
2. Anencletus	79–91
3. Clement	91–99
4. Euaristus	99–109
5. Alexander	109–119
6. Sixtus	119–128
7. Telesphorus	128–138
8. Hyginus	138–142
9. Pius	142–154
10. Anicetus	154–165
11. Soter	165–173
12. Eleutherius	173–188
13. Victor	188–198

St Irenaeus seems not to have counted into his list of *bishops* the 'two most glorious apostles who founded the church'. His numeration 'from the apostles' is precise. In another passage he describes Hyginus and Anicetus as eighth and tenth in the episcopate:[2] at another place, however, he dates Cerdon from Hyginus 'who occupied the ninth place in the succession from the apostles'.[3] Some think that St Irenaeus may have copied the list of Hegesippus and, from this isolated reference to Hyginus as ninth, it has been conjectured that 'his own normal practice was to think and write of St Peter as first Bishop of Rome',[4] but there seems to be nothing else in his writings to confirm this guess.

Bishop Victor, who succeeded Eleutherius, is referred to incidentally by a Roman presbyter,[5] writing about A.D. 210, as 'the 13th bishop at Rome from Peter'.

[1] Ibid., III, iii, 3. [2] Ibid., III, iv, 3. [3] Ibid., I, xxvii, 1.

[4] Dom Gregory Dix in *Laudate,* September 1938, xvi, 175.

[5] Or perhaps by St Hippolytus himself; Euseb., V, xxviii, 3; Lightfoot, *Clem.*, ii, 377 ff.

After all, the omission of St Peter and St Paul in the earliest episcopal enumerations 'from the apostles' may have little significance. Linus, Anencletus, and Clement also, the first three 'bishops' of Rome, were evidently not called 'bishops' in their own days. Yet from earliest times the Church has regarded all bishops as successors of the apostles in general, and the bishops of 'apostolic sees' (such as Ephesus, Antioch, Rome, or Smyrna) as successors of their apostle-founders in particular.

(iii) '*The twenty-five years' episcopate*'

None of the writings of the first two centuries describes St Peter as a *bishop* of Rome. He and St Paul are coupled as the joint founders of that Church.

In the third century, we find St Peter claimed as the founder, St Paul retaining a subordinate place in memory. This marked change of emphasis is attributed by some to the influence of the 'Clementine Romance', of which mention must be made later;[1] that explanation is conjectural, but the change is obvious.

In the fourth century, we find an explicit statement that St Peter was bishop of Rome for twenty-five years: it appears earliest in a list of Roman bishops called the Liberian Catalogue, which was compiled in A.D. 354.[2] According to this late 'tradition',[3] St Peter went to Rome twelve years after the Crucifixion, left it because of the decree of Claudius which expelled the Jews, and was absent from it for long years.[4] This theory of a twenty-five years' episcopate has great difficulties to meet.[5] Its beginning has to be brought back to the year 42. St Peter was in Jerusalem towards Easter 44, again in 51, and at Antioch some time after. Some scholars think that the words of St Paul in writing to the Romans in A.D. 58[6] are inconsistent with the idea of Rome as a church already presided over by St Peter. At every

[1] Infra, ch. xv.

[2] It is thought to have been a recension of an earlier list written about A.D. 235, but it contains some bad blunders, and the statement about St Peter cannot be traced with certainty to the earlier list.

[3] Lactantius, at the beginning of the fourth century, says 'Nero was already in power when Peter came to Rome', i.e. not before A.D. 54. *De mortibus persecutorum*, p. 11.

[4] Barnes, *CR*, supports it with careful argument.

[5] See Duchesne *Origines Chrétiennes*, p. 73.

[6] Rom. i, 7–11. Some consider that his being 'hindered hitherto' (i, 13) was because Rome was 'another man's foundation' (xv, 20, 22; Barnes, *CR*, pp. 41–4). In a contrary view, St Paul said he was no longer 'hindered' from coming to Rome because of 'having no more place in these countries'—Illyricum, etc.(xv, 19, 23).

point in the Acts and St Paul's Epistles where some mention of St Peter might have been expected, if indeed he were Rome's bishop, support for the theory is lacking. Origen of Alexandria (186–255) says[1] that St Peter, after preaching in other regions, 'came also to Rome at last', and was there crucified.

Although it is reasonably certain that St Peter was at Rome before his martyrdom, for an unknown period of time, the theory of a twenty-five years' episcopate is not now strongly maintained by Roman scholars: a recent verdict is that 'The so-called tradition of the twenty-five years of Peter's Roman episcopate rests on no historic data. This tradition may have originated in a confusion.'[2] Abbot Chapman has put the matter in a true light when he says:

> That St Peter and St Paul died at Rome is not seriously doubted. For our present purpose it is quite unimportant when St Peter first went thither. In what sense he could be called 'bishop' of Rome need not trouble us either. It is obvious that in his day the local episcopate was at the very most a new conception, scarcely anywhere carried out. The simple question is this: *Did St Peter deposit the primacy in the see of Rome?*[3]

(iv) *Precedence of St Peter and St Paul*

These two great names, so closely linked together in our history, are familiar to us in the order 'Peter and Paul'; we recognize St Peter's 'firstness'. But in early writings this order is sometimes reversed, we find references to 'Paul and Peter'. St Irenaeus, according to one reading,[4] wrote 'Paul and Peter'. Eusebius did so when writing his history at the beginning of the fourth century: 'Now Linus was the first, after the martyrdom of Paul and Peter, to receive the episcopate of the church of the Romans.'[5] 'Clement occupied the third place of those who were bishops after Paul and Peter.'[6]

There are some indications that in popular estimation, even in Rome in early times, St Peter's precedence over St Paul was not appreciated. About two miles outside Rome, on the Appian Way, is the Basilica of S. Sebastiano, with catacombs beneath it. It has been from the fourth century a 'basilica of the apostles'; Pope Damasus (366–384) placed an inscription there stating that at one time the two apostles

[1] *Comm. on Genesis*, iii; Euseb., III, i, 1.

[2] Lebreton and Zeiller, i, 238–9.

[3] *GCC*, p. 61.

[4] Adopted by Duchesne, *CS*, p. 79. The Clermont and Vossian mss. read, 'Paulo et Petro'—'which in view of the later tendency to prefer St Peter may represent the original order'. Jalland, *CP*, p. 114.

[5] III, ii, 1.

[6] III, xxi. Elsewhere, however, he says that Linus was the first after Peter.

dwelt there; some scholars think that it had actually been a temporary resting-place of their bodies. On what remains of the walls, and on fragments, have been found a large number of *graffiti*, inscriptions that had been scratched on the walls by pilgrims to the place, perhaps in the third century. It is interesting to notice that on a number of these *graffiti* the order of the names is not Peter and Paul, but Paul and Peter, thus:

> Paul and Peter, pray for Victor.
> Paul and Peter, pray for Eratus and ask . . .
> Paul and Peter, keep in mind Sozomenus and . . .
> Paul and Peter, pray for Nativus for ever.[1]

Notwithstanding the greatness of St Paul, there can be no equal comparison between his apostleship and the tremendous office of St Peter which, according to the Doctrine of the Papacy, resided in him as the true Vicar of Christ Himself. Such instances as these, where the two names are coupled with what seems a disregard of St Peter's preeminence, are thought by some to indicate that the incomparable greatness, implicit in that exalted office, was not clear to the generality of Christians in the first two or three centuries.

Throughout the second century, indeed, the 'two most glorious apostles' were revered together as martyrs at Rome, and *joint* founders of the church there.[2] In the middle of the third century, however, the Roman bishop was claiming succession from St Peter individually; and by the fourth century, St Paul was eclipsed, and his share in the Roman foundation comparatively little thought of. Yet since the time of Pope Nicholas I[3] (858–67), the popes have been accustomed to promulgate decrees in name of the apostles St Peter and St Paul.

[1] Turner, *CA*, pp. 224–5; Hughes, i, 79; L. E. Elliott-Binns, *Beginnings of Western Christendom*, p. 95; *Corpus Inscriptionum Latinarum*, viii, 18656; G. M. Bevan, S.Th., *Early Christians of Rome*, 1927, pp. 32–3.

[2] St Iren., III, iii, 2; infra, ch. x.

[3] Roy, p. 196.

CHAPTER V

Clement of Rome, A.D. 96

According to firm tradition, Clement was the third to preside over the Church of the Romans after the martyrdom of St Peter and St Paul, approximately from A.D. 91 to 99. He was probably a freedman, as were his two predecessors, Linus and Anencletus; 'among these freedmen were frequently found the most intelligent and cultivated men of their day'.[1] He may have been a Hellenist Jew, and perhaps one of the household of Flavius Clemens, the consul who became a Christian and was put to death by his cousin, the Emperor Domitian;[2] but Clement, like Anencletus, was a common servile name.[3]

Our knowledge of St Clement is derived entirely from the famous letter sent from the Roman Christians to the Corinthians about A.D. 96. The letter itself does not say who wrote it, but it has always been attributed to St Clement. St Dionysius of Corinth, writing to the Romans *circa* A.D. 170, refers to 'the former letter written to us through Clement',[4] and St Irenaeus a little later notes that 'in the time of this Clement, the Church in Rome wrote a most adequate letter to the Corinthians'.[5]

There is no reference in the letter to any bishop of Rome, but the name of 'bishop', in Rome at all events, had apparently not yet become attached to the office of ministry held by Clement; presbyters are still described in it as 'bishops', as they were in the New Testament. It seems that the early bishops of Rome were not called bishops until some time, probably early, in the second century.

In St Paul's time, forty years before, disorders at Corinth had drawn from him the great teaching of 1 Cor. x, 14–22, and xi, 17–34. Good is oft brought out from evil. This later letter to the Corinthians mentions

[1] Lightfoot, *Clem.*, i, 62. [2] Ibid., pp. 59, 61. [3] Turner, *Studies*, p. 224 n.
[4] Euseb., IV, xxiii, 11. [5] III, iii, 3.

that they had made sedition against their duly appointed presbyters and had replaced them by other men. It is addressed from 'The Church of God which sojourneth in Rome to the Church of God which sojourneth in Corinth, to them who are called and sanctified by the will of God through our Lord Jesus Christ', and it was written during the persecutions of the Emperor Domitian:[1] 'By reason of the sudden and repeated calamities and reverses which are befalling us, we consider that we have been somewhat tardy in giving heed to the matters of dispute that have arisen among you, dearly beloved.' It is not said that the Corinthians had asked for help from the Romans.[2]

Corinth had close associations with Rome. It had been refounded as a Roman colony in 44 B.C., its colonists were freedmen, with some Roman citizens. 'In its official life, whether political or religious, Corinth appears in the first century as a city entirely and exclusively Roman.'[3] 'The communication between Rome and Corinth was easy and frequent. If the journey were rapidly accomplished, it need not take more than a week; though the average length was doubtless greater.'[4]

Mgr Duchesne observes that St Clement's letter 'is an admirable testimony to the wise and practical spirit animating Roman piety, even in these remote days. From end to end it is inspired by a fine simplicity of faith and pious wisdom'.[5] He thus summarizes it:

'First he dwells on the unseemliness of discord and strife (3–6), then he counsels obedience to the Will of God (7–12), points to the greatness of the reward promised to simple and righteous souls (23–26) and the need for order in the Church. He takes his illustrations from the discipline of the Roman armies, and from the sacerdotal hierarchy of the Old Testament (37–42). Then turning to the New Covenant, the author points out that the Ministry of the Church comes from the apostles and Jesus Christ, that its authority is lawful and to be obeyed (42–47). He entreats the Corinthians to repent, to return to peace and order, and to submit to salutary chastisement; if certain people are an obstacle to peace, they must not shrink from exiling them. The Church should pray for those who are seditious (48–58). With rather an abrupt transition, he at once adds example to precept, formulating (59–61) a long prayer, which has but a remote connection with the Corinthian troubles.'[6] Lightfoot says that 'the whole letter is a great

[1] Mgr A. S. Barnes (*CR*, pp. 209–11) supposes the date to be *circa* A.D. 70, in the troubles which followed the death of Nero; but the internal evidence of the Epistle tells strongly against the earlier date (Lightfoot, *Clem.*, i, 348–52).

[2] Duchesne, *CS*, pp. 84–5. [3] Clarke, p. 19. [4] Lightfoot, *Clem.*, i, 82.

[5] *EH*, i, 162–3. [6] Duchesne, *EH*, i, 162

eucharistic psalm which gathers about its most practical aim—the restoration of order at Corinth'.[1]

The messengers who carried the letter to Corinth, Claudius Ephebus and Velrius Bito, are described in it as faithful men 'who have walked among us from youth unto old age unblamably'.[2] The letter seems to have been well received, and to have brought about peace among the Corinthians for, some seventy years later, St Dionysius their bishop said that it was an old custom with them to read it in church.[3]

This important letter has features that are relied upon both for and against the historical claims of papal jurisdiction. Although it does not call attention to any supposed privilege of the Roman Church, 'it is strenuous, even peremptory in the authoritarian tone which it assumes'.[4] On the other hand 'it pleads the authority, not of the chief minister, but of the whole body'.[5] St Peter is mentioned only as one of the two 'good apostles' whose martyrdoms are spoken of as noble examples. There is nothing to indicate that the Church in Rome, or its chief minister, had derived any peculiar authority from either of these two apostles. Indeed, there is nothing in all the letter to show that this Church even possessed a chief minister of the order afterwards called episcopal.

If St John was still living at Ephesus, in advanced old age, and if news had reached him of the disorders at Corinth, and if he did not send them admonition, the effective action taken by the Romans would stand out in contrast; these are conjectures. Yet the letter suggests that 'the Roman church was already conscious of some degree of external responsibility, such as does not appear to have been realized by the geographically neighbouring churches of Thessalonica or Philippi'.[6]

Conflicting views are taken of this letter, and opposite inferences are drawn from it:

A. 'In the very first document belonging to Christian history, outside the pages of Holy Scripture, the Church of Rome steps to the front in a manner that is suggestive of supreme authority, and that tallies with the whole future attitude towards the rest of the Church.'[7] It was 'undoubtedly the first step towards papal domination'.[8] It was 'The Type Set'.[9] It was 'the *epiphany* of the Roman primacy'.[10] 'The least

[1] Lightfoot, *Clem.*, i, 82.
[2] Section 63. The 'we' and 'us' of the letter are true plurals for the brotherhood at Rome. Allnatt (p. 121 n.) seems to read into it the much later 'we' of royalty.
[3] Euseb., IV, xxiii. [4] Lightfoot, *Ign.*, i, 398 [5] Ibid. [6] Jalland, *CP*, p. 103.
[7] Rivington, *PC*, p. 1. [8] Ibid., p. 7, citing Lightfoot, *Clem.*, i, 70.
[9] Ibid. (title of ch. i). [10] Batiffol, *PC*, p. 123.

that can be said of this first disclosure of Rome's position in the Church is that it fits in with her present position in Roman Catholic Christendom.'[1]

N. The piety and the influence of the great Roman Church clearly appears. But the content of this important letter is just as clearly negative of the later Roman claim. There is no hint of any Petrine authority in the local church; nor is there any reference to its chief pastor, or any suggestion of an office resembling what was later claimed for the Roman bishops.

'Not only have we no traces of a bishop of bishops, but even the very existence of a bishop of Rome itself could nowhere be gathered from the letter. Authority indeed is claimed for the utterances of the letter in no faltering tone, but it is the authority of the brotherhood declaring the mind of Christ by the Spirit, not the authority of one man, whether bishop or pope.'[2] 'The later Roman Theory supposes that the Church of Rome derives all its authority from the bishop of Rome as the successor of St Peter. History inverts this relation and shows that, as a matter of fact, the power of the bishop of Rome was built upon the power of the Church of Rome. It was originally a primacy, not of the episcopate, but of the church.'[3]

[1] Rivington, *PC*, p. 20
[2] Lightfoot, *Clem.*, i, 352.
[3] Ibid., p. 70.

CHAPTER VI

Papal Titles

The interest of this chapter is partly antiquarian, and the reader may prefer to pass it by; but it may be useful to glance at the headings, which show the approximate dates at which various titles have become attached to the Roman bishopric. In the chronological arrangement of this book, and in the quotations from contemporary sources, the bishops of Rome are referred to in the language of their period. Thus it was not until the fourth century that they adopted the Eastern title of 'pope', although the earlier bishops also are now spoken of retrospectively as popes.

BISHOP (*circa* A.D. 110 onwards)

The earliest bishops of Rome were apparently not distinguished by the epithet of 'overseer' or bishop, for it was often applied in the New Testament to presbyters, and they were still so described when St Clement was writing in A.D. 96.[1] Afterwards, probably very early in the second century, the name of 'bishop' came to distinguish the chief pastor of the city, and it was no longer applied to presbyters in general.

SAINT (A.D. 79 to 530)

Although this, of course, is not a papal title, it should be noted that all the first fifty-three bishops of Rome after the martyrdom of St Peter and St Paul were revered in memory as martyrs and saints; many of the earliest bishops attained actual martyrdom. Since the death of St Felix IV in A.D. 530, only twenty-three have been accounted saints in the full sense; the most recent of these was St Pius V, who died in 1572.

[1] Supra, ch. iv (ii).

METROPOLITAN or ARCHBISHOP (*circa* A.D. 300)

Such titles were in use by the time of the Council of Nicaea in A.D. 325, and were applied indiscriminately to all presidential bishops, i.e., primates and patriarchs, including of course those of Rome.[1] This usage continued for long; thus the Council of Chalcedon in 451 described Pope St Leo I as 'archbishop of the great and elder Rome'.

PAPA or POPE (*circa* A.D. 314 onwards)

'Pope' was an Eastern and African title, and in early times it was applied to the bishops of the primatial sees of Carthage and Alexandria. Thus in A.D. 250, the clergy of Rome address St Cyprian of Carthage as 'Pope Cyprian', and refer to him as 'most blessed and glorious pope'.[2] Alexandria, a few years later, called to remembrance 'our blessed Pope Heraclas'.[3] The contemporary bishops of Rome were not so styled.

As applied to a Roman bishop, the epithet first occurs in a memorial inscription referring to 'my papa Marcellus' (304), but rather as a term of affection than as a title.[4] In the fourth century the word comes into general use for the bishops of various important sees, such of course as Alexandria, and also of Rome,[5] Salamis, Jerusalem, Aquileia, and others.[6] The clergy of Rome call Zosimus 'Pope of the catholic church of the Roman city'.[7] In the fifth century, the title is used still more generally; Sidonius Apollinaris (431–89) speaks thus of the bishops of Rheims, Lyons, Arles, Vienne, Marseilles, and others.[8] The Sixth General Council in 680 refers to 'the pope of Old Rome', and 'the pope of Alexandria'.[9] Pope St Gregory VII (1073–85) decreed that the title should be confined to the Roman popes,[10] but its traditional use continued in the East, and still continues there.

PATRIARCH (*circa* A.D. 450)

This title came into general use for the bishops of the most important sees about the fifth century. There were patriarchates of Alexandria and Antioch before Nicaea (A.D. 325); 'the organization of provinces and metropolitans followed, as a matter of obvious convenience, the organi-

[1] *Cath. Enc.*, vol. I, s.v. 'Archbishop'.
[2] St Cyprian, Ep. xxx, also viii, 8; xxiii; xxxi; xxxvi.
[3] Euseb., VII, vii, 4.
[4] Batiffol, *PC*, p. 290; G. B. de Rossi, *Inscr. Chr. Urb. Romae*, I, p. cxv; II, 55.
[5] Council of Arles, 314.
[6] St Jerome, Epp. lxxxi (66), lxxxvi (70), lxxxviii (71), and *Contra Johann, Hierolymit*, p. 4.
[7] Coll. Avell., p. 63.
[8] See Denny, sects. 1195–7.
[9] Mansi, xi, 214.
[10] Funk, i, 392; *Cath. Enc.*, xii, 270.

zation of the empire arranged by Diocletian'[1] (*circa* A.D. 300), and these were the second and third greatest cities in the empire. As a Christian title of honour in Rome, 'patriarch' appears first as applied to Pope St Leo I, *circa* 450.[2]

SERVANT OF THE SERVANTS OF GOD (*circa* A.D. 450 onwards)

This beautiful description of his pastoral office was adopted by Pope St Leo I (440–61), and has been ever since retained.

APOSTOLIC SEE (sixth century onwards)

'Apostolic see' was a general description for each of 'the Apostolical Churches in which the very seats of the apostles at this very day do preside in their own places'; thus Tertullian, writing early in the third century; he instances Corinth, Philippi, Ephesus, and Rome.[3] Pope St Siricius (384–98) applies the epithet to the principal or metropolitan see of any province.[4] St Augustine more than once speaks of the 'apostolic sees' in the plural,[5] and so does Pope Pelagius I (555–60).[6]

But the great see of Rome was the only apostolic see in the West, and it came in time to be thought of as *the* apostolic see. So Pope St Celestine I is referred to as 'bishop of the apostolic chair' by the Council of Ephesus in 431. Latin, unlike Greek or English, has no definite article, no *a* or *the*. *Sedes apostolica* may sometimes mean no more than one of a number of sees recognized as apostolic. But the double martyrdom of St Peter and St Paul 'suffices to make Rome the Apostolic See *par excellence*'.[7] By the time of Pope Hormisdas (514–23) the expression was claimed as a peculiar title of the Roman see.[8] Nevertheless, down to the time of Charlemagne (crowned in A.D. 800), 'it must be confessed that the name of pope, of apostle, of apostolic prelate, of apostolic see, was still common to all bishops'.[9]

VICAR OF PETER

This designation was often used in the centuries before 'Vicar of Christ' came to be used specifically of the popes of Rome.

[1] *Cath. Enc.*, xi, s.v. 'Patriarch'. [2] Ibid.; Döllinger, *Hist.*, ii, 233.
[3] *De praescr. heret.*, p. 36. [4] Ep. iv, 1, 2; Labbe, ii, 1029.
[5] Ep. cxxxii, 3; *Contra Faustum Manich.*, xxviii, 2; *PL*, xlii, 485.
[6] Ep. vii, *ad episcopos Tusciae*; *PL*, lix, 598. [7] Lebreton and Zeiller, i, 242.
[8] Pope Damasus (366–84) was the first to do so, PBLPB, p. 668.
[9] Thomassin, *De l'ancienne discipline de l'église*, Pt. I, book I, cap. iv, 39; Denny, sect. 12.

BISHOP OF BISHOPS (*circa* A.D. 1073)

This is less a formal title than a description sometimes applied to the papal office. St Gregory VII (Hildebrand, 1073–85) seems to have been the first pope to use it.

VICAR OF CHRIST (*circa* A.D. 1200)

This title has an interesting history, and perhaps marks the developing recognition of the papal sovereignty. The phrase is elastic, and can convey widely different meanings. In the early Church, it was sometimes used to describe the character of the Holy Ghost. About A.D. 200, Tertullian used it thus, with particular reference to St John's Gospel, xiv and xv.[1] On the other hand, any priest can be spoken of aptly enough as a vicar of Him in whose Name he pronounces absolution.[2] The epithet became a usual description of bishops. About A.D. 380, 'the most learned and most illustrious of the Latin fathers' wrote: 'A bishop has the *persona* of Christ, he is Vicar of the Lord.'[3] Some time later, another Latin theologian wrote: 'God's bishop [*antistes*] must be purer than other men, for he is His Vicar . . . for he must daily act in Christ's place, . . . pray or offer for the people.'[4] The phrase occurs in the 'acclamations' with which Pope Gelasius was greeted at the close of a Roman synod in A.D. 495'[5] but it was not yet a specially papal epithet; Pope Hormisdas in A.D. 517 still applies it to all bishops: 'As Christ is the Head of the Church and bishops are the Vicars of Christ, manifest care ought to be taken in selecting them.'[6] Archbishop Amalarius of Trèves, *circa* 800, wrote that 'the bishop has the *persona* of Christ, . . . he is the Vicar of the Lord'.[7] The Council of Compiègne in 833 declared that: 'Bishops are Vicars of Christ and key-bearers of the kingdom of heaven; on them Christ has bestowed authority, that whatsoever they shall bind on earth', etc.[8] The Council of Meaux in 845 declared that 'We are Vicars of Christ by divine authority . . . by virtue of the sevenfold Holy Spirit we all, although unworthy, are Vicars of Christ and successors of the apostles'.[9] In those

[1] *De praescr. heret.*, xxviii; *PL*, ii, 40.

[2] Thus Pope Pius XII, in 'Menti nostrae', 23 September 1950, 'sacerdos Iesu Christi partes agit'.

[3] Lightfoot, *Diss.*, p. 229; Ambrosiaster, *Comm. on* 1 *Cor.* xi, 10; *PL*, xvii, 240.

[4] Pseudo-Aug. (perhaps Hilary the Deacon), *Quaestiones de utraque mixt.*; *PL*, xxxv, 2386.

[5] Mansi, viii, 184; Hardouin, ii, 941.

[6] Ep. xxv, to the bishops of Spain; *PL*, lxiii, 423–4.

[7] *De ecclesiasticis officiis*, Lib. II, cap. ii; *MBVP*, xiv, 980.

[8] Mansi, xiv, 647.

[9] Mansi, xiv, 814–15.

days, the title certainly denoted an authority divinely given, but incomparably less than what it has come to denote when appropriated solely to the single holder of a unique office.

It is not easy to discover exactly when this great title became attached distinctively to the pope and detached from bishops in general. Pope Innocent III (†1216) was perhaps the first pope to claim the title for himself alone, and Pope Boniface VIII declared in 'Unam Sanctam' (1302) that 'Christ and His Vicar constitute only one Head'. Yet as late as the thirteenth century, St Thomas Aquinas could still write that 'the Apostles and their successors are Vicars of God';[1] and at the Council of Trent in 1562 a daring claim was still voiced that all bishops are vicars of Christ as much as the pope, though he be the chief.[2]

SUPREME PONTIFF (*circa* 1464)

This now-familiar title also has an interesting history. *Pontifex Maximus* was a title of the pagan Roman emperors, and by it were addressed such monsters of vice and tyranny as Caligula and Commodus. So, at the beginning of the third century, Tertullian (after he became a Montanist) used it as a sarcastic insult to some bishop, probably the bishop of Rome.[3] The Christian emperors of the West continued to use the title, but they died out in the fifth century. *Pontifex* had already come into Christian use in the West as equivalent to *sacerdos*, and until about A.D. 1000 *summus pontifex* was a style of archbishops in general.[4] Gradually this became restricted to the popes,[5] and it was a settled papal title by the time of Pope Paul II (1464–71).

It need hardly be said that the great office of the Bishop of Rome is neither demeaned by the simplicity of early address, nor enhanced by the many honorific forms dear to later times. A collection of these can be found in De Maistre,[6] such as Father of Fathers, Pastor of All Pastors, Heir of the Apostles, Most Happy Lord, Sovereign Priest. Not all of them were countenanced; to decribe anyone—patriarch, pope, or bishop—as 'oecumenical' or 'universal' was condemned by Pope

[1] *Summa*, iii, 235 (pars iii, q. lxiv, art. ii, conclusio).
[2] *Acta Trid.*, ii, 157, 600; infra, ch. lxx. [3] Infra, ch. xvi.
[4] Baronius ad an. 397 (v, 42); Du Cange *Glossarium*, and Smith and Cheetham, *Dict. Christian Antiqq.*, s.v. 'pontifex'. The pagan title, 'Pontifex maximus', was finally dropped by Gratian, A.D. 382; PBLPB, 703–5.
[5] Pope Theodore I was addressed as 'supreme pontiff of all prelates' in A.D. 649: Epp. of bps. of Africa *ad pap. Theod.*, Labbe, vii.
[6] Pp. 52–3.

St Gregory I (590–604) as haughty and Satanic.[1] 'Holy Father' is now, of course, the commonest title.

A. As appears in the New Testament, titles of dignity were not in use at the first; there was no need for them, although St Peter and his earliest successors fully possessed the great authority afterwards indicated by titles of reverence; they accompanied the developing organization of the Catholic Church. Some of these titles give expression, in becoming terms of honour and reverence, to the unique greatness of the office of the Supreme Pontiff, as it came to be more fully understood and universally acknowledged.

The words quoted from Pope Nicholas I were obviously meant to prove that the ecclesiastical power, being directly concerned with God, is above secular power. Expressions such as those of Arnaldus were purely individual and unauthoritative.

N. Rome gradually monopolized the name of Apostolic See, which had also described other sees, and the old style of Supreme Pontiff. Its bishops appropriated the name of Vicar of Christ, which had previously been given to all bishops. This process went on, step by step with the gradual aggrandizement of the Roman bishop into 'bishop of bishops', and the corresponding subordination of all other bishops.

The name of 'Vicar of Christ' illustrates this long process. It was a seemly figure of speech for the sacred office common to all bishops. But when it is monopolized, its possible implications are tremendous; when it is appropriated to express a divinely given and unique authority in one single bishop as *the* Vicar of Christ, as the individual representative and mouthpiece of our Lord, it can be understood to hold him out as virtually divine, and has been so understood. Pope Nicholas I indeed claimed for the Roman Pontiff that 'the pious Emperor Constantine called him God, and it is manifest that God cannot be judged of men'.[2] Arnaldus of Villanova in 1300 said 'which of the faithful does not know that the Roman Pontiff is Christ on earth?'[3] and a bishop at the Lateran Council of 1517 called him 'a second God on earth'.[4] These may be deprecated as medieval extravagances; yet

[1] Infra, ch. lvi. But according to the *Dictatus papae*, Pope Gregory VII claimed that the Roman pontiff alone is to be called universal; Mirbt, 5th ed., no. 278, p. 146; *PL*, cxlviii, 407.

[2] Ep. lxxxvi, to the Emperor Michael III, A.D. 864; *PL*, cxix, 960–1. This was only an embroidery of the Silvester-Constantine legend; infra, ch. lx.

[3] Mirbt, p. 211. [4] C. B. Moss, D.D., *The Old Catholic Movement*, 1948, p. 26.

less than a hundred years ago the enthusiasts whom Abbot Butler calls 'neo-ultramontanes' were substituting the name of the reigning pope for the Name of God, or of the Holy Ghost, in the hymns of the Church.[1] And although it was a medieval pope who declared that 'Christ and His Vicar constitute only one Head', the present pope has renewed that pronouncement, which sounds to non-Roman ears a startling echo of St John x, 30 ('I and the Father are one').[2]

If indeed the bishop of Rome were our Lord's true and unique vicar, no disciple of Christ could deny him absolute authority or withhold absolute obedience. If the pope were actually One Head with Christ, then unlimited infallibility might be thought a detail needing no council to endorse it. But the early Church knew of no such title and no such authority for the Roman bishop. A metaphor applicable to all bishops in common has been monopolized by the Roman bishop, and perverted to ascribe to him a semi-divine status and authority.

[1] Butler, i, 76–7, 228.
[2] Boniface VIII, 'Unam sanctam' A.D. 1302, Mirbt, p. 148; Pius XII, 'Mystici corporis Christi', 29 June 1943.

CHAPTER VII

Ignatius of Antioch, A.D. 110

Within twenty years after Clement's letter to the Corinthians, a Syrian bishop, journeying to his martyrdom at Rome, wrote seven vivid letters which have been preserved to us. St Ignatius, the second bishop of Antioch, was condemned to death in the persecutions under Trajan, and was sent to Rome to help to supply the demand for victims for the sports of the arena. The provinces were put under requisition to furnish convicts to be 'butchered to make a Roman holiday'. He was not a Roman citizen, or he would not have been thrown to the beasts. He journeyed through Asia Minor in the custody of a maniple of ten soldiers, passing through Philadelphia and Smyrna. Brethren from Ephesus, Magnesia, and Tralles also sallied out to cheer him and give what little help they could. Before he sailed from Troas he had written letters to the Churches of these five cities, and to St Polycarp, the bishop of Smyrna (who himself received the martyr's crown in his old age, some forty-five years later). Some brethren from Ephesus carried on another letter from the saint, in advance, to the Romans.

These seven letters were written down to dictation, probably in haste. The dominant note is the writer's intense humility and self-depreciation, and his burning desire for martyrdom. There are two chief topics in the letters to the Churches in Asia Minor: (1) He gives repeated warnings against the then flourishing Docetic and Gnostic heresies, which denied the reality of the Incarnation and maintained that both the birth and death of Christ, and His whole life on earth, were apparitional, not real. St John had written against this same heresy.[1] (2) He treats the threefold ministry of bishop, presbyters, and deacons as the centre of order, the guarantee of unity in the Church. Again and again he exhorts the Churches to loyalty and obedience, using language that sounds exaggerated to modern ears:

[1] 1 John ii, 22–3; iv, 2, 3; 2 John 7.

> Be ye zealous to do all things in godly concord, the bishop presiding after the likeness of God and the presbyters after the likeness of the council of the apostles, with the deacons also who are most dear to me, having been entrusted with the diaconate of Jesus Christ.[1]
>
> It is therefore necessary, even as your wont is, that ye should do nothing without the bishop; but be ye obedient also unto the presbytery, as the apostles of Jesus Christ our hope. . . . In like manner, let all men respect the deacons as Jesus Christ, even as they should respect the bishop as being a type of the Father, and the presbyters as the council of God and as the college of the apostles. Apart from these there is not even the name of a Church.[2]

The main theme of the saint's letter to the Romans is his entreaty that the Roman brethren will not try to procure his deliverance from death. 'Christianity had already forced its way upwards to the highest ranks of society in Rome. . . . The intercession of powerful friends in the metropolis, whether open Christians or secret sympathizers, might have procured, if not a pardon, at least a commutation of his sentence.'[3]

> I dread your very love, lest it do me an injury. . . . Ye never grudged any one; ye were the instructors of others.[4] I write to all the churches, and I bid all men know, that of my own free will I die for God, unless ye should hinder me. I exhort you, be ye not an 'unseasonable kindness' to me. Let me be given to the wild beasts, for through them I can attain unto God. I am God's wheat, and I am ground by the teeth of wild beasts that I may be found pure bread of Christ. . . . I do not enjoin you, as Peter and Paul did. They were apostles, I am a convict; they were free, but I am a slave to this very hour. . . . Bear with me, brethren. Do not hinder me from living; do not desire my death. Bestow not on the world one who desireth to be God's, neither allure me with material things.

In writing to the Romans, the saint makes no reference to any bishop or other minister. From this silence some opponents of episcopacy have drawn an inference that the Church in Rome at that date had no bishop. It may be that the name of 'bishop' was not as yet applied in Rome to its chief pastor, that even if he was 'bishop' in the nature of his office he was not so in name.[5] But the emphatic words of St Ignatius already quoted make it difficult to suppose that the Church in Rome, which he praised so highly, had 'not even the name of a Church', for lack of the triple ministry.

Each of his letters begins with many laudatory epithets in honour of

[1] *Magnesians*, p. 5. [2] *Trallians*, pp. 2, 3. [3] Lightfoot, *Ign.*, ii, 196.

[4] 'We may suppose that he had in his mind the Epistle of Clement, which contains several references to confessors and martyrs, with exhortations to patient endurance founded on these examples.' Lightfoot, *Ign.*, ii, 203.

[5] Supra, chs. iv and vi.

the Christian Churches to whom he wrote, but for the Church of the Romans his praise is greatest:

> Ignatius, who is also Theophorus, unto her that hath found mercy in the bountifulness of the Father Most High and of Jesus Christ His only Son; to the church that is beloved and enlightened through the will of Him who willed all things that are, by faith and love towards Jesus Christ our God; even unto her that presides in the country of the region of the Romans, being worthy of God, worthy of honour, worthy of felicitation, worthy of praise, worthy of success, worthy in purity, presiding in love, walking in the law of Christ and bearing the Father's name; . . . being filled with the grace of God without wavering, and filtered clear from every foreign stain.

Thus clearly the saint sets out the eminence of the Church in Rome in piety and good works. The phrases, 'which presides in the country of the regions of the Roman' and 'presiding in love',[1] suggest, in the view of some Roman scholars, an official presidency of the local church in Rome over all other churches of the world.[2] 'The country of the region of the Romans' may, however, refer to early Christian communities in southern Italy. By the following century they had become very numerous, with sixty bishops, and they 'were bound by close ties to Rome, from which, evidently, they had received their first apostles and their organization'.[3] The phrase 'presiding in love' resembles another, 'presiding in truth', which does not easily bear so extended an application.[4]

A. The meaning of St Ignatius is, 'She presides in the country of the Romans; she presides at the love-feasts', or 'the charities'. 'The love' means the whole Christian brotherhood everywhere. 'The most natural meaning of such language is that the Roman Church presides over all the Churches. As the bishop in his diocese presides over its works of charity, so does the Roman Church preside over those same works throughout Christendom.'[5] The words 'filtered clear from every stain' may refer to the renowned purity of the Roman faith (Rom. i, 8).

N. 'If the meaning were as suggested, it is difficult to see why Ignatius should write "in the country of the district of the Romans" in place of

[1] καὶ προκάθεται ἐν τόπῳ ʽΡωμαίων . . . προκαθημένη τῆς ἀγάπης.

[2] E.g., Döllinger, *Hist.*, i, 255; but the ancient Latin translation is *praesidens in caritate*, which hardly supports that view.

[3] Duchesne, *CW*, pp. 15, 16; *EH*, i, 184.

[4] Ep. Clem., ii, *ad Jacobum*, cap. xvii, Προκαθέξεσθαι ἀληθείας: see Lightfoot *Ign.*, ii, 192–3, 558; Symonds, p. 65.

[5] Duchesne, *CS*, pp. 85, 86.

"in Rome", which alone would be natural to describe merely the locality. The idea of the "cathedra Petri" therefore has no place here.'[1]

'The presidency of this church is declared to be a presidency of love. This then was the original primacy of Rome—a primacy not of the bishop but of the whole church, a primacy not of official authority but of practical goodness, backed however by the prestige and advantages which were necessarily enjoyed by the church of the metropolis.'[2]

Whatever may be the exact shade of meaning in St Ignatius' eulogy of the Church in Rome, it is the Church and its membership that he refers to. There is no slightest hint of a presiding chief pastor, or of any Petrine office.

[1] Lightfoot, *Ign.*, ii, 190. [2] Lightfoot, *Clem.*, i, 71.

CHAPTER VIII

Polycarp of Smyrna and Anicetus of Rome, A.D. 155

Some facts in the life of St Polycarp, Bishop of Smyrna, have been preserved for us with unusual certainty and exactness. When he suffered martyrdom by burning at the stake on 23 February 156, he was eighty-six years old; he was born therefore about A.D. 70. St Irenaeus, who in his youth had been a disciple of Polycarp,[1] records that Polycarp 'had not only been trained by the apostles, and had conversed with many who had seen Christ, but had also been constituted by the apostles bishop over Asia in the Church of Smyrna'.[2]

St Ignatius, in the letter mentioned in the last chapter, because he had not had time to write to certain other churches, asked Polycarp to write for him to them.[3] We have also a letter from St Polycarp to the Philippians, asking for particulars of the martyrdom of Ignatius.

A year before his own martyrdom, Polycarp visited Rome, while Anicetus was its bishop. At that time the Church was already troubled by the dispute as to the right date for the keeping of Easter.[4] It came to a head about forty years later, when Irenaeus thus relates what had taken place between Polycarp and Anicetus:

> When the blessed Polycarp stayed at Rome in the time of Anicetus, although they had some trifling disagreements on other matters, they immediately made peace, nor did they care to quarrel on this head [the dispute about the date of Easter]. For neither could Anicetus persuade Polycarp not to observe what he had always observed with John the disciple of our Lord and the other apostles with whom he consorted; nor yet did Polycarp persuade Anicetus to observe it, for he said that he ought to hold to the custom of the elders before him. And though such

[1] Iren. to Florinus, Euseb., V, xx; Lightfoot, *Ign.*, i, 445.
[2] Euseb., III, iii, 4. [3] *Polycarp*, 8; Lightfoot, *Ign.*, ii, 357, 574.
[4] Following old tradition, the Churches of Asia kept Easter on a day other than that kept in Rome and most other Churches; infra, ch. ix.

was the case, they held communion with one another, and in the church Anicetus yielded the [celebration of the] eucharist to Polycarp, manifestly out of respect. So they parted from one another in peace.[1]

A. Polycarp must have come to Rome as an ambassador from the Orientals in order to take the decision of Anicetus on the point in dispute, so that he might submit to it as being authoritatively binding on the Church as being the decision of the Supreme Judge of all the faithful.[2]

N. Notwithstanding the undoubted primacy of the see of Rome and the great importance of its bishop, these two bishops, of Rome and Smyrna, met as equals. Neither could persuade the other on this serious and troublesome question. Yet 'they did not care to quarrel', and 'parted from one another in peace'.

'On Papalist principles Polycarp ought to have submitted the question to Anicetus as the one who possessed *jure divino* full power of jurisdiction over the whole Church, whose decision as Supreme Judge would be final, and when that decision had been given obeyed it; and in the event of disobeying it he would have been separated from the Church, no longer being in communion with the Supreme Pastor of the One Flock. Polycarp's action proves that neither Anicetus nor himself knew anything of the Papal Monarchy; and St Irenaeus, by the way he records the facts, shows that he was equally ignorant.'[3]

[1] Iren. Ep., *ad Victorem*, Euseb., V, xxiv; Lightfoot, *Ign.*, i, 555; tr. Lawlor and Oulton, i, 170.

[2] F. X. Funk, *Historisch-politische Blätter*, p. 745; Denny, sect. 527.

[3] Denny, sect. 527.

CHAPTER IX

Early Greatness of the Roman See

It is difficult to exaggerate the greatness of the metropolis of the Roman Empire, the 'eternal city' of the Caesars, conquerors of the Old World. Moreover, all the countries within the Empire, as well as those on its fringes, had been brought into a great and effective system of communication well suited to the metropolis of the Church which Rome became. 'A vast system of roads bound together the different parts of the empire; along them travelled both private carriages and the imperial posts. The Mediterranean itself formed a great waterway, where travelling was safe and rapid; intercourse between the various parts of the empire, being made easy, became incessant.'[1] 'All movements of thought throughout the Empire acted with marvellous rapidity on Rome, the heart of the vast and complicated organism.'[2]

The secular greatness of the imperial metropolis contributed to its greatness as the metropolis of the Church; the secular greatness of a see city tends to enhance the standing of its bishop. Thus for a time in the fourth century the bishop of Milan seemed to share a twofold hegemony with the pope; 'the real reason was that Milan was the Imperial official residence, the capital of the Western Empire'.[3] So also, after the rise of the Byzantine Empire, when Constantinople had become an exact counterpart of the old metropolis of the Empire from the civil point of view, the General Council of 381 decreed that 'the Bishop of Constantinople shall hold the privilege of honour after the Bishop of Rome, because Constantinople is the New Rome'; and the Council of Chalcedon in 451 asserted in a canon (which, however, Rome repudiated) that 'the Fathers naturally assigned privileges to the See of Elder Rome because it was the Imperial City'. On the other hand, Jerusalem itself, the Mother Church of the world, sank into insignificance when Hadrian

[1] Duchesne, *EH*, i, 5. [2] Ramsay, *St Paul*, p. 346.
[3] Duchesne, *CW*, pp. 32, 35.

destroyed the city in A.D. 135.[1] Aelia, built on the ruins, was only a humble see, suffragan to the provincial capital, Caesarea.[2]

But great as was the position of the Church in the imperial metropolis, the Church itself was great. 'The Roman church was the greatest, the most numerous, and in regard to the West, the most ancient of all the Christian establishments, many of which had received their religion from the pious labours of her missionaries.'[3] 'When St Paul wrote his Epistle to the Romans (A.D. 58 at the latest), their church had already been in existence, and he had been wishing to visit it, for several years. Whose hands had sown the Divine seed in this ground, where it was to bring forth such a tremendous harvest? We shall never know. There is nothing to prove that the Roman Jews, present at the first Pentecost, were converted; still less that they became missionaries.'[4] Yet St Paul could say, 'your faith is spoken of in the whole world.'[5]

A hundred years after Pentecost, the Mother Church of Jerusalem was a memory, and Rome had become the metropolis of the whole Church. From early times, two special reasons were recognized for the pre-eminence of Rome: (1) the peculiar greatness of its apostolic foundation and (2) the conspicuous charity, piety, and orthodoxy of the early Roman Christians.

(1) The foundation of a church by an apostle was looked upon in every church that could claim it with reverence and pride, the more so if he had been martyred there. There were other 'apostolic sees' in the East, but Rome, the only such see in the West, had an undisputed claim to *two* apostle founders, and these the 'two most glorious apostles', both martyred also at Rome. Rome was a pre-eminently 'apostolic see'.

(2) There is ample testimony to the outstanding Christian virtues of the faithful in Rome. 'It was not merely owing to the superior authority of her tradition that the Church of Rome was known and esteemed. For the faithful, in general, her most striking pre-eminence was the pre-eminence of her charity. Let the ecclesiastical disputes of every country resound in Rome; what most easily found a hearing there were the sufferings of the other Churches. Rome was at once affected by even the most distant calamities, whether caused by ordinary adversities, by the scourge of war, or by persecution. Messengers were sent off in her name to console the afflicted, and to carry to them abundant alms.

[1] Dr S. G. F. Brandon dates the eclipse of the see from A.D. 70 and the destruction of the Temple; *The Fall of Jerusalem*, 1951, p. 180 and passim.

[2] Three centuries later, at Chalcedon, Jerusalem was promoted to be the fifth and smallest patriarchate.

[3] Gibbon, ii, 48 (ch. xv). [4] Duchesne, *EH*, i, 41. [5] Romans i, 8.

Such was her constant tradition.'[1] Dionysius, Bishop of Corinth, writing to the Romans *circa* A.D. 175, says:

> For this has been your custom from the beginning: to do good in divers ways to all of the brethren, and to send supplies to many churches in every city: now relieving the poverty of the needy, now making provision, by the supplies which ye have been in the habit of sending from the beginning, for brethren in the mines; and thus as Romans ye observe the hereditary custom of Romans, which your blessed bishop Soter has not only maintained, but even advanced, by providing in abundance the help that is distributed for the use of the saints, and by exhorting with blessed words, as a loving father his children, the brethren who come up [to Rome].[2]

The great Epistle to the Corinthians, written 'through Clement', established the fame of the Romans in doctrine and exhortation. The terms of high praise in which St Ignatius addressed the Romans have already been quoted.[3]

Church life in Rome was extraordinarily cosmopolitan. At the time when St Polycarp visited Rome, he may have met there Christian teachers, orthodox or heretic, from all parts of the world: Hegesippus, a Palestinian, the earliest historian of Christianity: Justin Martyr, a Samaritan by race, champion of the Gospel against Jew and Gentile alike; his own earlier pupil, Irenaeus, afterwards the greatest Christian writer of his age; Hermas, author of the earliest Christian allegory, may still have survived there: heretical teachers likewise gathered in force, Cerdon, the heresiarchs Marcion and Valentinus, and the influential lady heretic Marcellina, another Gnostic: there too studied Tatian, still the disciple of the orthodox Justin, but later the founder of the Encratic sect of Gnostics. 'It must have been a strange and sad experience for one whose memory travelled back to the first ages of the Church, to witness this rank and rapid growth of excrescences on the pure teaching of the Gospel.'[4]

In the Vatican is the *stele* of a Phrygian bishop named Abercius, who in the latter part of the second century was a renowned champion of the Catholic faith against the Montanists:

> The citizen of a notable city I made this [tomb] in my lifetime; that in due season I might have here a resting-place for my body. Abercius by name, I am a disciple of the pure shepherd, who feedeth his flocks of sheep on mountains and plains, who hath great eyes looking on all sides; for he taught me faithful writings. He also sent me to royal Rome to behold it

[1] Duchesne, *CS*, p. 102. [2] Euseb., IV, xxiii, 10; tr. Lawlor and Oulton, i, 130.
[3] Supra, ch. vii. [4] Lightfoot, *Ign*., i, 451, 452.

> and to see the golden-robed, golden-slippered queen. And there I saw a people bearing the splendid seal. And there I saw the plain of Syria and all the cities, even Nisibis, crossing over the Euphrates. And everywhere I had associates. Taking with me [the epistles of] Paul, I followed where faith led me and set before me for food the fish from the fountain, mighty and stainless (whom a pure virgin grasped), and gave this to friends to eat always, having good wine and giving the mixed cup with bread. . . .[1]

This stone-carved epitaph 'is couched in highly mystical phraseology. . . . At a time when persecution was still constant, and when the Church was surrounded on all sides by hostile pagans, it was clearly quite impossible to depict the mysteries of the Catholic faith in any obvious manner. . . . The style of the whole epitaph demands a mystic interpretation.'[2] The symbolism of the Fish is well known. Probably the 'golden-robed queen' is the Church at Rome, and the 'splendid seal' denoted the baptism of the people. Sir William Ramsay, who discovered the *stele* in 1883, describes it as 'the testimony of Abercius in favour of the one and indivisible Church Catholic, and against the separation and nationalism of Montanus'. In the sending of Abercius (by the Good Shepherd) to see 'royal Rome', Mgr Barnes sees 'the doctrine of the Primacy of the Roman Pontiff'.[3] In any view, this venerable monument gives a striking testimony to the early greatness of Rome in the Church, and its far-reaching magnetism.

A. 'Even if it be true that the situation of Rome, as capital of the empire, contributed to increase the importance of its Church, have we not a right to see therein a means prepared by Divine Providence for assuring a centre to Christianity at its very inception? Believers all agree in seeing the finger of God in the marvellous history of the Roman Empire, and in the services which her peaceable institutions rendered to the propagation of the faith. Why should it not be allowed to us to perceive the designs of Providence in the selection of Rome as the abode of St Peter and the See of his successors?'[4]

N. We may well believe that the imperial greatness of Rome was used by Divine Providence. It is true also that the imperial greatness of the city was only a contributory cause of the greatness of the local church. Of that greatness there is ample contemporary evidence in the first two centuries. But none of the evidence associates the pre-eminence of the

[1] Barnes, *Mon.*, pp. 94–100; Lightfoot, *Ign.*, i, 492–501; Euseb., V, xvi, 3; Lawlor and Oulton, ii, 171.
[2] Barnes, *Mon.*, pp. 81, 96, 99. [3] Ibid., p. 99. [4] Duchesne, *CS*, p. 83.

Church in Rome with the martyrdom of St Peter rather than of St Paul, or suggests that importance was attached to its foundation more by one than by the other of its two glorious apostle-founders, or that anyone during these two centuries attributed its influential greatness to a Petrine office inherited by its bishops.

CHAPTER X

Irenaeus of Lyons 'against Heresies', A.D. 185

St Irenaeus, born about A.D. 120–30, was a Greek of Smyrna. He recalls in a letter how, in his youth, he often listened to the teaching of Polycarp (who had been trained by apostles, and by them appointed Bishop of Smyrna), 'concerning the Lord, His mighty works and teaching, as having received them from the eyewitnesses of the life of the Word'.[1] He is said to have been teaching in Rome at the time of the martyrdom of St Polycarp, i.e., 156. He appears to have paid repeated visits to Rome.[2] He became a presbyter of Lugdunum, now Lyons, in Gaul. At the time of the fierce persecution under the Emperor Marcus Aurelius, the Churches there wrote to other Churches, as distant as Asia and Phrygia, telling of the sufferings of their martyrs. Irenaeus carried one letter to Rome, to Bishop Eleutherus. On his return he was made Bishop of Lyons, in 177 or 178,[3] in succession to the martyred Pothinus. His great treatise *Against Heresies*, in five books, was written *circa* 180–5. Only fragments of the Greek original have been preserved, but the whole work survives in a very early Latin translation.

It is a searching examination of heresies, and especially of the doctrines of the Gnostics. These were weird and mythological imaginings, which varied in various schools of Gnostics, but agreed in one assertion, i.e., that the life, death, and resurrection of our Lord were all illusory, mere semblance and apparition; behind them was inner truth that the apostles knew but kept hidden from the many; they had handed it down by word of mouth as a secret tradition which the Gnostics claimed to possess. St Irenaeus exposed the many absurdities of the pernicious cult, and firmly stressed the true tradition of the Faith.

[1] Euseb., v, 20. [2] Lightfoot, *Clem.*, ii, 495. [3] Batiffol, *PC*, p. 198.

How was the earnest inquirer to know what was the true Christian tradition? Where should it be looked for? In the Churches founded by the apostles, says St Irenaeus, and from the bishops and presbyters there who are their successors. In all the Churches the tradition is the same, proving its truth, even in the farthest of them. There is no other belief 'in the regions of Germany, nor do they hold any other tradition in the parts of Spain, nor among the Celts, nor in Egypt, nor in Libya, nor in the middle parts of the world'.[1] 'The tradition is guarded by the successions of presbyters in the Churches.'[2] It cannot be supposed, he argues, that the apostles kept back a secret tradition of truth from their own successors whom they chose and appointed to govern and guide the Churches:

> All who wish to look back on the truth can see the tradition of the apostles clear and manifest in every Church in the whole world. We can enumerate those who were appointed as bishops in the Churches by the apostles, and their successors down to our own time, who neither knew nor taught anything like these ravings. Yet surely, if the apostles had known hidden mysteries which they were teaching secretly and apart to the perfect, they would assuredly have handed them on to these men to whom they committed the very Churches themselves, for they desired them to be perfect and irreproachable in all things whom they left as their successors, handing on their place of authority.[3]
>
> But since it would be very long in a volume of this sort to give the successions of all the churches, we confound all those who, from self-pleasing, vain-glory, blindness, or perverse will, gather where they ought not, by [pointing to] that Church, very great, very ancient, and known to all, founded and established in Rome by two most glorious Apostles Peter and Paul,[4] its tradition which it has from the Apostles, its 'faith announced to all men',[5] its faith proclaimed to men through the successions of bishops coming down to our time. *Ad hanc ecclesiam propter potentiorem principalitatem necesse est omnem convenire ecclesiam, hoc est eos qui sunt undique fideles, in qua semper, ab his qui sunt undique conservata est ea quae ab apostolis traditio.*[6]
>
> The blessed apostles then, having founded and established the Church, committed the ministry and episcopate to Linus . . . (St Irenaeus here enumerates the bishops of Rome)[7] . . . Anicetus having been succeeded by Soter, the bishop's office is now held in the twelfth place from the apostles by Eleutherius. By the same order, and in the same succession, both the tradition from the apostles in the Church, and the preaching of the truth, has come down to us. And this is a very full demonstration of the unity and sameness of the life-giving faith, which from the apostles even unto now hath been preserved in the Church and passed onward in the truth.[8]

[1] Iren., I, x, 2.
[2] Iren., III, ii, 2; 'presbyters' used here in the sense of 'reverend seniors'.
[3] Iren., III, iii, 1. [4] Or 'Paul and Peter', supra, ch. iv (iv). [5] Rom. i, 8.
[6] Iren., III, iii, 2. [7] Supra, ch. iv (ii). [8] Iren., III, iii, 3.

> And Polycarp too, who had not only been trained by the apostles, and had conversed with many who had seen Christ, but had been constituted by the apostles bishop over Asia in the Church of Smyrna, whom also we saw in the first age of our life, . . . having always taught these things which he learned from the apostles, which the Church delivers, which alone are true. These things are witnessed by all the Churches in Asia and by those who to our time have succeeded Polycarp. . . . Yea and the Church in Ephesus, having had both Paul for its founder, and John to abide among them until the times of Trajan, is a sure witness of the apostles' tradition.[1]
>
> The proofs therefore being so abundant, we ought no more to look for the truth elsewhere which it is easy to obtain from the Church, the apostles having therein most abundantly deposited, as in a rich storehouse, whatsoever appertains to the truth. . . . Wherefore we ought, shunning them [the heretics], with all diligence to love what belongs to the Church, and to lay hold of the tradition of the truth. Even if a trifling matter was in question, would not it be necessary to resort to the oldest Churches, where the apostles went in and out, and obtain from them a clear and definite ruling on the matter of dispute? And what if the apostles themselves had not left us the Scriptures: should we not need to follow the order of tradition which they delivered to those to whom they delivered the Churches?[2]

The sentence in italics has been left in the Latin here because its exact meaning has been much debated; the Latin is tortuous and obscure. 'The original Greek text of this phrase is missing; so that we have here only a translation with the risk of its being more or less inexact in its renderings, a risk not lessened by the fact that this Latin translation is quite old, dating perhaps from the time of Tertullian.'[3] Its meaning has been endlessly discussed; attempts are made by scholastic guesswork to restore the original Greek; a note on some of these will be found at the end of this chapter. The following two translations are typical, but they vary considerably.[4]

A. For with this Church, on account of its greater princedom (*or*, pre-eminent authority), it is necessary that every Church, that is, the faithful who are everywhere, should agree, in which the tradition which is from the apostles has been preserved by those who are everywhere.[5]

N. For to this Church, on account of its more influential pre-eminence

[1] Iren., III, iii, 4. [2] Iren., III, iv, 1. [3] Batiffol, *PC*, pp. 207–8.

[4] The various conjectures of scholars, such as Thomassinus, Waterworth, Bonner, Funk, Wilhelm and Scannell, and Chapman on the one hand, and Keble, Hitchcock, Bright, Dix, and Jalland on the other, do not conform to controversial type.

[5] Dogm. Const., cap. ii, translations in Rivington, *PC*, p. 23; Chapman, *GCC*, p. 64; Butler, ii, 283.

(*or*, superior nearness to the source, *or*, superior origin), it is necessary that every Church should resort—that is to say the faithful who are from everywhere—in which the tradition which is from the apostles has always been preserved by those who are from everywhere.[1]

Of this great work *Against Heresies*, Mgr Batiffol observes[2] that 'It expounds the theory of the Church and of her doctrinal function with such fullness and firmness that the third book is a veritable treatise on the Church, and the oldest in existence'. The passages that have here been quoted, including the debatable sentence, are all in the whole five books that seem to have any bearing upon 'the ancient faith of the universal Church' regarding Rome and its bishops. St Peter is mentioned only in this passage, jointly with St Paul as a founder of the Church in Rome. In *The Demonstration of the Apostolic Preaching*,[3] a shorter treatise written *circa* A.D. 190, St Irenaeus does not mention or allude to St Peter or to Rome.

A. 'This text [the debatable sentence], however translated, ever remains a full and complete proof of the tradition which we believe was received from the Apostles, namely, that Rome is the centre of the Church and the infallible throne of truth.'[4]

It would be difficult to meet with a clearer assertion:

1. Of unity of doctrine in the universal Church,
2. Of the sovereign importance of the Church of Rome,
3. Of her superior pre-eminence over the whole of Christianity.'[5]

'The justification of the central authority recognized in the Roman Church is the deposit of Faith which it preserved in safety and in the principalitas which it held from Peter. It is Irenaeus who says this, and Irenaeus is a Greek.'[6]

Although all the Churches founded by the apostles preserved pure doctrine, Rome, says St Irenaeus, was the greatest, because of its superior pre-eminence; it is not Rome which agrees with the other Churches, but others with Rome.

N. That Rome held any principalitas through St Peter individually is exactly what St Irenaeus nowhere said or suggested, although he testifies to the outstanding greatness of the Church in Rome, a fact well

[1] See Puller, p. 19; Symonds, p. 274. [2] Batiffol, *PC*, p. 198.
[3] E.T. by J. Armitage Robinson, D.D., 1920.
[4] Chapman, *Revue Bénédictine*, année xii, p. 64.
[5] Duchesne, *CS*, p. 80. [6] Batiffol, *CP*, p. 111.

known and undisputed. 'A see founded by two apostles is not necessarily the see of both or either.'[1]

For the true tradition of faith, he refers to the apostles (in the plural) and the Churches (in the plural) founded by them. The unbroken series of their successors *in each Church* authenticates the tradition, and, above all, the fact that all the Churches agree in the one tradition.

In the debatable sentence (which alone is quoted in support of the modern Roman view), the apostolic tradition is said to be preserved by the faithful who are, or come from, everywhere, not by any inherent prerogative of Rome.

If St Irenaeus had any idea that the Roman bishop was 'the true Vicar of Christ, Head of the whole Church, the Father and Teacher of all Christians', possessing 'in virtue of the Apostolic primacy, which as the successor of Peter, Prince of the Apostles, he holds over the whole Church, the supreme power of teaching', it is unthinkable that no hint of anything resembling such momentous doctrine should be given in the whole five books of St Irenaeus' great work 'expounding the doctrinal function of the Church'. He can have heard nothing resembling it either in Rome itself, or from St Polycarp. St Polycarp can have heard nothing resembling it from St John or other apostles.

Some suggested restorations of the original Greek of St Irenaeus' 'Against Heresies', III, iii, 2

Convenire ad

In the Latin of the Vulgate, *convenire* alone means 'resort to' or 'assemble' in 97 out of 111 instances; in only ten it means 'agree with'. But *convenire ad*, which occurs twenty-six times, means 'to resort to' every time.[2] The Encyclical 'Satis cognitum', in quoting the sentence, omits the *ad*. Yet the translator from the Greek may perhaps have used it clumsily to render συμβαίνειν πρὸς if he found that in the original, and that Greek phrase undoubtedly means 'agree with.'[3]

Necesse est

It seems to be agreed that this represents ἀνάγκη not δεῖ (*oportet*) and implies a natural necessity, not a moral obligation.

Potentior principalitas

'*Potentiorem* presents some difficulty. It ought to mean "more powerful". But probably it represents ἱκανωτέραν, for "potentissimas" is used to translate ἱκανωτάτην found in the following paragraph of the original as applied to the letter of Clement to the Corinthians. Here "adequate" or

[1] Rivington, *PC*, pp. 23, 24. [2] Puller, p. 26. [3] Symonds, p. 272.

"satisfying" would seem to be its meaning. On the other hand, *potiorem* has been conjectured instead of *potentiorem*. . . . *Potiorem*, meaning "special", may represent ἐξαιρέτον or διαφορωτέραν in the lost original.'[1]

Principalitas may stand for αὐθεντία, authority, but a careful study of comparative uses by Irenaeus tends against this view. Dr Funk and Abbot Chapman prefer πρωτεῖα, the first place. It may stand for ἀρχή[2] or ἀρχαιότης.[3] 'The very careful documentation of D. Van den Eynde[4] makes it as near a certainty as we can get in these things that the word is ἀρχαιότητα, not in the sense of "age" but of "source".'[5] 'Irenaeus will therefore mean that Rome's nearness to the source of Apostolic tradition is more adequate or satisfying to the inquirer than that of any other Apostolic Church. The Greek original will then be, as Stieren conjectured, διὰ ἱκανωτέραν ἀρχαιότατα.'[6]

Undique

The primary meaning of the word is *from* all quarters or from everywhere, not *in* all quarters, etc. So 'the faithful will come from every place, *undique*'.[7] But it can also be used loosely to mean 'everywhere'. Some consider that the words *sunt undique* are due to a copyist's error, and they propose to substitute others, such as *praesunt ecclesiis*.[8]

In qua

If it represents ἐν ᾗ, then it ought grammatically to refer to *omnem ecclesiam*, not *hanc ecclesiam*. 'If *in qua* refers to the Roman Church it suggests that the apostolic tradition as to truth is preserved there by "those of the faithful" who "resort there" for business or pleasure, and bring it with them, rather than find it there. It is thus because the Roman Church is Christendom in miniature that truth may best be found there.'[9] But Dom Gregory Dix suggests that *in qua* represents ᾗ, 'inasmuch as'.[10] 'Harnack, Mgr Duchesne, and Funk, think that *in qua* refers, not to the Roman Church, as has been long thought, but to the Churches other than Rome.'[11]

[1] Symonds, p. 274. [2] Keble. [3] Symonds, pp. 272–4.

[4] *Les Normes de l'Enseignment Chrétien dans la Littérature Patristique des Trois Premiers Siècles* (1933), pp. 163 sq. (Completed by J. Madoz, *Potentior Principalitas*: Estud., Ecles., V [1936], 360–6).

[5] Dom G. Dix, Jurisdiction in the Early Church, *Laudate*, September 1938, xvi, 180.

[6] Symonds, p. 274. [7] Batiffol, *PC*, p. 208. [8] Batiffol, *PC*, p. 209.

[9] Kidd, *RP*, p. 15. [10] Loc. cit. [11] Batiffol, *PC*, p. 208.

CHAPTER XI

The Dispute about Easter, A.D. 195

The feast of Easter was not celebrated on the same date everywhere in the Church. The Churches of Asia, who claimed that they followed the rule of St John and other apostles, kept it on the fourteenth day of the first Jewish month, Nisan, on whatever day of the week that might fall. At Rome, and throughout the greater part of the Church, it was kept always on the Sunday following the fourteenth day of Nisan.[1] This caused difficulty, especially when Christians of one tradition found themselves living among others. Dispute grew tense when Victor was bishop of Rome (189–98). He was an African and the first Roman bishop of pure Latin race.[2] Our knowledge of what occurred comes from the narrative of Eusebius, which must therefore be fully examined.[3] After naming those who were bishops of the principal sees at the time, Eusebius continues:

> Now a question of no small importance arose in their time. For the communities of the whole of Asia, relying on a tradition of great antiquity, thought that they ought to observe the fourteenth day of the moon—the day on which the Jews were ordered to sacrifice the lamb—as the day for

[1] The exact point at issue was whether the Vigil of Easter should be kept on the night 13–14 of the moon, or on the following Saturday-Sunday; F. E. Brightman, in *Essays on Early History of the Church*, ed. H. B. Swete, 1918, p. 234, n. 3.

[2] Jalland, *CP*, p. 123; Lightfoot, *Diss.*, p. 223.

[3] V, xxii–xxv; translation by Lawlor and Oulton, i, 168–70. Some scholars lay stress on the actual documents which Eusebius quotes, and mistrust his own interpretation of the dispute. In a careful study of the conditions in Rome in the time of Victor, by G. la Piana (*Harvard Theological Review*, 1925, pp. 207–70), he suggests that the Roman community included heterogeneous elements, and that the dispute chiefly concerned a group of Asiatics settled in Rome who kept to their own observances. Similarly, Dr N. Zernov considers that the letter of Polycrates 'can be properly understood only as the protest of the Asiatic churches against the excommunication by a Roman synod of their brothers settled in Rome'. (*CQR*, April 1933, p. 30).

the festival of the Saviour's Pascha; since they deemed it necessary at all costs to put an end to their feast on that day, no matter on what day of the week it should fall. But it was not the custom for the churches throughout all the rest of the world thus to celebrate it, preserving as they did by an apostolic tradition the custom which had obtained hitherto, that it was not proper to end the fast on any other day than on the day of the resurrection of our Saviour.

So then, synods and assemblages of bishops came together, and unanimously drew up in letters an ecclesiastical decree for the faithful everywhere, to the effect that the mystery of the Lord's resurrection from the dead should never be celebrated on any other but the Lord's day, and that on that day alone we should observe the close of the paschal fast. Now there is still extant to this day a letter from those who were assembled in Palestine.[1]

These synods had been convoked by the various metropolitans at the request of Bishop Victor; 'He was the first bishop in the Church, and it was most fitting that he should take the initiative'.[2] Eusebius then refers to letters from the bishops of Palestine, presided over by Theophilus, bishop of Caesarea, and Narcissus, bishop of Jerusalem, from those in Pontus, Palmas as senior presiding, from the communities in Gaul, Irenaeus their bishop presiding, from the bishops in Osrhoene and the cities in that part, from Bacchyllus, bishop of the Corinthians, 'and from great numbers of others who pronounced one and the same opinion and judgement, and gave the same decision'.[3]

But of those bishops in Asia who confidently affirmed that they ought to keep to the custom which they had received from days of yore, Polycrates [bishop of Ephesus] was the leader. And he too sets forth the tradition which had come down to him, in the letter he penned to Victor and the church of the Romans, in the following words:[4]

'As for us, then, we keep the day without tampering with it, neither adding nor subtracting. For indeed in Asia great luminaries have fallen asleep, such as shall rise again on the day of the Lord's appearing, when He comes with glory from heaven to seek out all His saints: to wit, Philip, one of the twelve apostles, who has fallen asleep in Hierapolis, also his two daughters who grew old in virginity, and his other daughter who lived in the Holy Spirit and rests at Ephesus; and moreover John too, he who leant back on the Lord's breast, who was a priest, wearing the sacerdotal plate, both martyr and teacher. He has fallen asleep at Ephesus. Moreover, Polycarp too at Smyrna, both bishop and martyr; . . . These all observed the fourteenth day for the Pascha according to the Gospel, in no way deviating thereform, but following the rule of faith. And moreover I also, Polycrates, the least of you all, [do] according to the tradition of my kinsmen, some of whom also I have followed closely.

1 Euseb., V, xxiii, 1–3. 2 Puller, p. 15. 3 Euseb., V, xxiii, 3, 4.
4 Euseb., V, xxiv, 1.

Seven of my kinsmen were bishops, and I am the eighth, and my kinsmen always kept the day when the people [the *laos*, i.e. the Jews] put away the leaven. Therefore I for my part, brethren, who number sixty-five years in the Lord and have conversed with the brethren from all parts of the world and traversed the entire range of holy Scripture, am not affrighted by threats.[1] For those better than I have said, We must obey God rather than men.'[2]

Then he goes on to add as follows, with reference to the bishops present at his writing who held the same views as he did:

'But I could mention the bishops present with me, whom I summoned when ye yourselves desired that I should summon them. And if I were to write their names, the number thereof would be great. But they who know my littleness approved my letter, knowing that I did not wear my grey hairs in vain, but that I have ever lived in Christ Jesus.'[3]

Thereupon Victor, the president of the Romans, endeavoured to cut off by a single stroke the communities of the whole of Asia, together with the neighbouring churches, from the common union, on the ground of unorthodoxy; and, indeed, denounced them in letters, proclaiming that the brethren in those parts were all wholly excommunicate. Howbeit this did not please all the bishops without exception. On the contrary, they exhorted him in reply to have a mind for the things which make for peace and neighbourly union and charity. And their words are extant also, in which they rebuke Victor somewhat severely.[4] One of these was Irenaeus, who wrote in the name of the brethren in Gaul, whose leader he was; and, while holding that the mystery of the Lord's resurrection should be celebrated on the Lord's day, and on that alone, he nevertheless gives Victor much suitable counsel besides, not to cut off whole churches of God for observing an ancient custom handed down to them.[5]

He then points Victor to the good example of his predecessors, Anicetus, Pius, Hyginus, Telesphorus, and Xystus; they were 'at peace with' those who followed the Asiatic tradition. Especially he commends the charitable behaviour of Anicetus and Polycarp towards one another, in the passage quoted already in Chapter VII.

The record of Eusebius makes it appear that Bishop Victor definitely and formally cut off the bishops of the province of Asia from communion with Rome, and that he did not rest on the threats to which Polycrates had replied. He did 'excommunicate in a kind of peremptory edict the Churches of the province of Asia'.[6] We must suppose that his edict was recognized by all the Italian bishops, but the Asian bishops stood firm and ignored it,[7] and he failed too to carry with him the other

[1] οὐ πτύρομαι ἐπὶ τοῖς καταπλησσομένοις. [2] Euseb., V, xxiv, 2–7.
[3] Euseb. V, xxiv, 8. St Jerome quotes this letter to show the 'genius and authority' of Polycrates, *De viris illustr.* 45.
[4] Πληκτικώτερον καταπτομένων. [5] Euseb., V, xxiv, 9–11.
[6] Batiffol, *PC*, pp. 226, 227; see also Duchesne, *CS*, p. 96.
[7] Batiffol, *PC*, p. 230.

bishops, notwithstanding that they agreed with his view on the Easter controversy, so although he 'endeavoured' to cut off the Asian bishops 'from the common union', he did not succeed.[1]

The reaction to Bishop Victor's edict, not only of the Asian bishops but of all, seems lacking in recognition of papal authority, so that some recent writers have suggested that Victor only threatened excommunication, without carrying it out; but this does not seem to tally with the narrative of Eusebius.[2] The fifth-century Church historian, Socrates, observes[3] that 'Irenaeus, bishop of Lyons in France, swept down nobly[4] upon Victor for his immoderate heat; telling him that although the ancients differed in their celebration of Easter, they did not desist from communion'.

In the long run, at all events, the Churches of Asia fell in with the Easter observance of the rest of the Church. 'By the fourth century, and notably at the Council of Nicaea, nothing more was said upon the subject.'[5] 'Gradually and silently they came over to the Catholic practice.'[6] Whether this harmonious outcome had been hastened or not by Bishop Victor's action, we cannot tell.

Considerable importance has been attached to the episode by modern historians, 'not less by those who assign a primitive origin to the Roman primacy than by those who deny it'.[7] In the 'A' view, the episode is an early example of papal jurisdiction rightfully exerted. In the 'N' view, it was an attempt by a masterful bishop, of the see which was already the undisputedly principal see of Christendom, to presume beyond his rightful primatial functions, and it was rebuffed.

A. 'The initiative of Pope Victor alone, an initiative proved to be effectual, suffices to show how evident in those ancient times was the exceptional situation and the oecumenical authority of the Roman Church.'[8]

In any view, it is significant that the Asian Councils met at the desire of Victor.

[1] Duchesne, *EH*, i, 211.

[2] 'The view that Victor after all only "threatened" to excommunicate the Asian Christians appears to be untenable in the face of Euseb., V, xxiv, 9. . . . The use of "στηλιτεύει", an almost technical term for the action of proscribing a condemned person or group of persons, shows this clearly enough. The fact that Eusebius uses "πειρᾶται" means that in his view the sanction was not adopted by the Church as a whole.' Jalland, *CP*, pp. 120 n. 3. See Puller, pp. 225, 437.

[3] V, xxiv.

[4] γενναίως κατέδραμεν; cp. Acts xxi, 32 (the chief captain) κατέδραμεν ἐπ ἀὐτούς.

[5] Duchesne, *EH*, i, 211.

[6] Batiffol, *PC*, p. 230.

[7] Jalland, *CP*, pp. 116

[8] Duchesne, *CS*, p. 95.

N. Bishop Victor's action was repudiated by the other bishops, and was apparently ineffectual.

To the threats of Victor that he would sever communion with Asia, Polycrates replied that he was not scared by them. 'Bishops who could thus act and write evidently know nothing of communion with the Roman bishop being an essential condition of membership of the Catholic Church; a breach of communion with him was like a similar breach with any other bishop, doubtless a matter for regret, but not involving the awful consequences of separation from the One Fold and exile from the Kingdom of God.'[1]

'The bishops to whom Victor wrote in announcing his action, in like manner were equally ignorant of any such sovereignty belonging to the Roman bishop. They declined to support his action, which consequently failed in its object. On papalist principles, they were bound to render Victor obedience: his judgement was given, they had no power to review it, carry it out they must: not only did they not do so but they severely rebuked him. They held themselves to be on an equality with him: he had erred by his action against peace, unity, and love, and they as brothers told him so. Papalism was certainly not "the venerable and constant belief" of their age.'[2]

[1] Denny, sect. 530. [2] Denny, sect. 533.

CHAPTER XII

Early Christian Treatises

We know the names and authors of early Christian writings that have long been lost. A considerable number, however, have been preserved. Except for those of St Clement of Rome, St Ignatius, and St Irenaeus, they contain next to nothing to assist the inquiry on which we are engaged.

There are several Apologies, written to maintain the truth of Christianity. The *Apology* of Aristides was addressed to the Emperor Antoninus Pius (138–61). So also were the two *Apologies* of Justin Martyr; his *Dialogue with Trypho* was directed against the Jewish religion. The *Oratio* of Tatian, in the same reign, is a defence of Christianity addressed to the pagan world. The *Apologies* of Athenagoras and Melito were probably addressed to the Emperor Marcus Aurelius (161–70). But it was not necessary in such writings to expound the constitution of the Church, and they contain nothing with any bearing on the bishopric of Rome.

There are a fair number also of writings made for the instruction of the faithful. One of the earliest of these is the *Epistle of Barnabas*. It is not 'apocryphal'. 'There is no indication, direct or indirect, that the writer desired to be taken for the Apostle Barnabas. . . . How the name of Barnabas came to be attached to the Epistle, it is impossible to say.'[1] It was probably written in Alexandria, about the end of the first century, and it is directed against Judaism.

Mention has already been made of the Epistle of Polycarp *to the Philippians*, a letter of instruction and exhortation, written soon after St Ignatius had passed through Philippi on his way to martyrdom. We have also the *Letter of the Smyrnaeans* forty-six years later, telling of the martyrdom of St Polycarp himself.

We have a very ancient homily, probably written and delivered at

[1] Lightfoot, *Clem.*, ii, 504.

Corinth, formerly ascribed to St Clement of Rome and known as his 'Second Epistle'. Its exact date, as well as its authorship, is uncertain; Lightfoot places it between A.D. 120 and 140.

The *Letter to Diognetus*, by an unknown author in the middle of the second century, is of the nature of an Apology, and is strongly anti-Judaistic.

The origin and date of the *Didache* or *Teaching of the Twelve Apostles* are so uncertain as to have made it a problem-piece for scholars. Opinions differ widely, but tend to date it early in the second century. It is thought by many scholars, however, that 'the work describes, not the conditions in the Church at large, but only those in a remote and backward district, where an imperfect Christianity was taught'.[1] In any view, it makes no reference to anything touching on the present inquiry.

We might expect to learn more from the *Shepherd* of Hermas. Like many leading Christians in Rome, including its bishops Clement, Pius, and Callistus, Hermas was a freed slave. 'Amongst these freedmen were frequently found the most intelligent and cultivated men of their day.'[2] According to bibliographical notes written *circa* A.D. 200,[3] Hermas wrote the *Shepherd* 'while his brother Pius the bishop was in the chair of the city of Rome', i.e., *circa* 142–56. The *Shepherd* was reverently treasured as the teaching of a seer; it was quoted with deference by Irenaeus and by Clement of Alexandria; down to the end of the second century it was read in church almost as Scripture, and it was used for the instruction of catechumens. It consists of three books of visions, in some of which there appears to Hermas an Aged Lady, who personifies the Church. In other visions appears a man dressed as a shepherd, from whom the work is named. These and other visionary personages instruct Hermas at great length on many subjects of morals and conduct.

In recent time the *Shepherd* has been minutely searched for any clues to the contemporary ministry of the Church in Rome. Thus in the course of long sections describing the building of a tower by six young men, who are angels, with various kinds of stones, the Aged Lady tells Hermas that 'the square white stones . . . are the apostles and bishops and teachers and deacons who walked in godly gravity, and ministered purely and gravely as bishops and teachers and deacons to the elect of God; of whom some are fallen asleep and some yet are'.[4] Thirty-five stones personify 'the prophets and ministers (or deacons) of the Lord',

[1] Bp. A. J. Maclean, *The Doctrine of the Twelve Apostles*, 1922, p. viii.
[2] Lightfoot, *Clem.*, i, 61.
[3] Probably by St Hippolytus; Lightfoot, *Clem.*, ii, 411.
[4] Vis., iii, 5, 1.

another forty 'the apostles and teachers of the preaching of the Son of God',[1] who at another place are distinguished.[2] The 'presbyters who preside over the Church'[3] seem to be the same as 'the occupants of the chief seat', who in one reference are distinguished from 'the rulers of the Church'.[4] One of the marks of a false prophet is that he desires a chief seat.[5] It is nowhere indicated that Hermas himself held any office of ministry.

Hermas does not name St Peter or any other apostle, nor does he mention Rome, so the *Shepherd* does not help our inquiry; but one curious passage must be noticed. At one point the Aged Lady, who personifies the Church, tells Hermas to write down her words in two little books, 'and thou shalt send one to Clement and one to Grapte. So Clement shall send it to the cities abroad, for this charge is committed unto him, and Grapte shall instruct the widows and the orphans: while thou shalt read it to this city together with the presbyters who preside over the church.'[6] It is generally understood that St Clement is meant, who presided in Rome *circa* A.D. 90 to 99. Some scholars therefore date the *Shepherd* in his time, and treat the later bibliographical note as mistaken. Others consider that the reference to St Clement should be understood as figurative only, in allusion to his epistolary fame. Grapte, however, seems to be a deaconess, and is coupled very strangely with St Clement.

This short survey of the early Christian treatises is included here so that no evidence from the first two centuries may be overlooked, but it is unproductive, for nothing in them seems to have any bearing on the papacy.

[1] Sim., ix, 15. [2] Ibid., pp. 16, 5. [3] Vis., ii, 4, 3.
[4] Vis., iii, 9, 7. [5] Mand., xi, 12. [6] Vis., ii, 4, 3.

CHAPTER XIII

Clement of Alexandria, A.D. 190-202

St Clement of Alexandria, an Athenian by training if not by birth, was the most outstanding Christian teacher and writer at the end of the second century, and 'the best acquainted with Christian literature of any one up to his time'.[1] From about A.D. 190 he was head of the great catechetical school of Alexandria, until 202, when the persecution under Severus drove him from Alexandria, and our knowledge of him ends.[2] He wrote many books of religion and theology, four of which are preserved, with fragments of five others. He was accounted a saint, and for fourteen centuries he was commemorated in the Western martyrologies on 4th December. A study of his works yields little pertinent to our inquiry. We find in them no reference to Rome. In one passing reference he speaks thus of St Peter: 'The blessed Peter, the elect, the chosen, the first of the disciples, for whom alone and for Himself the Lord pays tribute.'[3] But he does not seem to notice a distinction between St Peter and the other apostles as regards their authority:

> Peter and James and John after the ascension of our Saviour did not lay claim to glory, as men who had been preferred in honour by Him; but selected James the Just as bishop of Jerusalem.[4]
>
> To James the Just and John and Peter the Lord after the resurrection committed the 'gnosis'; they committed it to the other apostles, and the other apostles to the Seventy, of whom Barnabas also was one.[5]

We have his *Stromateis* or *Miscellanies*, in eight books, in which Clement recorded 'an image and outline of those vigorous and animated discourses which I was privileged to hear, and of blessed and truly

[1] Döllinger, *FA*, ii, 162–3.
[2] He was still alive nine years later; Euseb., VI, xi, 6; Lawlor and Oulton, II, 196.
[3] *Quis Dives salvetur*, xxi; *PG*, ix, 625.
[4] *Hyptyposis* in Euseb., II, i. [5] Ibid.

remarkable men; of these the one in Greece, an Ionic, the others from Coelo-Syria, Egypt, and Palestine. Preserving the tradition of the blessed doctrines derived directly from the holy apostles Peter, James, John, and Paul, . . . they came by God's will to us also to deposit those ancestral and apostolic seeds.'[1]

The seventh book of the *Stromateis* contains several chapters upon the distinguishing of true doctrine and heresy. In Chapter XV, on 'The objection to join the Church on account of the diversities of heresies discovered', he says:

> From the very reason that truth is difficult and arduous of attainment, questions arise from which spring the heresies, savouring of self-love and vanity. . . . With the greater care, therefore, are we to examine the real truth, which alone has for its object the true God. On account of the heresies, therefore, the toil of discovery must be undertaken. . . . By the exercise of contemplation, and by reasoning of the most decisive character, we must distinguish the true from the seeming.

Chapter XVI is entitled 'Scripture the criterion by which truth and heresy are distinguished'; truth is to be found not by selecting ambiguous texts as the heretics do, but 'in the consideration of what perfectly belongs to and becomes the Sovereign God, and in establishing each one of the points demonstrated in the Scriptures again from similar Scriptures'. Chapter XVII is upon the thesis, 'The tradition of the Church prior to that of the heresies'. He is content to show that the teaching of the apostles, including the ministry of St Paul, ends with Nero, whereas the heresies began in the times of Hadrian and later.

A. The subjects on which Clement wrote did not involve the constitution of the Church, and did not call for an explanation of the papacy.

N. This outstanding theologian and teacher, even when distinguishing true faith and heresy, never refers to the Roman Church, or to its bishop.

[1] *Strom.*, I, i; *PG*, viii, 700.

CHAPTER XIV

Survey at A.D. 200

Our search is for the earliest evidence of belief in the Doctrine of the Papacy which, in the words of Pope Pius IX at the Vatican Council, 1870, was 'the ancient and constant faith of the universal Church'. The foregoing Chapters IV to XIII set out all the historical events of the first two centuries, and all the quotations from the contemporary Fathers, that seem to have a bearing upon the inquiry. Some important facts may be regarded as established beyond reasonable doubt.

1. St Peter (and St Paul) were martyred at Rome *circa* A.D. 67.

2. St Peter (as well as St Paul) preached and taught in Rome before martyrdom for a length of time that is wholly uncertain.

3. St Peter was not called 'bishop' in his lifetime, or during the first century; but he, or St Paul, or any other apostle resident in a city, must have held there a position of honour and authority only differing from the office afterwards distinguished as 'bishop' by being still greater.

4. After the destruction of Jerusalem in A.D. 135, Rome was the greatest Church in Christendom. The city of Rome was the metropolis of the Empire, and virtually the world-centre.

5. Apart from the greatness of Rome the city, its Church was very early renowned for the Christian faith and virtues of its members, for their charity, generosity, and steadfastness in the faith.

6. Before the end of the first century, the influence of the Church in Rome extended over a sister Church in Corinth, in guiding and exhorting its disorderly members.

7. St Ignatius honoured and praised the Church in Rome much more highly than the other Churches to which he wrote.

8. Although there were other 'apostolic sees' founded by apostles, Rome had been founded by *two* apostles, and these 'two most glorious

apostles', who also sanctified Rome with their blood. Moreover, Rome was the only apostolic see in the Western Empire.

9. St Irenaeus distinguishes the Church in Rome as principal and pre-eminent among the apostolic Churches to which the apostles had entrusted the *paradosis*, the tradition of the true faith, unanimously held and taught in all of them.

Beyond the important body of evidence, the results of which are here summarized, we are left to inference, and to the arguments advanced from opposite sides of opinion.

A. The indisputable facts show that St Peter deposited the primacy in the see of Rome.[1] No rival claim was ever made for Antioch or Jerusalem.

St Irenaeus proves the tradition received from the apostles, that Rome is the centre of the Church, and the infallible throne of truth.[2]

The initiative of Bishop St Victor (in the dispute about Easter) shows 'how evident in those ancient times was the exceptional situation and the oecumenical authority of the Roman Church'.[3]

Although the papacy developed in organization in subsequent centuries, we see it here already 'in substance, in principle, in essential features'.[4] 'Yet the doctrine was not held explicitly as it is today. The primacy and authority of Rome, in a general way, was widely if not generally understood, but its extent was not yet realized, and it was not easily applied in all parts of the world on account of various difficulties of communication, etc.'

N. 1. The theory that St Peter deposited a primacy in Rome is an inference based on the assumption that he was its first bishop. There is no other evidence of 'deposit' of his individual pre-eminence among the apostles. The inference is weakened by the fact that neither he nor St Paul was 'bishop', the office of an original apostle being greater and different.

2. There is no evidence to suggest that St Peter's relation to Rome was ever in the first two centuries regarded as different in kind from that which he possessed in relation to the Churches in Jerusalem or Antioch, except that his (and St Paul's) martyrdom, and the possession of their relics, were the unique glory of Rome.

3. Similarly, there is nothing to suggest that St Peter was then regarded, any more than St Paul, as having transmitted an individual Petrine (or Pauline) office to Rome.

[1] Chapman, *GCC*, p. 61. [2] Chapman, *Revue Bénédictine*, année xii, 64.
[3] Duchesne, *CS*, p. 95. [4] Rivington, *PC*, p. xix.

4. The 'argument from silence' depends for its force upon the context, and the surrounding circumstances, but:

(*a*) It is significant that in all the Fathers and Christian literature of the first two centuries—St Clement, St Ignatius, St Irenaeus, St Clement of Alexandria, and others—there is no mention or suggestion of any Petrine authority or infallibility attached to the office of bishop of Rome.

(*b*) The attempt of Bishop St Victor to enforce his solution of the Easter Dispute by excommunicating the bishops who disagreed with him was ineffectual, and was rebuffed. The attitude of the other bishops in East and West, both those who agreed with his view on the question and those who disagreed, shows that nothing resembling the Doctrine of the Papacy had been heard of by them.

(*c*) In the great treatise of St Irenaeus on the Church and against heresies, he mentions St Peter only coupled with St Paul as a joint founder of the Church in Rome. He could not have omitted some indication or hint of what is now claimed as 'the ancient and constant faith of the universal Church' if he knew it. The inference is difficult to resist, that he knew nothing resembling it.

5. 'The later Roman theory supposes that the Church of Rome derives all its authority from the bishop of Rome as the successor of St Peter.'[1] There is not a particle of evidence that this theory was ever heard of in the first two centuries. 'History inverts this relation and shows that, as a matter of fact, the power of the bishop of Rome was built upon the power of the Church of Rome.'[2]

[1] Lightfoot, *Clem.*, i, 70.

[2] Lightfoot, loc. cit.

PART THREE

THE THIRD CENTURY

CHAPTER XV

Spurious Scriptures

'The curiosity of the little world of Christians led them to give too ready a welcome to gospels which were not officially recognized, and especially to pious romances about the apostles which claimed to be genuine history.'[1] An amazing quantity of such spurious stuff began to be put out in the second century, and grew prolifically in the third. Dr M. R. James[2] selects for notice over a hundred documents of this kind. There were 'Gospels' of *Philip*, *Thomas*, *Peter*, *Nicodemus*, *Bartholomew*, *according to the Hebrews*, or *the Egyptians*. There were '*Acts*' of *Peter*, *John*, *Paul*, *Andrew*, *Thomas*, *Philip*, *Matthew*, *Barnabas*, and others. Most of these strange writings were produced in heretical circles with the object of fostering Gnostic, or Ebionite, or Manichaean views. They worked on a natural popular taste for the romantic and the marvellous, in an age that was uncritical of their absurdities. Many of them reappeared again and again in fresh versions. Sometimes the worst and most heretical bits were cut out, leaving only 'orthodox' romance. From them comes much mediaeval saint-lore. The origin of the various documents cannot be dated exactly: the very early date of some is proved by references to them in serious writings such as those of Tertullian and Origen.

The *Gospel of Thomas*, one of the earliest, contains stories of marvels in our Lord's childhood, such as that of His forming sparrows out of clay and setting them to fly off alive. The *Acts of Paul* is said by Tertullian to have been written by a presbyter of Asia whose imposture was found out. It includes a long, thrilling, and popular tale of Thecla, a holy virgin, converted by St Paul, and her miraculous preservation through all manner of attempts to put her to death. The *Apocalypse of Peter* is assigned to the first quarter of the second century. The *Acts of Peter*, probably late second-century, contains the *Quo Vadis* episode; so does

[1] Duchesne, *EH*, p. 370. [2] *The Apocryphal New Testament*, 1924.

the *Acts of the holy apostles Peter and Paul*, which relates St Paul's martyrdom, the story of St Perpetua, the miracle of her handkerchief, and her own martyrdom. Simon Magus of Samaria (Acts viii) is found in Rome in both versions, and there he contends with St Peter before Nero in disputation and miracle-working; by magic art, Simon soars in air, but Peter's prayer brings him crashing down.[1]

This mass of spurious popular literature yields nothing to throw light upon the authority of St Peter as contrasted with that of the other apostles, except for the important group of writings forged under the name of St Clement, which calls for closer attention. 'The posthumous fame of Clement presents many interesting features for study. Notwithstanding his position as a ruler and his prominence as a writer, his personality was shrouded in the West by a veil of unmerited neglect. ... His personal history was forgotten—so entirely that his own church was content to supply its place with a fictitious story imported from the far East.'[2] Dr von Döllinger points out St Clement's noticeably Jewish and Old Testament habit of thought, which, together with his eminence and literary fame, made him 'the right man for the Ebionite or Gnostic Judaizing party to choose for their hero. . . . Thus in the Clementines, an Ebionite production of the second century, where Christianity is represented as a purified Mosaism, he is the principal personage after St Peter, and his family history forms the basis of this didactic romance.'[3]

We have this romance in the famous *Clementine Recognitions*. Faustus and his wife Mattidia, relations of the Emperor of Rome, had twin sons Faustinus and Faustinianus, and a younger son Clement. All were separated and lost to each other by a variety of misfortunes. The twins were captured by pirates and sold to Justa, the Syrophenician woman of the Gospels, and they became disciples of Simon Magus. But Zacchaeus converted them, and they joined St Peter and accompanied him in his missionary circuits. The orphaned Clement hears in Rome a rumour of an inspired Teacher who had appeared in Judea. He sails, via Alexandria, where Barnabas instructs him, to Caesarea; there St Peter instructs him further and baptizes him, but he and the twins do not yet recognize one another. St Peter publicly debates against Simon Magus, follows his migrations, and counters his baneful influence. A maimed beggar-woman on the island of Aradus turns out to be really Mattidia. She is converted and baptized, as is also an old man

[1] For a full account of the Simon Magus legend, see Shotwell and Loomis, pp. 120–207.

[2] Lightfoot, *Clem.*, i, 98.

[3] *FA*, ii, 155–6; also *Hist.*, i, 118.

who is looking on, who of course turns out to be Faustus. All but Clement had been living under assumed names, but the Recognitions unite them.

Such is the famous popular romance in bald outline. It is the basis of both the Clementine *Recognitions* and *Homilies*, which are generally attributed to Ebionite heretics in Syria or Palestine.[1] (The Ebionites were Jewish pseudo-Christians, who held that our Lord was the son of Joseph, and that the whole Mosaic Law was binding on Christians.[2] They hated St Paul and his teaching.) In the *Homilies*, the dramatis personae appear again in Rome. 'The chief villain of the story, Simon Magus, combines in himself all those teachers whom the writer wished to stigmatize as heretical—notably St Paul and Marcion',[3] although he hardly dared to identify St Paul by name as 'enemy', so that the heretical animus escaped the notice of early and uncritical Christians.

Attached to early MSS. of the *Homilies* is the *Epistle of Clement to James the Lord's Brother*.[4] This gives an account of Clement's appointment by St Peter as his successor in the see of Rome, and the earliest mention of St Peter's chair; St Peter says, 'the day of my death is approaching, I lay my hands on this Clement as your bishop, and to him I entrust my chair of discourse'.[5]

In these writings, the office of Clement is monarchical, he is represented as a bishop not of his own Church only, but in some degree also of Christendom. St Peter is the missionary of the whole world, St Paul being ignored, and St Clement inherits his position. Yet a still higher authority is over them, that of James, 'the Lord's brother', occupant of the mother-see of Christendom, to whom even St Peter is required to give an account of his labours. One might suppose that the heretical Ebionite teaching, and the subordination of St Peter and St Clement to the bishop of Jerusalem, should debar these writings from popularity in Roman circles,[6] yet it seems that they did not do so. In the fourth and fifth centuries the romance had still a great vogue in orthodox circles,[7] even among scholars; Rufinus made a Latin translation of the spurious Clementine writings already mentioned, together with some others, although he ignored the one genuine Epistle to the

[1] Extant versions are not earlier than late third century (James, p. xxiv), but some scholars date their origin in the second century, Döllinger, *FA*, ii, 156; Lightfoot, *Clem.*, i, 55, 157, 361; Duchesne, *CS*, p. 87; Funk, i, 30.

[2] Euseb., VI, xvii. [3] Lightfoot, *Ign.*, i, 347. [4] Hinschius, pp. 30 sq.

[5] τὴν ἐμὴν τῶν λογῶν καθέδραν, as we should say, his pulpit.

[6] Rivington, *PC*, p. 17.

[7] Duchesne, *Les Origines Chrétiennes*, Leçons d'Histoire Ecclésiastique, Premier partie, Nouvelle édition, p. 98.

Corinthians. The *Letter to James* was quoted as genuine at the Synod of Vaison in 442, and it is cited by popes and councils from that time onward.[1] The important *Liber Pontificalis* adopts it; in the ninth century it was reissued in the pseudo-Isidorian Decretals,[2] which successive popes held out as authoritative; in 1562, at the Council of Trent, it was still authoritative scripture.[3]

The confused order in which the early bishops of Rome are named in the Roman lists of the third and fourth centuries may have been due partly to the Clementine literature. In the second century the true order had been recorded by St Irenaeus as Linus, Anencletus, Clement; that order is also preserved from early antiquity in the Canon of the Roman Mass. In the pseudo-Clementines, however, Clement is represented as ordained by St Peter himself to succeed him, and St Jerome says that 'most of the Latins think' that Clement came next after St Peter.[4] The date by which the stories found in the *Recognitions*, *Homilies*, and *Letter to James* began to influence opinion in the West is unknown; it may have been before the end of the second century. However that may be, they had an influence upon the 'accepted' history of the primitive Church which endured for many centuries.

[1] Labbe, iv, 717; Lightfoot, *Clem*., i, 415.
[2] Hinschius, p. 252; *PL*, cxxx, 245; infra, ch. lxi.
[3] Acta Trid., e.g., ii, 157, 191, 600.
[4] *De viris illustr*., p. 15.

CHAPTER XVI

Tertullian of Carthage, †circa 230

Tertullian, 'the first of Latin theological writers', was a Carthaginian, born perhaps about A.D. 160. Brought up to be a Roman advocate, he was converted to Christianity some time before 197. He was ordained a priest, but about 206 he lapsed to Montanism, driven, according to St Jerome, by the envy and abuse of the Roman clergy.[1] About six years later he became definitely separated from the Catholic Church;[2] St Jerome says also that he lived to very old age.

'Tertullian the Theologian' continued to be held in high respect notwithstanding his lapse from the Church. St Cyprian, in the next generation, never passed a day without reading Tertullian, and used to say, 'Give me the master'.[3] He was a voluminous writer; we have the full text of many of his works. Only a few passages here and there touch upon our inquiry.

Both in his *Praescription of Heretics* and *Against Marcion* he repeatedly uses the same argument that St Irenaeus had urged against Gnostics and others who claimed to possess peculiar knowledge of the truth. The touchstone of the true faith, he says, is the tradition of all the apostolic churches.[4] The doctrine revealed by Christ to the apostles can rightly be proved only by those very churches which the apostles founded in person:

> All doctrine which agrees with the apostolic churches—those wombs and original sources of the faith—must be reckoned for truth, as undoubtedly containing that which the churches received from the apostles.[5]
>
> To them (the apostles) it was given to know those mysteries which it was not permitted the people to understand. Was anything hidden from Peter, who is called the rock whereon the Church was to be built, who obtained the keys of the kingdom of heaven and on earth? Was anything,

[1] *De viris illustr.*, p. 53. [2] Approximate dates in *Cath. Enc.*, xiv, 520 sq. [3] St Jerome, loc. cit. [4] *Adv. Marcionem*, i, 21. [5] *De praescr. haeret.*, 21.

again, hidden from John, the Lord's most beloved disciple, who used to lean upon His breast . . . whom He commended to Mary as a son in His own stead?[1]

Let them (the heretics) produce the original records of their churches. . . . For this is the manner in which the apostolic churches transmit their registers: as the church of Smyrna, which records that Polycarp was placed therein by John: as also the church of Rome, which makes Clement to have been ordained in like manner by Peter. In exactly the same way the other churches likewise exhibit those whom, having been appointed to their episcopal place by apostles, they regard as transmitters of the apostolic seed.[2]

That comes down from the apostles which has been kept an inviolate deposit in the churches of the apostles. Let us see what milk the Corinthians drank from Paul; to what rule the Galatians were brought for correction; what the Philippians, the Thessalonians, the Ephesians read: what utterance also the Romans give, who are nearest to us, to whom Peter and Paul conjointly bequeathed the gospel sealed even with their own blood. We have also John's foster-churches.[3]

Run through the apostolic churches, in which the very chairs of the apostles still preside in their very places. . . . Is Achaia near to thee? thou hast Corinth . . . Philippi . . . Thessalonica . . . Ephesus. . . . Since moreover you are close upon Italy, you have Rome, whence too we have an authority close at hand. That happy church, into which the apostles poured all their doctrine with their blood.[4]

Of St Peter he remarks that it was the Lord's pleasure 'to communicate to the most highly esteemed of His disciples, in a peculiar manner, a name drawn from the figure of Himself'.[5] In one reference to the keys, which he seems to identify with the power of binding and loosing, he represents the gift as personal to St Peter and completely fulfilled in him.[6] In another book he seems to be referring again to the keys: 'Heaven lies open to the Christian . . . and he who reaches it will enter. What powers, keeping guard at the gate, do I hear you to affirm to exist in accordance with Roman superstition? If thou thinkest heaven is closed, remember that the Lord left to Peter and through him to the Church the keys of it, which every one who has been put to the question and also made confession will carry with him.'[7]

The Montanist sect originated in Phrygia and was named after one Montanus, who was regarded by them as an inspired prophet. The Montanists taught new precepts of austerity, forbidding second marriage, imposing rigorous fasting on all, and denying the power of the bishops, the successors of the apostles, to grant absolution for grave sins. Tertullian, in one of his later writings, inveighs against what he

[1] *De praescr. haeret.* 22: cp. St Iren., III, iii, 1. [2] *De praescr. haer.*, 32.
[3] *Adv. Marcion.*, iv, 5. [4] *De praescr. haer.*, 36. [5] *Adv. Marcion.*, iv, 13.
[6] *De pudicitia*, 21. [7] *Scorpiace*, 10.

deems as a wicked laxity, an episcopal power to absolve even from grave sin. The particular bishop against whom he directs his sharpest satire is unnamed; some think that it is his own bishop of Carthage,[1] but the point of the sting strongly suggests that the bishop he rails against is the bishop of Rome:

> I hear that an edict has been set forth, and a peremptory one too. The Supreme Pontiff (*Pontifex Maximus*), that is the bishop of bishops, proclaims: 'I remit to those who have done penitence the crimes of adultery and fornication.' ... But this is read in the Church, and the Church is a virgin.[2]

The bitterness of this sarcasm does not immediately strike our ears, because for the last five centuries the modern popes, since Paul II (1464–71), have adopted the style of Supreme Pontiff. But to Tertullian and his readers Pontifex Maximus was the pagan-religious title of the Roman Emperors, and it suggested a vicious monster such as Commodus, under whose despotism they had been living. The actual bishop of Rome at the time was Callistus; the sarcasm also suggests that by his time novel styles of dignity, such perhaps as 'archbishop', may have begun to attach to the see of Rome, in view of its eminence and unmistakable primacy.[3]

There is another interesting point to notice. Tertullian remarks that Rome believes Clement to have been ordained by St Peter, just as Polycarp was ordained by St John.[4] That may be true, although it is found in the pseudo-Clementines, for among those fictions may be buried crumbs of truth,[5] and although Clement did not attain to the chair of Rome until after Linus and Anencletus, it should be remembered that 'mon-episcopacy' and diocesan jurisdiction had not been generally organized at that early date; Clement may have been ordained to the highest apostolic ministry, like Timothy, Titus, and others, without immediately succeeding to the chair of Rome. This observation is the earliest that makes any distinction between St Peter and St Paul in the foundation of the Church in Rome. Hitherto these apostles had always been referred to as joint founders, and 'never before the third century is the name of one mentioned without the other'.[6] Many scholars attribute this mention of St Peter to the ideas of the pseudo-Clementines; von Döllinger considered that Tertullian derived it 'either directly or indirectly' from one of them, the *Preaching of Peter*, a second-century writing.[7]

[1] Benson, pp. 29–31. [2] *De pudicitia*, 1. [3] Lightfoot, *Diss.*, p. 224 n.
[4] *De praescr. haer.*, 32; *PL*, ii, 44–5. [5] Rivington, *PC*, p. 29.
[6] Turner, *CA*, p. 219. [7] *FA*, ii, 157–8.

Tertullian appears to think of the Church in Rome as only one, though doubtless the greatest, of the various apostolic churches, in all of which the authentic deposit of faith, the *paradosis*, is preserved. He gives no suggestion either of an individual Petrine office, inherited by the bishops of Rome, or an individual Johannine office inherited by the bishops of Ephesus or Smyrna.

CHAPTER XVII

Hippolytus of Rome, †circa 237

St Hippolytus was the most learned member of the Church in Rome at the beginning of the third century. He had been a disciple of St Irenaeus, and he made great use of the work of that Father in his own *Refutation of All Heresies*. In 235, when he was an old man, Maximinus became Emperor, and at once began a persecution that singled out the Christian leaders. Pontianus, bishop of Rome, and Hippolytus were transported to the pestilent mines of Sardinia, and it seems likely that they did not survive for long.[1] Their remains were translated to Rome, probably a few years later, and were buried on one day, August 13th, those of Hippolytus on the Via Tiburtina. He has always been revered as a martyr and saint. His life-history has been something of a puzzle. Eusebius and St Jerome both record that he was a bishop, but of what see they did not know; according to an old tradition, it was Portus, at the mouth of the Tiber. At the beginning of the first book of the *Refutation of All Heresies* Hippolytus includes himself among 'the successors of the apostles, and participators in this grace, high-priesthood, and office of teaching'. In the sixteenth century, a marble statue of Hippolytus, of contemporary date, was unearthed at the Via Tiburtina; it represents him seated as a bishop, and names of his works are carved on the chair.

Until 1842, only Book I of the *Refutation* was known, but in that year the last seven of the ten books were found at Mount Athos. They revealed the startling fact that Hippolytus had opposed Bishops Zephyrinus (202–17) and Callistus (218–22), charging them with the Modalist heresy, and moreover that he had received schismatic consecration and himself claimed to be the rightful bishop of Rome. (He violently attacked Callistus, both as to his character and his career.)

[1] Although 263 is the date set against his name in the Calendar of the Eastern Orthodox Church. See also Benson, pp. 169 sq.

There our knowledge ends. The schism may have endured through the reign of Urbanus (222–30) and that of Pontianus. Seeing that Pontianus and Hippolytus were equally revered as martyrs by the Church in Rome, it is natural to suppose that the schism had been healed before the end; but it has been suggested that only the joint martyrdom brought reconciliation.[1]

In the extant writings of Hippolytus there is little to call for notice here. In a short list of 'The Twelve Apostles: where each of them preached, and where he met his end', he says that 'Peter preached the gospel in Pontus, and Galatia, and Cappadocia, and Betania, and Italy, and Asia, and was afterwards crucified by Nero in Rome with his head downward, as he himself had desired to suffer in that manner'. In another place he refers to 'Peter, the rock of faith, whom our Lord called blessed, the teacher of the Church, the first disciple, he who has the keys of the kingdom'.[2]

In the books of his *Refutation of All Heresies* there is no reference to Rome or to its bishops, either as custodians of truth or governors of the Church.

[1] B. S. Easton, *The Apostolic Tradition of Hippolytus*, 1934, p. 24.
[2] *De fine mundi et de antichristo*, p. 9.

CHAPTER XVIII

Origen of Alexandria, †243

Origen, an Alexandrian of Greek family, was sixteen years old when his father died a martyr at Alexandria in the persecution under Severus, A.D. 202. He himself, after suffering prolonged torture in the persecution of Decius, died at Tyre, aged sixty-nine.[1] He was a pupil of Clement of Alexandria, and he heard St Hippolytus preach at Rome; among other places, he visited Greece and Ephesus. From 231 onwards, he made his home at Caesarea. He was a notable scholar, 'the best acquainted with Christian literature of any one up to his time'.[2] and a voluminous writer of commentaries on Scripture and theology; in the Paris edition of 1733 his works fill four huge folios. When referring here and there to St Peter, he recognizes his priority and greatness as a matter of course, often following the words of Scripture.

> Although there may be a Paul, of whom it is said 'he is a chosen vessel unto me', or a Peter, against whom the gates of hades prevail not, or a Moses, the friend of God, . . . yet not one of them could stand against the powers of Darkness (Eph. vi, 12) unless in the might of Him who said, 'I have overcome the world'.[3]
>
> See what is said by the Lord to that great foundation of the Church and most solid rock upon which Christ founded the Church—'O thou of little faith, why didst thou doubt?'[4]
>
> Is it as if the rock and the Church were one and the same? This I think to be true, for neither against the rock, upon which Christ builds the Church, nor against the Church, shall the gates of hades prevail.[5]
>
> Peter the first of the apostles.[6] More honoured than the rest.[7]
>
> 'Charity never faileth.' . . . And when to Peter was delivered supreme power to feed the sheep, and upon him, just as upon the earth, the Church

[1] Euseb., VI, xxxix; VII, i.
[2] Döllinger, *FA*, ii, 162–3.
[3] *De principiis*, III, ii, 5; Opera i, 141.
[4] *In Exod.* v, 4; Opera, iii, 145.
[5] *In Matt.* xii, 11; Opera, iii, 526; sim. *In Joann.*, Euseb., VI, xxv, 8.
[6] *In Lucam.* xvii; Opera, iii, 952.
[7] *In Joann.* v; Opera, iv., 413.

was founded, confession of no other virtue than charity is required of him, and John also says, 'He that abideth in charity' . . . (1 John iv, 16).[1]

Although the other apostles also received the power of the keys, and of binding and loosing, yet St Peter had pre-eminence:

> We may discover much difference and pre-eminence in the words spoken to Peter (Matt. xvi, 19) over and above those spoken to the apostles generally in the second place (Matt. xviii, 19). It is no small difference that Peter received the keys not of one heaven but of many, and that whatsoever things he should bind upon the earth should be bound not in one heaven only but in them all. . . . For they do not transcend in power as Peter so as to bind and loose in all the heavens.[2]

He seems to teach that the Petrine promises were diffused among the other apostles, and now among the faithful of the Church:

> But if you suppose that upon that one Peter only the whole Church is built by God, what would you say about John the son of thunder, or each one of the apostles? Shall we otherwise dare to say that against Peter in particular the gates of hell shall not prevail, but that they shall prevail against the other apostles and the perfect? Does not the saying previously made, 'the gates of hades shall not prevail against it', hold in regard to all, and in the case of each of them? Are the keys of the kingdom given by the Lord to Peter only, and will no other of the blessed receive them? . . . For all bear the surname of 'rock' who are imitators of Christ, that is, of the spiritual rock which followed those who are being saved . . . these bear the surname of the rock just as Christ does. But also as members of Christ deriving their surname from Him they are called Christians, and from the rock, Peters.[3]

In an historical note, Origen says that 'Peter preached in Pontus, Galatia, Bithinia, Cappadocia, and Asia, to the Jews of the Dispersion. He came also to Rome at last and was crucified head-downwards, for he requested that he might suffer thus.'[4] That is Origen's only mention of Rome. He does not refer to the jurisdiction or doctrinal authority of its bishops.

[1] *In Ep. ad Rom.* v; Opera, iv, 568. [2] *In Matt.* xiii, 31; Opera, iii, 613–14.
[3] *In Matt.* xii, 11; Opera, iii, 524. [4] *In Genesis,* Euseb., III, i.

CHAPTER XIX

Cyprian of Carthage, †258

(i) *His great episcopate*

The ten years of St Cyprian's episcopate are an outstanding part of the third century. In A.D. 246, nearly four centuries after Carthage had been 'deleted', but long after it had been rebuilt as the capital of Roman Proconsular Africa, Cyprian was converted to Christianity. Carthage had been evangelized from Rome, from which it was 340 miles distant; a vessel sailing from the port of Rome with a fair wind could arrive the second day out. It was well established as the chief see of Africa, with primacy over more than eighty bishops. Its bishop, as in Alexandria, was known as the pope.

Cyprian was a cultivated man and a famous orator; in middle age he was converted, and he 'instantly translated thought into life'. Possessed of great wealth, he sold all and distributed the proceeds. He gave his energy to scriptural study and to doctrinal writing. He was soon ordained deacon and priest; when Donatus died, he was called to the episcopate 'by the suffrage of the whole people' in A.D. 248.

The ten following years, ending with his martyrdom, were full both of glory and of tragedy for the Church. They are illuminated for us in St Cyprian's correspondence, which he carefully preserved, and in his treatises.

When Cyprian became bishop and pope of Carthage, Fabian was bishop of Rome. Early in A.D. 250, the persecution by the Emperor Decius began, and St Fabian was martyred in January. There were many heroic martyrs, both in Rome and at Carthage; but many too were the *lapsi*, who yielded to torture or the prospect of death, and who 'sacrificed' to the pagan deities. When that storm of persecution was lulled, a new problem arose; should those who had fallen be received back into the Church? What of the *libellatici* too, those who had not actually sacrificed, but had contrived to get official 'libels', certifying untruly that they had complied and sacrificed?

Great regard was paid to recommendations that were made by martyrs and confessors for the restoration of their weaker and fallen brethren, but Cyprian had to deal with some unruly and hostile presbyters who began to readmit the *lapsi* to communion without the bishop's authority and even without genuine penitence and penance. Cyprian in his treatise *De Lapsis* laid it down that the lapsi should be readmitted, but only after careful inquiry and proof of penitence. During the Roman vacancy, several letters on this matter passed between him and the Roman clergy (who address him as 'Pope Cyprian', 'most blessed and glorious Pope'.)[1]

Because of the persecution, the see of Rome was left vacant until in April 251 Cornelius was elected bishop 'by the testimony of almost all the clergy and by the suffrages of the people', as Cyprian declares.[2] Almost immediately, the Church was afflicted by another tribulation, schism at Rome. Cornelius, like Cyprian, readmitted the *lapsi* after careful inquiry as to their penitence; but a faction among the Roman clergy held rigidly that these could never be readmitted to the Church in the world. The leader of the faction was Novatian, 'the first great puritan'. They denounced the 'laxity' of Cornelius, and purported to elect Novatian to the see of Rome; they procured his consecration at the hands of three 'very simple' Italian bishops (who were deposed together with all Novatian's supporters).[3] But the Novatian sect spread quickly through East and West, and endured in schism for more than four centuries. Cornelius says that Novatian had received clinical baptism during sickness, and did not receive Confirmation ('the sealing by the bishop'), 'so how could he obtain the Holy Spirit?'[4]

Cyprian gave his stalwart support to Cornelius as the rightful bishop of Catholic election. His famous treatise, the *De Unitate Ecclesiae*, was written at this time. He wrote a number of letters to his fellow-bishops, to his own clergy, to the Roman clergy, and to Cornelius himself, powerfully upholding the true episcopate of Cornelius and spurning the pretensions of Novatian and the schismatics. In 253, St Cornelius was exiled, and in June he died, accounted as a martyr. Lucius, who was soon elected bishop of Rome, died in March of the following year. In May 254, Stephen was elected.

Another grave trouble then arose. When those who had been baptized by schismatics or heretics sought admission to the Church, was

[1] Epp. xxx, xxxi, xxxvi. [2] Ep. lv, 6. [3] Euseb., VI, xliii, 8.
[4] Ep. to Fabius of Antioch, Euseb., VI, xliii, 15.

it enough to admit them with the imposition of hands only (as was customary in Rome and many parts of the Church), or was it necessary that they should receive Catholic baptism? That was the custom in most Churches in the East, in Africa, and apparently in Alexandria.[1] An embittered controversy took place between Cyprian and Stephen. Stephen seems to have severed communion with the Asian Churches. Relations with Cyprian too were greatly strained, although it is not certain that there was a formal severance of communion.[2] St Stephen died, however, on 2 August 257. Just then a fierce new persecution began, that of the Emperor Valerian. Xystus II was elected bishop of Rome, and it seems clear at least that Cyprian was in communion with him. But on 6 August 258, St Xystus was martyred, and on September 14th. St Cyprian also received the martyr's crown at Carthage.

Thus during Cyprian's episcopate of ten years he was involved in three anxious disputes:

1. As to the readmission of the *lapsi*.
2. His support of Cornelius against Novatian.
3. His controversy with Stephen of Rome as to the baptizing of converted heretics.

His name is linked in pious memory with that of Cornelius who, curiously enough, is commemorated on the same day, September 14th. Their effigies, side by side, were painted on the walls of Cornelius' sepulchre. Cyprian alone of all the saints throughout the Church has been joined with the few saints of Rome commemorated in the Roman Canon. 'The blessed Cyprian, whom the holy Mother, the Church, counts among those few and rare men of most excellent grace', says St Augustine of him,[3] and 'If my sins do not disable me, I will learn, if I can, from Cyprian's writings, assisted by his prayers, with what peace and what consolation the Lord governed His Church through him'.[4] St Gregory of Nazianzum (†390) says, 'Not only over the Church of Carthage and Africa does he preside, but over all the regions of the West, and almost all parts of the East, and South, and North, wherever his wonderful reputation spread'.[5]

[1] In the one view, heretics and schismatics had *potestas* in sacrament, although not *jus*. In the other view, they had neither. Afterwards a distinction was drawn: the baptism by anti-Trinitarian heretics only was deemed a nullity (sixth canon of Nicaea, 325), and this remained the rule in the fifth century (Hefele, ii, 368).

[2] But see ch. xx. Von Döllinger thought it probable that Stephen excommunicated all the African bishops too. (*Hist.*, i, 210).

[3] *De bapt.*, vi, 2; *PL*, xliii, 198. [4] Ibid., v, 23; *PL*, xliii, 188.

[5] Or. xviii, 21, *in laud. Cypr.; Opp.* i, 281. See Newman, *Development* (1845 ed.) p. 266.

This rather full outline of St Cyprian's episcopate is necessary in order that the application and meaning of his correspondence and treatises may be clear. The weight of his authority needs no emphasis. In regard to the present inquiry, however, it must be observed that a question as to the relationship of Rome and its bishops to the rest of the Church was not directly raised.

(ii) *The doctrine of Cyprian in his writings*

Cyprian speaks repeatedly of St Peter's outstanding greatness, always with reference to his own great doctrine of unity:

> To Peter first, on whom He built the Church, and from whom He appointed and showed that unity should spring, the Lord gave that power that whatsoever he should loose on earth should be loosed in heaven.[1]
>
> The Church, which is one, and was by the voice of the Lord founded upon one, who also received its keys.[2]
>
> Peter, on whom the Church has been built by the same Lord, one speaking for all, and answering in the voice of the Church, says, 'Lord, to whom shall we go' . . . (Matt. xv, 13).[3]
>
> There is both one Baptism, and one Holy Ghost, and one Church, founded by Christ the Lord upon Peter, for the origin and principle of unity.[4]

He seems to teach that this fundamental unity, when thus originated and established, was diffused throughout the apostolate:

> Certainly the rest of the apostles were that which Peter was, endued with equal partnership both of honour and power, but the beginning sets out from unity.[5]
>
> We (i.e., he and Cornelius of Rome, to whom he is writing) strive to hold fast as much as we can the unity appointed by the Lord and through the apostles delivered to us their successors.[6]
>
> For neither did Peter, whom the Lord chose first, and on whom He built His Church, when Paul afterwards disputed with him about circumcision, claim to assume anything insolently and arrogantly to himself; so as to say he held the primacy and should rather be obeyed of those late and newly come.[7]

The unity of the Church is embodied in an inseparable unity of all bishops. To explain this, Cyprian uses a technical phrase of the Civil Law which expresses a joint proprietorship, both equal and inseparable:

> The episcopate is one, so that each shares the whole, and the whole is in each part.[8]

[1] Ep. lxxiii, 7. [2] Ibid., 9. [3] Ep. lix, 8. [4] Ep. lxx, 5.
[5] *De unitate*, 4. [6] Ep. xlv, 2. [7] Ep. lxxi, 2.
[8] *De unitate*, 5; episcopatus unus est, cuius a singulis in solidum pars tenetur.

The Church, which is catholic and one, is not separated nor divided: but is in truth connected and joined together by the cement of bishops mutually cleaving to each other.[1]

One episcopate, diffused throughout an harmonious multitude of many bishops.[2]

Cyprian clearly regards the Roman bishop as a successor of St Peter in particular. His reference to the chair of Peter is the earliest reference we have to the *cathedra Petri* outside the pseudo-Clementines, although Tertullian had already written of 'the very chairs of the Apostles in Corinth, Philippi, Thessalonica, Ephesus, and Rome'.[3] Cyprian too may have thought of a 'chair of Paul' at Philippi, but it is the 'chair of Peter' that he speaks of. Writing 'to his brother, Cornelius', Cyprian observes that a group of Novatianists from Carthage:

dare to set sail and to carry letters from schismatic and profane persons to the chair of Peter, and to the principal Church whence the unity of the priesthood took its rise without reflecting that the Romans are the people whose faith was commended by the Apostle, to whom faithlessness can have no access.[4]

In an extended sense, the 'one chair', like the 'one altar', seems to be thought of as pertaining distributively to each diocesan bishop. Referring to schismatics in his own diocese, not at Rome, he says:

They who promise to bring back and recall the lapsed to the Church are they who themselves have departed from the Church. There is one God, and one Christ, and one Church, and one chair founded by the word of the Lord on a rock. Another altar cannot be set up, nor a new priesthood made, besides the one altar and one priesthood.[5]

'And there shall be one flock and one shepherd' (John x, 16). And does any one believe that in one place there can be either many shepherds or many flocks?[6]

(iii) '*De Unitate*', *Chapter IV*

All the writings of Cyprian so far quoted are extant in their original, undisputed wording; we must now consider one of the twenty-seven chapters that compose his *De Unitate*. He wrote this treatise when there was some schism at Carthage, but the much greater schism of Novatian was beginning at Rome. He read it out at the first Council of Carthage soon after Easter 251; he sent a copy to the Church in Rome, together with the *De Lapsis*.[7] One chapter only of the *De Unitate*, Chapter IV, presents a curious textual problem, because it is found in two different

[1] Ep. lxvi, 7; so also Ep. lxviii, 3. [2] Ep. lv, 20 [3] *De praescr. haer.*, 36.
[4] Ep. lix, 18 [5] Ep. xliii, 4. [6] *De unitate*, 8. [7] Ep. liv, 2.

versions. What is printed below in ordinary type is known as the 'Received Text'; the 'Primacy Text' contains also the words printed in italics, including the reference to the 'primacy' (a word which Cyprian uses elsewhere in regard to Esau and his birthright).[1]

The Lord saith unto Peter, 'I say unto thee that thou art Peter . . . and whatsoever thou shalt bind on earth shall be bound in heaven'. *And to the same (apostle) He says after His resurrection 'Feed My sheep.'* He builds *His* Church upon *that* one, *and to him entrusts His sheep to be fed.* And although after His resurrection He assigns equal power to all His apostles, and says 'As the Father sent Me even so I send you . . . whosesoever sins ye retain they shall be retained', nevertheless in order to make the unity manifest, he *established one chair, and* by His authority appointed the origin of that same unity beginning from one. Certainly the rest of the apostles too were that which Peter was, endued with equal partnership both of honour and power, *and primacy is given to Peter that one Church of Christ and one chair may be demonstrated; and all are pastors and one flock is shown, to be fed by all the apostles with one-hearted accord,* that one Church of Christ may be demonstrated. It is this one Church which the Holy Spirit in the Person of the Lord speaks of in the Song of Songs, saying, 'My dove is one, my perfect one, one she is to her mother, elect to her who brought her forth'. He that holds not this unity of the Church, *he who deserts the chair of Peter on which the Church was founded,* does he trust that he is in the Church? Since the blessed Apostle Paul teaches the same thing, and sets forth the sacrament of unity, saying, 'There is one body and one spirit and hope of your calling, one Lord, one Faith, one baptism, one God'?[2]

The literary problem presented by the two versions has been pored over and debated by scholars for several centuries past. There are three possible solutions: (1) That the passages italicized were interpolated into Cyprian's text, perhaps through the copying-in of marginal notes.[3] This has been generally believed. A reading of the whole passage does convey an impression of interpolations.[4] (2) That both versions were written by Cyprian, the 'Received Text' first, then the other, with additions specially adapted for the schism at Rome. (3) That Cyprian wrote the 'Primacy Text' first, and afterwards re-issued it in the other version.

An odd feature in the problem is that some early MSS. set out both versions, one after the other, the 'Primacy Text' first. Any attempt to decide between these alternatives is beyond the province of this book.

[1] Ep. lxxiii, 22; *De bono patientiae*, 19.

[2] The last sentence is not in the 'Primacy Text'.

[3] E.g., Hergenröther, p. 149. A 'forger' would have been more thorough and would not have preserved a phrase such as that about the rest of the apostles (Bévenot, p. 6).

[4] Bévenot, p. 3.

The recent very exhaustive study of the MSS. by Father Bévenot led him to favour the third alternative solution,[1] and has tended to win support for it.[2] Many scholars consider that it makes little difference to our estimate of Cyprian's theory of the Church whether he wrote the 'Primacy Text' or not; in the undoubted writings of Cyprian, already quoted, there are phrases parallel to the 'interpolations' of the 'Primacy Text'.[3]

(iv) *Cyprian and Roman authority*

It remains to be considered whether St Cyprian understood the bishop of Rome to possess a right of jurisdiction over other bishops of the Church in general (as distinct from a primacy of honour and initiative). As has been said, the subject was never directly broached, and it is only by inference that we may discern what would have been his teaching on the matter. He refers to Rome as 'the principal Church',[4] and in writing to Cornelius he observes that 'Rome for her greatness[5] ought to have precedency of Carthage'. Correspondence between him and the Roman bishop is couched in terms of simple equality; it is always 'Cyprian to Cornelius his brother, greeting', 'Cornelius to Cyprian his brother, greeting'—'Fare thee well, dearest brother'.[6] In writing to Cornelius he calls him his brother priest,[7] and he refers to him elsewhere as 'our colleague Cornelius, a peaceable and righteous priest'.[8]

Although he strongly maintains that heretical baptism ought not to be regarded as valid, he also asserts the independent right of each bishop to follow the dictates of his own conscience and judgement. To this effect he writes both to Jubaianus, a bishop of Mauretania,[9] and also to Stephen, bishop of Rome; Cyprian and his Council assure the bishop of Rome that he, Stephen, like every other bishop, 'hath in the government of the Church his own choice and will free, hereafter to give account of his conduct to the Lord'.[10] Cyprian does not seem to recog-

[1] Pp. 12, 61.

[2] E.g., Jalland, *CP*, pp. 163–5; see also Denny, sect. 1246. *Sed contra* Dr H. Koch, 'Cyprian und der Römische Primat' in *Texte und Untersuchungen*, Leipsig, 1910, xxxv; Abp. J. H. Bernard in, *Early Hist. of the Church and Ministry* (ed. H. B. Swete, 1921), at pp. 250–3.

[3] Bévenot, pp. 5, 6, 8; Chapman, *Studies*, pp. 36–7. But elsewhere Cyprian repeatedly rests the significance of Matt. xvi, 18, on the fact that the Church is built on *one* man, and he nowhere else suggests that the Lord's words indicate a peculiar authority for St Peter personally, or for the see of Peter.

[4] Ep. lix, 18.
[5] Ep. lii, 3; *pro magnitudine sua.*

[6] Epp. xlv, xlix, lii, lix, lx; similarly to Stephen, Ep. lxviii.

[7] Ep. lx, 1.
[8] Ep. lxvii, 6.
[9] Ep. lxxiii, 22.
[10] Ep. lxxii, 3.

nize a superior doctrinal authority in his brother of Rome; when Stephen appealed to tradition, Cyprian called it 'a human tradition, and not legitimate'.[1]

Two of Cyprian's epistles are concerned with heretical bishops in Spain and in Gaul, and with the relations between these Churches and Rome.

Two Spanish bishops, Basilides and another, had become *lapsi*, and other bishops had been consecrated to replace them. Basilides had resigned and submitted to penance.[2] But both appealed to Rome,[3] and 'deceived Stephen, residing at a distance and ignorant of what had been done and of the real truth'.[4] Stephen 'demanded that Basilides should be restored to his bishopric, although Sabinus had been already elected to succeed him'.[5] Basilides then returned to Spain and claimed to be reinstated. Two bishops of Spain were therefore sent with letters to Carthage. Cyprian and the fourth Council of Carthage replied, upholding the excommunication of the two lapsed bishops and the valid appointment of their successors.[6]

A. St Cyprian 'showed his acceptance of the principle of Papal jurisdiction', although 'he objected to the particular exercise in this case'. 'Not a word has St Cyprian to say against the possibility of a bishop being replaced in his bishopric by the Pope'.[7]

N. St Stephen was disregarded; if indeed he had given a decision, it was not recognized as authoritative, and was brushed aside.

Some time before this, seven missionary bishops had been sent from Rome to Gaul, which was not yet organized with a metropolitan of its own.[8] So when Marcianus, bishop of Arles, joined the Novatians, the other bishops wrote to inform Stephen of Rome. His reply seems to have been slow in coming, and they appealed for help from Cyprian. He wrote at considerable length 'to his brother, Stephen'. 'It is ours, dearest brother, to advise and come in aid. . . . Wherefore it behoves you to write a very full letter to our fellow-bishops established in Gaul, that they no longer suffer the froward and proud Marcianus to insult our college. . . . For therefore, dearest brother, is the body of bishops so large, united together by the cement of mutual concord and the

[1] Hefele, i, 105; Ep. lxxiv. [2] Ep. lxvii, 6. [3] Hefele, i, 98.
[4] Ep. lxvii, 5. [5] Hefele, i, 98. [6] Ep. lxvii, 9.
[7] Rivington, *PC*, pp. 72, 74.
[8] Döllinger, *Hist.*, p. 236; Chapman, *Studies*, p. 11, n. 1; nor even a century later, PBLPB, p. 638.

bond of unity, that if any of our college should attempt to introduce heresy, the rest may come in aid.'[1]

A. St Cyprian here recognized the papal authority of St Stephen.

N. Rome stood in a kind of metropolitan relationship to Gaul (where there was as yet no metropolitan). St Cyprian exhorted St Stephen as bishop of Rome to act more vigorously.

Near the end of the period came the painful breach between Cyprian and Stephen in the Baptismal Dispute. Cyprian speaks of the 'arrogant, extraneous, or self-contradictory' things Stephen had written, his 'blindness of mind, perverseness, and obstinacy'.[2] At the seventh Council of Carthage in 256, each of the eighty-seven bishops severally upheld the opinion of their president, Cyprian, who declared that 'no one of us setteth himself up as a bishop of bishops, or by tyrannical terror forceth his colleagues to a necessity of obeying; inasmuch as every bishop, in the free use of his liberty and power, has the right of forming his own judgement, and can no more be judged by another than he can himself judge another'.[3]

In St Cyprian's teaching, although the 'one chair' is an endowment in common of the whole Church, like the 'one altar and one priesthood',[4] the 'chair of Peter' is a special glory of Rome in more than a symbolic sense; Rome has 'precedency'.[5] His writings before his relations with Stephen of Rome became strained do not contemplate the possibility that he might himself become involved in a rift in that great unity of the episcopate which he always preached. The few letters written in the remaining months of his life leave us without any restatement of his teaching on that unity.

As Mgr Batiffol analyses the doctrine of St Cyprian, it was that 'each church is one since the first of all the churches, that founded by Christ on Peter, is one . . . every church reproduces this primordial unity'.[6] The bishop of Rome has no more right than any other bishop to secure the Catholic unity by means of a sovereign intervention in the question of faith. . . . 'There is a universal episcopate which comprises all the bishops; there is no universal bishop. . . . The bishop of Rome is the one who holds in his hands, so to speak, the threads of the universal communion; but . . . it is beyond his province to determine by himself the conditions of a communion of which he is not the head but the

[1] Ep. lxviii, 1–3.
[2] Ep. lxxiv, 1, 4, 9.
[3] *Sententiae episcoporum.*
[4] Ep. xliii, 4
[5] Ep. lii, 3.
[6] *PC*, p. 358.

official representative.'[1] Mgr Batiffol, of course, regards these views as gravely defective, and he attributes them to St Cyprian's 'misunderstanding of the text *Tu es Petrus*', and to his 'strained interpretation' of it.[2] Abbot Chapman remarks that 'On an important matter Cyprian refused to accept the judgement of the Pope, and enunciated the absurd doctrine that bishops must agree to differ on all points where the faith does not come in. . . . His outlook was extremely narrow, and his logic was very short-sighted.'[3]

[1] *PC*, pp. 363–4.
[2] Ibid., pp. 363, 365.
[3] *Studies*, p. 40. (There is verbal anachronism here; at that time the bishop of Carthage was called pope, but not the bishop of Rome).

CHAPTER XX

Firmilian of Cappadocia, †268

Firmilian was bishop of Caesarea in Cappadocia. He appears to have been a disciple of Origen. St Dionysius the Great of Alexandria calls him one of 'the more eminent bishops in the East'.[1] He was 'among the most distinguished bishops' at the Synod of Antioch in A.D. 264, which tried Paul of Samosata, and at which he presided.[2] St Gregory of Nyssa calls him 'an ornament of the Church of Caesarea',[3] and St Basil quotes him as an authority in doctrine.[4] Cardinal Baronius says that 'scarcely any of his contemporaries appeared to surpass him in learning and sanctity'.[5] Born, probably, *circa* A.D. 200, he died in 268. The Greek Church commemorates him as a saint on October 28th.

The bishops of the Church in the East agreed in opinion with St Cyprian and Carthage that heretical baptism ought not to be deemed valid; as to mere numbers, it seems likely that they were in a considerable majority, 'Christians were incomparably more numerous in the East than in the West'.[6] Firmilian took a leading part in the dispute; our knowledge is derived chiefly from his bitterly worded letter to Cyprian in A.D. 256, of which Cyprian kept a Latin translation in his file of correspondence.[7]

In the first place, Firmilian expresses indignation that Stephen accepts heretical baptism, and he refers ironically to the title of 'chair of Peter' now applied to the Roman see:

> Stephen, who boasts of the seat of his episcopate and contends that he holds the succession from Peter on whom the foundations of the Church

[1] Euseb., VII, v.
[2] Euseb., VII, xxviii; cp. VII, xxx, 3; VI, xxvii.
[3] Greg. Nyss., *vit. S. Greg. Thaum.*; *Opp.*, Paris, 1638, iii, 542.
[4] *De Spiritu Sancto*, c. 29; *Opp.*, iii, 63.
[5] *Sub an.* 258, n. 47 (ii, 522).
[6] Duchesne, *Origines du Culte Chrétien*, p. 21. Later, in the fifth century, there were 470 bishops in Africa as against about 300 in the seventeen provinces of Italy (Bingham, IX, v, 1).
[7] Ep. lxxv.

> were laid, introduces many other rocks, and buildeth anew many Churches, in that by his authority he maintains baptism among them. . . . Stephen, who proclaims that he occupies by succession the 'chair of Peter', is roused by no zeal against heretics.[1]

In the second place, Firmilian refers to Stephen's having severed communion with the Eastern Churches, and (as he believes) with Cyprian. So far as regards the Churches of Asia, Firmilian is corroborated by the record of St Dionysius that 'Stephen had formerly written to Firmilian and all from Cilicia and Cappadocia, and in fact Galatia and all the provinces that border on these, to the effect that he would not hold communion with them in future'.[2]

Firmilian, indeed, says also that Stephen called Cyprian 'false Christ and false apostle and deceitful worker', and not only excluded Cyprian's episcopal legates at Rome from communion but even denied them shelter and hospitality.[3] No doubt 'the evidence of embittered opponents is never a reliable source for the conduct of an adversary',[4] but Cyprian himself seems to have made the Latin translation of Firmilian's letter retained in his file.[5]

Firmilian's attitude to the excommunication by Stephen of himself and the other Eastern bishops is contemptuous. Addressing Stephen rhetorically, he says:

> How great sin hast thou heaped up when thou didst cut thyself off from so many flocks. For thou didst cut thyself off; deceive not thyself; for he is truly the schismatic who has made himself an apostate from the communion of the unity of the Church. For while thou thinkest that all may be excommunicated by thee, thou hast excommunicated thyself alone from all.[6]

A. 'There is not sufficient ground for asserting that things were proceeded with beyond a threat of excommunication.' 'Why were both St Cyprian and Firmilian so disturbed if their communion with Rome was not essential?'[7]

N. 'It is plain that St Cyprian and the African bishops, St Firmilian and the Eastern bishops, knew nothing of the Papal Monarchy, and did not consider that separation from communion with Rome cut them off from the Unity of the Fold so that they were no longer within "the fold".[8]

Even if it were true that St Stephen stopped short at threatening his

[1] Ep. lxxv, 18. [2] Euseb., VII, v, 4. [3] Ep. lxxv, 26, 27.
[4] Jalland, *CP*, p. 132. [5] Döllinger, *Hist.*, i, 212.
[6] Ep. lxxv, 25. [7] Rivington, *PC*, pp. 107, 111. [8] Denny, sect. 584.

excommunication, two facts remain clear: (1) The contemptuous disregard of the threat, by St Cyprian and St Firmilian and the other bishops, proves that they knew nothing of what (according to the Doctrine of the Papacy) would be the dreadful consequence of the threat fulfilled. (2) It was equally unknown to the Saints and Fathers who tell of these transactions without troubling to mention whether St Cyprian and the others incurred such terrible condemnation, or only just escaped it.

CHAPTER XXI

Dionysius of Alexandria and Dionysius of Rome, †265, †269

St Dionysius 'the Great' was born probably about A.D. 200. He succeeded Heraclas as head of the Catechetical School of Alexandria in 233, and succeeded him again in 248 as archbishop or patriarch and pope of Alexandria. He lived through the persecutions of Decius and Valerian, not without suffering. He corresponded with three bishops of Rome (Stephen, Xystus II, and his namesake Dionysius) regarding the Baptismal Dispute, consulting them, but urging that differences between Churches should not be allowed to create separations between them.[1] He refers to the baptismal practice of his predecessor, 'our blessed pope Heraclas'.[2]

When two bishops of Pentapolis (part of Cyrenaica, in his own patriarchate) fell into the Sabellian heresy,[3] what he wrote in reproving them seemed open to criticism as if it leaned towards the opposite heresy.[4] 'Some of the brethren, . . . without asking him so as to learn from himself how he had written, went up to Rome; and they spoke against him in the presence of his namesake Dionysius the bishop of Rome', who wrote to the Alexandrians against the Sabellians and Arians, together with a noble exposition of the Nicene faith. He wrote 'also to Dionysius (of Alexandria) to inform him of what they had said about him. And he to clear himself promptly published the books which he called "A Refutation and Defence".'[5]

This episode has been claimed as an instance of a Roman prerogative of supervision over Alexandria. Our information of what took place is derived from what is recorded by St Athanasius; he does not indicate

[1] Euseb., VII, ii–ix. [2] Euseb., VII, vii, 4.
[3] Which the Athanasian Creed condemns as 'confusing the Persons'.
[4] 'Dividing the Substance', and not confessing the 'equal, and co-eternal'.
[5] Athan., *de sententia Dionysii*, 13; *Opp.*, i, 252.

that an actual supervising jurisdiction was either claimed by Rome or recognized by Alexandria. St Cyprian urged the principle that an interest and responsibility for maintaining orthodoxy in all parts of the Church lies on every bishop; but in any view it rests in full measure on the bishop of Rome. This doctrinal elucidation between Alexandria and Rome seems to have been recalled eighty years later, when in 340 Pope Julius I claimed for Rome a peculiar prerogative over the affairs of 'the Church of the Alexandrians',[1] and again in 430 when St Cyril of Alexandria spoke of a custom of communication with Rome.[2]

St Dionysius the Great was a prolific writer, but in what has been preserved to us of his doctrinal writings and commentaries there is nothing further to assist us. He died in 265, age and infirmity having prevented his attendance[3] even at the first of the Synods of Antioch which sat to try Paul of Samosata, its corrupt and heretical patriarch. 'The deposition of Paul of Samosata was notified to the Church of Rome as to the Church of Alexandria; but it had not been called upon to take any share in the proceedings.'[4] For two or three years after Paul had been excommunicated and deposed, he retained possession of the bishop's house at Antioch, helped, it is supposed, by the patronage of the celebrated Zenobia, Queen of Palmyra.[5] On her downfall, it was recovered for Domnus, who had been appointed to succeed Paul, on an application to 'the temporal power'. The Emperor Aurelian gave what Eusebius calls 'an extremely just decision',[6] ordering possession to be given 'to those to whom the bishops of the dogma in Italy and in the city of the Romans should send written appointment'.

So far as this inquiry is concerned, the last thirty years of the third century seem to have been uneventful and uninstructive. We possess patristic literature of the period, but again nothing to assist us. Thus we find nothing to the point in all the writings of St Gregory Thaumaturgus of Neocaesarea in Pontus (275). A treatise written in 277 by Archelaus, bishop of Carchar in Mesopotamia,[7] entitled 'Acts of the Disputation', is an orthodox Catholic challenge of the Manichaean heresy; but it does not refer to authority in the Church of Rome, or its bishop.

[1] Infra, ch. xxvi (i).
[2] St Cyril, Ep. ix; *Opp.*, V, ii, 36; Mansi, iv, 1011.
[3] Hefele, i, 119.
[4] Duchesne, *EH*, ii, 521.
[5] See Gibbon, i, 325 sq. (ch. xi).
[6] Euseb., VII, xxx, 19.
[7] Or, as some think, by Hegemonius.

CHAPTER XXII

Survey at A.D. 300

The position at the beginning of this third century was summarized in Chapter XIV. Throughout the course of the century there has been little to throw light on our inquiry beyond the teaching of St Cyprian, during his episcopate of ten years.

There is nothing to the purpose in the *Spurious scriptures*, except for the pseudo-Clementines (which, in their earliest editions, probably date from the previous century); they are regarded by some[1] as the source of Tertullian's belief that St Clement was ordained by St Peter. *Tertullian* refers to Matt. xvi, 18, but he seems to regard the promises and privileges as inherited by all the 'Apostolic Churches' collectively. *St Hippolytus* makes no reference to Rome or its bishops. *Origen* fully recognizes St Peter's firstness and greatness in his various commentaries; the other apostles, he teaches, received the same power of the keys, and of binding and loosing; while St Peter retained his preeminence, the promised powers were diffused through the Church. He does not refer to jurisdiction or to doctrinal authority.

St Cyprian's doctrine of unity is difficult to summarize. The Church was founded on *one* in order to manifest its lasting unity, in which all bishops share as equals; yet 'Rome for her greatness ought to have precedency'. St Peter's chair is the especial glory of Rome, yet it seems to be possessed in common by all bishops. He seems to take for granted a perfect equality with his brother bishop of Rome, both in his writings and in his actings. The difficulty of assessing his precise doctrine regarding Rome as a centre of unity is that, until some two years before his death, and after he had written most of his great treatises and letters, no idea of any possible rift in unity, such as could affect his relations with the Roman bishop, had apparently occurred to him. So we do not know his mind on this matter after the painful

[1] E.g., Döllinger, *FA*, ii, 157, 158.

breach with St Stephen of Rome. He makes no reference to any individual doctrinal authority of the Roman bishop.

St Firmilian's epistle gives us the earliest record of the invocation by a Roman bishop of 'the chair of Peter' as conferring an individual authority on him. This is a notable feature of the third century.

The last thirty years of the century were comparatively uneventful, but the claim of individual successorship to St Peter, based on occupancy of his chair, was now plainly recognized in the West: it does not clearly appear whether it was recognized so soon in the East.

A. 'The power of the Roman pontiff, and his relation to the universal Church, were not yet fully developed. Like all other essential parts of the constitution of the Church, the supremacy was known and acknowledged from the beginning as a divine institution, but it required time to unfold its faculties: it assumed by degrees the determined form, in which the bishop of Rome exercised systematically the authority entrusted to him for the preservation of the internal and external unity of the Church. . . . As the union of the Churches became more formal and more close, the supremacy came forth, . . . it displayed itself the more evidently the more the unity of the Church was, in later times, shaken by dangerous assaults, and the more it was torn by heresy and schism.'[1]

N. The 'supremacy', except in a sense of simple primacy, was still unheard-of. The third century affords no evidence of anything resembling the Doctrine of the Papacy, either as to jurisdiction or infallibility. But the individual successorship to St Peter, now being claimed in prerogative by the Roman bishops, who already had all the prestige and influence of the greatest see in Christendom, paved the way for the developments of the next two centuries.

[1] Döllinger, *Hist.*, i, 263.

PART FOUR

THE FOURTH CENTURY

CHAPTER XXIII

Introductory

(i) *Persecution, and the conversion of Constantine*

This fourth century was notable and eventful for the Church, and saw great developments. It opened in a burst of fierce persecution under Diocletian, followed by others under Galerius, Maximin, and Licinius. In 312, Constantine defeated his rival Maxentius, and his progress towards Christian belief is dated from the traditional appearance in the sky of a cross, on the eve of battle, with the words 'In this sign conquer'. Next year, the tolerating 'Edict of Milan' was a dawn after darkness for the suffering Church. But from that time onward the Church came under a new danger, that of imperial patronage and mastery. The emperors took much control of ecclesiastical affairs, even in questions of doctrine. Councils were convoked by them, or at their command, and they often took part in the proceedings. When emperors adopted the Arian heresy, it all but prevailed. The subjection of the Church to secular sway, Erastianism as it is now called, has had ill effects all through the centuries. It has even been said that Constantine's conversion, hailed by the tortured Christians as their joyous deliverance, was the greatest disaster to befall the Church.

(ii) *Sees, provinces, and patriarchates*

During this century, there began an inter-organization and grouping of the local Churches which matured in later centuries. The system took shape from the civil organization of the Empire. As Christianity spread, there had come to be generally a bishop for each city, together with the territory attached to it in the census.[1] (What we now call a see was originally called *parochia*, a parish.) These areas, however, were very unequal, and in some countries, such as Gaul, they were really

[1] Duchesne, *CW*, p. 12.

provinces. In others, sees were small and numerous; thus in 'Africa' there were over five hundred Catholic sees, a greater number than in all the other parts of the West.[1]

Although diocesan bishops were at first wholly independent, the intervention of neighbouring bishops was necessary at times, as for example when a bishop died, or in case of disputes. Custom therefore banded the sees into groups, which also followed the civil geography; bishops were grouped into a province for ecclesiastical purposes exactly as the districts already were for civil purposes. So also, as each province had its chief city or metropolis for its civil government, the bishop of that city usually came by custom to be the president of the group. The group was called a province, and its president the metropolitan or archbishop, although some provinces, Spain for instance,[2] for a long time had no metropolitan, and the senior bishop presided.

The patriarchates of Rome, Alexandria, and Antioch came into existence much in the same way, provinces being federated into larger groups for the sake of unity, on similar lines to what the emperors Diocletian and Constantine had ordained on the civil side. Rome was the first, and Alexandria and Antioch were the second and third greatest cities in the Empire. Constantinople was founded later as 'the second Rome'. These patriarchates, with the later addition of Jerusalem, embraced the main part of the Roman Empire, but not the whole of Christendom.[3]

Custom also settled the metropolitan's powers, which were to decide controversies among their provincial bishops or suffragans, to take appeals from them, to call provincial synods, to take care of vacant sees in the province,[4] and to ordain their provincial bishops. A patriarch had a similar authority over the metropolitans within his customary jurisdiction.

The whole system developed bit by bit. An important milestone was the ninth of twenty-five canons enacted by a synod held at Antioch about A.D. 341,[5] which 'have always been held by the Church as great authorities', and among 'the Canons of the Sacred Fathers'.[6] It declared that 'The bishop presiding in the metropolis (the civil capital) has charge of the whole province because all who have business come together[7] from all quarters to the metropolis. For this reason it is decided

[1] Döllinger, *Hist.*, ii, 242. [2] Hefele, i, 162; Döllinger, *Hist.*, ii, 236.
[3] Bp. W. H. Frere, *Collection of Papers* (posthum., 1940), pp. 1–3.
[4] Bingham, II, xvi, 13; i, 207–15. [5] Hefele, ii, 56–82.
[6] Ibid., p. 59; Canon 1 of Chalcedon, A.D. 451, confirmed them.
[7] πανταχόθεν συντρέχειν, Hardouin, i, 596. This is perhaps an echo of the well-known passage in St Irenaeus.

that he should also hold the foremost rank.'[1] The nomenclature is often confusing, for it was uncertain and variable. *Protos* or *kephalos*, first and head, were early names for the metropolitan;[2] 'archbishop' and 'patriarch' came into use gradually, and were not clearly distinguished; 'exarch' was an alternative name. 'Diocese' originally meant a province, and even a patriarchate could still be called a diocese at the beginning of the fifth century.[3] Moreover the extent of the provincial and patriarchal jurisdictions was rearranged occasionally, sometimes because of rivalries and ambitions.[4]

(iii) *Synods and councils*

'Synod' and 'council' represent synonymous Greek and Latin words. The first Church Council was held at Jerusalem about the year 52 (Acts xv). In the fully developed organization of the Church, it is possible to distinguish (1) the Diocesan Synod of a bishop with his clergy, (2) the Provincial Synod of a metropolitan with his suffragan bishops and other privileged clergy, (3) Patriarchal Councils, also called national, or universal, or primatial, (4) Semi-general Councils, i.e., General Councils of either the Latin or the Greek Church, and (5) General (or universal, or oecumenical) Councils.[5] Synods of some kind had been held as early as the second century, concerning the Montanist schism,[6] and in the third century concerning the Easter Dispute[7] and the heresy of Paul of Samosata;[8] but the fourth century was the period of their great development and, more especially, of the first representative General Councils. They were never in fact classified so precisely. Disciplinary matters, especially with regard to grave sins and to the repentance of heretics, were a frequent concern of synods and councils, but the great work of the General Councils of the fourth and fifth centuries was to define the Catholic Faith and to correct the Christological heresies that sprang up.

(iv) *Convoking of councils*

Just as the synod of a diocese is convoked by its bishop who also presides in it, a provincial synod is convoked and presided over by its metropolitan, and a patriarchal synod by its patriarch. Semi-general

[1] Hefele, ii, 69
[2] Bingham, II, xvi, 5; i, 198.
[3] Innocent I, Ep. xviii, *ad Alex. Antioch.*, Hefele, i, 394; cf. PBLPB, p. 603.
[4] See Puller, p. 130 n.
[5] Hefele, i, 2–5.
[6] Euseb., V, xvi, 10.
[7] Supra, chs. xix and xx.
[8] Supra, ch. xxi.

Councils of East or West ought appropriately to have been convoked always by the sole patriarch of the West (the bishop of Rome) and the chief patriarch of the East (latterly the bishop of Constantinople). Similarly, the Roman pope, as first bishop of Christendom, was the appropriate authority for the convoking of a General Council; actually, the emperors took a great deal into their own hands. Bishops attending General or Semi-general Councils were often accompanied by presbyters and deacons who signed the decrees, either after their own bishop, or else after all the bishops.[1] Sometimes presbyters or deacons attended as legates of their bishop in his absence. (In these early centuries, deacons stood high in importance. A custom peculiar to Rome[2] even limited their number there to seven, although presbyters were ten times as many, and a new pope was commonly elected from among the deacons.)

(v) *Two conflicting interpretations of the history*

Historians have written much about the complicated events of the century. In the present inquiry, we may fail to see the wood for the trees unless two opposite points of view are marked out. For although some precise incidents are disputed, a trend can clearly be seen towards a wider jurisdiction and fuller authority of the Roman popes (as by this time the bishops of Rome may now be called without anachronism).

In one view, (A), this progress was nothing else than a growing recognition of those who had been from the beginning, by divine right, the Vicars of Christ and Sovereign Pontiffs of the whole Church. Whereas in the other view (N), it was a plain aggrandizement of the presidential authority, allowed by natural custom to the bishops of the greatest and most powerful see in Christendom.

This divergence of view is fundamental.

[1] Hefele, i, 20.

[2] Sozomen, VII, xix.

CHAPTER XXIV

The Council of Arles, A.D. 314

Four synods or councils of some note were held in the early years of the century. These were at Elvira (near Granada in Spain) in 305; Arles (at the mouth of the Rhône) and Ancyra (which is now Angora in Turkey), both in 314; and Neocaesarea in Cappadocia (now Niksar, forty miles south of the Black Sea). At all of these synods, numbers of disciplinary canons were agreed upon but, except at Arles, they were synods of a local or provincial type.

The Council of Arles was assembled because of the schism of the Donatists, who challenged the consecration of Cecilian, the bishop of Carthage.[1] They appealed against him to the Emperor Constantine, and he remitted the cause to 'Miltiades, bishop of the Romans', together with ten other bishops, three of whom from Gaul he 'ordered to hasten to Rome' for the purpose.[2] Judgement was given in favour of Cecilian. The Donatists appealed to Constantine, alleging that the Roman council was too small and its proceedings casual. Constantine then convoked the Council of Arles to retry the question; he summoned bishops from all parts of the West;[3] the council was of a semi-general type. These disgraceful dissensions, said the emperor, had made it necessary for him to provide for a larger assembly to settle the matter.

Marinus, bishop of Arles, presided at this council.[4] The new pope, Sylvester I, was represented by two priests and two deacons. From the British Church came the bishops of York, London, and Lincoln.

After the council had reviewed the decision of the Roman council

[1] Alleging that he had been consecrated by a *traditor*, and insisting that the unworthiness of the minister *does* render the sacraments ineffective, they elected their own bishops (Donatus was the second of these), and excommunicated the rest of Christendom. For a full account of the Donatists, see G. G. Willis, *Saint Augustine and the Donatist Controversy* (1950); cf. PBLPB, pp. 35–8, 257–72.

[2] Euseb., X, v, 18, 19.

[3] Euseb., X, v, 21–4 has preserved the imperial summons.

[4] Hefele, i, 181.

under Miltiades, it gave judgement again in favour of Cecilian. (The Donatists appealed once more; the emperor heard it at Milan, and upheld the council's decision, but they remained stubbornly in schism, and formed a separate sect, which endured for several centuries.) Marinus and the council also enacted twenty-two canons of a disciplinary kind, and reported all to the emperor and to the pope, 'the most beloved pope Sylvester, most glorious pope, dearest brother'. They note that he was 'by no means able to leave that region where daily the Apostles sit and their blood bears witness'.[1] They wish their decrees to be 'brought to the knowledge of all', whether by the pope or the emperor.[2]

[1] Mansi, ii, 469; Hardouin, i, 261–2.

[2] The codices vary and are defective; C. H. Turner reads '*annuente qui maiores dioceses tenet*' which, at that time, he thinks, would point to the secular administration, *Ecclesiae occidentalis monumenta juris antiquae*, tom. i, 1899, p. 383 b; cf. Jalland, p. 196, PBLPB, p. 31.

CHAPTER XXV

Nicaea, A.D. 325. The First General Council

Arius was a presbyter of Alexandria who gave his name to the great Arian heresy; he declared that the Logos and the Father are not of the same *ousia* (essence or being). This heresy began to rage in Alexandria about A.D. 323. The Emperor Constantine had now turned his attention to his Eastern Empire, and his zeal for order and uniformity led him to intervene. He first sent Bishop Hosius, whom he 'greatly loved and held in the highest estimation',[1] on a mission to Alexandria. Hosius was bishop of Cordova in Spain, and St Athanasius describes him as 'of all men the most illustrious'.[2] 'Unhappily, Hosius did not succeed in his mission'[3] and Constantine convoked the great council[4] to meet at Nicaea (now Isnik, a decayed townlet, sixty miles from Constantinople across the Sea of Marmora). Hosius presided; five other bishops from the West attended, with two presbyters representing Pope Sylvester I (who was too old to come);[5] they 'supplied his place'.[6] The other bishops, about 318 in all, were Easterns; some of them bore scars and mutilations suffered in the persecutions fifteen years before.

The great work of Nicaea was, of course, the condemnation of Arianism and the framing of the creed which (with some amplification by later councils) is the Nicene Creed of the universal Church. The council also decreed twenty canons. Most of them are disciplinary; we are only concerned with three of them.

By Canon 4, 'The bishop shall be appointed by all [the bishops] of

[1] Socrates, i, 7; Hefele, i, 260. [2] *Apol. de Fuga*, 5; *Opp.*, i, 322.
[3] Hefele, i, 261; Socrates, i, 8 [4] Hefele, i, 268; Euseb., *de vita Constant.*, iii, 6.
[5] F. Hayward, *A History of the Popes*, E.T., 1931, p. 44.
[6] Euseb., *de vita Constant.*, iii, 7; *PG*, xx, 1061.

the eparchy [i.e., the civil province].[1] The confirmation of what has been done belongs by right, in each eparchy, to the metropolitan'. Bishop Hefele observes that 'in the Latin Church, this right of confirmation passed in course of time from the metropolitan to the Pope'.[2]

> Canon 6. Let the ancient customs prevail which are observed in Egypt, Libya, and Pentapolis, that the bishops of Alexandria have authority over all these [provinces], since this is customary also for the bishop of Rome. In like manner, the old [rights] of the churches must be preserved throughout Antioch and the other eparchies. This is quite plain, that if anyone has become a bishop without the metropolitan's approval, the Great Synod commands him not to remain a bishop. . . .

Canon 7 again deferred to 'custom and ancient tradition'. Caesarea had become the metropolis of Palestine when Jerusalem was destroyed, and it was therefore the ecclesiastical metropolis also. But afterwards Aelia Capitolina had been built on the rubble of Jerusalem. This canon awarded to Aelia a special 'honour', but 'without prejudice to the dignity of the metropolis'. Subsequently, Aelia recovered the venerable name of Jerusalem, and after a period of uncertain equality with Caesarea, was acknowledged as a patriarchate at Chalcedon, A.D. 451.

There has been endless discussion and debate about Canon 6. Does it afford any evidence either for or against a universal jurisdiction of the Roman bishop? In later centuries, when the organization of the Church had matured and largely crystallized, it has been expounded that 'The Pope unites in himself several ecclesiastical dignities: he is bishop, metropolitan, patriarch, and lastly, primate of the whole Church',[3] although the distinction between these characters was not always observed.[4]

Two opposite views of Canon 6 have been argued with energy and ingenuity:[5]

A. 'Each one of these dignities (i.e. bishop, metropolitan, patriarch, and primate) may be regarded separately, and that is what the canon has done: it does not consider the pope as primate of the universal Church, nor as simple Bishop of Rome; but it treats him as one of the great metropolitans, who had not merely one province, but several, under their jurisdiction.'[6] The council had no occasion in this canon to consider the pope's universal primacy, and the absence of reference to the primacy in no way derogates from it.

[1] Hefele, i, 382.
[2] Hefele, i, 386.
[3] Hefele, i, 397.
[4] Döllinger, *Hist.*, ii, 234.
[5] E.g., Rivington, *PC*, pp. 166–72; Hefele, i, 388–404; Denny, sects. 311–22; Puller, pp. 138 sq.
[6] Hefele, i, 397.

N. It is true that the council was referring to the Roman bishop as a patriarchal primate (which he certainly was), who had, by settled custom, an authority similar to that which Alexandria also had. It is true also that the council was not legislating for him as primate or first bishop of the universal Church. If indeed the Fathers of Nicaea had understood his primacy in anything like the sense of the modern claim ('. . . Head of the whole Church', with 'full and supreme power of jurisdiction over the Universal Church') there must have been some indication of it in these canons, and there is none.

It has been keenly maintained that Pope Sylvester I collaborated somehow with the emperor in convoking the Council of Nicaea, and also that Hosius represented him in the chair, so that he presided by deputy. No one, perhaps, will deny that these things would have been appropriate enough; later on, when the inter-organization of the Church had become more settled, that appropriateness (or, in one view, that necessity) was recognized.

Western theologians formerly considered papal summons and presidency to be necessary requirements of a valid General Council. It was accordingly maintained that these requirements must have been satisfied at Nicaea, although the contemporary records omit to say so. The following later testimony was cited:

(1) Rufinus, a Roman historian writing about A.D. 400, says that Constantine summoned this council 'at the suggestion of the priests'.[1]

(2) The Roman *Liber Pontificalis*, which was compiled in the sixth and later centuries, says that this council was summoned by the pope and the emperor.

(3) This was asserted also at the Council of Constantinople of A.D. 680.

The earliest suggestion that Hosius represented Pope Sylvester, as his two legates expressly did, is found in a late fifth-century account by Gelasius[2] which, unfortunately, is erroneous on other matters, and is not very trustworthy.[3] Pope Sylvester's legates added that description to their signatures; they followed the signature of Hosius, but he is not so described. Later popes[4] claimed that the third and fourth general councils were under papal presidency, but not Nicaea.

[1] *Eccl. Hist.*, lib. i, cap. i; Sulpicius Severus, writing about the same time, says that Hosius suggested it, *Hist.*, ii, 55.

[2] *Historia Concilii Nicaeni*, ii, 5; *PG*, lxxxv, 1229.

[3] Hefele, i, 263; Bardenhewer, p. 534.

[4] E.g., Vigilius in 552, and Pelagius II (578–90); see Puller, pp. 171–2.

In any view, it would be natural[1] for the first of the patriarchs of the Church to convene a general council and preside at it, either personally or by deputy. It has been argued that the theory which held these things to be a *sine qua non* cannot stand in face of the fact, which all contemporary evidence strongly suggests, that these conditions were not satisfied at Nicaea (which was everywhere regarded as oecumenical) or indeed at any of the seven general councils to Nicaea II in 787.[2]

Nowadays, however, Roman theologians look upon confirmation of a council's decrees by the pope as the only indispensable warrant of validity, though they still claim for him the sole right to convoke and preside. Without now asserting that the pope convoked the Council of Nicaea, or that his legates presided there, they hold that he confirmed it either explicitly or implicitly. Although there is no trace of an explicit approbation, papal approval of Nicaea seems to be assumed by Pope Liberius in 363, by Pope Innocent some forty years later,[3] and it was asserted by the Italian bishops in 485.[4]

[1] Denny, sect. 297.

[2] Jalland, *PC*, p. 424: save that papal legates presided at the fourth and had the place of honour at the sixth and seventh.

[3] Ep. viii; *PL*, viii, 1372; Ep. v; *PL*, xx, 493.

[4] Hefele, i, 44.

CHAPTER XXVI

Athanasius of Alexandria, A.D. 296–373

(i) *Nicaea,* A.D. 325, *to Sardica,* A.D. 343

The great St Athanasius was born in Alexandria and, as a young man, became secretary to the archbishop Alexander. His life-history is so closely interwoven with the events of the half-century after Nicaea, that they form part of it. They make a crowded story, from which those events must be picked out that have a bearing on our inquiry. An outline of the years next after Nicaea will be useful.

325 Council of Nicaea, at which Athanasius, then an archdeacon, was present and active.

326 On the death of Alexander, Athanasius elected and consecrated archbishop and pope of Alexandria.

330 Eusebius of Nicomedia (now Ismid, at the east end of the Sea of Marmora), a semi-Arian and the lifelong enemy of Athanasius, prevailed on Emperor Constantine: Arius recalled from exile.

334 Constantinople founded as 'New Rome'.

335 Constantine convoked a council of bishops at Tyre, the majority being supporters of Eusebius: it condemned and deposed Athanasius: he was banished to Trier (Trèves on the Moselle).

337 Constantine died.

338 Constantine II restored Athanasius to Alexandria. Throughout the next twenty-eight years, the Eusebians attacked Athanasius with every kind of slander.

340 The Emperor Constantius, won over by the Arians, sent one of them to Alexandria as archbishop.

Athanasius sailed to Rome, where he stayed eighteen months. St Ambrose observes that he 'had recourse to the judgement of the Church of Rome, and of all the West'.[1]

The Arians at Alexandria had sent envoys to Rome with accusations against him, which they were quite unable to justify, and the Eusebian

[1] Ep. xiii, 4; *PL*, xvi, 850.

(pro-Arian) bishops, who had been in council at Tyre, had written fierce denunciations of Athanasius to Pope Julius and invited him to call a council. He did so, by letter of summons to the Italian bishops and the Eusebians from the East, and also to Athanasius himself.

The Eusebians refused to attend and, after much delay, sent back a reply (says Sozomen) 'in language elegant and suave, but ironical and threatening'. Rome was a home of apostles and had become the metropolis of religion from the first, yet their Church, which excelled otherwise, should not rank lower for not exceeding in magnitude; Julius had acted unjustly and contrary to ecclesiastical law; they threatened him with loss of their communion if he went against them.[1]

A synod at Rome under Pope Julius examined all the calumnies against Athanasius and declared that he (and certain other persecuted bishops) had been wrongly deposed.

St Julius then wrote a famous and often-quoted letter to the Eusebian bishops.[2] In lengthy and dignified argument he justified the proceedings of the Roman synod, yet invited the Eusebians to come and support their judgements, for the Fathers of Nicaea, he said,[3] allowed the acts of one synod to be reviewed by a later synod. He stressed the unanimity of the Western bishops rather than the authority of his own office:

> I must tell you that though I alone wrote, the opinion was that of all the bishops in Italy and these regions, not mine only. Indeed I did not wish them all to write lest their numbers should weigh with you overmuch. . . . If you think you can prove anything against them (Athanasius and Marcellus) then let whoever will come to us. . . . Give us notice, beloved, that we may write to them and to the bishops who will meet here again. . . . For if they were wholly in fault, as you say, it should be judged according to ecclesiastical rule, not in this way. You ought to have written to us all, so that a just decision might be given by all; because those who suffered were bishops, and not ordinary Churches but those the apostles themselves governed.[4] And why was nothing written to us about the Alexandrian Church in particular? Do you not know the custom is that word is written to us first and then what is just is decided from hence?[5] Indeed, if any suspicion fell on the bishop there, intimation should be written to this Church. But without telling us, they did as they

[1] Sozomen, III, viii, 44–8; Athan., *Apol. c. Arian.*, 25; *Opp.*, i, 145; Hefele, ii, 53; Duchesne, *EH*, ii, 161; Shotwell and Loomis, p. 506.

[2] Athan., *Apol. c. Arian.*; *Opp.*, i, 141 sqq.; *PG*, xxv, 281 sqq.

[3] There is nothing of this in the Nicene canons.

[4] St Mark traditionally founded the Church at Alexandria; St Paul may have preached at Ancyra, the city of Marcellus.

[5] This may recall the examination by the Roman synod, eighty years before, of the orthodoxy of St Dionysius of Alexandria, supra ch. xxi.

saw fit, and wish us to support them without examining the accusations. Not such are Paul's instructions, not such the traditions of the Fathers; this is a new kind of proceeding, a new practice. I beseech you readily to bear with me; what I write is for the good of all. What we have learned from the blessed apostle Peter, this I declare to you, and if these doings had not so disturbed us I should not have written what all might be expected to know....

We hear of no reply from the Eusebian bishops to this letter of Pope St Julius, which is not referred to in the proceedings of the subsequent Council of Antioch in 341.

A. This letter of St Julius 'affords irrefragible witness to the existence, in the Nicene period, of the entire claim on the part of Rome to a divinely instituted authority over East and West alike'.[1]

It 'plainly declared that the Church of Rome, and no other, was able to judge the bishop of Alexandria, who ranked in order next after the pope. St Julius solemnly states that he is giving the tradition handed down from Peter, as the successor of whom he speaks.'[2]

'This is the first letter in which a Pope speaks as the mouthpiece of Peter, though this is common enough later on.'[3]

N. The claim of St Julius is inconsistent with an authority either universal, or divinely instituted, or possessed by himself individually. He claims none of these. Custom, he says, called for word 'to us all' and decision by all, 'i.e., the episcopate acting as a body, so far is Julius from claiming the prerogative of judging by himself alone'.[4]

Moreover he claims that Alexandria is affected by a custom peculiar to it; he does not lay claim to any general right of divine institution, either papal or Roman. That claim was special, not universal, attributed to custom, not divine institution, and it was not in fact acknowledged.

St Julius, writing as he says individually, refers (in the first person singular) to the instructions of Paul and of blessed Peter 'learned by us' (plural) generally in the Roman Church. Later popes developed the idea that they are individually St Peter's mystical mouthpiece.

(ii) *The Council of Sardica*, A.D. 343

This council was convoked by the two emperors Constans and Constantius,[5] at the desire of several bishops, especially Hosius, Julius,

[1] Rivington, *PC*, p. 175. [2] Chapman, *Studies*, p. 59.
[3] Ibid., p. 15, n. 13. [4] Kidd, *RP*, p. 48. [5] Hefele, ii, 90, 160.

and another,[1] to remove dissension concerning Athanasius, and to root out false doctrine. Hosius presided and signed first, 'Hosius of Spain', followed by 'Julius of Rome by his presbyters Archidamus and Philoxenus, Protogenes of Sardica', etc. Sardica (now Sofia, the capital of Bulgaria) was inside the margin of the Western Empire, and although many of the bishops were Easterns, the council is not accounted as General. The Eusebian bishops arrived, but saw that they would not obtain support. Sitting apart, they wrote an encyclical letter, addressed to the whole episcopate, in which among other things they declared Hosius of Cordova, Julius of Rome, and three other Western bishops to be deposed and excommunicated.[2] They then departed. Nevertheless, the council carefully investigated the charges against Athanasius, vindicated him completely, and deposed and excommunicated the Eusebian bishops for their slanders and for other offences. They issued an encyclical letter, writing on the copy for Rome, 'This will seem to be most good and very proper if to the head, that is to the see of Peter the Apostle, the bishops of the Lord shall refer from all provinces'.[3]

There is a little obscurity about the canons of Sardica.[4] The encyclical letter from the council does not mention them. They remained for very long unknown throughout a great part of the Church both in East and West, and they were not generally recognized in the East.[5] Mgr Duchesne believes that the canons were sent to Pope Julius who 'ordered them to be inscribed on his registers following those of Nicaea'.[6] Three of these canons have engaged much attention.

> Canon 3. Hosius, the bishop, said: . . . That if any bishop be judged adversely in any cause, and consider that he has a good cause for a fresh decision, if you agree, let us honour the memory of Peter the Apostle, let those who tried the cause write to the bishop of Rome, so that the judgement may be reviewed, if it ought to be, before bishops of a neighbouring province, and he appoint judges. If however the matter do not appear to him to need revision, the first judgement shall stand. Is this generally agreed? The Synod replied: Agreed.[7]

Canons 4 and 5 apply where the bishop has been deposed by the other bishops of the province. He may himself petition the most blessed

[1] Hefele, ii, 84. [2] Duchesne, *EH*, ii, 173–4. [3] Hardouin, i, 653.

[4] According to two theories, extreme and opposite and not widely held, they were (1) really canons of Nicaea, in spite of strong internal evidence, or else (2) a fifth-century forgery: Rivington, *PC*, pp. 467–75; Denny, sects. 331–5.

[5] Duchesne, *CS*, pp. 136–7. Their inclusion in some Byzantine collections did not imply an operative effect in the East; PBLPB, p. 155. The West did not trouble about them and they remained a dead letter, ibid., p. 292.

[6] *EH*, ii, 179, 180. [7] Hefele, ii, 112–13.

bishop of the Roman Church, who may then appoint fresh inquiry to be made by the bishops of the adjoining province. If so desired by the petition he may, but only if he sees fit, send a presbyter from his suite to sit and judge with these bishops.[1] Canon 4 directs that the see of a deposed bishop who has appealed shall not be filled until the bishop of Rome has decided. (By medieval Western development, the right of deposing a bishop was taken from provincial synods in the West and entirely transferred to Rome.[2]) Canon 14 gives to a presbyter or deacon, condemned by his bishop, a right of appeal to the metropolitan.

A. 'These canons suppose a mode of unity which is irreconcilable with any but the Papal form of government. They do, indeed, condition appeals to Rome, but they assume their necessity. They do not inaugurate them.'[3]

'The right of the Pope to receive appeals was involved in the idea of the Primacy as a divine institution.'[4]

'The Pope has an inherent right to hear appeals if he chooses: the manner in which he exercises this right, and the classes of persons whose appeal he will consent to hear, are questions to be settled by canon law.'[5]

N. These canons conceded to the Roman bishop, in certain cases arising in the West, a regulated discretion to direct a rehearing, and also to appoint those who should review the deposition of a bishop, with or without the help of a member from Rome. They were an early step in the steady progress by which Rome gradually absorbed total authority in the West.

The proposals were novel ('if you agree . . . honouring St Peter's memory') in contrast with a declaration of ancient custom as at Nicaea.[6]

If St Athanasius and the other Fathers had any idea that the Roman pontiff had always possessed, by divine appointment, sovereignty and power of immediate jurisdiction in the discipline and governance of the Church, the proposals would have seemed impertinent, and could not have been framed as they were.[7]

[1] Canon 5 is sometimes numbered as 7. [2] Hefele, ii, 122.
[3] Rivington, *PC*, p. 181. [4] Hefele, ii, 122. [5] Chapman, *Studies*, p. 66.
[6] 'The words of the canon prove that the institution of this right was new. . . . He says not that the ancient tradition was to be confirmed, as was wont to be done in matters which only require the renewal or explanation of an ancient right.' De Marca, *De Concordia Sac. et Imp.*, vii, iii, 8.
[7] Puller, p. 143.

Nothing resembling the Doctrine of the Papacy was then 'the venerable and constant belief'.[1]

(iii) *His last thirty years*

In 345, Gregory, the intruded pope of Alexandria, died. Constans persuaded his brother Constantius to end the exile of Athanasius, who travelled home in 346 via Rome, Antioch, and Jerusalem. At Rome he was welcomed by Pope St Julius, 'who now poured forth his generous heart in a letter of congratulations for the Alexandrian Church'.[2] The next ten years can be outlined as follows:

350 Constans killed: Constantius left sole emperor.
351 Constantius won over by the Semi-Arians.
252 Pope Julius died; Liberius elected.
353 Constantius convoked a synod at Arles, and forced all, including the papal legates,[3] to sign a decree condemning Athanasius.
355 Synod of Milan: more than 300 Western bishops coerced into signing an Arian declaration. Five who stood firm, including the legates of Liberius, were exiled. Pope Liberius bravely withstood Constantius, and was exiled to Beroea. Felix II made (Anti-) Pope.[4]
356 Athanasius, forced out of Alexandria, sought refuge in the desert.

In 358, Pope Liberius was allowed to return to Rome to share rule with Felix, after he had signed a formula of belief approved by the Semi-Arians.[5] 'A matter which seems of graver character is the fact that he repudiated communion with Athanasius, and allied himself with that of the Easterns. . . . It was a weakening, a downfall';[6] its full extent has been disputed,[7] but 'were it desirable to enlarge on this miserable apostacy', says Cardinal Newman, 'there are abundant materials in the letters which Liberius wrote in renunciation of Athanasius, to his clergy, and to the Arian bishops'.[8] Athanasius, although not on very friendly relations with Liberius during that pope's last years,[9] defends his memory, saying that he only succumbed after two years of exile and

[1] Denny, sect. 330 [2] Canon W. Bright, in DCB. [3] Hefele, ii, 204.
[4] In the *Liber Pontificalis* and some earlier catalogues, Felix is included as a pope; Duchesne, *EH*, ii, 361.
[5] Hefele, ii, 245; cf. PBLPB, p. 188.
[6] Duchesne, *EH*, ii, 226. Baronius (*ad an.* 357, n. 56) says that the people of Rome held him utterly sundered from Catholic communion by communion with the Arian heretics.
[7] See Rivington, *PC*, pp. 185–90; Denny, sects. 758–69; Puller, pp. 275–87.
[8] *Arians*, p. 322; but his epithet of 'renegade' (ibid., p. 352) seems too harsh.
[9] Duchesne, *EH*, ii, 318.

affliction, and under fear of death; 'he supported me as long as he had free choice.'[1]

After this, the emperor convened a pair of councils in 359 in the East and West, at Seleucia (now Selefke in Turkey, near the shore north of Crete), and Rimini in Italy. By manœuvres and coercion he got them to adopt semi-Arian confessions.[2] St Jerome remarks that at this time 'the whole world groaned, and wondered to find itself Arian'.[3] These councils, had they been free, would have ranked high as semi-general. As it was, they had neither ecclesiastical validity nor moral authority, and they were treated as nullities by all later councils.

The death of Constantius in 361, and the two-year reign of Julian the Apostate, began the overthrowing of the Arians. St Athanasius was able to return to his see. In 362 he presided over an important Council of Alexandria which determined, says St Jerome, 'that with the exception of the authors of the heresy, who could not be excused on the ground of having made a mistake, those who repented should be admitted to communion with the Church. The West assented to this decision, and it was by means of this most necessary decree that the world was snatched from the jaws of Satan.'[4]

Athanasius ruled his see thereafter in peace until his death in 373. Some fifteen of his forty-seven years of episcopate had been passed in exile, most of it in endurance of malignment and persecution, all of it in steadfast striving for the Catholic faith against odds so great as to make the saying proverbial 'Athanasius against the world', *Athanasius contra mundum*. Yet throughout the long struggle against Arian heresy, imperial domination over the Church, 'Caesaro-papism', was greater in the Eastern than in the Western Empire. It was in the East that majorities of Arian bishops were easily found. Rome and the West take pride that, save for these temporary coercions, they held to the faith of Nicaea.

St Athanasius has left us many writings. They relate chiefly to the Arian heresy, and the history of the times in which he took so great a part in combating it. There are two references to St Peter as the leader (*coryphaeus*) 'who had received the keys'. He says of the Arians that 'they have spared neither the great confessor Hosius, nor the bishop of Rome, nor so many others from the Spains and the Gauls and Egypt

[1] *Hist. Arian. ad Monach.*, 41; *Apol. c. Arian.*, 89; *Opp.*, i, 368, 204.
[2] Hefele, ii, 246 sq.
[3] *Dial. adv. Luciferianos*, 19; *PL*, xxiii, 172.
[4] Ibid., 20; *PL*, xxiii, 174–5.

and Libya'.[1] 'They spared not even Liberius, bishop of Rome . . . they did not reverence his see as an apostolic throne, nor Rome as the metropolis of Romania';[2] Milan, in contrast, he calls 'the metropolis of Italy'.[3]

[1] *Apol. de Fuga*, 9; *Opp*., i, 325. [2] *Hist. Arianorum*, 35; *Opp*., i, 364.
[3] Ibid., 33; *Opp*., i, 363.

CHAPTER XXVII

Communion and Excommunion

Throughout the fourth century, the Church was afflicted by heresies; the greatest of these was the Arian heresy in all its varieties of error. Another trouble was the continual intervention and domineering of the emperors, many of whom inclined towards Arianism.

Under these conditions, the relationship of the Churches was chaotic. 'Patronized by the secular power, the great Churches of Christendom conceived a jealousy of each other, and gradually fortified themselves in their own resources.'[1] The three great patriarchates of Rome, Alexandria, and Antioch were intermittently out of communion with each other. The relations of the Churches, the greater and the weaker, at this time somewhat resemble the modern international relations of the various Powers, great and small. Indeed, the accession of a patriarch was intimated to other Churches just as monarchs have been accustomed to intimate their accession to other Courts. When bishops, even patriarchal bishops, were being exiled and replaced by synods and councils, the occupant of a see coveted 'recognition' by other Churches, and more especially by the great Churches, and by Rome as the greatest and most influential. All this is paralleled to some extent in modern international relations.

Whenever there was a sharp difference of orthodoxy and heresy, a definite breach followed, often with express and reciprocal excommunication. There might be some disunion, and recognition might be withheld, without any formal excommunication, but at times synods formally deposed and excommunicated bishops with whom they were in disagreement, even patriarchs, not excepting the bishop of Rome. At Sardica, as has been noticed, the Western bishops and the bishops of the Eusebian party in the East solemnly deposed and excommunicated each other.

[1] Newman, *Arians*, p. 375.

Out of the complicated history of the fourth century some particular episodes have been relied upon to support opposing contentions. In particular, there has been much controversy regarding the schismatical state of affairs at Antioch, and the position of St Meletius its bishop.

In the modern teaching of Rome, dating back at least to 1303, the Catholic Church is coextensive with the pope's communion, and no one outside that communion can be within the Church. Schism from Rome *ipso facto* involves excommunication, at least in modern Roman doctrine.[1] For many years there was sharp schism at Antioch. One party, whose bishop was St Meletius, were out of communion with another party which acknowledged Paulinus as bishop. Now Paulinus was in communion with Rome, and was recognized by Rome as bishop of Antioch.

Some maintain, therefore, that St Meletius lived and died out of communion with Rome.[2] He died at Constantinople while presiding at the second General Council there in 381. He has always been revered as a saint, both in East and West. They argue from this that the doctrine of the necessity of communion with Rome cannot have been part of the teaching of the Church in the fourth century.[3] In a contrary view, the events of that time cannot be rightly judged by the mature disciplinary system of Rome, and Rome's rejection of St Meletius was not equivalent to excommunication.[4]

Moreover, the Catholic bishops in the East, including St Basil the Great and St John Chrysostom, were in full communion with St Meletius, and recognized him as the rightful bishop of Antioch. They did not so recognize Paulinus; and yet they were not out of communion with Rome. This created a curious triangular discord for which a modern parallel could hardly occur.

The state of communion of certain Churches with others in those days remains a little obscure. Some general principles, however, seem plain enough. A clear conflict between Churches or their bishops, as to their orthodoxy or heresy, put them out of communion with each other *ipso facto*. The function of a formal denunciation was to pronounce a judgement of heresy; excommunication was an automatic consequence. This fatal result of heresy, or what was adjudged to be heresy, is amply illustrated from St Cyprian's time onwards. On the other hand, it was urged by St Cyprian and others after him that lesser differences, not

[1] *Cath. Enc.*, v, 681; xiii, 529.
[2] Puller, pp. 165, 166, 293–5, 350, 353, 502; Denny, sect. 289.
[3] Puller, p. 166; Denny, sect. 289.
[4] Rivington, *PC*, p. 267; cp. *Cath. Enc.*, v, 679.

involving heresy, ought not to be allowed to break communion between Churches.

Letters from a Church or its bishop acknowledging the orthodoxy of another Church had the positive effect of establishing a state of communion between them. When communion was not positively established, the relations between Churches seem sometimes to have been uncertain and indefinite. Especially where the orthodoxy of some Church was doubted by others, it may be difficult to affirm that it was in positive communion with them. On the other hand, unless a definite charge of heresy had been made against it, it may be equally difficult to affirm that there was positive excommunion.

CHAPTER XXVIII

Meletius of Antioch: Saints and Schism, A.D. 331–98

The tangled story of the schism at Antioch begins in 331 when St Eustathius, its orthodox Catholic bishop, was deposed by Arian bishops (on false charges of Sabellian heresy) and was exiled by the Emperor Constantine. Before he departed, the saint enjoined on his flock to continue patiently in the Church, even if Arianizing bishops were set over them. This so fell out until, thirty years later, Meletius, who had previously been consecrated bishop of Sebaste (in Armenia), was elected bishop of Antioch. In his first sermon he openly professed the Catholic faith in its fullness. The Arians were infuriated; we get an odd side-light on the ecclesiastical manners of the time. The archdeacon rushed up and thrust his hand over the bishop's mouth; St Meletius held up three fingers, and then one finger, thus dumbly reasserting the doctrine he had declared.

It is necessary here to mention Marcellus, a storm petrel of the Church, who hovered uncertainly between orthodoxy and heresy. Most Fathers, and most scholars, regard him as a heretic,[1] but for a time he persuaded both St Athanasius and Pope St Julius to receive him in their communion (although St Athanasius in his last years seems to have withdrawn it).[2] Marcellus was regarded as a heretic at Antioch, and by St Basil and the Easterns generally. He was afterwards stamped as a heretic by the general councils of Constantinople and Chalcedon.[3]

Although the great majority of the Catholics at Antioch had obeyed St Eustathius and remained in communion with the heretical bishops who succeeded him, a small group had kept apart under a faithful priest named Paulinus. These 'Eustathians' or 'Paulinians', as they

[1] Hefele, ii, 29–32; Hergenröther, p. 75.

[2] Dom Maran, *Vit. S. Basil*, xxxvii, 6; see Rivington, *PC*, p. 224, Puller, p. 290.

[3] Hefele, ii, 367; ii, 351.

were called, were recognized by Alexandria, and St Athanasius was in communion with them. In 362, now that Meletius was bishop, Athanasius and the Council of Alexandria saw that the schism could be healed, and they sent two bishops to Antioch 'to effect a reconciliation between the Meletians and the Eustathians'.[1] But unluckily an impetuous and wrong-headed bishop, Lucifer of Cagliari, arrived before them and consecrated Paulinus, uncanonically and wrongly;[2] the proposals of Alexandria were 'rendered futile by Lucifer's hasty action'.[3] (Lucifer then renounced communion with Athanasius, 'causing a fresh schism, called the Luciferian', which lasted fifty years).[4]

Next year, St Athanasius himself visited Antioch: 'The most blessed Pope Athanasius,' says St Basil, 'when he arrived from Alexandria, exceedingly desired that communion should be brought about between Meletius and himself; but through wretched counsellors their union was deferred to another occasion; would this had not happened.'[5] What went wrong is not known; the communion of Athanasius with Marcellus, whom Meletius (like St Basil) regarded as a heretic, may have had to do with it. St Athanasius was grieved,[6] but admitted Paulinus to his communion.

In 365, Pope Liberius, in the name of the bishops of Italy and all the West, sent a letter addressed to sixty-four named Eastern bishops, and generally 'to all the orthodox bishops of the East', receiving them into their communion.[7] Meletius was not one of those named, and although it has been suggested[8] that he was 'recognized among the bishops of the East', some think that he himself would not at that time have accepted communion with the Western bishops, who had not yet repudiated Marcellus.[9]

During the next ten years, St Meletius was twice exiled by the Arian Emperor Valens, as was also St Athanasius, both as confessors of the orthodox faith. Pope Damasus, elected in 366, refrained for nine years from any relations with either Paulinus or Meletius.

In 375, Vitalis, a priest of Antioch who had broken away from Meletius and led the Apollinarians there, went to Rome and visited Pope Damasus. According to St Gregory of Nazianzum, he deceived Damasus as to his actual doctrine.[10]

[1] Hefele, ii, 278. [2] Theodoret, iii, 2; PBLPB, pp. 287, 309.
[3] Rivington, *PC*, p. 199. [4] Hefele, ii, 279; Newman, *Arians*, p. 364.
[5] Ep. cclviii, 3; *Ad Epiphanium*, *Opp*., iii, 394.
[6] St Basil, Ep. lxxxix, *Ad Meletium.*, *Opp*., iii, 181. [7] Socrates, iv, 12.
[8] Rivington, *PC*, p. 250. [9] Puller, p. 295.
[10] Ep. *Ad Cledonium*, cii; Puller, p. 315; Merenda thinks Damasus actually admitted Vitalis to communion, *De S. Damasi Opusc. et Gestt*., x, 1; *PL*, xiii, 168.

Near Antioch at this time was residing a remarkable young layman who had been a catechumen baptized nine years before at Rome, and who was later on to become renowned as the great Biblical scholar St Jerome. He wrote two much-quoted letters[1] to Pope Damasus, asking for direction. Even allowing for St Jerome's florid and extravagant style of writing (he described a nun's mother as 'mother-in-law of God'),[2] they afford striking evidence of the strongly 'papal' teaching imparted to him in Rome:

> Since the East tears in pieces the Lord's coat, and foxes lay waste the vineyard of Christ, so that among broken cisterns which hold no water it is difficult to understand where the sealed fountain and enclosed garden are . . . therefore by me is the chair of Peter to be consulted . . . thence now seeking food for my soul where of old I received the robe of Christ. . . . At present the Sun of Righteousness rises in the West; but in the East the fallen Lucifer has placed his throne above the stars. You are the light of the world; you are the salt of the earth. . . . Therefore though your greatness terrifies me, yet your kindness invites me. From the priest the sacrifice claims salvation, from the shepherd the sheep claims protection. Let us speak without offence; I court not the Roman height. I speak with the successor of the Fisherman and the disciple of the Cross, I who follow none as my chief but Christ am associated in communion with thy Blessedness, that is, with the see of Peter. On that rock the Church is built, I know. Whoso shall eat the Lamb outside that house is profane. If any one shall not be in the Ark of Noah, he will perish when the flood prevails. . . . I know not Vitalis, Meletius I reject. I am ignorant of Paulinus. Whoso gathereth not with thee scattereth; that is, he who is not of Christ is of Antichrist.
>
> If any one is joined to the see of Peter, he is mine. . . . Wherefore I conjure your Blessedness . . . that you would signify to me by your letters with which bishop in Syria it is my duty to communicate.

Pope Damasus replied to Jerome in three letters, the first of which he dispatched by the hand of 'my son, Vitalis'. (Next year Apollinarius consecrated Vitalis heretically as a third bishop of Antioch, there being already two orthodox bishops, Meletius and Paulinus). We have the third letter of Damasus only.[3] He accepted Paulinus as 'joined with us in the communion of the same faith', and he ignored St Meletius. He even allowed him to be described as an Arian heretic.[4]

St Meletius presided over the Council of Antioch of 379, which was attended by more than a hundred and fifty Eastern bishops (among whom were Gregory of Nyssa, Eusebius of Samosata, and others afterwards canonized); it is described by Tillemont[5] as one of the most

[1] Epp. xv, xvi; *PL*, xxii, 355 sq. [2] Ep. xxii, 20; *PL*, xxii, 407.
[3] *PL*, xiii, 356. [4] St Basil, Ep. cclxvi, *ad Petrum*, *Opp*, iii, 412–13.
[5] viii, 367.

illustrious councils ever held. One main object was to proclaim to the Western bishops their adherence to the orthodox faith, and to assist the Church to overcome Arianism. The bishops adopted and signed as their own the dogmatic 'tome' published by a Roman synod ten years before, and they sent it with a Synodal Letter 'to the bishops of Italy and Gaul'.[1] The president signed first: 'I, Meletius, bishop of Antioch, consent to all things which are written above, so believing and holding: and if any one holds otherwise, let him be anathema.'[2]

This important declaration of faith, which duly reached the Roman archives,[3] ought to have cleared up any Western doubts as to the perfect orthodoxy of Meletius. Yet it does not appear that it affected the attitude of Pope Damasus towards him. Next year (380) the fourth Roman Synod under Damasus issued a fresh confession of faith, with nineteen anathemas annexed to it, all of which were sent to Paulinus. The ninth paragraph says that 'those who have migrated from churches to churches we regard as aliens from our communion'.[4] Now Paulinus' rival, Meletius, had undoubtedly been consecrated first to Sebaste and afterwards to Antioch.[5]

Further than this, it does not appear that Meletius received either recognition or notice from Rome. He was continuously and fully in communion with St Basil the Great and the Catholic bishops of the East, and he presided at the second General Council at Constantinople in 381. He died there while the council was in session, and he is revered as a saint both in East and West. If all the known facts had to be read in the light of later centuries, it might seem that he lived and died out of communion with the Roman see (and therefore outside the peace of the Church, according to the Roman doctrine). Some take that view;[6] Dr Rivington, on the other hand, maintains that 'St Meletius died in communion with Rome',[7] although it is difficult to see any positive indication of this. In the circumstances of those times, was there room perhaps for a neutral position that amounted neither to definite communion nor definite excommunion?

Before St Meletius set out for Constantinople, he and Paulinus had agreed between themselves that the survivor of them should be recognized as legitimate bishop of both their flocks. But the Council of

[1] Hefele, ii, 291; Rivington, *PC*, p. 230. [2] *PL*, xiii, 353. [3] *PL*, xiii, 354.
[4] *a communione nostra habemus alienos*, *PL*, xiii, 361, 362.
[5] Hefele, ii, 291, 292; Mansi, iii, 486 sq.; *PL*, xiii, 360, 361; Theodoret, vii; it is generally thought that this was aimed at Meletius, see authorities cited Puller, pp. 330–4.
[6] Puller, p. 350; Denny, sect. 593. [7] *PC*, p. 267.

Constantinople ignored this[1] and made St Flavian bishop of Antioch; so when Paulinus was on his death-bed, six years later, he consecrated another, Evagrius, as bishop to succeed him. After the latter's death, St John Chrysostom, in 398, persuaded the then patriarch of Alexandria to become reconciled with Flavian and to send a joint embassy entreating Pope St Siricius also to recognize St Flavian as canonical bishop of Antioch. This mission succeeded,[2] and the schism between Rome and Antioch was healed at last, although a few 'Eustathians' kept apart for seventeen years more.

In the same year that St Meletius died, the bishops at the Council of Aquileia in Italy wrote to the Emperor Theodosius in favour of Paulinus, who 'has been put in great anxiety by the dissensions of other persons whose faith in former times was undecided'—apparently the 'great Church' of St Meletius—desiring 'that these persons, if it be possible, and if they are recommended by sufficient faith, should be added to our fellowship',[3] yet preserving their own prerogative 'to those colleagues who have enjoyed our communion from of old', i.e., the Paulinians.[4] They suggest that the two sides should agree that on the death of one bishop 'the rights of the Church should remain with the survivor'.[5] It appears from this that, even then, the Westerns still regarded the Meletians of Antioch as not yet in communion with them.[6]

A. The disorders at Antioch cannot be fairly read in the light of later centuries. The actual autonomy enjoyed by great sees at that time did not exclude the recognition of Roman supremacy.

'It must be remembered that the refusal to acknowledge a person as bishop is by no means equivalent to excommunication, and again, that the refusal of letters of intercourse may mean something much less than a decision that the person to whom they are refused is under the *excommunicatio major*.'[7] Pope Damasus never expressly condemned or excommunicated Meletius.

N. The 'great Church' at Antioch had been out of communion with Rome and the West for a generation; there was no occasion for a new

[1] In spite of the opposition of St Gregory of Nyssa.
[2] Socrates, v, 15; Sozomen, viii, 3. [3] *ad consortia nostra.*
[4] Ep. inter Ambrosianas, xii, 4; *PL*, xvi, 988, 989. [5] Ibid, xii, 5.
[6] Dr Rivington (*PC*, pp. 263–8; cp. Puller, pp. 347 sq.) thought that the letter relates only to a fresh breach of communion resulting from the election of St Flavius and the injustice to Paulinus, but the terms of the letter indicate that the writers had not yet heard of this event, as they had when they wrote again later (Ep. xiii).
[7] Rivington, *PC*, p. 267.

or formal excommunication of St Meletius (although he was actually one whom the Roman synod of 380 pronounced as 'alien from our communion'). He remained throughout in episcopal rivalry with Paulinus, with whom Rome held communion as bishop of Antioch. According to the later Roman doctrine, St Meletius lived and died in schismatic rebellion against 'the supreme jurisdiction of the Roman Pontiff', and self-excluded from Roman communion.

CHAPTER XXIX

Basil the Great of Caesarea, †379

St Basil, known as 'the Great', was born in 329 at Caesarea[1] in Cappadocia. In 370 he became its archbishop, and he died in 379. His writings are held in high esteem, and he is one of those Fathers whose writings were declared (by the synod of 496 under Pope Gelasius) to be entirely orthodox. They include twenty-seven commentaries on Scripture, some twenty-one dogmatic books, and 365 letters which unfold for us the events of his time.

His works contain several references to St Peter:

> The Church of God, whose foundations are upon the holy hills; for it is built upon the foundations of the apostles and prophets. One of these mountains was Peter, on which rock the Lord promised that He would build His Church.[2]
>
> On account of the pre-eminence of his faith he received on himself the building of the Church.[3]
>
> He saith, 'Peter, lovest thou Me more than these. Feed My sheep'; granting the same authority to all shepherds and teachers thenceforward; and the token of this is that all bind and loose exactly as he did.[4]

He does not seem to speak of 'the chair of Peter', but he congratulates St Ambrose on being 'translated to the chair of the Apostles at Milan'.[5]

Passages in his correspondence have been invoked (both A and N) to throw light on his attitude towards Rome and his relations with the contemporary popes. It is said on the one hand[6] (i) that he recognized the restoration of a bishop by Pope Liberius, and on the other hand (ii) that he regarded Pope Liberius with disdain, and moreover (iii) re-

[1] Now Kaisarié, 180 miles north of Antioch.
[2] *Comm. in Isai.*, ii, 66; *Opp.*, i, 427.
[3] *Adv. Eunom.*, ii, 4; Allnatt, p. 8; *PG*, xxix, 580.
[4] *Constitutiones Monasticae*, xxii, 5; *PG*, xxxi, 1410; *Opp.*, ii, 573.
[5] Ep. cxcvii., *Opp.*, iii, 288.
[6] Rivington, *PC*, p. 225.

mained in close communion with St Meletius as bishop of Antioch, and rejected Paulinus, the other bishop, who enjoyed communion with Rome.

(i) Eustathius (not the saint-bishop of Antioch) was a Semi-Arian bishop of Sebaste[1] who ended his days, after a chequered career, as an out-and-out heretic.[2] He was more than once deposed from his see. Having been sent, however, with two other bishops from Asia Minor as ambassadors to the Western Emperor Valentinian and Pope Liberius, and having given a written adhesion to the Nicene Creed, he was received into communion by Liberius. No mention was made of the new Macedonian heresy,[3] then rife in the Eastern Church, of which these three were among the chief promulgators. On their return, a synod of orthodox bishops was assembled in 367 at Tyana[4] to receive the letters of communion from the West.[5] Eustathius and his fellow delegates, being now recognized as true Catholics, were at that time acknowledged as the rightful bishops of their sees. But five years later, St Basil wrote to the Westerns, his 'most honourable brethren', that Eustathius had become a cause of great sorrow:

> Having been ejected . . . he hit upon a journey to you as a means of restitution for himself. What propositions were made to him by the blessed bishop Liberius, and to what he agreed, I am ignorant. I only know that he brought a letter restoring him, which he showed to the synod at Tyana, and was restored to his see. . . . As it is from the West that he derives his power to injure the Churches, and uses the authority given him by you to the overthrow of many, it is necessary that his correction should come from the same quarter, and that a letter be sent to the Churches stating on what terms he was received, and in what manner he has changed his conduct and nullifies the favour given him by the Fathers at that time.[6]

Dr Rivington[7] understands this to mean that the bishops at Tyana dutifully obeyed a papal letter restoring Eustathius, 'and St Basil has not a word to say against their attitude in the matter'.

(ii) Only one of St Basil's letters is addressed to Pope Damasus.[8] Depressed by the desolation of the Churches 'from Illyricum to Egypt', he besought help from the West, and asked in particular for a strong deputation of Western bishops to visit and show sympathy with the East. Nothing was done. His later letters are addressed to 'the bishops of the West', or to his 'fellow-ministers of like mind, the bishops of

[1] Sivas in Armenia, 245 miles north of Antioch.
[2] St Basil, Ep. ccxliv; *Opp.*, iii, 380. [3] Denying 'the Holy Ghost uncreate'.
[4] In Cappadocia, sixty miles north of Tarsus. [5] Hefele, ii, 287.
[6] Ep. cclxiii, *Opp.*, iii, 406. [7] *PC*, p. 225. [8] Ep. lxx, *Opp.*, iii, 163.

Gaul and Italy'.[1] He refers to Damasus as 'their leader' (*coryphaeus*)[2] as he also refers to 'the coryphaeus of the Arian party'.[3] He looked askance at the orthodoxy of Damasus for his support of Marcellus.[4] Damasus is 'a man proud and exalted, and therefore quite unable to hear those who preach the truth to him';[5] 'the man is arrogant . . . what help is there for us in Western pride . . . they do now just as they did before in the case of Marcellus . . . they themselves support heresy'.[6]

(iii) The see of Antioch was all-important in Basil's view. He wrote to St Athanasius imploring him to use his influence to restore harmony there: 'What part is more vital to the Churches throughout the world than Antioch?'[7] Basil was in close communion with Meletius as its bishop, undisturbed by the fact that Rome repudiated him and supported Paulinus as bishop. In 375, after Pope Damasus had sent letters of recognition to Paulinus, Basil wrote to Meletius:

> We received letters from the East telling that Paulinus' people had received certain letters from the West, tokens of authority as it were, and that his partisans were greatly elated and exulted in the letters, and were next putting out a form of creed and on those terms were ready to join with our Church.[8]

At this time he wrote also to Terentius, a nobleman of Antioch:

> I hear that the Paulinians are now carrying about letters from the Westerns assigning to them the episcopate of the Church in Antioch and wronging Meletius, that most admirable bishop of the true Church of God. . . . Yet since we accuse no one, but desire to have love towards all, and especially towards them who are of the household of faith, we congratulate those who have received the letters from Rome. . . . But I can never persuade myself on that account to draw back because somebody is much elated at getting a letter from man; no, not even if one should come from heaven, but walk not by the sound word of faith, can I regard him as of the communion of saints.[9]

Dom Maran[10] and others have considered that St Basil was not in communion with Paulinus. It is plain that he rejected Paulinus as bishop (despising his 'Western' credentials), and that they were not on friendly terms. Yet the orthodoxy of Paulinus is implied, he is 'of the household of faith', as he would not have been (by whomsoever supported) if he had been heretical. With St Basil it seems that communion

[1] Epp. xc, xcii, ccxlii, ccxliii.
[2] Ep. ccxxxix; *Opp.*, iii, 368.
[3] Ep. ccxliv; *Opp.*, iii, 381.
[4] Epp. lxix, ccxxxix; *Opp.*, iii, 162, 368.
[5] Ep. ccxv; *Opp.*, iii, 323.
[6] Ep. ccxxxix; *Opp.*, iii, 368.
[7] Ep. lxvi, 2; *Opp.*, iii, 159.
[8] Ep. ccxvi; *Opp.*, ii, 324, *PG*, xxxii, 792.
[9] Ep. ccxiv; *Opp.*, iii, 321; *PG*, xxxii, 783.
[10] *Praefat. in S. Basil*, Vit., ii, 2; St Basil, *Opp.*, III, xi; Puller, pp. 321, 322.

depended entirely upon the mutual holding of the orthodox faith. He was not out of communion with Pope Damasus in spite of some suspicion of the latter's orthodoxy. Nevertheless, he did not feel in the least bound by the decision of Damasus regarding Antioch and Meletius.

It was possible at that time for one bishop to be in communion with others who were not in communion with each other. St Basil, wholeheartedly in communion with St Meletius, was not out of communion with the Westerns. A century later, such a strange triangle would probably not have stood the tension. Tillemont[1] comments that: 'All the arguments of Gelasius[2] are based on his contention that whoever communicates with one who is excommunicate is defiled, and defiles those who communicate with him. If this maxim were to allow of no exception, it is hard to see how St Athanasius, Pope Damasus, and St Ambrose, who would not at all communicate with St Meletius of Antioch, were able not to excommunicate St Basil, St Gregory of Nazianzus, and all the other Catholics of the East who communicated with that Saint.'

A. Obviously Rome had the right, according to St Basil, to decide upon the person who was to be in charge of Antioch. In his indignant letter about Meletius being passed over he never disputes Rome's right in itself.[3]

As to his complaint of 'supporting heresy', he considered that the Westerns had done it through ignorance of the real state of things, and not by any actual decision. 'He was at liberty to consider it to be so, and yet might believe the pope as the divinely appointed monarch of the Church.'[4]

St Basil could believe in the primacy of the pope although he did not look upon him as he would today. 'The doctrine developed much in clarity.'

N. Obviously St Basil considered that Rome was free to decide (wrongly, as he thought) for itself only, and not for him or other Eastern bishops. There is nothing to suggest that St Basil had ever heard of a dogma that the bishop of Rome is the divinely appointed monarch of the Church. All that he wrote and did suggests that he would have repudiated such a dogma if it had ever been asserted in his time.

'It is clear that St Basil, St Meletius, and the whole Eastern Church

[1] xvi, 642.
[2] Pope, A.D. 492–6.
[3] Rivington, *PC*, pp. 221, 222.
[4] Ibid., p. 223.

were either consciously guilty of abominable rebellion against their divinely appointed head, or they did not acknowledge that view of the papacy, which is set forth in the Vatican decrees, and which has been summed up in the assertion that the pope, even in the fourth century, enjoyed a "lordship over the universal Church". The Church, by the extraordinary veneration which she has always manifested for the memory of St Basil, has practically decided in favour of the latter alternative.'[1]

[1] Puller, p. 323.

CHAPTER XXX

Constantinople, A.D. 381. The Second General Council

This was actually a semi-general council of Eastern bishops, although it was afterwards recognized as the second General Council. It was summoned by the Emperor Theodosius, with the purpose of establishing the Nicene faith and completing the overthrow of Arianism. Pope Damasus does not appear to have been consulted or invited; he was not present or represented.[1] One hundred and fifty bishops attended; St Meletius of Antioch presided until his death. He was not 'in diplomatic relations' with Rome, whether or not there was definite excommunion. Paulinus of Antioch, recognized as patriarch of Antioch by the pope, was not invited.

The chief work of the council was to approve the creed of Nicaea in its slightly amplified form, which was reaffirmed at Chalcedon in 451 and has ever since been known as the Nicene Creed.[2] It also enacted several canons, of which Canon 3 declares that 'The bishop of Constantinople shall hold the first rank after the bishop of Rome, because Constantinople is the new Rome'.[3] The whole proceedings of the council received formal confirmation from the emperor;[4] confirmation or approval by Rome or the West was not asked for.

The council pronounced against Maximus the Cynic, a queer character who had been irregularly and surreptitiously consecrated to the see of Constantinople, and it appointed St Gregory of Nazianzus (against his will). On the death of Meletius, Gregory became president of the council. After he resigned the see, Nectarius succeeded him and also became president. The council's appointment of Flavian to the see of Antioch has already been mentioned.[5] They announced it in a

[1] Hefele, ii, 342. [2] Ibid., p. 351. [3] Ibid., p. 357; see PBLPB, p. 606.
[4] Ibid., p. 369. [5] Supra, ch. xxviii.

synodical letter 'to the very honoured lords and most reverend brethren and fellow-ministers Damasus, Ambrose, Britonius, Valerian', etc. They 'have canonically consecrated the most reverend and most God-beloved Flavian to be bishop of the very ancient and truly apostolical Church of Antioch'.[1] There seems to have been no indefiniteness about the excommunion that resulted from this action; according to Sozomen,[2] 'the bishop of the Romans and all the priests (i.e., bishops) of the West were not a little indignant . . . they treated . . . the consecrators of Flavian as guilty persons, and held them to be excommunicate'.

According to the former precedence of the great sees, Alexandria and Antioch, the second and third cities of the Empire, came next after Rome. But Timotheus, the new patriarch of Alexandria, did not preside at the council; in passing over him it gave effect to the new precedence now accorded by it to Constantinople.[3]

The whole proceedings of the council were at once recognized as authoritative by the East. The council came to be recognized as the second General Council by the West also, early in the sixth century,[4] in respect of the Creed. Pope Gregory the Great declared that he received and revered 'the four councils (Nicaea, Constantinople, Ephesus, and Chalcedon) as the four books of the Holy Gospel'. But Rome and the West never assented to the canons and, indeed, were not asked to assent. The proceedings were marked by complete independence of Rome and the West.

[1] Theodoret, v, 8. [2] vii, 11. [3] Hefele, ii, 344, 345.
[4] Ibid., p. 374; Puller, p. 360.

CHAPTER XXXI

Popes Damasus and Siricius, †384, †398

Pope St Liberius died in 366, nine months after the rival pope, Felix II, and 'as a quarrel had arisen at Rome among the orthodox themselves, Damasus was chosen pope by one party, and Ursinus by the other. This occasioned bloody contests between the two parties',[1] in which a hundred and thirty-seven persons were killed. The Prefect of Rome decided in favour of the regularity of the ordination of Damasus, and Ursinus was exiled for a time;[2] but he remained in active opposition throughout the reign of Damasus.

The Church of the Metropolis had now got great wealth, to which the pagan historian, Ammianus, attributed these troubles,[3] but 'he was not the only man to deplore the progress of comfort among the Roman clergy; St Jerome has censured with much vigour the strange abuses which the increasing prosperity of the Church of Rome introduced into its midst'.[4] 'The Roman Pontiff had need of riches, and riches abounded; he had need of *éclat*, and the most extraordinary splendour was seen to radiate from the throne of St Peter, to such a degree that already, in the third century, one of the greatest nobles of Rome observed playfully, as St Jerome relates, "promise to make me Bishop of Rome, and I shall at once become a Christian".'[5] Moreover, with the rise of Constantinople, Rome had lost much of its imperial standing, and its Church had grown in secular authority; the pope had now great power in the city.[6]

Damasus has been called the greatest of the early Roman bishops: he was 'a man of much practical shrewdness and self-assertive energy'.[7] He venerated Rome's Christian antiquities (although with very limited

[1] Hefele, ii, 287. [2] Coll. Avell., pp. 48, 49.
[3] Ammianus Marcellinus, xxvii, 3; Gibbon, iii, 31, 32 (ch. xxv).
[4] Duchesne, *EH*, ii, 385. [5] De Maistre, p. 135.
[6] F. Hayward, *A History of the Popes*, E.T. 1931, p. 52.
[7] Shotwell and Loomis, p. 595.

knowledge, for the early documents, such as St Clement, St Irenaeus and Tertullian, had become literary rarities and were not at his disposal),[1] and he caused inscriptions in honour of the martyrs to be engraved on their tombs.

He had grave difficulties to surmount; Rome still harboured numerous sects and heresies—Valentinians, Marcionites, Montanists, Sabellians, Luciferians, as well as the Donatists, who were organized under their own bishops.[2] 'His victory had cost him too dear: his promotion had been accompanied by too much police action, too many imperial rescripts, too many corpses. The whole of his pontificate felt the effects of it. And besides, Ursinus had never laid down his arms.'[3]

Damasus 'was above all a ruler'.[4] Early in his reign, an imperial constitution of Valentinian I granted praetorian support to ecclesiastical discipline in the West. His son and successor, Gratian, whom Gibbon describes as gentle and amiable, soft and tractable,[5] was an orthodox Catholic who upheld the Church in every way, 'her first thoroughly filial subject amongst the line of the Roman emperors'.[6] In 382 a Roman synod under Damasus petitioned Gratian for additional legislation, and in response Gratian issued the rescript *Ordinarium sententiae*.[7] It applied to the two praetorian prefectures of the West (viz., 'Italy', which included the 'dioceses' of Rome, Northern Italy, Western Illyricum, and Africa, and 'Gaul', which included Gaul proper, Spain, and Britain).

In the suburbicarian districts or 'provinces' of Rome itself, charges against bishops were to be tried either at Rome, or by synods elsewhere (such as were usual in Sicily). Elsewhere in the West, bishops under accusation were to be remitted by the local magistrate to the court of their metropolitan. 'Thus Gratian made the execution of episcopal judgements easier than it had hitherto been. He did not create a patriarchate, but found one in existence.'[8] He also made two important provisions of some novelty; to bishops in the West he gave a right of appeal from their metropolitan 'to the bishop of Rome or to a council of fifteen of the neighbouring bishops', and an accusation against a metropolitan himself was to be taken 'to Rome or to those judges whom the Roman bishops shall appoint'. This legislation strengthened the internal jurisdiction of the Roman patriarchate. Moreover, Damasus laid fresh emphasis on his primatial supremacy. In his later letters he

[1] Duchesne, *CS*, p. 106. [2] Duchesne, *EH*, ii, 366. [3] Ibid.
[4] Rivington, *PC*, p. 106. [5] Gibbon, iii, 140–1 (ch. xxvii).
[6] Rivington, *PC*, p. 234.
[7] *PL*, xiii, 581, 583–8; Dr Jalland dates it 378, *CP*, p. 244, n. 2.
[8] Rivington, *PC*, p. 236

began to write in the 'plural of majesty'. In one of them he addressed bishops for the first time as 'sons', instead of 'brothers'.[1] Acknowledging the letter from the Council of Antioch in 379,[2] he writes as from 'the holy Church in which the Apostle sat and taught us . . . how we ought to handle the helm which has been entrusted to us. . . . Most honourable sons, in that your charity accords to the Apostolic See the reverence due, you confer the greatest honour upon yourselves.'[3]

A document known as the *Decretum Gelasianum*, which has been described as 'the first official definition of papal claims',[4] is attributed by some eminent scholars to the Roman synod of 382 under Damasus, although its source is uncertain and was possibly much later.[5] It bases Rome's supremacy on the promise to St Peter, not 'on synodal decisions' (perhaps a hit at the third canon of Constantinople of the previous year), and it depicts the three chief Nicene sees as a Petrine hierarchy, with its first, second, and third sees at Rome, Alexandria, and Antioch. It does not explain why Alexandria took precedence of Antioch, which was traditionally St Peter's first see; Alexandria was, of course, the second city of the Empire. Under the pontificate of Damasus, a long step forward was taken in formulating the claim of the Roman Church as the exclusive inheritor of the prerogative of St Peter.[6]

The Emperor Theodosius I, on recovering from a dangerous illness, received baptism in February 380, and immediately became zealous for the purity of the faith. In the same month he issued the famous decree *Cunctos populos*:[7]

> We will that all the peoples who are governed by Our Clemency and Moderation should practise the same religion which the divine apostle Peter delivered to the Romans, as the religion proclaimed by him up to this time declares it, and which it is clear the pontiff Damasus follows and Peter the bishop of Alexandria, a man of apostolic holiness. We order that those who follow this law shall assume the name of Catholic Christians; and as we judge that all others are extravagant madmen, we brand them with the infamous name of heretics.

He followed this by *Nullus hereticus*:[8]

> Perpetual observance is to be made of the Nicene faith, handed down by our forefathers and confirmed by the testimony and assertion of divine

[1] Shotwell and Loomis, p. 618, n. 283. [2] Supra, ch. xxviii.

[3] Damasus, Ep. vii; *PL*, xiii, 370; Allnatt, p. 113; Kidd, *RP*, p. 63. Damasus was first to use this style of 'the Apostolic See', PBLPB, p. 668.

[4] CMH, i, 173; Chapman, *Studies*, p. 20, n. 2; Kidd, *RP*, p. 69.

[5] Batiffol, *Le Siége Apostolique*, pp. 149 sq.; PBLPB, pp. 669.

[6] Turner, *CA*, p. 233. [7] *Cod. Theod.*, xvi, 1, 2. [8] Ibid., 5, 6.

religion . . . the Catholic churches throughout the world are to be restored to the orthodox bishops who hold the Nicene faith.

These were specified as:

the bishops who believed in the Catholic doctrine of the Holy Trinity, and were in communion with Nectarius of Constantinople, or in Egypt with Timothy of Alexandria, in *Oriens* with Pelagius of Laodicea, etc.[1]

This last provision was made on the advice of the Council of Constantinople,[2] and appears not to have referred to Rome or the West.

On the death of Damasus in 384, Siricius succeeded him and reigned until his own death in 398. He followed the example of Damasus in maintaining the authority of the Roman see. He was perhaps the first to put forward the mystical conception of St Peter living on in the person of the Roman bishop, which will be found constantly recurring in later centuries.[3] Thus in 385, in an epistle to the bishop of Tarragona in Spain, which is the first authentic papal 'decretal', he wrote: 'We bear the burdens of all who are heavily laden; or rather the blessed Apostle Peter bears them in us; for he, as we trust, in all things protects and defends those who are the heirs of his administration.'[4] Nearly seventy years earlier, however, the Council of Arles had visualized the two apostles, Peter and Paul, 'sitting daily in Rome and witnessing with their blood'.[5]

The century ended in the short pontificate of St Anastasius (399–401), in whose letter occurs this significant passage:

Care shall not be lacking on my part to guard the faith of the Gospel as regards my peoples, and to visit by letter, as far as I am able, the parts of my body throughout the divers regions of the earth.[6]

Under Damasus and his successors there was a marked strengthening of the papacy, not confined to Italy, Gaul, Africa, and Spain, where 'at any moment the secular authority was to be found at the service of the Roman Church'.[7]

A question remains outstanding, on which opinions differ sharply, whether (A) all this was nothing more than a growing clearness in the enunciation of a truly primitive and original authority, or whether (N) there was aggrandizement, and the accretion of a new authority.

[1] *Cod. Theod.*, I, 3. [2] St Greg. Nyss., Ep. i; *PG*, xlvi, 1009.

[3] Although in Abbot Chapman's view it 'is not a natural way of expressing the authority of the Apostolic See', *GCC*, p. 94.

[4] Ep. i; Mansi, iii, 655; *PL*, xiii, 1132 sq.; Denzinger, 87. Twenty 'salutory ordinances' on discipline follow; for a full translation, see Shotwell and Loomis, pp. 699 sq. This first use of the term 'decretal' 'is indicative of the progress of the Roman Church', PBLPB, p. 665.

[5] Supra, ch. xxiv. [6] Ep. i; Allnatt, p. 75; *PL*, p. xx. [7] Duchesne, *EH*, iii, 453.

CHAPTER XXXII

Ambrose of Milan, †397

Ambrose was a conscientious, high-minded, and much respected consular magistrate, an earnest Christian although still unbaptized in his early middle age, as was then not unusual. On the death of the previous archbishop of Milan there was strife over the choice of a successor. At the height of this a cry was heard, traditionally the voice of a child, 'Ambrose for bishop'; it caught the mood of the multitude. Against his will, Ambrose was unanimously acclaimed; he was baptized, was speedily given the intermediate ordinations, and on the eighth day was consecrated. As archbishop of Milan he toiled indefatigably for twenty-three years until his death in 397. His single-minded goodness and zeal strongly influenced three emperors, Gratian, Valentinian II, and the great Theodosius, whom indeed the saint so deeply moved to penitence that the emperor did public penance, stripping himself of his royal insignia, and praying for pardon with groans and tears.

St Ambrose has left to us a large collection of his religious works, and some more general writings, including ninety-one letters; he also composed many hymns.

Here and there he alludes to the three 'charter texts'. Sometimes he identifies the Rock with St Peter,[1] sometimes with the faith he confessed;[2] sometimes Christ Himself is the Rock.[3]

He groups together St Peter, St John, and St James as 'everlasting doors' of the Church.[4]

> Nor was Paul inferior to Peter, though the latter was the foundation of the Church, and the former a wise builder knowing how to make firm the footsteps of the nations who believed; Paul was not unworthy of the

[1] *De Fide*, IV, v, 57; *De Spiritu Sancto*, xiii, 158.
[2] *De Incarnat.*, iv, 33; v, 34.
[3] Ep. *ad Horontianum*, xliii, 9; *PL*, xvi, 1132; *Expos. in Lucam* (ix, 20), vi, 97; *PL*, xv, 1594.
[4] *De Fide*, IV, ii, 26.

fellowship of the Apostles, but is easily comparable with the first, and second to none.[1]

But St Peter was 'chosen to be a shepherd of the Lord's flock';[2] 'chosen to feed the flock by the judgement of the Lord Himself'.[3] He associates the command and the triple question with forgiveness of the triple denial.[4]

The following passages are often quoted to show St Ambrose's high esteem for the Roman see:

> This is that Peter to whom Christ said, 'Thou art Peter, and upon this rock I will build My Church'. Wherefore, where Peter is, there is the Church; where the Church is there is no death, but life eternal. . . . That blessed Peter, against whom the gates of hell prevailed not, did not close the gates of heaven against himself, but, on the contrary, the entrances of hell, and made manifest the entrances of heaven. Being therefore placed on earth, he opened heaven and closed hell.[5]

He refers to St Peter and his chair as a source of unity in a way that recalls St Cyprian. Thus he observes that the Novatians, in saying that they ought not to remit sins, rightly confess *their* inability, 'for they have not the succession of Peter, who hold not the chair of Peter, which they rend by wicked schism'.[6]

His brother Satyrus had been shipwrecked in Sardinia, which was infected at that time by the Luciferian heresy. In narrating this event, St Ambrose says that Satyrus anxiously inquired whether the bishop of the place 'agreed with the Catholic bishops, that is with the Roman Church?'[7]

Writing to Pope Siricius, he says: 'We have recognized in the letter of thy holiness[8] the watchfulness of a good shepherd, who dost faithfully keep the door committed to thee, and guardest the fold of Christ with pious care.'[9]

At the Council of Aquileia in 381, St Ambrose 'was the most active member, and the soul of the whole affair'.[10] It was composed of Western bishops from different countries; only Spain and Rome were unrepresented.[11] It was convoked by Gratian in order to adjudicate on charges

[1] *De Spiritu Sancto*, II, xiii, 158. [2] In Ps. xliii, 40. [3] *De fide*, V, i, 2.
[4] *Apol. David*, ix, 50; *PL*, xix, 871; *De fide*, IV, v, 2.
[5] In Ps. xl, 30; *PL*, xiv, 1082. [6] *De poenitent.*, I, vii, 32.
[7] *De excessu fratris*, i, 47.
[8] 'Your holiness', then a usual form of address to any bishop: thus, for example, Pope Damasus addresses Acholius, bishop of Thessalonica (Ep. vi, *PL*, xiii, 369–70), and St Ambrose thus addresses the bishops of Macedonia (Ep. xv, 2).
[9] Ep. xlii, *Siricio*. But he did not treat the pope's judgement on heresy as conclusive; he retried the question with his own council, PBLPB, p. 661.
[10] Hefele, ii, 375. [11] Ibid.

of heresy against two Illyrian bishops; it pronounced an anathema upon them and deposed them, and addressed a circular letter to Western bishops announcing the sentence.[1]

It also addressed a letter to the Emperor Gratian in regard to Ursinus, the Antipope. A false accusation of a most offensive kind had been brought against Pope Damasus, on which the Prefect of the City had reported indecisively; the emissaries of Ursinus were stirring up trouble also in Milan. To Gratian therefore the Council wrote:

> It were fit that Your Clemency should be besought not to suffer the Roman Church, the head of the whole Roman world, and that sacred faith of the Apostles, to be disturbed, for thence emanate the rights of venerable communion to all . . . we therefore entreat you to get rid of this most importunate person, and thus restore the sense of security which has been interrupted, both to our bishops and to the people of Rome who, ever since the Prefect of the City has sent in his report, have remained in uncertainty and suspense.[2]

Later in the year, 'Ambrose and the bishops of Italy' wrote (probably from Milan)[3] to the Emperor Theodosius, upholding Maximus the Cynic as the rightful bishop of Constantinople, and protesting against the appointment of Nectarius by the Council of Constantinople.[4] They knew that Maximus had come to Italy to plead his cause before the synod:

> and to do this was competent for him, lawfully and according to the custom of our predecessors, as also Athanasius of holy memory, and quite lately Peter, both of them bishops of the Church of Alexandria, and a considerable number of the Easterns have done, so that they appeared to have recourse to the decision of the Churches of Rome, of Italy, and of all the West. . . . We do not claim a prerogative right of examination, but we ought to have had a share in what should be a common decision.[5]

Pope Damasus, indeed, had emphatically rejected the Cynic and his ordination,[6] although it does not appear that St Ambrose and the bishops with him knew this.

The power and importance of the see of Milan in the fourth century is remarkable. It began at the close of the previous century on the reorganization of the Empire under Diocletian and Maximian into *dioeceses*, of which one was 'Italy', i.e. Northern Italy, with Milan its capital; the imperial court moved there and it became the secular capital

[1] Mansi, iii, 599, 615.
[2] Ep. *ad Gratianum Imp.* inter Epp. S. Ambrosii, xi, 5; *PL*, xvi, 986.
[3] Hefele, ii, 377; Puller, p. 538.
[4] Supra, ch. xxx.
[5] Ep. inter Epp. S. Ambrosii, xiii, 4; *PL*, xvi, 9,91–3; Puller, pp. 532–3.
[6] Damasus, Epp. v. and vi; *PL*, xiii, 365–70.

of the West. 'Milan was therefore without a rival and its ecclesiastical position was becoming established on the same lines as that of Constantinople.'[1] By the middle of the fourth century, Milan had become a metropolitical see. 'Particularly in Gaul and Spain the ecclesiastical authority of Milan seems to have been accepted as a superior and natural tribunal.' Towards the end of the century the bishop of Milan was appealed to jointly with the pope for the settlement of disputes, by the bishops of Spain, Gaul, and Africa.[2] 'For a short but important period it would thus appear that the Western episcopate recognized a twofold hegemony—that of the Pope and that of the Bishop of Milan.'[3] 'This extraordinary position ascribed to the Bishop of Milan did not owe its existence to the antiquity of the Church, which did not date further back than the end of the second century, nor to the celebrity of its founders, for they are quite unknown to us.... The real reason was that Milan was the Imperial official residence, the capital of the Western Empire.'[4]

In 404, however, the Emperor Honorius took up his abode at Ravenna. After a time it was detached from Milan and became another metropolitical see. Milan lost its peculiar supremacy; but it remained outside the Roman patriarchate until 1059.[5]

A. St Ambrose plainly recognizes St Peter as Rock and Foundation of the Church and head of the apostles, and the Chair of Peter as the necessary centre of unity of the whole Church, 'whence emanate the rights of venerable communion to all'.

Moreover (i) The Council of Aquileia simply deposed and anathematized. 'At the time this would not need the explicit approval of Rome, or at least that would not be seen.' (ii) St Ambrose eventually suggested that a general council should be held at Rome under Pope Damasus.

N. St Ambrose wrote nothing and did nothing to support the later theories of papal jurisdiction. The independent outlook of the bishops at Aquileia, among whom he was a leader, and at Milan itself, is very noticeable.

(i) They deposed the Illyrian bishops without any reference whatever to Rome, and then notified the whole West. 'The Aquileian Fathers therefore could not have meant that the Bishop of Rome had alone the right to decide who were to be in communion with the Church;

[1] Duchesne, *CW*, p. 36. [2] Ibid., pp. 33–6; Mansi, iv, 482–3.
[3] Ibid., p. 32. [4] Ibid., pp. 35–6. [5] See Mansi, xix, 885–96.

they separated those heretics . . . and therefore the Bishop of Rome was no longer to hold communion with them.'[1]

(ii) 'It is clear that the synod did not recognize any right of final appeal to the Bishop of Rome as the Supreme Judge of the Faithful, whose judgement can be reviewed of none. The Churches of Rome, Italy and the whole West are classed together as forming the proper authority from which Easterns in the past had a just right to obtain the opinion of the Westerns. They knew of no unique prerogative of the Bishop of Rome of finally deciding any disputed question belonging to ecclesiastical jurisdiction, as they denied that "all" the Westerns, including the Bishop of Rome, had any such right.'[2]

The remarkable hegemony of Milan at this epoch proves the effect of a city's greatness upon its ecclesiastical prestige and status. The great position held by the see of Milan 'was attained by it in the same way as the other great sees of the Church—those of Rome, Alexandria, and Antioch—attained their pre-eminence in the Church, viz., through the position occupied by those See Cities in the Roman Empire'.[3]

[1] Denny, sect. 537. [2] Ibid. sect. 543. [3] Ibid., sect. 1178, n. 3.

CHAPTER XXXIII

Chrysostom of Antioch, †407

(i) *His life and death*

St John Chrysostom was born at Antioch in 347; he belonged to the 'great' Church there, and it was by St Meletius that he was baptized and ordained deacon. He was ordained priest by St Flavian in 386. The 'great' Church of Antioch was not recognized by Rome and the West until 398; whether or not there was a state of definite excommunion has been discussed already.[1] In 398, however, the schism was healed, and it was in that year also that St John was made bishop and patriarch of Constantinople, much against his will. He was 'the most prominent doctor of the Greek Church and the greatest preacher ever heard in a Christian pulpit'.[2] Long after his death he came to be known as Chrysostom, i.e., golden-mouth.

His great work as a theologian and preacher was mainly done at Antioch. At Constantinople he found corruption in the Court and among the clergy. The Empress Eudoxia became his enemy, and although he was greatly beloved by the people, opposition grew, secretly and openly, until in 404 he was deposed by synods of hostile bishops, assembled under the influence of Theophilus of Alexandria, always his enemy.[3] He was banished by the emperor, and died in exile in Pontus at the east of the Black Sea in 407, after suffering pitiless cruelties.

As patriarch, Chrysostom held a high and independent authority. Thus he deposed Gerontius, bishop of Nicomedia,[4] and 'going into Asia, he deposed fifteen bishops and consecrated others in their stead'.[5] His own deposition, although the patriarch of Alexandria was behind it, was irregular. From exile, he wrote three letters in similar terms to Pope Innocent I of Rome and the two other great prelates of the West, Venerius of Milan and Chromatius of Aquileia, telling of his unjust ill-

[1] Supra, ch. xxviii. [2] *Cath. Enc.*, viii, 452. [3] Hefele, ii, 430–9.
[4] Fleury, XXI, vii; v, 151. [5] Mansi, vii, 293.

usage, and complaining of the conduct of Theophilus, and the breach of the Canons of Nicaea and Constantinople. He asked them to use their influence with the Court to get his banishment recalled.

Pope Innocent wrote to Theophilus—'Brother Theophilus, we hold both thee and brother John as communicating with us, as Theophilus has been clearly told before and now again. Communion with John cannot be left off without reason. If Theophilus is confident in his case, let him establish it at a lawful synod according to the Nicene canons; the Roman Church recognizes no other canon.'[1]

St Innocent wanted an impartial general council to be assembled to do justice by Chrysostom, and he asked Honorius, the emperor of the West, to urge this on Arcadius, the emperor of the East;[2] but his efforts failed.

On the death of Chrysostom, 'the bishops of the West' refused communion to the bishops of the three Eastern patriarchates 'until the name of that holy man had been inserted among those of deceased bishops'[3] (i.e., written in the 'diptychs' or hinged tablets placed on the altars and read aloud on solemn occasions). Pope Innocent too was insistent on this.[4] Theophilus died in 412, still out of communion with Rome and the West. Several more years passed before the other two patriarchs, of Constantinople and Antioch, brought themselves to comply with this demand, and so resumed communion with the West.[5]

It is remarkable that the memory of Theophilus was honoured not only in the East, in such terms as blessed Theophilus, most holy bishop, of blessed memory, pillar of the Church, and saint,[6] but also by Latins in the West. St Vincent of Lerins[7] calls him St Theophilus, and St Leo the Great mentions him as a 'bishop of holy memory' among 'the excellent pastors of the Church of Alexandria'.

A. The supreme authority of the Roman pontiff in the universal Church is illustrated by the action of Pope St Innocent I in support of St John Chrysostom, and in his disciplinary directions to the patriarchs of Alexandria, Antioch, and Constantinople.

Constantinople and Antioch consented to restore St John's name in 413 and communion was restored.

N. In Chrysostom's letters from exile to the bishops of Rome, Milan,

[1] St Innocentius, P. I. Ep. v, *ad Theophilum Alex.*; *PL*, xx, 493.
[2] Palladius, *Dial. Histor. de vita S. Joann. Chrysost. Opp.*, *PG*, xlvii, 14.
[3] Theodoret, v, 34.
[4] St Innocentius, P. I. Ep. xxii, *De Attico Const. Episc.*; *PL*, xx, 544; cp. *Cath. Enc.*, viii, 455.
[5] In 415 and 417. [6] Refs. in Denny, sect. 1257. [7] Cap. xxx.

and Aquileia, 'there is not the slightest trace of any "appeal" to "the Roman Pontiff" as the "Supreme Judge of the Faithful" to whose jurisdiction the Synods at Constantinople were necessarily subject jure divino. The three bishops are each asked to declare for St Chrysostom and to use their influence'.[1] Moreover Pope Innocent made no suggestion of any such authority or claim. His action 'was diplomatic, but at the same time entirely incompatible with Papalism'.[2]

'Pope Innocent's procedure shows that he admitted that a Council was the proper authority in these Eastern dissensions. At about the same time he was making great claims of authority over certain Western Churches within his own patriarchate, fortified by Gratian's Rescript. It would have been useless for him to assert them in the East. His action was diplomatic, but incompatible with Papalism, and is thus a witness against its historical character.'[3]

In modern Roman doctrine, Theophilus was a recalcitrant schismatic who died out of communion with the 'Supreme Pastor', and was therefore 'separated from the fold' and from membership of the 'one flock'. It is evident that the later Roman doctrine was not the doctrine of those days.[4]

(ii) *His writings*

St Chrysostom has left us a mass of writings more voluminous than those of any other Father. (They fill thirteen folios in the Benedictine edition and include sixty-seven homilies on *Genesis*, ninety on *St Matthew*, eighty-eight on *St John's Gospel*, and fifty-five on *Acts*.) Because of this profusion and the greatness of his authority, they are widely appealed to. Among the many references to apostles, Sts Peter, John, James, and Paul are mentioned most often, as a matter of course, and St Peter most of all. Abbot Chapman has collected them.[5] The following are typical examples:

> Peter, that head of the apostles, the first in the Church, the friend of Christ, who received the revelation not from man but from the Father . . . this Peter, and when I say Peter, I mean the unbroken Rock, the unshaken foundation, the great apostle, the first of the disciples, the first called, the first to obey.[6]
>
> Peter the coryphaeus of the choir of the apostles, the mouth of the disciples, the foundation of the faith, the base of the confession, the fisherman of the world, who brought back our race from the depth of error to

[1] Denny, sect. 720 [2] Ibid., sect. 723. [3] Ibid. [4] Ibid., sects. 1257, 593.
[5] *Studies*, pp. 72–98. [6] *De eleemos.*, ii, 300; *Studies*, p. 74.

heaven, he who is everywhere fervent and full of boldness, or rather of love than of boldness.[1]

Peter, the first of the apostles, the foundation of the Church, the coryphaeus of the choir of the disciples.[2]

This holy coryphaeus of the blessed choir, the lover of Christ, the ardent disciple, who was entrusted with the keys of heaven, he who received the spiritual revelation.[3]

After that grave fall (for there is no sin equal to denial), after so grave a sin, He brought him back to his former honour and entrusted him with the presidency (*epistasia*) of the universal Church.[4]

He saith to him, 'Feed My sheep'. Why does He pass over the others and speak of the sheep to Peter? He was the chosen one of the apostles, the mouth of the disciples, and the coryphaeus of the choir; for this reason Paul went up to see him rather than the others. And also to show him that he must have confidence now, since his denial had been purged away, He entrusts him with the presidency (*prostasia*) over the brethren. Nor doth He recall the denial, or upbraid him, but saith 'If thou lovest Me, preside over thy brethren'.[5]

'After three years I went up to Jerusalem to see Peter' (Gal. i, 18). Wanting nothing of Peter, not even his assent, but being of equal dignity with him (for at present I will say no more) he comes to him as to a greater and elder. . . . Thus he pays due respect to the apostles, and esteems himself not only not their better but not their equal. . . . He first addresses himself with great humility to James, as to a greater and more honourable.[6]

The commonest title of all is *coryphaeus*, 'the head-man, or (of a chorus) leader, conductor'.[7] On 1 Cor. ix, 5 he says that St Paul 'puts the coryphaeus last, for the strongest of the heads of argument are reserved for that place',[8] and on 1 Cor. i, 12 ('I am of Paul, I of Apollos', etc.), 'he has arranged his statement on an ascending scale'.[9] He frequently calls the other great apostles *coryphaei*. 'The word of itself implies no idea of jurisdiction. . . . Still the coryphaeus *par excellence* is Peter'.[10]

On the choice of Matthias, he says:

Then why did it not rest with Peter to make the election himself? This, that he might not seem to bestow it of favour. And besides, he was not yet endowed with the Spirit. And they appointed two. . . . Not he appointed them, but it was he that introduced the proposition to this effect, at the same time pointing out that even this was not his own, but from old time by prophecy; so that he acted as expositor, not as preceptor. . . . Again consider the moderation of James. He it was who

[1] *Hom. de decem mille talentis*, 3; *Opp.*, iii, 4.
[2] *Ad eos qui scandalizati sunt*, 17; *Opp.*, iii, 504.
[3] *In Acta Apost.*, vi, 1; *Opp.*, ix, 48. [4] *De poenitentia*, Hom. v, 2; *Opp.*, ii, 311.
[5] *In Joann.*, Hom. lxxxviii, 1; *Opp.*, viii, 525. [6] *In Gal.* i, 18; *Opp.*, x, 677–8.
[7] Chapman, *Studies*, p. 75. [8] On 1 *Cor.*, Hom. xxi, 2; *Opp.*, x, 181.
[9] On 1 *Cor.*, Hom. iii, 2; *Opp.*, x, 16. [10] Chapman, *Studies*, p. 75.

received the bishopric of Jerusalem, and here he says nothing.... And yet he (Peter) had the same power to ordain as they all collectively.'[1]

'The rock on which the Church is to be built is regularly taken by St Chrysostom to be the confession made by St Peter, or the faith which prompted the confession.'[2] This, as has more than once been noticed, is usual with the Fathers. Abbot Chapman observes[3] that 'he has no idea of the two notions, "Peter is the Rock" and "his faith is the Rock" being mutually exclusive, as, in fact, they are not'.[4]

St Chrysostom speaks in many places of the other great apostles also in words similar to all those he uses of St Peter. He describes the apostolate generally as 'in the chief place of all . . . not only the chief of the other dignities but also their root and foundation, all the apostles being entrusted with the world in common'.[5] St John is 'the pillar of the Churches throughout the world, who hath the keys of the kingdom of heaven'.[6] He and St Peter together 'were about to receive the charge of the whole world'.[7] He speaks too of 'Paul and Peter, renowned in heaven, the coryphaei of the apostles'.[8] St Paul had 'the care of the whole world',[9] and 'excelled all men who have been since men first were'.[10] St Paul 'declares himself to be equal in honour to the apostles, and by comparing himself with the coryphaeus, not with others, he shows that each hath the same dignity'.[11]

At the Council of Jerusalem (Acts xv, 6–21) St James 'was invested with the chief rule . . . Peter, indeed, spoke more strongly, but James more mildly, for thus it behoves one in great power to leave what is unpleasant for others to say, while he himself appears in the milder part.'[12] Elsewhere, Chrysostom asks and answers the question 'Why then was it James who received the see of Jerusalem? . . . He made Peter the teacher not of that see but of the world.'[13] But he also calls St Paul 'the teacher of the world'.[14]

Throughout all varieties of expression, there remains a special pre-

[1] *In Acta Apost.*, Hom. iii, 2, 3; *Opp.*, ix, 25–6; see Chapman, *Studies*, pp. 86–9.
[2] Chapman, *Studies*, p. 77. [3] Ibid., p. 79. [4] On this point, supra, ch. iii (ii).
[5] *De utilitate lectionis Scripturarum in Princip. Actorum*, iii, 3; *Opp.*, iii, 75.
[6] *In Joann.*, Hom. i, 1; *Opp.*, viii, 2; *PG*, lix, 25.
[7] *In Joann.*, Hom. lxxxiii, 2; *Opp.*, viii, 528.
[8] *De precatione*, Oratio ii., *Opp.*, ii, 504. [9] On 2 *Cor.*, Hom. xxv; *PG*, lxi, 571.
[10] *De laudibus S. Pauli*, Hom. ii; *Opp.*, ii, 485; *PG*, lx, 5.
[11] *In Gal.*, Comm. ii; *Opp.*, x, 684–5; *PG*, lxi, 638.
[12] *In Acta Apost.*, Hom. xxxiii, 2; *Opp.*, ix, 255; see Chapman, *Studies*, pp. 89, 90. Cp. St Hesychius, 'Peter orates but James legislates'; *In Jacobum fratrem Dom.*, viii; *PG*, xciii, 1480.
[13] *In Joann.*, Hom. lxxxviii, 1; *Opp.*, viii, 527.
[14] *De petitione filiorum Zebidaei*, viii; *PG*, xlviii, 772.

eminence for St Peter. It may be summed up in the words *prostasia* and *epistasia*, of which probably the nearest equivalent is presidency. *Protostates*, too, of which the primary meaning is the right-hand man in the front line, is used by him both of St Peter and St Paul. No doubt pre-eminence and firstness can shade into authority and jurisdiction, but there is nothing more to show how far Chrysostom had that in mind.

In all the abundance of his works there is little mention of Rome, and he gives us no clear teaching concerning its bishop. 'There is no direct passage in favour of the primacy of the pope.'[1] 'When he speaks of the sheep handed over by the Lord to Peter and his successors',[2] he 'does not mean the Popes, but all bishops'.[3] There are two special references to Rome. The first occurs in a sermon preached at Antioch:

> In speaking of Peter, another Peter occurs to me [viz., St Flavian, his bishop], our common father and teacher, who has succeeded to the virtue of Peter and also to his chair. For this is one great privilege of our city, that it received the coryphaeus of the apostles as its teacher in the beginning. For it was fitting that the city which was first adorned with the name of Christian should receive as pastor the first of the apostles. But though we received him as teacher, we did not keep him to the end, but gave him up to imperial Rome. We have not indeed the body of Peter, but we keep the faith of Peter as himself, and having the faith of Peter, we have Peter himself.[4]

The other occurs in the fine peroration of his last homily on *Romans*:

> There (in heaven) we shall behold Paul. . . . There, with Peter, we shall see Paul the coryphaeus and protostates of the choir of the blessed. . . . And it is for this I love Rome; though I might praise her on other grounds, for her greatness, her antiquity, her beauty, her numbers, her power, her wealth, her victories in war; but passing over all these, I bless her because Paul, when living, wrote to the Romans, and loved them so much, and was among them, and spoke to them, and there ended his life. Whence also the city is more renowned for this than for all else; and like a great and mighty body, she has two eyes, the bodies of these two saints. . . . It is for this that I admire the city, not for its much gold, for its columns, or any other phantasy, but because of these two pillars of the Church.[5]

A. St Chrysostom 'believed and taught, and was ever anxious and careful to teach, that St Peter was really the chief ruler of the Church'.[6]

[1] *Cath. Enc.*, viii, 457.
[2] *De sacerodotio*, ii; quoted in Satis Cogn.
[3] Chapman, *Studies*, p. 83.
[4] *In inscriptionem Actiorum*, Hom. ii, 6; *Opp.*, iii, 70; *PG*, lii, 86.
[5] *In Rom.*, Hom. xxxii, 2; *Opp.*, ix, 757.
[6] Chapman, *Studies*, p. 73.

Nowhere does St Chrysostom dispute the authority and jurisdiction of the pope. His writings 'contain nothing positive against' that doctrine.[1]

'He did not think that he was out of communion with Rome through supporting Flavian, though the West might have thought so.'

N. St Chrysostom recognized a firstness, a pre-eminence, of St Peter. But the close similarity of character and position he attributes to the other great apostles depicts St Peter as *primus inter pares*, a president, not a governor or ruler with 'sovereignty of ordinary power.'

Are his writings consistent with any doctrine of the supremacy and sovereignty of 'the Roman pontiff'? Or that the bishop of Rome is the Supreme Pastor and Teacher of all Christians? Had he known of any such doctrine, could he have omitted to give the slightest indication of it?

The significance of his words regarding Antioch and Rome, and his bishop St Flavian, is enhanced by the fact that St Flavian was, in the judgement of Rome, an intruder into the see of which Rome recognized Paulinus as the legitimate bishop.[2] 'In preaching at Antioch in A.D. 395, he denounced the act of "those who are deserting from" St Flavian's flock as an "act of adultery".'[3] 'Such is the way in which this great doctor characterizes the conduct of those who, to use the language of our day, "went over" to what on Papalist principles was "the Church" at Antioch.'[4]

[1] *Cath. Enc.*, viii, 457.
[2] Denny, sect. 187.
[3] On *Eph.*, Hom. xi; PG, lxii, 88.
[4] Denny, sect. 689.

CHAPTER XXXIV

Other Saints and Fathers

Some of the other Fathers of the fourth century describe St Peter in words similar to those that have now been often quoted; references to Rome are very few.

(i) From the early part of the century there remain considerable works of five writers:

St Methodius, bishop of Patara in Lycia, is said to have suffered martyrdom about A.D. 312. He does not refer to St Peter.

St Peter I of Alexandria, martyred in 311, says that 'Peter, the preferred of the apostles, having been often apprehended and imprisoned and shamefully treated, was last of all crucified at Rome'.[1]

Arnobius, an African who taught in the reign of Diocletian, wrote seven books of *Disputations Against the* [*Pagan*] *Nations*. In one place he refers to the story of St Peter's victory over Simon Magus at Rome.

Lactantius, †*circa* 325, was also an African. He lived for a time near Constantinople, and later at Trier (Trèves). His greatest work was the *Divine Institutions*, in seven books, which has been described as 'the first attempt at a systematic exposition of Christian theology in Latin',[2] but it throws no light on our inquiry. Elsewhere he observes that:

> The apostles were dispersed throughout the earth to preach the Gospel; and during twenty-five years, and until the beginning of the reign of Nero, they occupied themselves in laying the foundations of the Church in every province and city. And while Nero reigned, the Apostle Paul came to Rome, wrought certain miracles, and by turning many to the true religion, built up a faithful and steadfast temple unto the Lord. . . . Nero crucified Peter and slew Paul.[3]

St James, bishop of Nisibis in Mesopotamia in 325, eighteen of whose treatises are preserved, was one of the bishops of the Council of Nicaea. He calls St Peter 'rock', 'foundation', and 'head of the apostles'.[4]

[1] Canon ix; Hardouin, i, 229.
[2] *Cath. Enc.*, viii.
[3] *De morte persecutorum*, ii.
[4] Allnatt, pp. 5, 42.

The Assyrian schism drew from him a long letter to the bishops of Seleucia and Ctesiphon, lamenting the divisions of the Church, and exhorting them to seek peace and concord;[1] he does not refer to Rome.

(ii) The latter part of the century is a little more productive.

St Hilary, bishop of Poictiers, †368, wrote a number of works, of which many survive. St Peter was 'the first of the apostolate',[2] 'the foundation-stone of the Church, who received the keys of the kingdom of heaven',[3] 'the foundation and rock'.[4] More than once, it is the confession that is the rock;[5] to him, as to so many Fathers, this seems a distinction without any important difference. The *Fragmenta*, which contain strictures and anathemas against Pope Liberius as a renegade and apostate, are attributed to St Hilary by nearly all scholars, but Bishop Hefele considers them spurious.[6]

Ambrosiaster, an unknown Latin Father, whose works go by this name, speaks of the Church throughout the world 'of which Damasus is at this day the ruler'.[7]

St Cyril, bishop of Jerusalem 351–86, left a number of *Lectures*, which have been called 'the earliest example extant of a formal system of theology'.[8] He says that 'Peter and Paul, a noble pair, arrived in Rome'.[9] 'Elias truly was taken up into heaven, but Peter has the keys of the kingdom of heaven . . . Elias was taken up only to heaven, but Paul both into heaven and into paradise'[10] (2 Cor. xii, 2–4). His favourite epithets for St Peter are *coryphaeus, protostates*,[11] and also 'keybearer of the kingdom of heaven'.[12]

St Optatus, bishop of Milevis in Numidia, who lived into the reign of Pope Siricius (384–98), says that St Peter 'alone received the keys to be communicated to the others'.[13] His principal work is a treatise in six books directed against the Donatists, and addressed to Parmenius, the Donatist bishop of Carthage. He was a Western bishop, and shows clearly the growing appreciation of the central supremacy in Rome as the chair of Peter:

> Thou canst not deny that the episcopal chair was first established by Peter in Rome, in which sat Peter, head of all the apostles . . . that in one chair unity might be preserved by all, . . . and that he might at once be condemned as a schismatic and sinner who against that pre-eminent chair should place another. . . . Peter, therefore, first filled that unique chair, which is the first of the endowments of the Church, to whom succeeded

[1] Caillau, *Patres Apostolici*, xxv, 254–543. [2] *In Matt.* vii, 6.
[3] *De Trinitate*, ii, 20. [4] *In Matt.* vii, 6. [5] *De Trinitate*, ii, 23; vi, 36.
[6] ii, 238 sq. [7] Allnatt, p. 117; *Comm. in Epist. i. ad Tim.* [8] *DCB.*
[9] *Catechetical Lectures*, vi, 15. [10] Ibid., xiv, 26. [11] Ibid., ii, 19; xi, 3.
[12] Ibid., xvii, 27. [13] *De schism. Donat.*, vii, 3.

> Linus (etc.) . . . and Siricius, who today is our colleague, with whom the whole world agrees together with us in one communion of fellowship of communion by exchange of letters of peace. . . . If Macrobius [a Donatist bishop] be asked where he sits in Rome, can he say 'In Peter's chair?'[1]

St Gregory of Nazianzus in Cappadocia, †389, successively bishop of Sasima, Caesarea, and Constantinople, is often called 'the great', 'the theologian', or 'the divine'. He describes St Peter as 'rock',[2] and 'most honoured of the disciples'.[3] He has left us 45 sermons, 243 letters, and 78 poems. In one long poem he seems to refer to Rome in speaking of the faith which binds the whole West by the saving Word 'as is fitting for the president over all, reverencing the whole harmony of God'.[4]

St Gregory, bishop of Nyssa in Cappadocia, was a brother of St Basil, and a leading theologian of the Eastern Churches. He occasionally refers to St Peter; 'through Peter He gave to bishops the key of the super-celestial honours';[5] St Peter is 'the rock',[6] 'most firm rock',[7] and also the *protostates* and *coryphaeus* of the apostolic choir, and head of the apostles. He does not seem to speak of Rome or its bishop.

St Epiphanius, bishop of Salamis in Cyprus, †403, has left many writings. He applies to St Peter the usual terms of respect, rock, foundation, 'who received the keys of heaven', 'to whom was entrusted the flock', also 'chief coryphaeus of the apostles'.[8] Although he does not seem to speak of Rome in a doctrinal sense, he makes an interesting and original historical remark that figures St Peter and St Paul as *joint* bishops. In giving a list of the Roman episcopate, he enumerates 'first Peter and Paul, apostles and bishops, then Linus, then Cletus, then Clemens, who was a contemporary of Peter and Paul', etc.[9] He says that Clement, although consecrated by the apostles, perhaps waived his claims for the sake of peace; Rufinus and other early writers took up this idea. Another ingenious suggestion built on this supposed joint-episcopate was that St Peter and St Paul were bishops of two distinct communities in Rome—a Jewish and a Gentile Church—with Linus and Cletus (Anencletus) as their suffragans, and that the two Churches were fused into one under Clement. But these theories have no support whatever apart from the uncorroborated remark of St Epiphanius.

A. The universal recognition of St Peter's primacy is manifest. Thus

[1] *De schism. Donat.*, ii, 2–4.
[2] Orat. xxxii, 18, etc.
[3] Orat., xix, 13.
[4] *Carmen de vita sua*, vs. 568–73.
[5] *De castig.*, iii, 314.
[6] Hom. xv., *in Cant. Cantic.*, i, 1088.
[7] *Alt. Orat. de S. Stephan.* iii, 734.
[8] See Allnatt, pp. 8, 21, 33, 44.
[9] *Haeres.*, xxvii, 6; Lightfoot, *Clem.*, i, 169, 329.

St Optatus shows how, whenever schism is in question, St Peter's chair at Rome, and the contemporary pope, are proclaimed as the necessary centre of unity, although 'many did not see the implications of St Peter's primacy'.

N. These other Fathers also, when they have occasion to refer to St Peter, recognize his pre-eminence, in accordance with Holy Scripture; but the associated references to the other great apostles portray him as *primus inter pares*, not as their sovereign. The omission from the doctrine of the Fathers of teaching concerning the bishop of Rome, or his authority, is striking, and is difficult to reconcile with any knowledge of the Doctrine of the Papacy.

CHAPTER XXXV

Survey at A.D. 400

To what extent does the history of the fourth century show development in the recognition of papal supremacy? Some points to which controversialists have attached weight may be recalled here.

On the one hand, there are the letter of Pope St Julius to the Eastern bishops, the strong assertions of authority by Pope Damasus and his immediate successors, and the striking language of St Jerome in his early letters to Damasus. St Ambrose of Milan, too, it is claimed, held the Roman Church to be 'the head of the whole world' and the necessary centre of unity. On the other hand, stress has been laid on the inefficacy of the papacy and Pope Liberius during the near-triumph of Arianism, and the rescue of the Church by the Pope of Alexandria, St Athanasius. The remarkable position in the face of Rome of St Meletius of Antioch, president of the second General Council, and the whole-hearted support of him by St Basil and all the Church in the East, is said to be incompatible with the Doctrine of the Papacy, of which also it is said that there is no trace whatever in all the doctrinal writings of St John Chrysostom.

The state of affairs in the Church towards the end of the fourth century has been summarized in the views of various Church historians. Thus Drs Shotwell and Loomis remark that:

> There are many signs during Damasus' pontificate that the Roman creed and the Roman Primacy were being accepted in principle by the churches abroad as never before.... To the generality of Christians it is plain that the faith of Rome was coming to mean the right faith of the apostles, and that the See of Rome was par excellence 'the Apostolic See'.[1]

Dr Kidd, summarizing the stage of development at A.D. 400, reached

[1] Shotwell and Loomis, pp. 626–7.

under Popes Siricius and Anastasius, remarks that 'both have a place above the episcopate. It is not contested; though it appears to be that, only as one among other great bishops.' He quotes the Latin ecclesiastical writer, Rufinus, as writing to Pope Anastasius, 'I declare in Christ's name that I never held any other faith but . . . the faith which is held by the Church of Rome, by that of Alexandria, and by my own Church of Aquileia, and which is also preached at Jerusalem'. The supremacy of Rome 'is limited; for the East goes on its own way and does not mind if out of communion with the West'.[1]

Mgr Duchesne shows that a 'State orthodoxy' had come about, obliging the State to recognize, in the midst of controversies, which party it ought to acknowledge and protect; the emperors organized religious inquiries and gathered together councils:

> If there had been, in the Church of the fourth century, a central authority recognized and active, it would have afforded a means of solution. But it was not so. Antioch and Alexandria were at variance; the Egyptian episcopate supports Athanasius, the Eastern episcopate opposes him. . . . There was not there a guiding power, an effective expression of Christian unity. The Papacy, such as the West knew it later on, was still to be born.[2]

[1] Kidd, *RP*, p. 76. [2] Duchesne, *EH*, ii, 521–2.

PART FIVE

THE FIFTH CENTURY

CHAPTER XXXVI

Jerome of Rome and Bethlehem, †420

St Jerome, the great biblical scholar, ascetic, and controversialist, was born in A.D. 347 in what is now Yugoslavia. He was brought up in Rome and baptized there as a lad; from the time he was nineteen years old, his bishop was Pope Damasus. While he was still a young layman, he went to Palestine, and in 375 he was living at Antioch, in the time of the famous schism.[1] There Paulinus, the bishop recognized by Rome, ordained him priest; but he never exercised the office of his order. In 382, he returned to Rome and became secretary to Pope Damasus. He was a marked man, and was pointed to as a likely future pope,[2] but on the death of Damasus, he was passed over and Siricius was elected. In 386 he left Rome for ever and went back to Palestine. At Bethlehem he lived a life of great austerity and vast literary energy until his death in 420.

The revision of the Latin Bible, the Vulgate, was the greatest of his many works, but he was continually in controversy, in which he was 'violent and acrimonious in a high degree'. 'Though well versed in works on Biblical exegesis, which was his specialty, he was otherwise extremely ignorant of early Christian literature.'[3]

From Antioch he wrote to his own bishop at Rome, Damasus, asking for directions, in the remarkable letters from which passages have been already quoted.[4] These letters are important, 'in spite of their affectations and exaggerations',[5] as evidence of the teaching imparted in Rome in the time of Pope Damasus.

[1] See ch. xxviii.

[2] Ep. xlv, 3; *PL*, xxii, 481.

[3] Lightfoot, *Ign.*, i, 157. He had no personal acquaintance with the letters of St Ignatius (ibid., pp. 156–7), and probably had not read St Clement's epistle to the *Corinthians* (Lightfoot, *Clem.*, i, 370, 410). His 'tendency to give too ready credence to unauthorized rumours is well known . . . he adopts the falsehoods spread abroad by the adherents of Paulinus to the prejudice of St Meletius of Antioch' (Bottalla, *Infallibility*, p. 185). Lightfoot says that he was 'not a writer to whom I should look for strict accuracy and frankness'. (*Clem.*, i, 410).

[4] Ch. xxviii.

[5] Chapman, *Studies*, p. 111.

Scholars have sifted St Jerome's later letters and other voluminous writings for more evidence of his beliefs regarding St Peter or the Roman bishopric. His style of writing was luxuriant, often angry and bitter, so that sometimes an impulsive passage must be balanced against what he says elsewhere.

There are many references to St Peter. On him 'the Church was founded in massiveness',[1] yet Christ Himself was the rock;[2] 'Christ is the rock, who bestowed it upon his disciples that they themselves also should be called rocks'.[3] He calls St Peter and St Andrew *principes apostolorum*,[4] and 'he speaks of St Peter and St Paul as *duo apostolorum principes*, elsewhere as *ecclesiarum principes*. But more often St Peter alone is *princeps apostolorum*.'[5] Such variety of expression never, of course, leaves it doubtful that St Jerome regards St Peter as the first or chief of the apostles, although there may be a question as to the degree of authority which he believes this priority to have carried with it. He puts forward particular reasons for the choice of St Peter as First Apostle; he is writing in praise of virginity, to confute a certain Jovinian (who had apparently questioned the celibacy of St John):

> If he was not a virgin, let Jovinian explain why he was more beloved than the other apostles. But you reply that the Church was founded upon Peter: though elsewhere the same is attributed to all the apostles, and they all together receive the keys of the kingdom of heaven, and the strength of the Church is made solid upon them all equally: yet one among the twelve is chosen so that when a head has been appointed there may be no occasion for schism. But why was not John chosen, who was a virgin? Deference was paid to age, because Peter was the elder, lest one who was still a youth and almost a boy should be preferred before men of advanced age: and lest the good Master, who should remove an occasion of strife from His disciples (and who had also said to them 'My peace I give unto you; peace I leave with you', and also 'Whosoever would be great among you, let him be the least of all') should seem to furnish a cause of grudge against the young man whom He loved.... Peter is an apostle, and John an apostle, the one married, the other a virgin. But Peter was an apostle only; John was an apostle, and an evangelist, and a prophet.[6]

Elsewhere, when St Jerome is arguing the need for a bishop in a diocese,[7] he says that the administration of baptism is subject to the

[1] *Dial. adv. Pelagian.*, i, 14.
[2] *Adv. Jovinian.*, ii, 37; *PL*, xxiii, 335; Comm. *in Matt.* (vii, 26), I, viii; *PL*, xxvi, 50.
[3] *In Amos*, vi, 12; *PL*, xxv, 1066. [4] Brev. *in Ps.* lxvii; *PL*, xxvi, 1019.
[5] Chapman, *Studies*, p. 129. [6] *Contra Jovinian*, i, 26; *PL*, xxiii, 247.
[7] Chapman, *Studies*, p. 104.

bishop's authority, although 'more by way of honouring the episcopate (*sacerdotium*) than from any compulsory law'. But:

> The well-being of a church depends on the dignity of the high priest (*summus sacerdos*). If to him is not given a certain independence and eminence of power, there will be made in the church as many schisms as there are priests. This is the reason that without a chrism and the command of a bishop neither a priest nor a deacon has the right to baptize.[1]

This passage, when quoted without its context and the last sentence (as in the Encyclical 'Satis cognitum') might be misunderstood to refer to the pope. Abbot Chapman,[2] however, draws an interesting comparison with the passage about St John and St Peter, and suggests that Jerome conceived the position of eminence given to St Peter, the 'elder apostle', as something akin to that of a bishop ('high priest') over the priests of his diocese. Jerome asserts that 'amongst the ancients, presbyters and bishops were the same', and insists that St Peter and St John were presbyters.[3] He supposes that when devil-brewed factions arose (I am of Paul, I of Apollos, etc., 1 Cor. i, 12), 'it was decreed throughout the whole world that one presbyter elected from among the presbyters should be placed over the others, and occasions of schism done away with, . . . and the weeds of dissensions eradicated'.[4] So these passages possibly show what St Jerome conceived to be the nature of St Peter's primacy, irrespective of any question as to the truth of his historical theories.

Regarding the authority of Rome and its bishop, we do not again find St Jerome using expressions as striking as those he wrote to Pope Damasus in his early days.

All bishops 'occupy the place of the apostles',[5] they correspond to apostles 'and have their honour and worth',[6] and are the successors of the apostles.[7] When Jerome is rebuking the deacons of Rome for forgetting they are less than priests, he argues that priests are almost equal to bishops, and 'wheresoever a bishop is—whether at Rome or Eugubium, at Constantinople or Rhegium, at Alexandria or Zoan—he is of the same worth, and also of the same priesthood. The power of riches and the lowliness of poverty do not make a bishop more exalted or more low; all are successors of the apostles.'[8] This is startling; in the fifth century it would be absurd to say that bishops of obscure sees were

[1] *Dialogus contra Luciferanos*, 9; *PL*, xxiii, 165–6.
[2] *Studies*, p. 105.
[3] Ep. cxlvi, 1; *PL*, xxii, 1193.
[4] Comm. *in Tit. I* (i, 5); *PL*, xxvi, 562–3.
[5] Ep. xli, 3; *PL*, xxii, 476.
[6] Ep. lviii, 5; *PL*, xxii, 583.
[7] Ep. cxlvi, 1; *PL*, xxii, 1193.
[8] Ep. cxlvi, 1; *PL*, xxii, 1193.

equal with their patriarchs; he means that they all alike share the priestly office.

'No one doubts that St Jerome believed St Peter to have been the first bishop of Rome, even though they think him mistaken.'[1] That had been the belief in Rome more than a century earlier, by the time of Bishop St Stephen, at least.[2] St Jerome refers to Rome naturally as Apostolic See;[3] 'let the chair of Peter the apostle confirm by its teaching that of the chair of Mark the evangelist'.[4] Throughout his life St Jerome remained staunchly Roman in allegiance and outlook. 'The Roman faith is praised by the mouth of the Apostle, of which faith the Church of Alexandria glories that she partakes.'[5] Rebuking the writer of a letter containing views he thought wrong, he writes from Palestine, 'Why do you try to teach us Romans? . . . Spare Roman ears'.[6]

The exact authority attributed by St Jerome to the Roman pope must be assessed from these writings. It was undoubtedly a high one. He was a devoted disciple of his master, Pope Damasus, and it has been seen how highly that pope exalted his great office.

A. The early witness of this great doctor of the Church, 'this famous pillar of orthodoxy, and storehouse of Eastern and Western learning',[7] amply testifies to the authority of Rome and the pope as the centre of authority in questions of faith.

N. As a Roman disciple of Pope Damasus, St Jerome had formed his opinions and beliefs with regard to the Roman see upon those which by that time had come to be taught and believed at Rome. If he had lived two centuries earlier, had his bishop been St Anicetus (with whom a visiting bishop was on terms of equality),[8] or had St Irenaeus been his teacher,[9] his outlook and beliefs would have been very far different.

Even so, there is a gulf between any views expressed by him and the later theories of the papacy that were developed in later centuries, culminating in the Dogmatic Constitution of 1870.

[1] Chapman, *Studies*, p. 110.
[2] See ch. xx.
[3] *Adv. Rufin*, ii, 15; Allnatt, p. 65. His own revered Pope Damasus was first to adopt this style, PBLPB, p. 668.
[4] Ep. xcvii, 4; *PL*, xxii, 792.
[5] Ep. lxiii, 2; *PL*, xxii, 607. Jerome 'divides Christendom into the Churches of the East, those of Egypt, and those of the Apostolic See, meaning thereby, the Western Churches'. PBLPB, p. 666.
[6] Ep. lxxxiv, 8; *PL*, xxii, 750.
[7] Chapman, *Studies*, p. 99.
[8] See ch. viii.
[9] See ch. x.

CHAPTER XXXVII

Augustine of Hippo, †430

(i) *His life and general writings*

The great theologian-bishop, St Augustine, was born in A.D. 354 in Roman Numidia. His father was a heathen until near the end of his life, but his mother, St Monica, was a most devout Christian. He began to study rhetoric at Carthage at the age of sixteen; a few years later, he joined the Manichaean heretics. At twenty-nine he migrated to Italy, first to Rome and then to Milan. In his famous *Confessions* he tells of his early life, and its sins and errors. He was converted to the Catholic Faith when he was thirty-two, and was baptized by St Ambrose. After living at Rome again for a time, he returned to Africa; he had already begun his theological writings. In 391 he was ordained priest at Hippo (170 miles west of Carthage), and he was consecrated bishop not many years later. After being Bishop of Hippo for about thirty-three years, he died in 430.

His writings fill eleven folios in the Benedictine edition. Many passages have been extracted from them concerning St Peter and Rome to explain his teaching.

St Peter is the first of the apostles;[1] who does not know this?[2] After the threefold questioning, to confirm him who had thrice denied,[3] he was made pastor of the Church;[4] 'and so were all the other apostles',[5] bishops being also apostles.[6]

His interpretation of the Rock-text changed. In some early alphabetical verses he figured the Rock as the see of Peter with its succession of bishops.[7] Afterwards he taught that the Rock is Christ:

[1] Sermo ccxcv, 4; *PL*, xxxviii, 1350.
[2] *In Joann. tract.*, lvi, 1; *PL*, xxxv, 1787. [3] Ibid., xlvii, 2; *PL*, xxxv, 1734.
[4] *Contra Faustum Manichaeum*, xxii, 70; *PL*, xlii, 445.
[5] Sermo ccxvi, 5; *PL*, xxxviii, 1354. [6] *In Ps.* xliv, 32; *PL*, xxxvi, 513.
[7] *Ps. abecedarius in Part. Donat.*; *PL*, xliii, 30.

> One gave the answer in behalf of many, unity in plurality. . . . Christ is the rock (Petra), Peter the Christian people. The rock is the original. Thus Peter is from Petra, not the Rock from Peter: just as Christ is not so called from Christian but Christian from Christ. Upon this rock which thou hast recognized . . . that is upon Myself, Son of the Living God, I will build My Church. Upon Me I will build thee, not Me upon thee.[1]

The Church was built 'not on the Petrus thou art but on the Petra which thou hast confessed',[2] and the Rock was Christ.[3]

Finally, in his *Retractations*, after saying that he had once referred to the rock as Peter,[4] he concludes:

> The rock was Christ, whom Simon confessing, as the whole Church confesses Him, was called Peter. But of these two opinions let the reader choose which is the more probable.[5]

St Augustine constantly teaches that the power of the keys, and of binding and loosing, and the pastoral charge, when given to St Peter, were given to all the apostles and to the whole Church, St Peter being its representative figurehead.

> Peter appears in many places of Scripture because he personates the Church, especially in the place where it is said 'I will give to thee the keys of the kingdom of heaven . . .'. Whether then, did Peter receive the keys and Paul not? Did Peter receive them and did not John and James receive them? But when in signification Peter represented the person of the Church, what was given to that one man was given to the Church. Peter therefore bore the figure of the Church.[6]
>
> The Church, symbolized in its generality, was personified in the apostle Peter on account of the primacy of his apostleship.[7]
>
> These keys not one man but the unity of the Church received.[8]
>
> Not without cause doth Peter sustain the person of this Church Catholic . . . and when it is said unto him, it is said unto all, 'Lovest thou Me? Feed My sheep'.[9]
>
> What was commended to Peter, what was enjoined on Peter, not Peter alone but also all the other apostles heard and held preserved, and most of all the partner of his death and of his day, the apostle Paul. . . . They heard, and transmitted to us that we should hear.[10]
>
> His pastoral office He hath imparted to His members also; for both Peter is shepherd, and Paul is shepherd, and the other apostles are shepherds, and good bishops shepherds.[11]

[1] Sermo lxxxvi, 1; *PL*, xxxviii, 479. [2] Sermo cclxx, 2; *PL*, xxxviii, 1239.
[3] *In Joann. tract.*, cxxiv, 5; *PL*, xxxv, 1974.
[4] *In Ps.* lxix, 4; *PL*, xxxvi, 869. [5] *Retractt.*, I, xxi; *PL*, xxxii, 618.
[6] Sermo cxlix, 7; *PL*, xxxviii, 802.
[7] *In Joann. tract.*, cxxiv, 5; *PL*, xxxv, 1974.
[8] Sermo ccxcv, 2; *PL*, xxxviii, 1349.
[9] *De agone Christiano*, xxx; *PL*, xl, 308.
[10] Sermo ccxcvi, 5 (Fest. P. and P.); *PL*, xxxviii, 1354.
[11] *In Joann. tract.*, xlvii; *PL*, xxxv, 1734.

Much of his teaching concerning St Peter recalls that of St Cyprian, and there is also an echo of St Irenaeus in what he says of the apostolic sees and the successions of bishops in them.

> The Christian society is diffused by propagation all over the world by the apostolic sees and the successions of bishops in them.[1]
>
> What has the chair of the Roman Church done to you (Donatists), in which Peter sat and in which Anastasius sitteth now? Or the chair of the church of Jerusalem, in which James once sat and in which John sitteth now; with which we are united in Catholic unity, and from which by your impious fury you have separated yourselves.[2]
>
> The authority of the Catholic Church, strengthened from the most foundational sees of the apostles unto this very day, by the chain of bishops succeeding to each other, and by the agreement of so many nations.[3]
>
> The universal Church, brought down by a sure succession from the apostolic sees to the present bishops.[4]

Yet Rome is the greatest apostolic see. For more than a century before his time, Rome's reverent pride in the 'two most glorious apostles' as its co-founders had been eclipsed by the individual glory of St Peter, regarded as its first bishop. St Augustine clearly based Rome's primacy upon this, together with its recognition by councils and general Christian assent. 'The pastoral watch-tower', he writes to Pope Boniface, 'is for all of us who fulfil the episcopal office, although you yourself are eminent on a loftier height.'[5] The grace of the chairs of those two glorious martyrs, Peter and Cyprian, is different: the primacy of the apostleship is to be preferred to any episcopate.[6] The primacy of the apostolic see 'has always been in force in the Roman Church'.[7]

> It is certainly the highest impiety or headlong arrogance to be unwilling to give the first rank to the Church which by acknowledgement of the human race, the heretics barking vainly, has continuously held the summit of authority, partly by the judgement of the common people, partly by the influence of councils.[8]

In all St Augustine's teaching, Christ is the Head of the Church:

> Since the whole Christ is the Head and the Body, which doubtless you know well, the Head is our Saviour Himself. . . . His body is the Church. . . . For the whole Church, consisting of all the faithful, because

[1] Ep. ccxxxii, 3, *Ad fratres Madurens*; *PL*, xxxiii, 1028.
[2] *Contra literas Petiliani*, ii, 51; *PL*, xliii, 300.
[3] *Contra Faustum Manichaeum*, xi, 2; *PL*, xlii, 246.
[4] Ibid., xxviii, 2; *PL*, xlii, 485.
[5] *Ad Bonifacium contra duas Epp. Pelagianorum*, I, i, 2; *PL*, xliv, 551.
[6] *De Bapt. contra Donat.*, ii, 2; *PL*, xliii, 127.
[7] Ep. xliii, 7; *PL*, xxxiii, 163.
[8] *De utilit. credend.*, 35; *PL*, xlii, 91.

all the faithful are members of Christ, has that Head situate in the heavens which governs His body: and although it is separated from sight, yet it is bound to them by love.[1]

He often gives this teaching;[2] he does not describe the Roman bishop as Head of the Church, or Vicar of Christ. Yet he clearly believed and taught that an apostolical primacy was inherited in Rome, and that its bishop had a peculiar weight and authority in questions of faith. It is more difficult to discern exactly what degree of authority he attributed thus to the Roman see: his general writings hardly make this clear.

On that subject, the controversies of his day have been closely studied, and particularly what was written regarding them by him, or by the African councils of which he was the leading member. This material has been confidently appealed to by scholars of widely different views. St Augustine has been claimed both as 'a witness against papalism',[3] and as assenting to 'the teaching of the Vatican Council entire'.[4]

(ii) *St Augustine and the Donatist schismatics*

'Africa', i.e. the modern Morocco, Tunis, and Tripoli, 'probably was the most Catholic province of all the West'. Its six civil provinces, with no less than 470 bishops, formed one autonomous ecclesiastical province under the customary primacy of Carthage. The African Church had a sturdy 'insularity'. Thus in the long fight with the Donatists, it never made appeal for help to other Churches.[5]

That great African sect of the Donatists had originated some ninety years before St Augustine was born,[6] and he wrote much against them. They claimed support for their views on baptism from the doctrine of St Cyprian, which he had maintained against St Stephen of Rome,[7] but which had at a later date been overruled by a general council. St Augustine says that Cyprian, 'whose dignity is only increased by his humility', would unquestionably have deferred to that authority; disagreeing with St Cyprian's baptismal views, he nevertheless upholds his orthodoxy and conduct. Although 'the primacy of the Apostleship is to be preferred to any episcopate whatever', Augustine seems to

[1] *In Ps.* lvi; *Opp.*, iii, 530; *PL*, xxxvii, 662.
[2] E.g., *In Pss.* lx, lxii; *Opp.*, iii, 585, 607; *PL*, xxxvii, 725–47.
[3] Denny, sect. 606. [4] Rivington, *PC*, pp. 288–9. [5] Hughes, ii, 39, 40.
[6] See ch. xxiv, and G. G. Willis, *St Augustine and the Donatist Controversy* (1950).
[7] See ch. xix.

imply that Cyprian was not in fault in rejecting the doctrine of the Roman primate.[1]

The Donatists complained of the decisions that were given against them in the year of the Council of Arles, A.D. 314.[2] St Augustine answers them thus:

> If it be said that Melchiades, bishop of the Roman Church, with his colleagues, the transmarine bishops, had no right to usurp the judgement which had already been decided by seventy African bishops under the presidency of the primate Tigistanus, the answer is—'What if he did not usurp it?' For the Emperor, being petitioned [by the Donatists], sent bishops to sit with him [i.e., with Melchiades] as judges and determine what appeared just concerning the whole affair.... What an equitable and complete decision was finally pronounced by the blessed Melchiades himself!... It might most justly be said to them—Suppose that those bishops who decided the case at Rome were not good judges, there still remained a plenary council of the universal Church, in which these judges themselves might be put on their defence.[3]

The point St Augustine is making is, that if the Donatists were dissatisfied with the judgement of Rome, there remained a general council, but they had not availed themselves of this.[4]

In his tract 'On the Unity of the Church', St Augustine urges the Catholicity of the Church, spread throughout the whole world, against the Donatist contention that they alone formed the Church (a contention which practically confined the Church to Africa). He does not refer to the bishop of Rome as supreme pastor of the flock, or as its necessary centre of unity.[5]

A. 1. St Augustine does not say that Cyprian stood out against a *de fide* ruling of St Stephen.

2. St Augustine was meeting and defeating the Donatists on their own ground, not on his.

3. A plenary council, such as St Augustine spoke of, would include the pope, through his legates or by his confirmation.[6]

N. It appears from St Augustine's teaching:

1. That in the Baptismal Dispute St Cyprian could without impropriety reject the doctrine declared by the Roman bishop.

2. That Melchiades, bishop of Rome, was clear from a charge of

[1] *De Bapt. contra Donatistas*, II, ii, 1, 5; *PL*, xliii, 127, 129. [2] See ch. xxiv.
[3] Ep. xliii, 14–19; *PL*, xxxiii, 161 sq. [4] Rivington, *PC*, p. 144.
[5] *Ad Catholicos*, Ep. c. *Donatistas vulgo De Unitate Ecclesiae Liber Unus*; *PL*, xliii, 391 sq.
[6] Rivington, *PC*, p. 144.

'usurping judgement', not by any inherent sovereignty or jurisdiction but by virtue of an imperial commission.

3. That if the Donatists considered the bishop of Rome and his colleagues 'bad judges', it was open to them to appeal to a general council.

4. That (notwithstanding the well-recognized primacy of Rome) the doctrine of 'one flock under one supreme pastor, through the preservation of unity' was so little known to St Augustine that it did not occur to him to refer to it in his theological tract on the Unity of the Church.

(iii) *Pope Innocent I and the Pelagian heretics*

Pelagius was a lay monk from Ireland or Wales, a big man described by St Jerome as 'weighted down with the porridge of the Scots'. Yet he was ascetic, studious, and learned. He and his chief disciple, Coelestius, went about teaching things that were ultimately condemned as heresies; especially they denied the effect of Grace, or man's need for it; 'man is virtuous entirely of his own merit, not of the gift of grace'.[1] It was peculiarly a heresy of the West.

A synod at Carthage in A.D. 411 excommunicated Coelestius for heresy; but a few years later, synods in Palestine acquitted Pelagius. (They did not understand Latin, and theological discussion through an interpreter became confused.)

The African bishops were gravely concerned, and in 416 synods at Carthage and Milevis wrote to Pope Innocent, urging him to condemn the heresy, in language of great respect, and telling him of their condemnation of Coelestius five years earlier. Pope Innocent replied to them, condemning Pelagius and Coelestius, and at the same time speaking in lofty terms of the authority of his see. Some expressions in these long letters, and in St Augustine's subsequent references to them, are often cited as evidence of the authority of the pope in a question of faith. The letters of the African synods were sent with another signed by the Primate and Augustine and three other bishops:

> To thy holy charity, lord brother, we confide the matter, in order that to the statues of our littleness may be added the authority of the apostolic see. . . . We fear lest by repeating to thee these very things which thou preachest with more grace from the apostolic seat we should seem to act inconveniently.[2]

[1] Hefele, ii, 446.

[2] Synod of Carthage, Ep. clxxv; inter Epp. Aug.; *PL*, xxxiii, 760–1.

> Those who hold such perverse and baneful opinions will more easily yield to the authority of thy Holiness, which has been taken from the authority of the Holy Scriptures.[1]
>
> The family of Christ . . . with suspense of heart, with fear and trembling, waits for the help of the Lord also by the charity of thy Reverence. . . . [They hope that the book of Pelagius will even be] condemned by himself on the authority of Catholic bishops, and especially that of thy Holiness, which we do not doubt will be of greater weight with him . . . we do not pour back our little stream for the purpose of replenishing thy great fountain.[2]

Pope Innocent replied to each of these three letters on 27 January 417, taking the view of the new heresy that was pressed on him by the African synods; 'Rome gave exactly the answer they wished'.[3] He spoke of the authority of his own office in impressive language:

> In making inquiry with respect to those things that should be treated with solicitude by bishops, and especially by a true and just Catholic Council, by preserving, as you have done, the example of ancient tradition, and by being mindful of ecclesiastical discipline, you have truly strengthened the vigour of our religion, no less now in consulting us than before in passing sentence. For you decided that it was proper to refer to our judgement, knowing what is due to the Apostolic See, since all we who are set in this place, desire to follow the Apostle from whom the very episcopate and whole authority of this name is derived.[4] Following whom, we know both to condemn what is evil and to commend what is good. So also, guarding the institutes of the Fathers by your priestly office, you judge that what they decreed, by a determination divine, not human, is not to be trodden under foot, that nothing be brought to finality, even in distant and remote provinces, unless it come to the knowledge of this see, so that by its authority the whole just pronouncement may be confirmed: and that from thence—like as all waters issue from their natal fount, and the pure streams of an incorrupt head flow through diverse regions of the whole world—other churches should take up what to order, whom to cleanse. . . . Therefore I rejoice, dearest brethren, . . . that you show concern for the good of all and ask for that to be decreed which may profit all Churches throughout the whole world:[5] . . . With due care and propriety you consult the secrets of the Apostolic office, that office I mean, to which belongs, besides the things that are without, the care of all the Churches.[6] . . .

[1] Synod of Milevis, Ep. clxxvi, 5; inter Epp. Aug.; *PL*, xxxiii, 764.

[2] (From five bishops) Ep. clxxvii; *PL*, xxxiii, 764; see Chapman, *Studies*, pp. 140–5.

[3] Chapman, *Studies*, p. 148.

[4] On this passage Pope Benedict XIV (1740–58) relies as evidence that the bishop's power of jurisdiction is derived mediately through the pope, not directly from Christ.

[5] St Innoc. P., Ep xxix; ad Epp. Carth. Conc.; *PL*, xx, 582; inter Epp. Aug., clxxxi, 1, 2; *PL*, xxxii, 780.

[6] 2 Cor. xi, 28.

> Especially as often as a question of faith is discussed, I think that all our brothers and fellow-bishops should refer to none other than to Peter, the author of their name and office. . . .[1]

St Augustine rejoiced that the condemnation of the Pelagians in Africa had been thus strongly confirmed, and he referred to it several times. He told the Pelagians that:

> Your cause has been ended by a competent judgement of the bishops in common.[2]
>
> Pope Innocent of blessed memory [he died soon after this episode] . . . answered in the manner which was right and the duty of the bishop of the Apostolic See.[3]
>
> My brethren, be of one mind with me. . . . Refute those who contradict, and bring to us those who resist. For already two Councils have sent to the Apostolic See concerning this matter: and thence too, rescripts have come. The case is ended: oh that the error may now end. Let us warn, teach, pray.[4]
>
> By the vigilance of Councils of bishops in support of the Saviour who guards the Church, and also by two venerable bishops of the Apostolic See, Pope Innocent and Pope Zosimus, Coelestius and Pelagius have been condemned by the whole Christian world unless, having amended, they do penance.[5]

A. 1. The language of the African bishops, including St Augustine, shows clearly the supreme authority which they attributed to the Apostolic See in this question of faith and heresy.

2. In Pope Innocent's replies to the African bishops, 'the whole of the Vatican teaching is contained'.[6]

3. The African bishops 'accepted without a murmur' all that he claimed. 'These bishops were either the tamest and most hypocritical of men, or they believed in papal supremacy.'[7]

4. St Augustine's words are epitomized in the common saying, 'Rome has spoken, the case is ended'.[8]

N. 1. The African bishops naturally addressed the patriarch of the West with great respect, but Pope Innocent, in tabling his own views, magnified what they said. His laborious assertions of his own authority are significant.

2. 'Like other Popes, Innocent knew how to make respectful language a basis for the acquisition of an authority whether or not recog-

[1] P. Innocent to Milevis Ep. clxxxii, 2; inter Epp. Aug.; *PL*, xxxiii, 784 (tr. Chapman, *Studies*, pp. 147–8).

[2] *Contra Julianum Pelagianum*, III, i, 5; *PL*, xliv, 704.

[3] Ep. clxxxvi, 2; *PL*, xxxii, 817.

[4] Sermo cxxxi, 10; *PL*, xxxviii, 734.

[5] Ep. cxc, 22, *Ad Optatum*; *PL*, xxxiii, 865.

[6] Rivington, *PC*, p. 289.

[7] Ibid., p. 288.

[8] Ibid., p. 291; Chapman, *Studies*, p. 156.

nized by the applicant, and to turn every occasion to advantage.'[1] Yet all his claim is only an embryo of the future Doctrine of the Papacy. The supposed 'decree of the Fathers' is quite unhistorical,[2] and he seems to forget that it was St Paul upon whom rested 'the care of all the Churches'.

3. The anxious wishes of the African bishops were completely gratified, and they were complimented for saying more than they had said. He knew that they would not be critical of his words. He did not put forward claims like this over bishops of the Eastern patriarchates, who might have criticized them.

4. This misquotation, of which controversialists have made a 'common saying', puts a false stress on this remark of St Augustine, as is shown by his other references to the matter.

(iv) *Pope Zosimus and the Pelagian heretics*

To say that 'the case is ended' was a little premature. In that same year, Pope Innocent died, and Zosimus succeeded him. To Rome went Coelestius, and Pelagius sent a letter. Pope St Zosimus was deceived by them into supposing that they had never taught the errors ascribed to them, or that they had sincerely recanted. He wrote to the African bishops that they were men 'of unimpeachable faith', although he postponed a final decision in their favour for two months.[3] In this letter he speaks of 'the authority of the Apostolic See, to which the decrees of the Fathers have, in honour of St Peter, sanctioned a peculiar reverence'. He seems to be referring to the canons of Sardica[4] (which he erroneously supposed to be of Nicaea).

The African bishops were again greatly disturbed. A synod of 218 bishops at Carthage in January 418 resolved that:

> We decide (*constituimus*) that the sentence against Pelagius and Coelestius published by the venerable Bishop Innocent from the see of the blessed Apostle Peter shall stand, until they confess, etc.[5]

Later, in May, the synod decreed eight or nine canons against Pelagian heresies.[6] In them they do not mention Pope Innocent's pronouncement, although they wrote to Pope Zosimus urging him to follow it.[7] Refer-

[1] Kidd, *RP*, p. 78. [2] Chapman, *Studies*, p. 16.

[3] St Zosimus P., Ep. ii, *ad Epp. Afric.*; *PL*, xx, 649; Chapman, *Studies*, pp. 157–64.

[4] See ch. xxvi (ii). In another letter he founds on 'the canons' and tradition of the Fathers, Ep. xii; *PL*, xx, 676.

[5] Mansi, iv, 376; Chapman, *Studies*, p. 152; *PL*, xliv, 1808.

[6] Hefele, ii, 458–60. [7] Ibid., p. 457.

ring to this anxious time, St Augustine wrote to Pope Boniface, who succeeded Zosimus, that if judgement had been pronounced in Rome approving of the opinions of Coelestius and Pelagius which Pope Innocent had condemned, 'it would have been a mark of prevarication to be branded on the Roman clergy'.[1]

But Pope Zosimus reconsidered the matter and condemned the Pelagians in a famous *Epistola Tractaria*, which is said to have been 'strengthened (*roborata*) by the subscriptions of the holy Fathers',[2] although nineteen Italian bishops refused to sign the *Tractaria*, drew up their own confessio, and offered to appeal to a Plenary Council;[3] some of them were deposed.

A. The mistake of Pope Zosimus as to the sincerity of Coelestius and Pelagius did not involve any question of the infallibility of his teaching when given *ex cathedra*.

N. In decreeing that the former decision was to stand (in the face of what Pope Zosimus said) and in making dogmatic decrees against Pelagianism without any reference to Pope Innocent's pronouncement, the African bishops acted with an independence inconsistent with any knowledge by them of the Doctrine of the Papacy.

Pope Zosimus ascribes the authority of his see to some supposed canonical grant, or patristic tradition, rather than to intrinsic papal sovereignty.

The dissent and lapse of Italian bishops in the papal provinces shows that the idea of the 'supreme pastor and teacher *jure divino*' was unknown even to them; it was not 'the venerable and constant belief' of the 'age' in which they lived.[4]

(v) *The case of Apiarius*

This affair 'remains one of the pièces de résistance of controversy'.[5] Apiarius was a priest of Roman Numidia who was excommunicated by his bishop for wicked conduct. (At that time the only court for the trial of a priest under African canon law consisted of his bishop and five others, and there was no appeal.)[6] Apiarius sailed to Rome, where

[1] *Contra duas Epp. Pelag.*, ii, 3; *PL*, xliv, 574.
[2] Marius Mercator, *Commonitorium*, vii; *PL*, xlviii, 93.
[3] *Libellus fidei a Juliano missus*, 16; *PL*, xlv, 1735. [4] Denny, sects. 778–80.
[5] Chapman, *Studies*, p. 185. [6] Ibid., p. 186; Hefele, ii, 391.

Pope Zosimus believed his story and demanded that he should be reinstated.[1]

The Africans were angry.[2] At the Synod of Carthage in 418, they made a canon giving a new right of appeal to the 'neighbouring bishops'—'But whosoever appeals to a court on the other side of the sea may not be again received into communion by any one in Africa'.[3]

The pope had begun to follow the Imperial method of sending out representatives *a latere*, and the case of Apiarius was now complicated by the arrival at Carthage of Faustinus, a bishop sent from Rome. He was overbearing and personally disagreeable.

The question then came into discussion of appeals to Rome by bishops. Pope Zosimus[4] (417–18), through this legate, erroneously put forward two canons of Sardica[5] as canons of Nicaea. They were unknown to the African bishops and, naturally, were not to be found among their Nicene canons. They wrote, however, to Zosimus that for the present, until further investigation of the Nicene decrees—which everyone accepted as binding—they would observe the two pretended canons.[6] (It appears that the Sardican canons had been written in the Roman register after those of Nicaea, without clearly distinguishing them.[7] Even such archives as escaped burning in the Sack of Rome, eight years before, were in some confusion.)[8]

Although Gratian's Rescript of A.D. 382[9] had greatly strengthened the arm of the popes in the West, it is not clear that it expressly covered the action of Pope Zosimus in hearing and granting the appeal of Apiarius at Rome. At all events Zosimus did not invoke it here. In discussion with Western bishops, later bishops would simply have claimed their supreme Petrine dictate as a warrant for the procedure that they chose. Pope Zosimus did not invoke that either. The *commonitorium* or Instructions, with which he briefed his legates, invoked the (Sardican) canons; and the directions of these canons do not cover the proceedings at Rome; even a bishop's appeal, if allowed, was to be heard locally. The African bishops drew attention to this courteously but pointedly.

Pope Zosimus died in December 418. Eulalius and Boniface were elected to the vacant throne on succeeding days; after some rioting, the

[1] Hefele, ii, 463. [2] Chapman, *Studies*, p. 187 [3] Hefele, ii, 461.

[4] 'The rash and hasty Zosimus, the rare pope of whom one is tempted to say he must have been a nuisance to all concerned' (Hughes, ii, 40).

[5] Canons 5 and 14, supra, ch. xxvi (ii). [6] Hefele, ii, 464.

[7] Duchesne, *EH*, ii, 180. The previous pope said that 'the Roman Church admits no canon but those of Nicaea' (St Innocent I, P., Ep. v; *PL*, xx, 493).

[8] Jalland, *CP*, pp. 289, 312; Hefele, i, 356. [9] Supra, ch. xxxi.

election was decided by the emperor.[1] The African bishops now wrote 'to the most blessed lord and honourable brother Boniface, bishop of the Roman city':

> As to two of these matters, i.e., that bishops may appeal to Rome, and that clerics' causes are to end with the bishops of their own provinces, we particularly said in our letter last year to Bishop Zosimus of blessed memory that we should concede them for a short time, until investigation of the statutes of the Nicene council.
>
> And now we beg thy holiness to cause us to keep whatever was really ordained by the Fathers at Nicaea, and also to take care that the rules in the Instructions brought [by the legates] be followed over there amongst you, i.e., [here they quote canons 5 and 14 of Sardica].[2]
>
> At all events, these have been inserted in our proceedings until the arrival of the authentic statutes of the Nicene council. Even if they are contained therein (as our brethren who were sent from the Apostolic See averred), as they are in the Instructions or in the series in your keeping in Italy, we cannot anyhow be forced to put up with or endure insufferable things, such as we do not even like to speak of.
>
> But we trust, through the pity of the Lord God, now that thy holiness presides in the Roman Church, we shall no longer have to endure such haughtiness, and that through the wisdom and justice which the Most High has given thee, such conduct as is fitting to usward will be maintained in brotherly charity, without our having to speak about it: unless perhaps the canons of the Nicene council stand otherwise.[3]

The question of the alleged Nicene origin of the (Sardican) canons remained unsettled between Carthage and Rome, although Carthage had obtained from Constantinople and Alexandria copies of the Nicene canons from their archives, and had forwarded them to Rome in November 419, together with short letters from the two Eastern patriarchs. Pope Boniface asserted an absolute authority: 'It was never lawful to discuss again anything that had once been decided by the Apostolic See.'[4]

In the next few years, several appeals went to Rome.[5] One of these was by Anthony, a bishop of Fussala whom a Numidian council deposed in 422. Pope Boniface sustained the appeal in a curiously conditional way, 'if he has declared the facts to us faithfully'. St Augustine, to whom the oversight of the diocese had reverted, wrote to the pope (now St Celestine) on behalf of 'the poor Catholic Christian people of Fussala', who were terrified by rumoured threats that the sentence of the Apostolic See was to be carried out by magisterial and military

[1] Funk, i, 195; Hughes, ii, 74; Baronius, an. 419, xxxiii–xli.
[2] Supra, ch. xxvi (ii). [3] Ep. ii, inter Epp. Bonifac.; *PL*, xx, 752.
[4] Ep. xiii, 2, *ad Rufum*; *PL*, xx, 776. [5] Tillemont, xiii, 1036–7.

force.[1] The secular arm was now strong in the West. Apparently, however, Anthony was not reinstated.[2]

In 424,[3] the Council of Carthage was still protesting to Pope Celestine that the disputed canons are not to be found among the originals of Nicaea; it does not appear that Rome ever admitted the mistake.[4] Apiarius had been pardoned, but he had been sent to a different charge. There he was again guilty of criminal behaviour and was again excommunicated. Pope Celestine sent him back to Carthage, in company with the obnoxious Faustinus, with a letter stating that he had found Apiarius innocent, and requiring that he be admitted to communion.

The African bishops replied 'to the most beloved and honourable brother Celestine', telling that Apiarius has at last confessed all his crimes and convicted himself, in spite of vehement opposition and affronts to them by Faustinus:

> We earnestly beg that henceforth thou wilt not too readily admit to thy ears persons coming from hence to Rome, nor consent henceforward to receive into communion those whom we have excommunicated; because thy reverence will easily perceive that this has been decreed even by the Nicene council. For though the rule affects the lower clerics and lay persons, how much more did the council wish the same to be observed in the case of bishops. . . .
>
> Let thy holiness reject, as is worthy of thee, the infamous harbouring of priests and lower clerics, both because the Church of Africa hath not been deprived of the right by any ordinance of the Fathers, and also because the decrees of Nicaea most plainly committed not only lower clerics but bishops themselves to their own metropolitans. For they ordained with prudence and justice that all matters should be terminated in the place where they arose. . . .
>
> Above all, because it is allowed to each, if he is offended with the judgement of the examiners, to appeal to the Councils of his province, or even to an universal Council [of Africa]. Unless perchance there is anyone who can believe that our God can inspire justice in examination to a single man, whoever he may be, and deny it to countless bishops assembled in a council. . . .
>
> We have not found it ordered in any synod of the Fathers that any should be sent from thy holiness' side (*a latere*); since of what thou sent before by the same Faustinus our fellow-bishop, as derived from the Council of Nicaea, we can find no sort in the true councils sent to us from the original. . . . And further, do not send, do not grant, thy clerical *exsecutores* to any who may ask, lest we seem to introduce the smoky

[1] Ep. ccix, 9; *PL*, xxxiii, 955–6.
[2] St August., Ep. ccxxiv; *PL*, xxxiii, 1001, and p. 956 n.
[3] So Hefele, ii, 480, but 426 according to Hughes, II, 41, and Puller, p. 190.
[4] Several popes, down to Gregory the Great (590–604) seem still to refer to Sardican canons as Nicene; see Denny, sects. 1057, 1124.

> haughtiness of the world into the Church of Christ. . . . As to our brother Faustinus . . . we are sure that through the uprightness and moderation of thy holiness Africa will suffer from him no more.[1]

The justice of 'a single man' has been thought to allude to the judgement of a pope: Abbot Chapman, however, objects that 'no one supposed Popes to decide important matters without a Council'.[2]

'To this extraordinary remonstrance—the most extraordinary surely it has ever received—Rome made no reply.'[3]

A. In all the proceedings connected with Apiarius, no question of faith was involved such as that which the Pelagian heresy had raised. The whole matter was one of canons and disciplinary jurisdiction.[4]

The popes regarded themselves as the custodians of general councils, and as bound in conscience to govern according to their requirements. It was, therefore, quite consistent with respect for the pope's supremacy to plead that he was in this instance departing from the canonical regulations.[5]

N. The African bishops had plainly never heard that the primacy of the Roman bishop gave him any inherent sovereign jurisdiction. The main question in the affair was what exact authority had been conferred by the councils. They asked the pope rather pointedly to comply himself with what the canons of Nicaea directed.

They were also quite unaware[6] of any 'immediate power of jurisdiction of the Roman Pontiff, to which all are bound to submit, not only in matters which belong to faith and morals, but also in those that appertain to the discipline and governance of the Church throughout the world'.[7]

[1] Ep. *optaremus*, inter Epp. Coelest., Ep. ii; *PL*, l, 422–7.
[2] *Studies*, p. 203.
[3] Hughes, ii, 42.
[4] Chapman, *Studies*, p. 184.
[5] Rivington, *PC*, p. 298.
[6] Denny, sect. 622.
[7] Dogm. Const., cap. iii.

CHAPTER XXXVIII

Ephesus, A.D. 431. The Third General Council

(i) *Cyril of Alexandria*

The three patriarchs of Alexandria, Antioch, and Constantinople fell out of communion with Rome and the West after the death of St Chrysostom (†407), whose name they struck off their diptychs.[1] When Theophilus of Alexandria died, still out of communion with the West, in 412, his nephew Cyril succeeded him as patriarch. According to Fleury,[2] communion with Rome was restored in 419, but several years after that Cyril was still refusing to restore Chrysostom's name, and said he would as soon enrol Judas. Mgr Duchesne found no evidence that he ever consented; but (according to Nestorius) he did so by 430.[3]

Cyril gained the fullest confidence of St Celestine I, notably so in connexion with the proceedings against Nestorius for heresy.

Notwithstanding some faults of vehemence and impatience, St Cyril remains famous for 'his high-souled struggle for doctrines which were to him, as to all thoughtful believers in Christ's Divinity, the expressions of essential Christian belief'.[4] His writings fill six folio volumes. What he says about St Peter much resembles the language of other Fathers already quoted. Thus, in one passage, St Peter is spoken of as the intended foundation of the Church,[5] and in another the Rock is Christ;[6] but more often he holds that the Rock is the faith confessed.[7] St Peter was 'equal in honour' with the other apostles:

[1] See ch. xxxiii. [2] Fleury, XXIII, xxvii, vol. v, p. 461.

[3] Nicephorus, xiv, 27, vol. ii, p. 496; Duchesne, *EH*, iii, 211; Nestorius' Sermon 12 December 430, Friedrich Loofs, *Nestoriana*, p. 300.

[4] Canon W. Bright in *DCB*. [5] *In Joann.*, i, 42, Lib. ii; *Opp*, iv, 131.

[6] *In Esai.*, xxxiii, 16; Lib., iii; *PG*, lxx, 722.

[7] *In Esai.*, xlii, 23, Lib. iv, Orat. ii; *Opp.* ii, 593; *PG*, lxx, 940; *De S. Trinitate dialogus*, iv; *Opp.*, v, 507; *PG*, lxxv, 865.

> Equality of honour doth not unite natures. And verily Peter and John were of equal honour one with another, in that they were both apostles and holy disciples, yet were not the two one.[1]

He expounds the *Pasce oves* text, in the usual interpretation:

> What is the meaning of Feed My sheep, and the like? We say then that Peter had been already appointed to the Divine Apostolate, together with the other disciples. . . . Peter, overwhelmed with terror, thrice denied the Lord. Christ heals the ill effects of what had happened, and demands in various terms the triple confession . . . therefore by the triple confession of the blessed Peter, the offence of triple denial was done away. But by the Lord's saying, 'Feed My sheep', a renewal, as it were, of the Apostolate already conferred upon him is understood to have taken place.[2]

He refers to Pope Celestine as 'archbishop of the whole inhabited earth, and father and patriarch of the great Church of Rome',[3] but addresses him as an equal: 'Let us narrate our affairs to each other as brothers to brothers, telling each other our actual plans.'[4]

St Cyril was on the highest pinnacle of doctrinal authority. Eight centuries after his time, many important spurious texts were concocted under his name, for controversial purposes,[5] and they deceived the best theologians of the West.

(ii) *Nestorius and his heresy*

Nestorius became patriarch of Constantinople in 428. He is said to have been eloquent and sincere, but almost at once he began to preach the false doctrine that is named after him, although it had been introduced a little earlier by others.

He and his followers distinguished two distinct persons in Christ, the one human, the other divine. This error was partly a reaction from both the Arian and the Apollinarian heresies, but it grew out of argumentation of the same human and fallacious kind that had misled the Arians. To say that the Word was born of Mary implied (so they argued) that only then did He take beginning, and therefore it denied His Godhead. No one, they insisted, should call the Blessed Virgin the God-bearer (*theotokos*), for she was a human being, and God could not be born of a human being. Nestorius laid an anathema on all who called her *theotokos*. 'Actually Nestorius only meant that the God-head pre-existed

[1] Ep. iii, *ad Nestorium*; *Opp.*, vi, 71.
[2] *In Joann*, xxi, 15, 17., Lib. xii; *Opp.*, iv, 1119, 1120; *PG*, lxxiv, 749–52.
[3] Hom. xi, *in S. Mariam Deip.*; *Opp.*, v, pars ii, 384.
[4] Mansi, iv, 1023.
[5] Infra, ch. lxv.

before the Incarnation and was, in its own nature, unaffected by that or any other event in the temporal sphere.'[1]

In 429, strongly worded letters passed between Cyril and Nestorius, Cyril remonstrating, Nestorius defending himself and counter-charging Cyril with other errors. The old enmity of Alexandria for Constantinople still burned, but 'the two thinkers were completely at cross-purposes. Their tragic misunderstandings blinded each other to the deep value of the facts which the opposite school was primarily anxious to secure and enforce'.[2] Nestorius wrote to Rome to explain and justify his views. Pope Celestine made inquiries of Cyril. After some delay, Cyril wrote to the pope:

> The ancient customs of the Churches[3] persuade us to communicate such matters to thy Holiness. I therefore write of necessity. . . . I was unwilling to break off communion with him (Nestorius) until I had laid these particulars before thee. Deign therefore to formulate thy opinion as to whether we ought to communicate at all with him, or to tell him plainly that no one communicates with a person who holds and teaches what he does. Further, the purpose of thy Holiness in this matter ought to be clearly explained by letter to the very religious and most God-loving bishops of the East; and that thy Holiness may be thoroughly informed both as to the opinions of Nestorius and those of the Fathers, I send thee books with passages marked.[4]

Celestine then held a council at Rome, and on 11 August 430 wrote to Nestorius that if he did not preach 'the things that the Roman, the Alexandrian, and the whole Catholic Church holds', and openly recant within ten days, he would be cast out of the communion of the universal Church.[5] To Cyril the pope wrote particularly:

> . . . Therefore taking to thee the authority of our see in our stead, thou wilt carry out this sentence with strict force, that unless within ten days after this admonition he anathematizes his foresaid perverse teachings in a written declaration, and affirms that he holds the faith concerning the birth of Christ our Lord which the Churches of Rome and of thy Holiness, and the universal Christian religion hold, then, if he do not this, thy Holiness having provided for that Church, let him know that he is in every way removed from our body. . . . We have written the same to our brothers and fellow-bishops (of Antioch, Jerusalem, Thessalonica, and Philippi) whereby our judgement concerning him, yea rather the judgement of Christ our Lord, may be manifest.[6]

[1] G. L. Prestige, D.D., *Fathers and Heretics* (1940), p. 261. [2] Ibid., p. 295.

[3] A reference, as some suppose, to Dionysius in A.D. 260 and Athanasius in 340; supra, chs. xxi and xxvi (i).

[4] Ep. ix; *Opp.* v, pars v, ii, 36, 39; Mansi, iv, 1011.

[5] Hardouin, i, 1307; Mansi, iv, 1026; Hefele, i, 25.

[6] Hardouin, i, 1323; Mansi, iv, 1019; Hefele, ii, 26–7.

Cyril did not take immediate steps to 'carry out the sentence'; perhaps it was not in his power. He summoned a council at Alexandria, and drew up a long and formidable Synodal Letter to Nestorius, expounding the orthodox doctrine at length, and appending his own twelve celebrated 'anathematizations'.[1] It requires that Nestorius will solemnly abjure what he has been teaching,

> and will hold and teach, as we all do, the bishops and doctors and heads of the people in the West and the East, and both the holy Church at Rome hath agreed and we all, . . . the faith of the Catholic and Apostolic Church in which the orthodox bishops of the West and East agree.[2]

Nestorius countered defiantly with twelve anathematizations of his own.[3] No further proceedings were taken against him before the meeting of the Council of Ephesus in the following year.

A. 'It would be impossible to express with greater clearness the claim involved in the Papal supremacy, as understood at this hour, than is done by these two letters' of Pope Celestine and Cyril. The pope claims that the sentence he has pronounced is Divine, that by this sentence, unless Nestorius retracts, he is cut off from the communion of the whole Catholic Church.[4]

N. Cyril and his synod refer to the authority of the Council at Rome, not of the pope its head. Nestorius is called on to accept the doctrine of Rome, Alexandria, of West and East, and in terms which the Alexandrian Synod themselves prescribed. They did not call on him to submit to an *ex cathedra* decision of Celestine as supreme judge, or to any supreme authority inherent in the Roman see by itself.[5]

What Pope Celestine called his sentence, they (and also the subsequent General Council) treat as an important and weighty doctrinal statement, but not as in itself an effective or operative sentence.

(iii) *The Council of Ephesus*

In November 430, the Emperor Theodosius II, who was a devout Christian, summoned an Oecumenical Council to meet at Ephesus at Pentecost of the following year. He was concerned for the peace of the Church, although he was prejudiced in favour of his own bishop, Nestorius, who indeed had suggested the holding of the council, and

[1] Hefele, iii, 31.
[2] Epp. iii, *ad Nestorium*; *Opp*., vi, 69; Hardouin, i, 1286; Hefele, iii, 28–34.
[3] Hefele, iii, 35.
[4] Rivington, *PC*, pp. 310, 314.
[5] Denny, sect. 356.

had hoped to preside at it.[1] In the circular letter to all Metropolitans, the emperor says nothing of a decision of Pope Celestine; he may not have heard of it. There is no indication that Celestine was consulted before the council was summoned. On 15 May 341, Pope Celestine wrote to the emperor that he could not attend the council himself, but that he would take part in it by commissioners.[2]

Cyril, the second patriarch of the whole Church, was president of the council. There has been some scholarly dispute as to whether the pope 'presided' at the council in the person of Cyril; it is something of a technicality. On the one hand, Celestine's letter to Cyril was written months before the council was in prospect, and it naturally does not make Cyril in express terms his proxy to preside at it. Then the three legates, not Cyril, are described as commissioned 'to supply the place of the most holy bishop Celestine'.[3] Moreover, on occasions when Cyril could not preside, Juvenal of Jerusalem, the prelate next in seniority to Cyril but certainly not a legate, signed first as presiding,[4] not the legates or any of them.

On the other hand, Dr Rivington claims that 'St Celestine was the real president of the Council . . . through St Cyril, who sat in his name'.[5] Throughout the proceedings Cyril was obviously looked on as possessing a special mandate from Celestine.[6] The minutes record him as 'holding also the place of the archbishop of the Church of the Romans' and 'acting also as proxy for Celestine'. Indeed he had in his pocket something like a 'power of attorney' to represent Celestine in condemning and deposing Nestorius. Celestine's opinions and letters were a dominating influence in the council, so that his name has remained linked with Cyril's, as if he had jointly presided.

The Council was to assemble on 7 June. John of Antioch sent to say that he was delayed and would arrive about six days later, but that the synod was not to await his arrival. The bishops actually waited for him in vain until 22 June, when they held their first session. Nestorius flatly refused to appear; yet in the usual ornate style the bishops still designate him 'most pious, most religious bishop'. The council proceeded to try the question of his orthodoxy or heresy.

The Nicene Creed was first recited. Afterwards the correspondence of Cyril and Nestorius, and the letter from Celestine and the Roman synod, were read,[7] followed by passages from the Fathers, and finally

[1] Hefele, iii, 40; Evagrius, i, 7; Rivington, *PC*, pp. 318, 325.
[2] Hefele, iii, 42; Hardouin, i, 1474; Mansi, iv, 1292.
[3] Mansi, iv, 1299, 1337.
[4] E.g., Hardouin, i, 1499.
[5] *PC*, p. 322.
[6] Hefele, iii, 46, 62.
[7] Mansi, iv, 1179.

twenty critical passages from what Nestorius himself had written. The sentence of the council, signed by more than two hundred bishops, concludes:

> Urged by the canons and in accordance with the letter of our most holy father and fellow-servant Celestine, the Roman bishop, we have come with many tears, to this sorrowful sentence against him, namely that our Lord Jesus Christ, whom he has blasphemed, decrees by the holy Synod that Nestorius be excluded from the episcopal dignity and from all priestly communion.[1]

They issued an edict to Nestorius informing him that he has been 'deposed by the holy Synod agreeably to the laws of the Church'. Their synodal letter to the emperor calls their decision a common sentence of the whole world inasmuch as the sentence of the holy synod of the whole West brought by the legates is in agreement with that of the synod.[2]

Before the end of June, John of Antioch did arrive. With support from two Imperial Counts he held an opposition council of about forty-three bishops, afterwards known as the 'Concilabulum'. This proceeded to 'depose' Cyril and Memnon the Bishop of Ephesus.

Soon afterwards, Pope Celestine's legates arrived; they were two bishops and a priest called Philip. They had the pope's written instructions how to behave in different eventualities, but they must 'watch over the authority of the Apostolic See'.[3] They also brought his letter to the council, saying that they were sent 'to carry out what has formerly been decided by us, to which we doubt not that Your Holinesses will agree'.[4] On 10 July the council held its second session. As one of the legates pointed out, this letter seemed to propose a mere confirmation by the council of Celestine's sentence, without further inquiry. Actually, the council had already carried out its own independent inquiry, and had pronounced its own sentence. But it came to the same thing, and the reported 'exclamations' of the bishops indicate their general and glad concurrence:

> That is a true judgement: we thank Celestine the new Paul, we thank Cyril the new Paul, Celestine the guardian of the faith, Celestine of one mind with the Synod, one Celestine, one Cyril, one faith in the whole Synod, one faith throughout the world.[5]

Reporting to the emperor, they say that 'our recent judgement was pronounced by common vote of the whole universe'.[6] During the remainder of July, the orthodox council held five more sessions and

[1] Hardouin, i, 1422; Hefele, iii, 51.
[2] Hardouin, i, 1482; Mansi, iv, 1301.
[3] Hardouin, i, 1347.
[4] Hardouin, i, 1467; Mansi, iv, 1283.
[5] Hardouin, i, 1471.
[6] Mansi, iv, 1301.

decreed certain canons. Dr Rivington draws attention to the markedly 'papal' protestations made at intervals by the legate Philip,[1] who was more prominent that his episcopal colleagues; and the records indicate only the general approval by the bishops of the legates' concurrence, and of all that they said. Philip carried out his instructions zealously, and some of his words still resound. Fifteen centuries later, Pope Pius IX enshrined them in the Dogmatic Constitution, and Leo XIII repeated them in the Encyclical 'Satis Cognitum':

> No one can doubt, and it is known to all ages, that the holy and blessed Peter, the prince and chief of the apostles, the pillar of the faith and foundation of the Catholic Church, received the keys of the kingdom from our Lord Jesus Christ, the Saviour and Redeemer of mankind, and lives, presides, and judges to this day always in his successors.[2]

We need not dwell on the subsequent proceedings and events, which were long and involved. The council and the concilabulum both appealed to the emperor, who impartially arrested and deposed Cyril, Memnon, and Nestorius. Cyril and Memnon, however, were restored before many weeks. Within the next two years, John of Antioch and Cyril were reconciled in agreement upon a sufficiently orthodox 'Union-Creed'.[3] In 435, the emperor banished Nestorius to Egypt, and ordered all his writings to be burned. He survived until 451 as a monk in Upper Egypt and welcomed the definitions of Chalcedon and the 'Tome' of Leo, asserting that it expressed exactly what he had always believed.[4]

Within the Roman Empire, Nestorianism hardly outlived the century; but it spread vigorously to Persia, Chaldea, Assyria, and even to India and China.[5] At one time, perhaps, Nestorians outnumbered the members of all other Christian communions, but the Mahommedan flood ultimately drowned and destroyed the once-flourishing Nestorian Churches, of which the tiny Assyrian Church survives.

A. The claim involved in the papal supremacy, as understood at this hour, was emphatically voiced by the legates and fully accepted by the bishops of the council.[6]

The council bases its sentence upon the pope's letter to Cyril and to itself. 'The council's action is stated to be the sequence of his; it is an actual exercise of judgement in the shape of an intelligent adhesion to the papal sentence; and the result of all is the exhibition of the Church's unity as a whole.'[7]

[1] *PC*, pp. 344–5. [2] Mansi, iv, 1295. [3] Hefele, iii, 129–39.
[4] Prestige, *op. cit.*, pp. 269, 270. [5] See Gibbon, v, 155 sq. (ch. xlvii).
[6] Rivington, *PC*, pp. 344–7. [7] Ibid., pp. 339–40.

'The doctrine of Papal Supremacy does not mean that there is no place for councils, but only that a council must finally have the pope's approval to be in order.'

N. It does not appear to have occurred to the emperor, or to the bishops in general, that the grave doctrinal question in dispute ought to be settled by the 'Supreme Pontiff'.

The Council did not accept and execute the 'sentence' of the pope, pronounced by him 'long ago' although Nestorius, far from recanting within ten days, remained stubbornly defiant. Instead of this, they carried out for themselves a fresh examination of his orthodoxy, and pronounced their own sentence.

They declare the deposition of Nestorius as the act of the council, not of Celestine, and they call it common to the whole world because 'the synod of the whole West' agrees with their (Eastern) sentence. A decision of the Eastern Church only, or of the Western, could not bind the whole Church; hence the importance of this agreement.

To infer from the fact that the Fathers did not vocally dissent from Philip's remarks, that they therefore understood them in the same way as the 'Satis Cognitum' and agreed with them, is absurd. The proceedings of the council itself are inconsistent with assent to, or belief in, any such claims as those in support of which 'Satis cognitum' quotes the words; 'dissent' from such claims, had they been aware of them, could hardly have been more practically or emphatically expressed.[1]

[1] Denny, sect. 741.

CHAPTER XXXIX

Leo the Great, A.D. 440–61

(i) *Papal authority formulated*

St Leo was the first of the only three popes who are popularly styled 'the Great'. He was 'above all the firm administrator and ruler, the touch of whose hands of steel an apostolic diplomacy kept ever from harshness. To this invaluable asset of a truly Roman spirit . . . he added intellectual attainments of a very high order.'[1] This great pope consolidated the primacy of his see; throughout his own patriarchate of the West he was not so much a primate as a spiritual sovereign with temporal armament. There had already been advance towards this under Popes Damasus (†384) and Siricius[2] (†398), in the authoritative claims of Popes Innocent (†417), Zosimus (†418), Boniface (†422), and Celestine (†432), and in the last-named pope's dominating influence over the Council of Ephesus.[3] Leo's immediate predecessor, Pope Sixtus III, had written to John of Antioch, after the agreement upon the Union-Creed:

> Now thou knowest what it is to think with us. What the blessed apostle Peter received, he has handed on to his successors. Who would separate himself from his doctrine whom first among the apostles the Master taught?[4]

When St Leo reached the papal throne, he began at once to assert its authority in downright language, and he took occasion to do so frequently. In early sermons he speaks of 'the well-ordered love of the whole Church which always recognizes Peter in Peter's see'.[5]

> Blessed Peter . . . has not left the helm of the Church which he took. Therefore if anything is rightly done and decreed by us, it is of his work and merits whose power lives and whose authority prevails in his see. . . . He is not only the president of this see but also the primate of all bishops,

[1] Hughes, ii, 68. [2] Supra, ch. xxxi. [3] Supra, ch. xxxviii.
[4] Ep. vi, 5; *PL*, l, 609. [5] Sermo ii, 2; *PL*, liv, 144.

wherefore . . . believe that it is he speaking to you whose office we occupy in his stead.[1]

In Peter the firmness of all is secured and the aid of divine grace so ordered that the firmness given by Christ to Peter should by Peter be bestowed upon the other apostles.[2]

Although pastors preside singly over their flocks, in individual care, . . . yet the care is for us in common with them all; and the administration of none is other than part of our task.[3]

He teaches that the other apostles received their powers, not directly from Christ, but mediately only through St Peter. It follows that bishops receive their powers mediately only through St Peter's Representative.

This sacred function the Lord wished to be indeed the care of all the apostles, but in such a way that He placed the principal charge on the blessed Peter, chief of all the apostles; and from him, as from the head, wishes His gifts to flow to all the body; so that any one who dares to secede from Peter's solid rock may understand that he has no part or lot in the divine mystery.[4]

The sovereignty of Rome is of divine appointment; Rome is 'that See which the Lord appointed to preside over all others'.[5] These examples of St Leo's constant teaching show the dogmatic basis that he formulated for the sovereign supremacy of his see. Except upon two matters–the pope's independent supremacy over any general council (which was still disputable in the seventeenth century), and his infallibility (which was not *de fide* until 1870), the Dogmatic Constitution of 1870 is largely an expansion of St Leo's doctrine.

Throughout the Western patriarchate of the pope, moreover, St Leo's claims were generally welcomed and acknowledged. Thus bishops in Gaul write to him that 'Through the most blessed Peter, chief of the apostles, the holy Roman Church holds the principate over all the Churches of the whole world'.[6] And in Italy, the archbishop of Ravenna, St Peter Chrysologus, wrote to Eutyches in 449, echoing his patriarch, that 'blessed Peter, who lives and presides in his own cathedra, gives the true faith to all who seek for it'.[7] Gaul and Spain had now been overrun and subdued by the Visigoths, Africa by the Vandals. These Barbarians professed Arianism, and the Vandals were bitter persecutors of Catholics. The Catholic Church in Africa was in straits, and was now no longer the vigorously independent province that had spoken so

[1] Sermo iii, 3, 4; *PL*, liv, 146–7. [2] Sermo iv, 3; *PL*, liv, 151–2.
[3] Sermo v, 2; *PL*, liv, 153. [4] Ep. x, *Divinae cultum*; *PL*, liv, 628–36.
[5] Ep. cxx (to Theodoret); *PL*, liv, 1047; Allnatt, 106.
[6] Inter Epp. Leon. Ep. lxv, 2; *PL*, liv, 881. [7] Ibid., xxv, 2; *PL*, liv, 743.

bluntly to popes less than a generation before. 'All that the Africans in 426 had protested the pope must not do—hear appeals from Africa, send legates into Africa to hold enquiries and execute his judgements—St Leo, twenty years later, continues to do, and this as simply as if none had ever questioned these rights of his see.'[1] It does not appear that he made any such immediate claims in the patriarchates of the East, but in his own patriarchate he asserted them roundly and almost without opposition. One man indeed, St Hilary, archbishop of Arles, dared to protest and, as will be seen, he was promptly suppressed.

St Leo is renowned as a theologian for the Dogmatic Epistle, known as his 'Tome', which dealt with the Eutychian heresy, and which the fourth General Council at Chalcedon in 451 incorporated in the teaching of the Church.

There was nothing petty or personal in his ambition, if ambition it can rightly be called. His set purpose was to establish firmly the high authority of his Petrine office, and under it the peace and unity of the Church in East and West. A sidelight is thrown on his character by a dispute about the date of Easter.[2] In the settled Roman rule, the latest possible date was 21 of April; in the Alexandrian rule it was the 25th. Now and then this difference came into effect. Thus in the year 455 the Alexandrian rule fixed Easter on 24 April, outside the limit of the Roman rule. The computation requires rather intricate chronological arithmetic.[3] It appears that the Alexandrians were the better mathematicians. Leo was not convinced of this, but he decided to give way and he agreed to adopt the Alexandrian rule, in the interests of peace and of uniform observance. 'A lesser man than Leo might easily have made of the whole question a cause of lasting schism.'[4]

St Leo's 'indomitable energy, his magnanimity, his consistency and his devotion to simple duty . . . make up a character of exceptional nobility. Like Ambrose in the preceding century he may be described as "the outstanding figure of his time".'[5]

(ii) *The Rescript of Valentinian III*, A.D. 445

St Hilary of Arles, a monk whom the people of Arles had insisted on choosing to fill that metropolitan see, continued to live with monastic simplicity as its zealous and devoted bishop. The extent of his archi-

[1] Hughes, ii, 69.
[2] Compare the Paschal Dispute in the time of Victor, ch. xi, supra.
[3] Jalland, *Leo*, pp. 350–72. [4] Ibid., p. 358.
[5] Ibid., pp. 420, 422.

episcopal jurisdiction was not clear;[1] he seems to have asserted a too-wide authority, and thus to have aroused opposition. Yet he was a notable and saintly figure.[2]

At a provincial synod in 444, Hilary deposed Celidonius, bishop of Besançon, as having been canonically barred from ordination.[3] Celidonius went to Rome and appealed against the sentence; Gratian's Rescript of 382 expressly allowed this.[4] Pope Leo at once admitted him to communion. Under canon 5 of Nicaea, appeals from excommunication were to be heard by provincial synods, and no one was to be admitted to communion while under sentence. Hilary, sturdy saint, marched in mid-winter across the Alps to Rome. In synod there he spoke so bluntly as to shock 'the extremely delicate Roman ears' (as the Prefect of Gaul afterwards said)[5] and anger Pope Leo, who complained that Hilary 'would not suffer himself to be subject to the blessed apostle Peter'.[6] The secular arm was at his disposal, and Hilary was put under arrest, but he got away and returned to Arles.

In synod in 445[7] Leo declared the sentence of the Gallic synod invalid and restored Celidonius. He then wrote to inform the bishops of Vienne, beginning with the exordium quoted above,[8] and severely condemning Hilary's exercise of metropolitical jurisdiction outside its due limits. Hilary, he said, was cut off from communion with the holy see, deprived of metropolitan authority, and only left in his own see as an 'act' of grace.[9]

St Hilary died four years later. St Leo himself spoke of him as 'a man of holy memory'. He is venerated as a saint and is commemorated in the Roman martyrology on 5 May.

We are not further concerned with the justice of the deposing of Celidonius, but only with the manner of the appeal, and its important sequel. The pope's procedure was not covered by the canons of Sardica,[10] and they were apparently not referred to. He was exerting what he plainly believed to be a comprehensive and supreme authority. This appears in the statements in the Rescript of the Emperor Valentinian, derived, as he says, from Pope Leo himself, although the accusations

[1] Jalland, *Leo*, pp. 159–64.
[2] Tillemont, xv, 36–97; Fleury, XXVII, v, vi; Jalland, *Leo*, pp. 113–28.
[3] On the facts, as alleged, that while a layman he had (i) married a widow, and (ii) while a magistrate, pronounced capital sentences.
[4] Supra, ch. xxxi. [5] Fleury, XXVII, vi, vol. vi, p. 266.
[6] Ep. x, 3; *PL*, liv, 630. [7] Hefele, iii, 172.
[8] Ep. x, *Divinae cultum*, 'This sacred function . . .', supra, p. 230.
[9] Ibid., x, 3; *PL*, liv, 630; Fleury, XXVII, v.
[10] Supra, ch. xxvi (ii). In accordance with them he could have ordered a rehearing in Gaul.

against Hilary are a highly coloured version of what Leo had written to Gaul.

Already, ever since the Constitution of Valentinian I, and the Rescript of Gratian in 382,[1] the authority of the popes throughout the Western patriarchate had been fortified by the secular arm. About the time of Pope Celestine, says the contemporary historian Socrates,[2] 'the Roman episcopate extended itself beyond the limits of ecclesiastical jurisdiction, and degenerated into its present state of secular domination'. Pope Leo now complained against Hilary to the emperor, with whom he had great influence. Valentinian III was a weakling, 'a miserable debauchee who recalls the last of the Valois'.[3] He issued the following Rescript at Rome, on 6 June 445, addressed to the Patrician and Commander-in-Chief Aëtius, whom he afterwards murdered:

> Seeing that the authority of a sacred synod has confirmed the primacy of the apostolic see, the due of St Peter, who is prince of the apostolic crown and the glory of the Roman state, let no presumption seek to attempt anything contrary to the authority of that see: for peace will be kept among the Churches only if the whole body acknowledges its ruler.
>
> Hitherto these things have been kept inviolable; but Hilary of Arles (as we learn by trustworthy report of the venerable man Leo, the Roman Pope) has with insolent daring ventured upon certain unlawful proceedings, with the result that hateful disorder has invaded the Transalpine Churches. . . .
>
> We do not repress this only, which is highly criminal, but in order that not even slighter disturbance may arise among the Churches, or religious discipline be threatened at all:
>
> We decree by this perpetual edict that it shall not be lawful for bishops of Gaul or of any other provinces, contrary to ancient custom, to do aught without the authority of the venerable Pope of the Eternal City; and whatsoever the authority of the Apostolic See has enacted, or shall enact, shall be law for them all. So that if any bishop who is summoned to the judgement of the Roman high-priest shall neglect to come, he shall be compelled to attend by the governor of the province: all [privileges] which our deified parents conferred on the Roman Church being preserved.
>
> Aëtius, dearest parent of Augustus, thy illustrious and excellent highness [conventional styles of rank] will cause what is above enacted to be observed by the authority of this present edictile law: a fine of ten gold pounds is to be exacted at once from any judge who may allow our commands to be infringed. May God with divine hand preserve thee for many years to come, dearest parent.[4]

The 'authority of a sacred synod' for the primacy of Rome may

[1] Supra, ch. xxxi. [2] vii, 11. [3] Hughes, ii, 54.
[4] Baronius, an. 445, vi, 31–2; *PL*, liv, 636–40.

allude to the Latin interpolation into the genuine Greek text of canon 6 of Nicaea;[1] Cardinal Baronius remarks that the Rescript was issued 'at the request of Pope Leo', and that it 'clearly shows the authority of the Roman Pontiff over all the Churches, and its recognition by the emperors to the extent of preserving it in good repair against all obstinate malefactors'.[2]

Throughout the Western patriarchate a virtually unlimited Petrine sovereignty was now recognized. 'For many a century after Leo's death Western Christendom accepted, for the most part without question, the voice of the Papacy and the voice of Peter, and that voice as the expression of the mind of God.'[3] Henceforward the popes were armed with a corresponding secular power to enforce it and to prescribe 'law for all'. No corresponding development had reached the East.

A. and **N**

There seems to be little occasion for arguments at this juncture. As usual, there are two clear and opposite views. The reign of St Leo the Great marks an important stage in development, but it is seen either as:

A. A stage in the unfolding and more effectual operation of a divine sovereignty in St Peter's successor, a sovereignty that was always the universal belief of the whole Church, although hitherto less clearly understood and enforced, or

N. A stage in the false development of Rome's simple primitive primacy into something utterly different, unwarranted by Scripture, unheard-of in the first centuries of the Church.

[1] Hefele, iii, 425; Jalland, *Leo*, p. 125 n., suggests canon 3 of Sardica.
[2] Baronius, loc. cit.
[3] Jalland, *Leo*, p. 424.

CHAPTER XL

The Robber-Council of Ephesus, A.D. 449

(i) *Eutyches and the Monophysite heresy*

Eutyches was the archimandrite or abbot of a monastery outside Constantinople, and a very old man in A.D. 448. He had taken a leading part in opposing the Nestorian heresy, reaction from which perhaps led him astray. He had come to teach that, at our Lord's Incarnation, His two natures, divine and human, were merged into one *physis*, one nature: he claimed that some expressions of Athanasius and Cyril supported this theory. At a synod of Constantinople in 448 he was charged with the teaching of heresy. He rejected a form of confession, proposed by Flavian, the archbishop and patriarch, to correct the error. At the seventh session, after much cross-examination, he was deposed and excommunicated. He had, indeed, professed his willingness to confess 'two natures', as was demanded of him, 'if my Fathers of Rome and Alexandria require me to do so', and he had given notice of his intention to lodge an appeal with the synods of Rome, Alexandria, Jerusalem, and Thessalonica.[1] His letter to Pope Leo is extant; he also wrote to the Bishop of Ravenna, part of whose reply has already been quoted.[2] Flavian sent the minutes of the synod to Leo, so that he might make the decision known 'to all the bishops in office under your reverence'.[3] Leo and Flavian were in agreement in thinking that there was no occasion for another council to dispose of the error of Eutyches.

(ii) *The 'Robber-Council'*

Eutyches was in favour at the Byzantine Court; moreover Dioscorus, now the patriarch of Alexandria, nursed a grudge against the patriarchate of Constantinople. At their request, the Emperor Theodosius II

[1] Jalland, *Leo*, p. 216; Mansi, vi, 817. [2] Supra, p. 230.
[3] Inter epp. Leon., xxii, 4; *PL*, liv, 732.

issued a summons for a council to meet at Ephesus in August 449. It was intended to be a General Council of East and West; all the great metropolitans were invited.[1] Pope Leo replied that he could not attend in person; there was no precedent, and things were too much unsettled at Rome (through dread of Attila the Hun) for him to leave the city.[2] He sent three legates to represent him, Julius a bishop, Hilary a deacon, and a presbyter who died on the way. They took with them a batch of letters from Leo dated 13 June 449.

The first of these was the celebrated dogmatic epistle to Flavian, known as the 'Tome' of Leo (a word that did not imply bulkiness). It was only a pamphlet of about twenty-seven hundred words, but it was great in content. It commented on and explained the Nicene Creed in vigorous language, remarkably free from the subtleties that were common in Eastern discussion. It dealt firmly with Nestorianism, and also with this new heresy of Eutyches:[3]

> It does not belong to the same nature to say: 'I and the Father are one' (John x, 30), and to say 'the Father is greater than I' (John xiv, 28). For although in the Lord Jesus Christ there is one Person of God and Man, yet from one nature comes the contumely that is common to both, from the other the common glory. From us He has the manhood, which is inferior to the Father; from the Father He has the Godhead, which is equal to the Father.

St Leo's first care was for the true faith and the removal of error, but he urged that the erring should be brought back and reconciled.[4]

The emperor appointed commissioners as usual to regulate the proceedings of the council, and he nominated Dioscorus to preside at it. The council duly met on 8 August 449. About a hundred and thirty-five bishops assembled, including the three patriarchs, Dioscorus of Alexandria, Domnus of Antioch, and Flavian of Constantinople. One of the legates, Bishop Julius, sat next to Dioscorus the president. The whole proceedings were dominated by Dioscorus and those who, like him, inclined to the Monophysite opinion. The emperor's brief was read, and his *commonitorium* or Instructions to the Commissioners. The legates asked repeatedly that Pope Leo's letters should be read, but the requests were ignored.

Then were read the minutes of the synod of the previous year at Constantinople. They showed that Flavian had asked Eutyches to subscribe a doctrinal statement which might plausibly be said to transgress

[1] Hefele, iii, 222; Mansi, vi, 588; Hardouin, ii, 71. [2] Ep. xxxvii; *PL*, liv, 811.
[3] Ep. xxviii; *PL*, liv, 755–82; Hefele, iii, 225–36.
[4] Epp. xxix, xxx, xxxiii; *PL*, liv, 781, 785, 797.

the canon of Ephesus by adding to or varying the faith. Dioscorus ruled that the council must consider whether these newly introduced statements agreed with the Fathers or not, and invited them to declare that men must simply abide by the established definitions of Nicaea and Ephesus.[1] According to the reports of the notaries, the assembled bishops loudly exclaimed:

> No one dare add anything or take anything away. . . . A great guardian of the faith is Dioscorus! . . . Anathema to him who makes changes in the faith of the Fathers. Anathema to him who ventures to discuss the faith. . . . The Holy Ghost speaks by Dioscorus. . . . Let him who teaches two natures be anathema.[2]

It is well to remember that at this council, as at others, it was the notaries of the dominant party whose reports are preserved. 'It is very probable that only some bishops thus exclaimed, and that the notaries put these words into the mouth of the whole synod.'[3] History is written by the winning side.

A resolution was agreed to condemning 'dyophytism', declaring Eutyches to be orthodox, and demanding his restoration as priest and abbot. Domnus of Antioch and Juvenal of Jerusalem headed the 114 who voted in favour of it. It does not appear that the legates or any others opposed it.[4] Thereafter, amid scenes of great disorder, Flavian was declared deposed, and also Eusebius of Dorylaeum, a bishop who had taken a leading part against Eutyches. The only recorded protests were by Flavian himself, and by Hilary the Roman deacon, who spoke one word, '*contradicitur*'. Flavian was actually beaten, and received serious hurt, from which he died not many days later.

At a subsequent session the 'Robber-Council' deposed various Eastern bishops on suspicion of Nestorianism (a charge that the Monophysites habitually made against their opponents). Among these was Theodoret of Cyrrhus. The legate Julius seems to have been absent; Hilary was under arrest, but he escaped, losing all his baggage, and got back to Rome. Later accounts tell of much irregularity and disorder in the proceedings of the council, and of illegality, tyranny, and *force majeure* on the part of Dioscorus. Some time afterwards, Dioscorus, as patriarch of Alexandria, declared Pope Leo excommunicate.[5]

Pope Leo called this council the *latrocinium* or robber-council, and the nickname stuck.

[1] Hefele, iii, 244.
[2] Hefele, iii, 244, 248; Mansi, vi, 625, 738; Hardouin, ii, 96, 162.
[3] Hefele, iii, 244. [4] Ibid., p. 250.
[5] Ibid., pp. 265, 329; Hardouin, ii, 323, 346; Mansi, vi, 1009.

A. The historical significance of the Robber-Council consists not so much in its outrageous doings, and disregard of the authority of the Apostolic See, as in the subsequent complete and emphatic condemnation of it by the much greater and Oecumenical Council of Chalcedon, and in that council's reaffirmation of all that the Robber-Council had denied and rebelled against.

N. No one seeks to justify the doings of the Robber-Council of Ephesus. But the wholesale flouting of Rome by all the bishops there assembled indicates that belief in the bishop of Rome as Supreme Pontiff and Vicar of Christ was not a 'universal' or even a general belief.

(iii) *The three appeals to Rome*

Of the four patriarchs, Alexandria and Antioch had joined against Flavian of Constantinople, and there remained only one, but that the first and greatest. In spite of Flavian's injuries, which soon proved fatal, he addressed a *libellus appellationis* 'to the most religious and holy Father and Archbishop Leo':

> It has become necessary for me at the present time to report to your Holiness by way of apostolic appeal, so that you may proceed to the East and bring help to the now-endangered faith of the holy Fathers, which they have handed down through their endurance of affliction. Behold all things are disordered.... The faith of the Fathers is no longer named, but by authority of Dioscorus, bishop of the Alexandrine Church, and those who opine with him, the doctrine of Eutyches is now proclaimed as the faith.... When I appealed to the throne of the apostolic see of Peter the prince of the apostles, and to the whole blessed synod which meets under your Holiness, a crowd of soldiers surrounded me at once, prevented me from taking refuge at the holy altar as I wished, and tried to drag me out.... Therefore I beseech your Holiness, do not let things rest... but rise up first on behalf of our right faith which has been wilfully destroyed: then to make the matter your concern because of the overthrow of Church order... stating the facts to the more honourable among the people, instructing suitably our faithful and Christian Emperor, and writing [to the clergy, monks, and people of Constantinople, Juvenal of Jerusalem, etc.] and to Dioscorus who, as it were, lorded it over the sacred synod of Ephesus: and also to issue a decree, as God shall inspire your mind, so that the faith may be proclaimed everywhere and the ordinances of the Fathers prevail, and that a united synod of the Fathers may be held, both of West and East, and the like faith proclaimed everywhere and all be brought to naught which has been evilly done by a sort of gamester's trick. Bring healing to this fearful wound.[1]

[1] Jalland, *Leo*, p. 242; Rivington *RP*, p. 174; Denny, sect. 727; Kidd, *RP*, p. 134.

Eusebius of Dorylaeum also sent a 'libel of appeal' to Pope Leo, asking him to declare his unjust condemnation by 'the most religious bishop Dioscorus' to be void, and to write saying that he is restored to his episcopal office and enjoys the communion of the Roman see.[1] Later that year he went to Rome himself, and remained there as a refugee.

Theodoret of Cyrrhus petitioned for legal permission to go 'to the West to be judged by the bishops of those parts',[2] as his only refuge and resource, and he appealed to Pope Leo in an interesting letter:

> If Paul, the herald of the truth, the trumpet of the Holy Ghost, betook himself to the great Peter, in order to obtain from him an answer for those at Antioch who were in doubt about conforming to the law,[3] much more do we, small and humble men, betake ourselves to your apostolic throne in order to obtain from you a remedy for the wounds of the Churches.
>
> On all accounts it is fitting for you to hold the first place. For your throne is adorned with many advantages. Other cities indeed are adorned by size, by beauty, by populousness; some that lack these are adorned by spiritual gifts. But the Giver of good things has bestowed a vast crop of blessings upon your city. She is the greatest of all, the most splendid, most illustrious, presiding over all the world, and swollen with inhabitants. She has, besides, reached her present hegemony and has given her name to those under her rule. Especially does faith adorn her, to which the holy Apostle witnesses, crying, 'your faith is spoken of throughout the whole world'. (Rom. i, 8). But if immediately after receiving the seeds of the message of salvation she was laden at once with such wonderful fruits, what words are enough to praise her piety now? She possesses the tombs that give light to the souls of the faithful, the tombs of Peter and Paul, our common Fathers and teachers of the truth. This thrice-blessed and divine pair arose in the East and sent out their rays in all directions. Now from the West, where they willingly found the setting of this life, they illuminate the world. They have made your throne most glorious; this is the culminating point of your privileges. Further, their God has even now shed light on their throne by placing on it your Holiness, shedding forth the rays of orthodoxy.[4]

He complains of his unjust condemnation, eagerly awaits a summons to Rome so that his teaching may be pronounced apostolic, and adds that he will accept whatever may be the decision. Theodoret clearly recognized an outstanding authority and primacy of Rome and its bishop. He was a distinguished writer on theology and history. Yet the terms of his letter suggest that the dogmatic basis which St Leo enunciated so

[1] Jalland, *Leo*, pp. 244, 277; Rivington, *RP*, pp. 176–8; Kidd, *RP*, p. 135.
[2] Ep. cxix, *ad Anatolium*; *PG*, lxxxiii, 1329.
[3] Confusing Gal. i, 18, ii, 14, and Acts xv, 15?
[4] Theodoret Ep. cxiii; *PG*, lxxxiii, 1312; inter epp. Leon., lii; *PL*, liv, 848; Jalland, *Leo*, pp. 244 sq.; Rivington, *RP*, pp. 212–15; Denny, sects. 731, 1267.

clearly, and which was now understood in the West, had not been fully assimilated in the East. He was writing to solicit Pope Leo's sympathy and support, but Leo can hardly have approved of the stress laid on imperial Roman power and greatness as a source of his own throne's authority, or the equalizing of the two great apostles, and the apparent failure to grasp the unique Petrine sovereignty which Leo himself constantly expounded; he afterwards instructed Theodoret that Rome was 'that See which the Lord appointed to preside over the rest'.[1]

'The chief importance of these three letters lies in the evidence which they afford as to the general acceptance in the East of the Roman see as the proper court of appeal in matters of doctrine. But in recognizing this we must not lose sight of the political circumstances of the time, nor of the fact that, with the loss of prestige by the other "greater churches" of the West, no other see remained to which an appeal could be addressed to any real advantage.'[2]

Later in the same year, Pope Leo held a considerable Council of the West which rejected everything that had been done at the Robber-Council.[3]

The Emperor Theodosius II confirmed the acts of the Robber-Council by a rescript.[4] Pope Leo wrote to him more than once, asking that all should remain *in statu quo* until revised by a General Council held in Italy—'all the Churches of our regions, all the bishops, entreat your Clemency to order a General Council to be assembled in Italy';[5] and he inspired Valentinian III to support him in a letter referring to the Roman bishop 'on whom ancient usage has conferred a pre-eminence in the episcopate above all others to judge in matters of faith and bishops'.[6] Theodosius ignored the request. He referred to Pope Leo as 'most reverend patriarch', or 'most reverend archbishop', but he failed to recognize a higher or paramount authority.[7]

A. (i) 'It is impossible not to see in these letters a unique position of authority assigned to Rome as the throne of the Apostolic See of Peter, the Prince of the Apostles, written too from the East.

'They swell the great body of proof, which we have seen to be accumulating, to the effect that Rome as the See of Peter held the sovereignty of the whole Church in its hands, however imperfectly at particular

[1] Ep. cxx, 1; *PL*, liv, 1047, quoted supra, p. 230.
[2] Jalland, *Leo*, p. 246. [3] Hefele, iii, 264–5. [4] Ibid., p. 263.
[5] Epp. xliv, lxix; *PL*, liv, 829, 892; Rivington, *RP*, p. 183.
[6] Inter epp. Leon., lv; *PL*, liv, 857; Rivington, *RP*, p. 192.
[7] Cod. Theod., xvi, 1, 2; inter epp. Leon., lxii, lxiv; *PL*, liv, 876, 878; Jalland, *Leo*, p. 287.

times and by particular persons the measure of its jurisdiction might be understood.

'There could be no reason for emphasizing the doctrine concerning the relation of Peter to the See of Rome, if it was not a dogma generally accepted.'[1]

(ii) St Leo's rescission of the acts of the Robber-Council of Ephesus exemplifies 'the office of the Roman Pontiffs to ratify or to reject the decrees of Councils'.[2]

N. (i) Rome was both the greatest patriarchal Church, and also at this juncture the only one remaining to which the wronged Patriarch of Constantinople and his fellow-victims could appeal for help.

The Easterns were fond of verbal embellishment: 'the use of the phrase, "the apostolic see of Peter", simply testifies to the fact that at that date the see of Rome was universally believed to have been founded by St Peter, and the title "the Prince of the Apostles" is naturally applied to the one who was pre-eminent in order among them'.[3]

'Restoration to the Episcopal dignity and to the communion of St Leo were requests that could be legitimately addressed to any Bishop, and, of course, were well within the power of Leo to grant as far as he himself was concerned, as it would be in the case of any other Bishop'.[4]

None of the applicants appreciates that he is addressing a spiritual sovereign with the awful authority of Christ's Vicar, and Supreme Judge of all the Faithful. Theodoret's eulogy of the imperial greatness of Rome, and his equalizing of the two great apostle-founders,[5] agreed more with primitive thought than with contemporary Roman ideas: he shows no knowledge of the uniquely Petrine claims which Pope Leo so incessantly stated.

(ii) It was the General Council of Chalcedon which annulled the doings of the Robber-Council:[6] Pope Leo said so himself: 'By the authority of the sacred Council of Chalcedon the Lord destroyed that detestable decision of the Synod of Ephesus.'[7]

[1] Rivington, *RP*, pp. 178, 217.
[2] Encyc. 'Satis cognitum'.
[3] Denny, sect. 728.
[4] Ibid., sect. 1266.
[5] Cp. St Irenaeus, supra, ch. x.
[6] See next chapter.
[7] Ep. cxxxix; *PL*, liv, 1103.

CHAPTER XLI

Chalcedon, A.D. 451.

The Fourth General Council

(i) *The Council convened*

But in 450, Theodosius was thrown from his horse and killed. The extraordinary system of nominally joint empires of East and West, ruled from Constantinople and Ravenna, left Valentinian theoretically sole emperor for the moment. Pulcheria, sister of Theodosius, a devout and orthodox woman who had vowed perpetual virginity, now took as her husband, in ceremonial marriage, the distinguished general Marcian, and he was solemnly crowned emperor on 24 August 450; he also was devout and orthodox. Anatolius had been elected to the vacant see of Constantinople; he had declared his orthodoxy, and had 'unhesitatingly subscribed' St Leo's dogmatic epistle to his predecessor Flavian, the 'Tome'.

Marcian entered into friendly correspondence with Pope Leo, and soon mentioned his intention to summon a general council in the East.[1] Leo did not now wish for a council, in the East at all events, and he told Marcian so; but Marcian had made up his mind, and on 17 May 451 he summoned all the metropolitans to a council to be held in the autumn. Nicaea was named as the meeting-place, afterwards changed to Chalcedon (now Scutari, close to Constantinople, across the Bosphorus). He appointed officers of state as his commissioners at the council; in the florid Eastern style, the acts repeatedly extol them as 'the most magnificent and most glorious judges and the most distinguished senate'.

Pope Leo assented with some regret, and appointed five legates, headed by Bishop Paschasinus, and including Julian of Cios, an Eastern bishop who regularly acted for him at Constantinople. To

[1] Inter epp. Leon., lxxiii, lxxvi; *PL*, liv.

Marcian he wrote that Paschasinus 'may represent my own presence... and preside at the synod in my stead'.[1] He furnished Paschasinus with a copy of the Tome, and gave full instructions for the conduct of the legates, telling them what matters should be transacted. Portions of these instructions were made public. The legates were particularly told to uphold Leo's authority:

> Do not in any way allow the ordinance of the holy Fathers [at Nicaea] to be infringed or threatened; in all ways maintain the dignity of our person in you whom we send in our stead. If any, perhaps, should try to arrogate aught to themselves for the splendour of their cities, rebuff this fittingly and firmly.[2]

He also explained his views to Marcian and to the Council: its primary duty was to arrange for the restoration of those who had been unjustly condemned, and for the reconciliation of the lapsed. The doctrinal decrees of Ephesus (A.D. 431) should be explicitly confirmed, but the council need not examine questions of doctrine; it need only enforce the view of the Incarnation set out in his Tome.

During the many sessions of the council, Dioscorus was condemned and deposed, Theodoret and others were restored; after full discussion the Tome was approved and signed, and a Definition of Faith was drawn up. The legates tried loyally and strenuously to carry out their instructions. In the various works of Church historians, two contrary lines of argument appear: (A) That the council merely carried out the duty of ratifying what Pope Leo had already decided (except for the famous 28th canon); the repeated utterances of the legates are referred to in support of this. (N) That the council in every instance arrived at its own decision after independent inquiry and debate.

(ii) *Dioscorus condemned*

The council met on 8 October and fourteen other days in the course of the next three weeks. There were about six hundred bishops, all of them Eastern with the exception of the Roman legates. There was a small opposition element of about sixty, from Illyria, Palestine, and Egypt,[3] but the great majority was of the orthodox opinion. Many who had been at the Robber-Council now repudiated Dioscorus and said that they had been overborne by him. Eighteen imperial commissioners sat in the centre of the church of St Euphemia, controlled the business,

[1] Ep. lxxxix; *PL*, liv, 930.
[2] Mansi, vii, 443; Hardouin, ii, 638; Hefele, iii, 283, 424–5.
[3] Rivington, *RP*, p. 226 n.

took the votes, and closed the sessions. On their left sat the legates, 'presiding in the proper and narrower sense'.[1] To one of their statements particular importance has been attributed. When Dioscorus, as second of the patriarchs, sat down with other bishops at the right hand of the commissioners, the legate Paschasinus said: 'We have a commission from the most holy and most apostolic Bishop of Rome, who is head of all the Churches, to see that Dioscorus shall have no seat or vote in the Council. . . . Either he or we depart.'[2] They complained that he held a synod without the consent of the Apostolic See, which they asserted had never been done before, and ought never to be done. The commissioners refused to expel him, but directed him to a lower place. They also ruled that Theodoret should be admitted, because Archbishop Leo had reinstated him and the emperor had commanded his presence.[3] This aroused vehement opposition and ejaculations (as at the Robber-Council, the voluble exclamations uttered during the proceedings were laboriously recorded), but Theodoret was placed in a subordinate position, beside Eusebius.

The first session was taken up with accusations against Dioscorus, of heresy and of misconduct in the chair at Ephesus. After nightfall, these ejaculations were reported:

> Anathema to Dioscorus. At this very hour he passed sentence; at this same hour let him be condemned. Holy Lord, avenge Thyself. Catholic Emperor, avenge Flavian. Long live Leo! Long live the patriarch![4]

The commissioners said it seemed right, if it so pleased the emperor, that Dioscorus should be deposed; then they closed the session. At the third session on 13 October, some two hundred bishops attended, apparently without the commissioners. Dioscorus refused to appear. After his misdeeds had been related in scathing detail, the legates summed up and concluded thus:

> Wherefore Leo, the most holy and blessed archbishop of great and Elder Rome, by us and by the present holy synod, one with the thrice-most-blessed and all-praiseworthy apostle Peter who is the rock and foundation of the Catholic Church and the foundation of the right faith, has stripped him of episcopal rank and excluded him from all sacred ministry. Therefore let this holy and great synod pass judgement on the said Dioscorus in accordance with the canons.[5]

[1] Hefele, iii, 296. [2] Mansi, vii, 443; Hefele, iii, 298–9, cp. 283, 424–5.
[3] Hefele, iii, 300.
[4] Rivington, *RP*, p. 239. The first record of the word 'Patriarch' used in a general council.
[5] Mansi, vi, 1038–48; Hardouin, ii, 346; Hefele, iii, 327–8.

The bishops[1] agreed on the sentence of deposition which was directly afterwards handed to him in the following terms:

> The holy and great and Oecumenical Synod . . . to Dioscorus. Learn that, on account of despising the divine canons, on account of thy disobedience to the Synod since, besides thine other offences, thou didst not respond to their threefold invitation, thou wast on the 13th of October, deposed by the holy Oecumenical Synod from the episcopal office, and deprived of all spiritual functions.[2]

'Three times had an Alexandrian "Pope" deposed a Bishop of Constantinople in this century: Chrysostom in 403, Nestorius in 431, Flavian in 449. Here at length a Bishop of Constantinople takes the the first place, under Rome, in deposing an Alexandrian "Pope".'[3]

A. The legates 'passed sentence',[4] in the name of the council as its presidents.

N. The declaration of the legates was as quoted, but the actual sentence also quoted was explicitly the sentence of the council.

(iii) *The Tome of Leo approved*

The main task of the council was to remove doubts as to the Faith, and was begun at the second session on 10 October. The Nicene Creed and an anathema against the Arian heresy were read, followed by exclamations: 'That is the orthodox faith. That we all believe. Into that we were baptized. Into that we baptize. Thus Cyril taught. Thus believes Pope Leo.'[5] The Creed of Constantinople was read and received with similar exclamations; then was read St Cyril's letter to Nestorius. After further exclamations came the turn of Pope Leo's Tome, and then:

> After the reading of the foresaid epistle, the most reverent bishops exclaimed:—This is the faith of the Fathers; this is the faith of the Apostles. Thus we all believe. Thus the orthodox believe. Anathema to him who believes not. Peter has spoken through Leo. The Apostles taught thus. Leo has taught righteously and truly. Cyril taught thus; eternal is Cyril's memory. Leo and Cyril have taught alike. Anathema to him who believes not so. This is the true faith, Catholics thus opine. This is the faith of the Fathers. Why was this not read at Ephesus? Dioscorus hid this.[6]

[1] Or at least 187 of them; Jalland, *Leo*, p. 294.
[2] Mansi, vi, 1094; Hardouin, ii, 378; Hefele, iii, 328–9.
[3] Rivington, *RP*, p. 252.
[4] Ibid., pp. 244, 221–56.
[5] Mansi, vi, 955; Hardouin, ii, 286 sq.; Hefele, iii, 316.
[6] Mansi, vi, 972; Hardouin, ii, 306; Hefele, iii, 317.

Some passages in the Tome were questioned by some of the bishops as verging on Nestorianism; they were defended by reference to passages in St Cyril. After further discussion, the commissioners adjourned the debate.[1]

A. The pronouncement of the council[2] was that 'Peter has spoken through Leo'; it is reported among the exclamations of all the assembled bishops.

N. Constant utterances of recent popes had made this a stock saying at Rome; that the papal legates made it a slogan is likely, other bishops may have repeated it. Such exclamations came easily, as when a few days later they hailed the emperor as 'a new Paul, a new David'.[3] It is remarkable that the Papal Encyclical of 1896, in referring to Chalcedon, should pick this out from the other ejaculations as the 'pronouncement of the Council'.[4]

The discussion was resumed a week later at the fourth session. The imperial commissioners called on the bishops to swear one by one on the Gospels 'whether the expositions of the 318 Fathers of Nicaea and the 150 of Constantinople agree with the letter of the most reverent archbishop Leo'.[5] The bishops declared their verdicts individually, beginning with Anatolius of Constantinople:

> The letter of the most holy and most God-loving archbishop Leo agrees with the creed of the 318 Fathers who were at Nicaea and of the 150 who afterwards assembled at Constantinople who confirmed the same faith, and with the proceedings at Ephesus under the most blessed and most holy Cyril by the Oecumenical and most holy Council when it condemned Nestorius. Therefore I have agreed to it and willingly subscribed it.
>
> Maximus, the most reverent bishop of Antioch of Syria, said: The epistle of the most holy archbishop of royal Rome agrees with the 318 at Nicaea and the 150 at Constantinople and with the exposition of the faith at Ephesus by the most holy bishop Cyril, and I have subscribed it.
>
> Seleucus, the most blessed bishop of Amasia, said: We have found the synodical letter of our most holy Father Cyril agreeing with the faith of the 318 holy Fathers. And in like manner we have found the letter of the most holy archbishop Leo agreeing both with the 318 and with those who were with the most holy Cyril.[6]

Each bishop expressed himself in similar terms, or in shorter expres-

[1] Hefele, iii, 319. [2] Encyc. 'Satis cognitum'. [3] See below, sect. (iv).
[4] *Concilii Chalcedonensis sententia*; so tr. auth. tr. 36, Messenger 63.
[5] Mansi, vii, 10; Hardouin, ii, 385 sq.; Hefele, iii, 330.
[6] Mansi, vii, 10–11; Hardouin, ii, 385, 387.

sions of approval, such as 'It agrees and I therefore subscribe it'. The bishops from Illyria and Palestine, who had raised doubts a week before, declared that their doubts had now been cleared up by explanations given to them by the legates, 'and we are persuaded that the most holy archbishop Leo is most orthodox', and they 'therefore assented to and subscribed his letter'.[1] Only the Egyptian bishops refused to sign, on the ground that they must await the judgement of their archbishop, that is to say him who should be elected in the room of Dioscorus.

A. The council was convened not to inquire whether the Tome of Leo was accordant with the Creed of Nicaea, but to bring the Eastern bishops into unity on the basis of Leo's teaching.[2]

'It was important that unity should be reached by common vote. If so many in the East had been willing to admit heresy in the Incarnation, it is not to be wondered at that they were not ready immediately to be as orthodox as the Vatican Council on Roman infallibility.'

N. The Tome of Leo was received with the respect due both to its authorship and its intrinsic value, but it was approved and adopted only after examination and comparison with the Nicene Creed, and with the dogmatic epistles of St Cyril. It was then given permanent rank with these earlier dogmatic epistles.

'Now on Papalist principle, "The Tome", as an *ex cathedra* definition on a point of faith, "irreformable of itself", given by the Pope exercising the supreme teaching office which he possessed *jure divino* in virtue of his Apostolic Primacy, was "of faith" from the date it was published to the world, 13 June, A.D. 449.'

The whole history and records of the council show that no such doctrine was known to the Fathers of Chalcedon.[3]

(iv) *The Definition of Faith*

The fifth session, five days later, on 22 October, was 'one of the most important in Christian antiquity'.[4] A doctrinal formula drafted in readiness caused much dispute, which was cut short by an imperial ruling; a committee was appointed to draw up a definition of faith, and this was done forthwith.[5] In it the Nicene Creed is pre-eminent, and the version issued by the 150 Fathers at Ephesus is confirmed. It sets

[1] Mansi, vii, 31. [2] Rivington, *RP*, p. 289. [3] Denny, sect. 452.
[4] Hefele, iii, 342. [5] Ibid., pp. 344–6.

out these two creeds in full. It endorses the letters of Cyril to Nestorius and to John of Antioch, and confirms the authority of the Tome of Leo on the explicit ground that it agrees with the confession of the great Peter. It goes on to define the doctrine of the Incarnation, incorporating much of the teaching of Leo.[1]

At the sixth session, three days later, the emperor and the empress attended with a large suite and all the commissioners and the senate. Marcian said in an oration that the synod had been summoned to establish the faith 'of the apostolic preaching and the decree in accordance therewith of the 318 holy Fathers, which was also testified by the letter of the holy Pope Leo of Rome to Flavian'.[2] After the Definition of Faith (now subscribed by 355 bishops) had been read, the emperor asked if it expressed the view of all, and the bishops replied with the usual profuse exclamations:

> We all believe this; there is one faith, one will. We are all unanimous and have unanimously subscribed; we are all orthodox. This is the faith of the Fathers, the faith of the Apostles, the faith of the orthodox; this faith has saved the world. Prosperity to Marcian, the new Constantine, the new Paul, the new David. You are the peace of the world; thou hast strengthened the orthodox faith. Many years to the Empress. You are the lights of the orthodox faith by which peace everywhere prevails. Marcian is the new Constantine, Pulcheria the new Helena. Thou art priest and Emperor together, conqueror in war and Emperor together, conqueror in war and teacher of the faith.[3]

The imperial confirmation of the Definition was immediately afterwards published by means of a proclamation, and later embodied in an edict.[4]

A. 'The Tome of Leo was from the first the standard of faith to which all were to give an intelligent adhesion. This had now been effected.'[5]

'But since they made their own definition, it needed the assent of the Pope before it could be fully oecumenical.'

N. The Definition of Faith was drawn up and deliberately adopted by the bishops of the council. They were indeed deeply indebted to the powerful theological epistle of St Leo. He, however, did not declare his assent to the Definition until two years later. It is not his assent, but the consent of the whole Church that has made the Definition oecumenical.

[1] Hardouin, ii, 453–6; Jalland, *Leo*, p. 298.
[2] Hefele, iii, 353.
[3] Ibid., p. 354; Hardouin, ii, 485–8.
[4] Jalland, *Leo*, p. 299.
[5] Rivington, *RP*, p. 291.

(v) *Theodoret restored*

Pope Leo had passed judgement on the orthodoxy of Theodoret, and had instructed his legates that Theodoret was to be restored to his see. At the first session the commissioners had allowed him to sit in the assembly, and he actually signed the Tome. At the eighth session, on 26 October, his case came up for final disposal. Because his orthodoxy had at one time been suspect, many bishops demanded that he should now expressly anathematize Nestorius, and ultimately he did so. The commissioners then said that doubt was removed and 'it only now remains that by your judgement he receive again his bishopric, as Leo has already assured him'. All agreed to this, and the commissioners declared that 'accordingly, by decree of the holy Council, Theodore shall receive again the Church of Cyrrhus'.[1]

A. Theodoret's restoration was presumably intended 'to be actually effected by a decree of the synod'.

'The rule of the Pope over the whole Church is not, on Vatican principles, a despotic sway. The Episcopate has a real office of judgement though in subordination to his.'

'There is nothing in the history of Theodoret's restoration to prejudice the doctrine of Papal supremacy, if that doctrine be understood according to the Vatican decrees.'[2]

N. 'The restoration of Theodoret to his see was the act of the Synod. On papist principles the supreme judge had given his decree, and this "judgement of the Roman Pontiff" *was* reviewed, nay entirely disregarded, by the Council. Theodoret was regarded as a heretic until he had satisfied the test by which the Fathers thought fit to try his orthodoxy. The whole proceedings of the Council in this case are, in fact, incompatible with the monarchical position which the Satis Cognitum declares to belong to the Roman Pontiff *jure divino*.'[3]

(vi) *The canons enacted*

At the fifteenth session, on 31 October, about two hundred bishops attended. Twenty-eight canons were enacted, all apparently on this day, although some may have been drafted beforehand.[4] Only three of them need be mentioned. Canons 9 and 17 gave to any bishop a

[1] Mansi, vii, 187; Hardouin, ii, 498 sq.; Hefele, iii, 357.
[2] Rivington, *RP*, pp. 299, 306–7. [3] Denny, sect. 401.
[4] Hefele, iii, 384.

right of appeal from his metropolitan to 'the exarch of the diocese[1] or to the see of imperial Constantinople'. If read literally, these canons seem to give a right of appeal to Constantinople even for Western bishops, but no one supposes that this was intended. At all events they leave no room in the East for the canons of Sardica, of which they show no knowledge. Yet these two canons have not aroused controversy, and they were included in the Western collection of canons compiled by Dionysius Exiguus in the following century.

But the 28th canon was quite another matter:

> Following in all things the rules of the holy Fathers, and acknowledging the canon of the hundred-and-fifty most God-fearing bishops which has just been read aloud (canon 3 of Constantinople, A.D. 381),[2] we too determine and adjudge by vote the same things in regard to the privileges of the most holy Church of Constantinople, New Rome.
>
> The Fathers justly granted the privileges to the throne of Elder Rome because that is the imperial city; and moved by the same consideration, the hundred-and-fifty most God-loving bishops awarded the like privileges to the most holy throne of New Rome, judging with good reason that the city which is honoured by the imperial power and the senate, and which enjoys equal privileges with the Elder imperial Rome, should be exalted like it in ecclesiastical affairs also, and be in the second place after it [so that the metropolitans of Pontus, Asia, and Thrace are to be ordained at Constantinople].[3]

Now the fat was in the fire. The Roman legates attended next day at the sixteenth and final session to express indignant disapproval. They were answered that the commissioners had placed the matter on the agenda, and that they themselves had declined to attend at its discussion on the previous day.

One legate read out some of Pope Leo's instructions to his legates. Then another, Paschasinus, recited a version of canon 6 of Nicaea. That important canon was found at Rome in a number of versions.[4] This version began, 'The Roman Church has always had primacy' (which was not in the original text);[5] but the variation was of small importance. For one thing, this version went on to ascribe primacies also to Antioch and the greater cities of the other provinces.[6] Moreover Rome was in

[1] Whether this is here equivalent to 'patriarch' is doubtful; Hefele, iii, 395; Denny, sect. 404; Funk, i, 191. Pope Nicholas I argued that it meant the Roman primate, Roy, p. 187; Denny, sect. 408.

[2] Supra, ch. xxx, p. 177.

[3] Mansi, vii, 370; Hefele, iii, 411; Kidd, *RP*, p. 144.

[4] See Hardouin, i, 325–6, 333, 431.

[5] Hefele, iii, 425.

[6] Labbe, iv, 812; Hardouin, ii, 638; Mansi, vii, 443; 'similiter autem et qui in Antiocha constitutus est, et in ceteris provinciis, primatus habeant ecclesiae civitatum ampliorum'. So it likened the primacies of Rome and of the Eastern patriarchates, as the Easterns always did.

fact the first Church of Christendom from the second century onwards, perhaps from the destruction of Jerusalem in A.D. 135, and in any view it ought to be acknowledged as the principal primacy or patriarchate.

The authentic Greek text of the canon was then read out, but the Latin variations do not seem to have been thought important. Any version of the Nicene canon, however, was enough to show that the new canon 28 broke the old order of the patriarchates, Rome-Alexandria-Antioch, laid down at Nicaea.

After a discussion, in which no objection to the new canon was raised by bishops whom it placed under Constantinople, the commissioners declared that it was decreed. The legates objected unsuccessfully, but got their protest recorded in the acts: they are to report 'to the Apostolic man, the principal guardian of the whole Church, so that he himself may make a decision either regarding the injury to his see, or the overthrow of the canons'.[1] The commissioners then closed the session with the words, 'Our interlocutory sentence has been approved by the whole Synod', and the famous Council of Chalcedon came to an end.

(vii) *Objection to Canon* 28

When the Council of Nicaea ranked the patriarchates as Rome-Alexandria-Antioch, Constantinople had not been founded. Canon 3 of Constantinople declared that 'the Bishop of Constantinople shall hold the first rank after the Bishop of Rome, because Constantinople is the New Rome'.[2] That was not recognized by Rome, but it had received effect in the East and had passed into practice there, as the pope 'was certainly not unaware'.[3]

This new canon 28 of Chalcedon affirmed it and ranked Constantinople over the two older patriarchs of Alexandria and Antioch. It did not directly encroach on the primacy of Rome, but expressly acknowledged it in placing Constantinople second. Yet its wording was open to objection; it suggested that Rome's primacy was due simply and solely to the civil and imperial greatness of the city. That was not true: the greatness of the Roman Church had always been referred especially to its foundation by the 'two most glorious apostles', and its fame as a stronghold of sound faith, even although the greatness of the imperial metropolis as a world-centre was a conducing cause.

But in the East, Church primacy had always attached to the civil

[1] Hefele, iii, 428; Hardouin, ii, 644. [2] Supra, ch. xxx. [3] Hefele, iii, 415.

metropolis. Thus Alexandria as the second city of the empire, although not founded by an apostle, always ranked above Antioch which claimed St Peter as its founder. Ephesus, founded by St Paul and then occupied by St John, never ranked as a patriarchate; Jerusalem was under Caesarea. The same principle had operated even in the West in the fourth century, when Milan had for a time enjoyed a 'twofold hegemony' with Rome, because it was then the imperial capital.[1] Ravenna had now become the seat of Western Empire, and Leo the Great had certainly no cause to fear any rivalry from its reigning archbishop. Yet that principle might have laid up trouble for the future if it were countenanced.

Moreover canon 28 implicitly denied Leo's *jure divino* claim in saying that 'the Fathers granted the privileges' to Elder Rome.

Mgr Batiffol observes that 'Undoubtedly, the papal legates at Chalcedon saw at once that the Twenty-eighth Canon inflicted a wrong upon the Apostolic See. But apparently they were over-excited, since Julian of Kos (or Cios) did not share their view.'[2] Both he and Abbot Chapman[3] think that Pope Leo saw in the canon no threat to the privilege or dignity of the Roman see. At all events, he never said so publicly.[4] He always took the point that the canon conflicted with canon 6 of Nicaea, as it obviously did. The canons of the Fathers at Nicaea, he said, 'shall endure until the end of the world'.[5]

Constantinople was extremely anxious to obtain Pope Leo's assent to the canon. The synodal letter to him was courtly and deferential and 'clearly shows the high esteem in which the Roman see was held at this time in the East'.[6] 'You were an interpreter of the voice of blessed Peter. . . . Your gracious leadership of us in the things which belong to orderliness was like the head is to its members.'[7] It was easy to write ingratiatingly about the Tome, or the condemnation of Dioscorus, 'who aimed his frenzy against him to whom the Saviour had committed charge of the vine',[8] but when they came to canon 28, they knew they were on thin ice. They professed to believe that the legates had 'vehemently essayed to oppose our proposals because they were eager that the credit for this beneficial act should be given to your watchful interest. . . . We beg you therefore to honour our decision with your approval.'[9] Anatolius also related the decisions of the council in a letter to Pope Leo, in the course of which he asked for Leo's assent to canon

[1] Supra, ch. xxxii. [2] C. & P., p. 118, n. 1. [3] *GCC*, p. 87.
[4] But see Ep. civ, 3 (to Marcian); *PL*, liv, 995. [5] Ep. cvi, 4; *PL* liv, 1005.
[6] Jalland, *Leo*, p. 311. [7] Inter epp. Leon., xcviii, 1; *PL*, liv, 951, 959.
[8] Ibid., 2; *PL*, liv, 953, 960.
[9] Ibid., 4; *PL*, liv, 955, 959; Jalland, *Leo*, p. 314.

28. The legates 'must have opposed it in ignorance of Leo's real wishes.'[1]

But Pope Leo was not to be cajoled by fine words. He flatly refused to give his assent, on the single stated ground that canon 28 ran counter to the order of patriarchates laid down at Nicaea. So he said in letters to the Emperor Marcian, Empress Pulcheria, and to Anatolius.[2] To Pulcheria he wrote 'I declare it to be invalid, and annul it by the authority of the holy apostle Peter'.[3]

Anatolius 'under pressure as it seems from the Emperor . . . presented his apology to Leo'.[4] 'All the force and confirmation of what was done was reserved for the authority of your beatitude.'[5] Leo graciously accepted the gesture as if it meant abandonment of canon 28;[6] Anatolius even submitted to what he complained of as 'interference' by Leo in the affairs of Constantinople.

The Eastern bishops cannot be acquitted of insincerity in what they wrote to Pope Leo, because, in spite of his flat refusal of assent, they quietly proceeded to give effect to canon 28 and to treat it as valid. 'In vain did Pope Leo protest.'[7] 'The Bishop of Constantinople assumed more and more the position of a sort of Pope of the Oriental Empire, and the obstacles he met with in so doing were one after another swept away.'[8] 'The Church of Constantinople thus took its place in the same category as those of Rome, Alexandria and Antioch. . . . The Roman Pontiffs, Leo I and others, protested vigorously, though fruitlessly. . . . The Bishop of Constantinople maintained his prerogative; and in proof of this, from the sixth century, he was called Oecumenical Patriarch. Justinian, in one of his edicts, calls the Church of Constantinople absolutely the head of all other churches.'[9]

A. 'If insincerely used, they (the definite statements of the bishops) testify to the necessity under which these bishops found themselves of crouching at the feet of a master in order to gain the object of their desires. If used in sincerity, they are the testimony of witnesses, naturally the most unwilling, to the position of headship which the East recognized in the occupant of the See of Peter.'[10] Anatolius eventually yielded to the rightful papal authority.

N. The then prevailing style of writing was flowery and insincere. At

[1] Inter epp. Leon., ci, 5; *PL*, liv, 981; Jalland, *Leo*, p. 320.
[2] Epp. civ, cv, cvi; *PL*, liv, 991–1009. [3] Ep. cv; *PL*, liv, 1000.
[4] Jalland, *CP*, p. 310. [5] Inter epp. Leon., cxxxii, 4; *PL*, liv, 1084.
[6] Jalland, loc. cit. [7] Duchesne, *CS*, p. 130. [8] Duchesne, *CW*, pp. 24–5.
[9] Funk, i, 191; Codex, I, ii, 24; Corpus J. C., ii, 26; Hefele, iii, 448.
[10] Rivington, *RP*, p. 356.

all times it was of great importance to win the support or assent of the first patriarch of the Church, and this was very much desired. He himself now claimed that his authority and approval were absolutely indispensable, but outside his own patriarchate that claim was denied in act even by those who flattered it in word.[1]

The apologetic attitude of Anatolius was forced on him by the imperial will, but canon 28 remained in force.

(viii) *More doctrinal disunity*

The doctrinal decree of Chalcedon was confirmed by the Emperor Marcian in February 452,[2] but rumours began to buzz that Pope Leo had repudiated it. This encouraged opposition, already simmering in some parts, and embarrassed the imperial government. In March 453, Marcian wrote to Pope Leo about it. 'The Emperor's letter was phrased in highly diplomatic terms, and revealed clearly enough the extent of the dependence of the eastern government upon the Roman see.'[3] He tactfully praised the Pope's firmness in defence of the canons, and suggested that it would be of weighty assistance in overcoming opposition to the doctrinal decisions if he would assent to them.[4] Pope Leo replied that 'Since the most religious will of your Piety must in all ways be obeyed, I have willingly added my judgement to the synodical constitutions, which have satisfied me as regards the confirmation of the Catholic faith, and the condemnation of heretics';[5] but he gave no assent to the obnoxious canon 28.

The sad fact remains that the Definition of Faith failed to bring about unity throughout the Church. There was widespread unwillingness to make definite confession of the Two Natures, and riots raged in Palestine, Egypt, and Antioch. A later sequel was the Acacian Schism of East and West. In modern times the Antiochene patriarchate has been the centre of the Monophysite Churches of Syria and elsewhere, Mesopotamia, Asia Minor, Armenia, Cyprus, Palestine. The Coptic Church of Egypt is Monophysite, together with Ethiopia.[6]

[1] Cp. Duchesne, *CS*, p. 145.
[2] Mansi, vii, 475 sq.; Hardouin, ii, 661–4.
[3] Jalland, *Leo*, p. 334.
[4] Inter epp. Leon., cxi; *PL*, liv, 1019; see Hefele, iii, 442, n. 2.
[5] Ep. cxv, 2; *PL*, liv, 1035.
[6] Hefele, iii, 449–62.

CHAPTER XLII

Later Papal Pronouncements of the Century

In what has been described as the *explicatio* or unfolding[1] of the papal sovereignty, this fifth century can be seen to have been momentous. A list of the popes of Rome during the century may be found convenient here.

Anastasius I	398–401
Innocent I	402–417
Zosimus	417–418
Boniface I	418–422
Celestine I	422–432
Sixtus III	432–440
Leo I	440–461
Hilarus	461–468
Simplicius	468–483
Felix III	483–492
Gelasius I	492–496
Anastasius II	496–498
Symmachus	498–514

The following quotations from those popes who followed next after St Leo show that his teaching with regard to the authority of the Roman see was earnestly continued. (Some passages relating to its canonical foundations are reserved for the next chapter.)

Pope Hilarus, who as deacon and papal legate at the Council of Ephesus had so stoutly proclaimed the sovereign supremacy of the papal throne, mounted that throne himself thirty years later, on the death of St Leo. He firmly upheld his power.

> It has been decreed by law of the Christian princes that whatever the high-priest of the Apostolic See has deliberately appointed for the Churches and their rulers, for the peace of all the Lord's priests and the observance of discipline, is to be reverently received and strictly observed . . . nothing fixed by decree both ecclesiastical and regal can ever be uprooted.[2]

[1] Humphrey, p. 48. [2] Hilarus P., Ep. xi; *PL*, lviii, 30–1; Labbe, iv, 1045.

> Most blessed Peter, the supremacy of whose vicar, as it is eminent so is to be feared and loved by all.[1]

Pope Simplicius observes in one passage that:

> The pattern of apostolic doctrine remains constant in the successors of him on whom the Lord laid the care of all the sheepfold.[2]

Pope Felix III wrote of:

> The Apostolic See, through which, by Christ's bestowal, the dignity of all priests (i.e., bishops) is consolidated.[3]

When Pope Gelasius acceded in 492, the great Acacian Schism of East and West had already gone on for eight years. The first of the following quotations is taken from some of his instructions for answering the Greeks:

> Christ . . . appointed Peter as first and principal in the principal city. . . . Peter granting to the see which he himself blessed, that in accordance with the Lord's promise, it should never be conquered by the gates of hell, and should be the safest harbour of those tossed by the waves.[4]
>
> We toil unceasingly in the government of the Apostolic See, engaged in the care of the whole flock of the Lord, which care was delegated to the blessed Apostle Peter by the voice of the Lord Himself. . . . (He cites Luke xxii, 32 and John xxi, 17.)[5]
>
> The First See both confirms every synod by its authority and guards by its continual rule, by reason to wit of its supremacy which, received by blessed Peter the apostle by the voice of the Lord, the Church nevertheless complying, has both always held and retains. . . . Just as that which the First See has not approved of cannot stand, so what it has thought well to decide has been received by the whole Church.[6]

The two remaining popes of the century do not appear to have added any particular teaching with regard to the Roman see.

A. The supremacy of the Apostolic See was consistently and unequivocally taught by the pontiffs. They showed that their authority was divinely bestowed upon them, as St Peter's successors, and as such they were charged with the care of the whole flock, the Church; that the 'pattern of Apostolic doctrine' was entrusted to them; and that no decrees of councils or synods could take valid effect without papal confirmation. These truths are redeclared in the Vatican Decrees.

What the pontiffs taught was indubitably true. Mgr Duchesne[7] shows

[1] Bishops of Tarragon, Inter, epp. Hilarii P.; *PL*, lviii, 15; Allnatt, p. 110.
[2] Ep. iv; *PL*, lviii, 40; Allnatt, p. 38. [3] Ep. xiii; *PL*, lviii, 972; Allnatt, p. 83.
[4] Ep. xiv; sive tractatus; *PL*, lix, 90; Allnatt, p. 68.
[5] Ep. v; *PL*, lix, 30–1; Labbe, iv, 1172; Allnatt, p. 30.
[6] Ep. xiii; *PL*, lix, 63, 67; Allnatt, p. 85; quoted also in Encyc. 'Satis cognitum'.
[7] *CS*, pp. 103–4.

that even before the time of Constantine, the influence of Rome, whether as to faith, discipline, administration, ritual or works of charity, was known everywhere throughout the known world. 'No competitor, no rival stands up against her; no one conceives the idea of being her equal. . . . Above the whole body of isolated Churches the Church of Rome rises in supreme majesty, the Church of Rome represented by the long series of her bishops, which ascends to the two chiefs of the Apostolic College; she knows herself to be, and is considered by all, the centre and the organ of unity.'

N. Pope Hilarus was exceptional in his frank reliance upon the authority conferred by imperial legislation. From the many other papal affirmations and claims, two things stand out plainly: (1) The utter contrast between these fifth-century papal claims and anything heard of in the early centuries, and (2) The power of propaganda and the effect of continually repeated assertion.

Nothing resembling these papal claims is expressed in Holy Scripture, and they were manifestly unknown to St Irenaeus or others in the second century. The idea of succession to an individually Petrine office is first discovered in the third century. Even in the fourth century, Pope St Julius put forward only a comparatively modest claim to be allowed a voice in Eastern decisions, and he relied also upon a supposed custom peculiar to Alexandria only.

There is no hint or suggestion in Scripture of a sovereignty or divine vicariate in St Peter, understood either by himself or by the other apostles. Scripture nowhere suggests that any one of the apostles' successors is to succeed St Peter individually. These things are now claimed as legitimate inferences from Scripture; but the papal assertions were calculated to build up a mass-belief that they were actual statements of Scripture, not mere inferences and arguments.

'It is but natural that the chief upholders of the prerogatives of the Roman See and of the Papacy should have been the Popes: the chief upholders of prerogatives of all kinds are commonly those most intimately concerned.'[1]

[1] Butler, i, 35.

CHAPTER XLIII

Canonical Affirmations of Roman Supremacy

(i) *The sources referred to*

The fifth century saw a notable advance in the clear statement of the Roman claims of supreme authority. In support of these, 'the canons' were constantly referred to. The canons of Nicaea are sometimes named (or the famous 'three hundred-and-eighteen', the traditional number of the bishops at Nicaea). No other canons are ever named. Pope Innocent I, indeed, declared that 'the Roman Church admits no canons but those of Nicaea'.[1] No particular canon is ever specified.

Only one of the actual canons of Nicaea has any reference to the position of Rome in the Church; that is canon 6:[2]

> Let the ancient customs prevail which are observed in Egypt, Libya, and Pentapolis, that the bishops of Alexandria have authority over all these (provinces), since this is customary also for the bishop of Rome.

This well-known canon does not refer to the Roman bishop as first bishop of Christendom, 'nor as primate of the universal Church, nor as simple Bishop of Rome; but it treats him as one of the great metropolitans, who had not merely one province, but several, under their jurisdiction'.[3] It recognizes Alexandria as having a similar 'patriarchate', to use the descriptive name that came later into use.

It will be remembered, however, that in one or more of the Latin versions of canon 6 found at Rome, the words 'The Roman Church has always had primacy' had been added to the original text, and it seems likely that many references to 'the canons' are based upon a recollection of these words, although it is true that they add little in effect to the original text.[4] It must also be remembered that the canons of Sardica in the Roman archives had been mixed up with those of

[1] Ep. v; *PL*, xx, 493. [2] Supra, ch. xxv. [3] Hefele, i, 397.
[4] Supra, ch. xli (vi); Hefele, iii, 425.

Nicaea,[1] so that 'or Sardica' may have to be read into any fifth-century Roman allusion to the 'canons of Nicaea'. Of the Sardican canons, only canons 3, 4, and 5 have any bearing upon the authority of the Roman see. It is convenient here to repeat canon 3:

> Hosius, the bishop, said: ... That if any bishop be judged adversely in any cause, and consider that he has a good cause for a fresh decision, if you agree, let us honour the memory of Peter the Apostle, let those who tried the cause write to the bishop of Rome, so that the judgement may be reviewed, if it ought to be, before bishops of a neighbouring province, and he appoint judges. If however the matter do not appear to him to need revision, the first judgement shall stand. Is this generally agreed? The Synod replied: Agreed.

By canon 5 of Sardica, a deposed bishop may himself petition the bishop of Rome, who may then appoint fresh inquiry to be made by the bishops of the adjoining province. If so desired he may also, at his discretion, send a presbyter from his suite to judge with these bishops.[2] Canon 4 directs that the see affected shall not be filled up until the appeal is disposed of. The canons of the (Western) Council of Sardica remained in strange obscurity—the bishops of Africa, for example, eighty years after Sardica, had never heard of them—yet all the following references to 'the canons of Nicaea', or 'of the Three-hundred-and-eighteen', ought in fairness to be construed as intended to apply to the canons of Sardica, and also to the words added to canon 6 of Nicaea.

(ii) *Appeals to 'the canons'*

Pope Zosimus (417–18) was the first to invoke the canons of Sardica against the bishops of Africa on the assumption that they were canons of Nicaea.[3] He evidently had in mind canon 3 of Sardica when he spoke of 'the authority of the Apostolic See to which the Fathers have, in honour of St Peter, sanctioned a peculiar reverence'.[4] So great is the authority of 'the canons', he says, that even 'the authority of this see cannot indeed assent or make alteration contrary to the statutes of the Fathers'.[5]

Pope Boniface I (418–22) continued to invoke the Sardican canons as Nicene. Pope Celestine I (422–32), who did so likewise, emphasized the binding character of 'the canons' (whether Nicene or pseudo-Nicene): 'The rules rule us, not we the rules; we be subject to the canons while we uphold their injunctions.'[6]

[1] Supra, ch. xxxvii (v). [2] Hefele, ii, 112–13. [3] Supra, ch. xxxvii (v).
[4] Ep. ii, *ad episcopos Afr.*; *PL*, xx, 649; see Chapman, *Studies*, pp. 157–64.
[5] Ep. v; *PL*, xx, 666. [6] Ep. iii; *PL*, l, 428.

Pope Sixtus III (432–40) does not furnish a quotation on this point, but in the histories written by his contemporaries Socrates and Sozomen there are passages which show it was coming to be widely supposed that 'the canons' (unidentified) had conferred a legislative veto on Rome. Socrates, writing of the Council of Antioch in 341, and the famous letter from Pope Julius to its bishops, observes that:

> Neither was Julius, bishop of Elder Rome, there (at Antioch), nor did he send any one in his stead. . . . Because they had not invited him to the Synod, he charged them with acting contrary to the canons, because the ecclesiastical canon commands the Churches not to legislate contrary to the mind of the bishop of Rome.[1]

There was no such canon: and Socrates cannot have had the actual letter of Pope Julius in front of him, because it makes no such statement and no reference to canons.[2] Sozomen borrows from Socrates as usual,[3] and imagines that the letter asserted 'a sacerdotal law that the things done against the judgement of the bishop of Rome are to be deemed null'.[4]

Pope Leo the Great (440–61) continually appeals to the canons of Nicaea,[5] with which he too still confuses Sardica.[6] No weight of numbers can be set against the venerable 'Three hundred and eighteen' of Nicaea:[7]

> The prerogatives of the Churches established by the canons of the holy Fathers and settled by the decrees of the Nicene Synod cannot be torn up by any depravity or altered by any innovation.[8]
>
> Since no one is allowed to listen to anything contrary to the Fathers' canons, which were established long ago by spiritual decrees in the city of Nicaea, so any one who would decide anything otherwise lowers himself rather than impairs them. If they are kept inviolate by all pontiffs, there will be calm peace and steadfast harmony throughout all the Churches.[9]
>
> The holy and venerable Fathers at Nicaea . . . established the ecclesiastical canons which shall endure until the end of the world.[10]
>
> Those statutes ought to be kept which were fixed by inviolable decrees at the Synod of Nicaea.[11]

The Emperor Valentinian III, in the Rescript written at Pope Leo's request, declares that 'The authority of a sacred synod has confirmed the primacy of the Apostolic See'.[12]

[1] ii, 5, 17.
[2] Supra, ch. xxvi (i).
[3] Duchesne, *EH*, II, x.
[4] iii, 10; Allnatt, p. 83.
[5] Besides the following quotations, see Epp. xliii, cvii, cxix, 2, 3, 4; cxx, cxxv; *PL*, liv, 825, 1009, 1042, 1043, 1054, 1096, 1098.
[6] Ep. xliv, 3, to Theodosius, A.D. 449; *PL*, liv, 831.
[7] Ep. cvi, 2; *PL*, liv, 1003.
[8] Ep. civ, 3; *PL*, liv, 995.
[9] Ep. cv, 2, to Pulcheria; *PL*, liv, 999.
[10] Ep. cvi, 4; *PL*, liv, 1005.
[11] Ep. cxiv, 2; *PL*, liv, 1009.
[12] Supra, ch. xxxix (ii).

Pope Felix III, in a Roman synod of A.D. 484, declares as follows:

> ... The Lord saying to the blessed Apostle Peter, *Thou art Peter*, etc. (Matt. xvi, 18, 19); following which voice the Three-hundred-and-eighteen Fathers assembled at Nicaea referred the confirmation and decision of affairs to the Roman Church, both of which, as the grace of Christ shows, all successions down to our own time retain.[1]

Gelasius (492–6) became pope during the Acacian Schism of East and West,[2] which continued long after his death. He laid stress on the authority conferred on his see by 'the canons'. He devoted particular attention to this in briefing his legate at Constantinople (which elsewhere he scornfully derides as 'in the diocese of Heraclea'):[3]

> The canons themselves willed the appeals of the whole Church to be referred to the examination of this see. From it, they decreed also, that no appeal whatever ought to be made, and thereby that it should judge the whole Church and come under the judgement of none. They determined that its sentence should not be annulled, but ordered its decrees to be complied with.... [4]
>
> Let them see therefore if they have other canons with which they pursue their fooleries.... But what religious and excellent men! They try to shatter the power which certainly has been granted to the Apostolic See under the canons, and strive to usurp to themselves what is contrary to the canons.... [5]
>
> We are in no fear lest the apostolic judgement be reversed, which both the voice of Christ, and the traditions of the Fathers, as also the authority of the canons support, in such wise that rather it may always judge the whole Church.[6]

Pope Gelasius in other writings also proclaims the canonical authority that has been conferred upon his see:

> The see of blessed Peter the Apostle has the right to unbind what has been bound by sentences of any pontiffs whatever, in that it has the right of judging the whole Church. Neither is it lawful for any one to judge its judgement, seeing that the canons have willed that it may be appealed to from any part of the world, but that no one may be allowed to appeal from it.[7]
>
> The first see of the most blessed Peter ... the honour of which was adjudged by the invincible and unique sentence of the Three-hundred-and-eighteen.[8]
>
> In accordance with the Scriptures, the tradition of the Fathers, and the

[1] Mansi, vii, 1138; Labbe, iv, 1126; Allnatt, p. 83.
[2] Infra, ch. xlv.
[3] Ep. xiii; *PL*, lix, 66.
[4] Ep. seu commonitorium, iv, *ad Faustum*; *PL*, lix, 28.
[5] Ibid., col. 29.
[6] Ibid., col. 30; Allnatt, p. 85.
[7] Ep. xiii, *ad episcopos Dardaniae*; *PL*, lix, 66; Allnatt, p. 85.
[8] Ep. sive tractatus, xiv; *PL*, lix, 89.

canons and rules of the Church, what the Apostolic See has appointed to be done, and has confirmed when done, is admitted by the whole Church for common faith and Apostolic truth.[1]

The *Decretum Gelasianum*, attributed to a Roman synod of 494, but possibly of a much earlier date,[2] contains a somewhat different pronouncement:

The holy Roman Catholic and Apostolic Church was preferred to other Churches by no synodical decrees but obtained primacy by the evangelic voice of our Lord and Saviour, *Thou art Peter*, etc. (Matt. xvi, 18, 19).[3]

At the date of the Council of Nicaea, when it declared 'Let the ancient customs prevail', Constantinople had not been founded. Pope Leo had a clear case therefore when he objected to Constantinople as an upstart patriarchate, intruded over the heads of older patriarchates. Yet neither Leo, nor any other of the popes, ever cited any specific canon to the Eastern bishops or councils in support of their downright claims to sovereign power under 'the canons'. A careful 'recension' of the canons of the first five centuries was made by Vicenzi, who found with astonishment that 'the prerogatives of the Roman Episcopate' were either left unmentioned or rejected. This was incredible, and he could only suppose that the canons had been mutilated by Eusebians and other heretics.[4] It does not appear that there was definite warrant in any actual canon for basing these claims on 'the canons'; some writers have argued that they could not therefore have been made in good faith, but the naïvety of Vicenzi suggests that early belief in them was no less sincere.

A. The supremacy of the Roman pontiff is based upon Holy Scripture, and constant recognition by ancient and immemorial custom of the Churches. These were the primary reasons given, when occasion arose for the giving of reasons. The references to the canons were purely secondary and, even though the actual canons were not specified in detail, the councils by which they were decreed substantially warranted all that was said about them by their other acts and declarations, and their entire deference to the Apostolic See.

The authority claimed for the Roman pontiffs was recognized in practice. 'If some of the arguments the popes appealed to are now known to lack the foundations they were thought to possess, this

[1] *Tomus de anathematis vinculo*; *PL*, lix, 102.
[2] Supra, p. 181. Hefele (iv, 45) attributes this section to Pope Damasus.
[3] Labbe, iv, 1261; Allnatt, p. 86.
[4] *De Hebraeorum et Christianorum Sacra Monarchia*, Rome, 1875, pars ii, cap. xiii, pp. 292, 298; Denny, sects. 654 sq.

should not be regarded as invalidating the case . . . though some are less strong than others and would often have been better omitted.'

N. Muddle and carelessness may account for the garbling of canon 6 of Nicaea, and the reckoning of Sardica as if it were Nicaea. Yet, even taking into account Sardica, and the words added to canon 6, it is evident to any reader of the actual canons that they give no warrant for what the popes were asserting about them. Habitual careless neglect to read or refer to the canons themselves is the best excuse that can be made.

These erroneous misrepresentations as to 'the canons' have two important aspects:

1. Inferences from Holy Scripture rest on opinion and argument, and are hardly susceptible of plain disproof. As to custom also, although history does not support the papal claims by positive evidence, the negative evidence cannot be decisive enough to put an end to argument. But the papal claims, so far as they were rested on the canons, were demonstrably baseless and false. It is reasonable to believe that the papal assertions of custom were no sounder and no better warranted.

2. These confident assertions by the first patriarch help to explain the fact that the papal claims not only grew mightily, but were also generally accepted in the West. Indeed the popes, as patriarchs of the West, truly enjoyed in the West much of the sovereign power that they went on to assert as universal; so that, for their own subjects in the West at all events, it would have been useless to dispute the claims made, even if doubts were felt. But constantly reiterated assertion has weighty effect, both on those to whom it is addressed, and on those who make it.

CHAPTER XLIV

Other Saints and Fathers of the Century

From the writings of the fifth century not much of importance remains to be quoted. Mr Allnatt gives quotations from eight popes, viz., Innocent I, Boniface I, Celestine I, Sixtus III, Leo I, Simplicius, Felix III, and Gelasius I, all of whose writings have already been quoted here rather more fully.

Of his other sources, the following also have been quoted here, viz., St Jerome, St Augustine, St Cyril, St Peter Chrysologus, Theodoret, the bishops of Tarragon, the Rescript of Valentinian III, and the historians Socrates and Sozomen.

He gives quotations from some ten other Western writers: Prudentius Bacchiarius, Cassian, Paulinus the Deacon, Zacchaeus, St Prosper of Acquitaine, St Proclus, St Maximus of Turin, Victor of Vite, St Avitus, and St Vincent of Lerins. With the exception of the last, of whose treatise something more should be said, the quotations from all these are chiefly allusions to St Peter, and express little that is instructive or out of the commonplace. Other fifth-century Western writers, such as Salvian, St Sidonius Apollinaris, Denis pseudo-Areopagite, and St Fulgentius, have not been found to touch upon our subject. Four Eastern writers are quoted by Mr Allnatt, viz., Victor of Antioch, St Proclus of Constantinople, St Nilus, and St Basil of Seleucia. They refer to St Peter in semi-Scriptural words, or describe him as a ruler of the apostles, or set over the others.

The famous *Commonitorium* of St Vincent of Lerins, written in A.D. 434, was considered in Chapter ii in connexion with the doctrine of development; it calls for some further notice. His theme, as he says at the outset, is the setting out of 'a general rule for distinguishing the true Catholic faith from wicked heresy'. This is to be achieved, 'first, by the authority of the law of God; secondly, by the tradition of the Catholic Church'; that tradition is to be recognized by 'universality, antiquity, and consent'.[1] But if any error be found in antiquity, then Christianus Catholicus is to 'prefer the universal decrees and determinations of an ancient General Council, if such there be, before the temerity and folly of a few'.[2]

In his clear-cut teaching, heresy is novelty, and novelty is heresy. 'Calamity entereth in when a novel doctrine is admitted.'[3] 'Whosoever preacheth a new dogma is to be accursed.'[4]

He gives special attention to the Nestorian heresy, and the Council of Ephesus which condemned it. The heroes and saints of the Church whom he names were those who spoke or wrote to resist innovation upon the faith. He mentions fifteen, of whom five were bishops or popes of Rome, viz., Stephen, Felix I, Julius, and his own contemporaries Celestine and Sixtus III. The other saints were Peter, Athanasius, Theophilus, and Cyril of Alexandria, Gregory of Nazianzus, Basil the Great, Gregory of Nyssa, Cyprian and Capreolus of Carthage, and Ambrose of Milan.[5]

St Stephen receives special praise in connexion with the controversy on the baptism of heretics. 'The more religious a man is, the more readily does he resist novel inventions: wherefore with great zeal did Pope Stephen resist rebaptization, . . . in common indeed with the rest of his fellow-bishops, but yet more than the rest, thinking it, as I suppose, reason so much to excel all other in devotion towards the faith, as he was superior to them in authority of place.'[6] He also praises 'the zeal of the Roman Pontiffs, Celestine and Sixtus, in proscribing novelty'.[7]

A. The chorus of saints and writers here briefly described is all in harmony with the other testimonies to the supremacy and dogmatic authority of the Apostolic See.

As regards the *Commonitorium* of St Vincent, 'The test *quod semper, quod ubique, quod ab omnibus*, is proposed by St Vincent in cases where the present teaching of the Church has been impugned or seems doubtful. He does not put it forward as the ordinary rule of faith, but as a test for emergencies.'[8] St Vincent also clearly enunciated a principle of development in doctrine.[9]

N. Great claims of sovereign authority were by this time being asserted by the popes. They obtained considerable support from within their own patriarchate of the West, especially from their own suffragans. Support from Eastern sources is conspicuously meagre.

[1] Cap. i. [2] Cap. iii. [3] Cap. iv. [4] Cap. ix. [5] Cap. xxx.
[6] Cap. vi; Allnatt, p. 116. [7] Cap. xxxii. [8] Chapman, *GCC*, p. 39 n.
[9] Supra, ch. ii (iv).

St Vincent in his *Commonitorium* (Instructions) for distinguishing heresy and true faith, praises indifferently those heroes of the Church who have resisted any new dogma, whether or not they happened to be Roman popes. He seems to be completely unaware that a Roman pontiff is the Supreme Pastor and Teacher of the whole Catholic Church, whose sole authority is all-sufficient to determine, beyond any doubt whatever, what is and what is not the Catholic Faith. He could not have written as he did if he had any inkling of the modern Doctrine of the Papacy.

CHAPTER XLV

The Acacian Schism, A.D. 484

(i) *East and West after Chalcedon*

In the latter part of the century conditions in the Western and Eastern Empires were very different.

In the West, after a succession of weak and short-lived emperors, their office flickered out in 476 when Augustulus yielded to Odeacer, the first of the Barbarian kings, who in turn was conquered and killed by Theodoric the Ostrogoth in 493. We are concerned only with the effect of these events upon the Church. The Roman see came into the power of these kings and their prefects, who supervised the appointment of popes, and adjudicated between rival candidates in a disputed election.[1] On the other hand, the Barbarian rulers (unlike the emperors in the East) interfered remarkably little with doctrine. They were Arians, and secured toleration for the Arian minority of the people, but they refrained from coercing the Catholic majority; under their rule the Roman bishops gradually rose to growing temporal influence.[2]

The state of the Church in the Eastern Empire was pitifully different.

In the first place, the settlement of the faith at Chalcedon failed to retain the general assent of the East. In the patriarchate of Alexandria, it was widely felt that, in Dioscorus, St Cyril had been condemned.[3] Alexandria leaned over more and more to the Monophysite heresy, and ultimately separated from Catholic communion. Very many of the bishops elsewhere in the East, although they disowned Eutyches and were not definitely Monophysite, were unwilling to accept the Chalcedonian definition of the Two Natures. It is fair to recognize that this sprang from mistaken loyalty to St Cyril, the Council of Ephesus, and recoil from the Nestorian heresy. To the uneasy Eastern theologians it seemed that the Two Natures, as defined, verged on the heresy of Nestorius, and robbed the Blessed Virgin of the title of *Theotokos*, the God-bearer.

[1] Gibbon, iv, 208 (ch. xxxix). [2] Milman, i, 283. [3] Hughes, i, 323.

In the second place, all ranks and conditions of men entered fiercely into the subtleties of religious strife. It ran in their blood. Thus in Constantinople, at an earlier time, 'There was not a street-corner in which men were not to be found discussing the most abstruse matters. The money-changer whom you asked for some money spoke to you of the Begotten and the Unbegotten; the baker, instead of telling you the price of bread, declared that the Father is greater than the Son, and that the Son is subject to Him.'[1]

Moreover the complete dominion assumed by the monks over the public mind was a strange phenomenon of the Eastern Church. 'They exercised complete tyranny, not merely over the laity, but over bishops and patriarchs, whose rule they threw off whenever it suited them. They swept the streets of the great cities in armed bodies. Ecclesiastical and civil authority were alike paralysed by combinations of fanatics ready to suffer or to inflict death, utterly unapproachable by reason.'[2]

Finally, the Emperors of the East took a leading part in the theological wars, as much from considerations of government and order as from religious zeal. At their dictation, patriarchs and bishops were elected or deposed, and doctrines were defined. They now inclined towards the Monophysite opinion.

(ii) *Acacius of Constantinople*

Acacius, who became patriarch of Constantinople in 471, stood out for the full Catholic faith of Chalcedon during the short reign of the usurping Emperor Basiliscus. 'Twenty-five years after Chalcedon it was on the Patriarch of Constantinople alone that the defence of orthodoxy depended.'[3] Six years after Zeno had recovered the imperial throne he issued his famous *Henoticon*, or Edict of Union, which is believed to have been written by Acacius. This was an attempt to bring about some sort of concord. It was drawn up as a letter from the emperor to the bishops, and it proclaims his faith to be that of Nicaea, Constantinople, and Ephesus. It condemns Eutyches, and reasserts St Cyril's twelve propositions against Nestorius. Nothing was asserted that a Catholic could not approve. Yet it ignored St Leo's Tome, the text-book of the orthodox; it carefully avoided the expressions 'One' or 'Two' Natures; the only mention of Chalcedon was casual and almost slighting. The attempted compromise really satisfied neither party.

About this time, Zeno had expelled from the see of Alexandria a

[1] Duchesne, *EH*, ii, 456. [2] Milman, i, 317–18. [3] Hughes, i, 326.

Monophysite patriarch, Peter Mongos. An orthodox Egyptian monk, John Talaia, was elected. He notified his accession to the other patriarchates, to Rome, Antioch, and Jerusalem, but not to Constantinople.[1] Acacius became hostile to him. Under his influence, the emperor reinstated Peter Mongos after he had signed the *Henoticon*. Talaia fled and sought refuge at Rome. 'There can be no question that Acacius was very much to blame, and . . . he richly deserved to be deposed and excommunicated.'[2]

Pope Simplicius had urged Acacius to use all his influence to prevent Zeno from acknowledging Peter Mongos, but Acacius ignored his letters. Early in 483, Simplicius died, and was succeeded by Pope Felix III. The hour had now struck for putting into force that sovereign jurisdiction which successive popes had been declaring with growing emphasis. Pope Felix dispatched two bishops as legates to Constantinople, with letters to Acacius and to the emperor, demanding that Acacius should repair to Rome to answer charges brought against him by Talaia.[3] This mission miscarried. The legates were arrested by command of the emperor and robbed of their papers. They were either coaxed or compelled to sign the *Henoticon*, which Felix had condemned out-and-out. They assisted publicly at the liturgy when the name of Peter Mongos was read from the diptychs as lawful bishop of Alexandria.[4]

Next year, when these unhappy legates had returned to Rome, Pope Felix held a synod at which he deposed them from the episcopate and declared Acacius excommunicate, together with all who stood by him, for his connexion with Peter Mongos, and for refusing to defend himself at Rome, although no direct heretical opinion was urged against him. The pope embodied this sentence in a letter to Acacius;[5] he also wrote to the emperor (whom he addressed with great respect and without any suggestion of rebuke), and to the clergy and people of Constantinople.[6]

The pope's messenger failed him again, and did not deliver the sentence of excommunication to Acacius; but one of the 'Sleepless' monks of a monastery[7] loyal to Rome fastened the fatal document to the robe of Acacius as he was about to celebrate mass. Acacius ordered the name of Felix, Bishop of Rome, to be struck off the diptychs of bishops in communion with the East. Except for this, he ignored the pope's letter. 'As the whole of the East that was not Monophysite supported

[1] It is said also (i) that Talaia broke a pledge not to accept election, and (ii) that he obtained it by bribery.

[2] Puller, p. 377.

[3] Epp. i, ii; *PL*, lviii, 893, 899.

[4] Hefele, iv, 30.

[5] Ep. vi; *PL*, lviii, 921.

[6] Epp. ix, xii, x; *PL*, lviii, 934, 969, 936.

[7] So called from its continuous offices.

him, the effect was a definite breach between Rome and the Eastern Church.'[1]

Regarded as a controversy in ecclesiastical law, the matter stood thus:

According to established custom, and any actual canons, the Patriarch of Constantinople might have been validly arraigned before (i) a synod of that patriarchate, or (ii) a full Eastern Council, or of course, (iii) a General or Oecumenical Council. According to the declarations by various popes throughout the century, the pope possessed an overriding sovereign jurisdiction. But this had not been accepted in the East. Except that Rome could certainly exclude Acacius or anyone else from communion with Rome, it seemed to the Church in the East that his excommunication and deposition by the pope was an empty fulmination and a nullity.

(iii) *Schism of the Diptychs*

Acacius died in 489. Pope Felix wrote that he had gone, like Judas, 'to his own place'.[2] In 490 Euphemius became patriarch. He was an orthodox Catholic, 'a courageous and holy man, full of zeal for the Catholic faith, and ready to suffer in its defence'.[3] He cut off communion with Peter Mongos of Alexandria and his successor there, for their anathematizing of the Council of Chalcedon. He replaced on his diptychs the name of Pope Felix, and sent to him the customary synodical letter announcing his accession. Pope Felix insisted, however, as a condition of resuming communion, that Euphemius should remove from the diptychs the names of Acacius and Fragitta.[4] Euphemius firmly refused to do this, on the ground that they had never been validly deposed. There are only sparse records of the dispute, but Euphemius seems to have argued that the alleged deposition was invalid, as the act of only 'one man', viz., the pope.[5]

Constantinople now held explicitly the full doctrine of Chalcedon. Its breach with Rome turned on the single issue of the pope's sovereign jurisdiction. The breach lasted on through the reigns of the next three popes, Gelasius I, Anastasius II, and Symmachus, purely on that issue. Anastasius, indeed, during his short pontificate, made some effort to heal the schism by taking a gentler line with the Easterns; but the more intransigeant of his clergy were indignant, and a legend grew that won for this peace-loving pope a place in the *Inferno* of Dante.[6] The Acacian

[1] Hughes, i, 329. [2] Ep. xiii; *PL*, lviii, 971. [3] Puller, p. 385.
[4] Acacius' first successor, who lived only four months.
[5] Gelas. I P., *Commonitor. ad Faustum*; *PL*, lix, 27. [6] xi, 9 ; Hughes, i, 329.

Schism, thus renewed and prolonged, lasted well into the following century, for thirty-five years altogether.

A. Alexandria and Antioch were under excommunication inasmuch as they had sadly lapsed from the Catholic Faith into the Monophysite heresy. Elsewhere in the East matters stood otherwise. The conduct of Acacius was outrageous, but he and his successors at Constantinople were excommunicated by the pope not for heresy but for their disloyalty to the Supreme Pontiff and disobedience to him. The submission of the Eastern bishops later on, when Constantinople was restored to communion with Rome in 519, recognized this, and admitted that Constantinople had been in the wrong and was solely to blame for its schism.

The action of Pope Felix 'meant, of course, nothing less than a declaration of open war between those who believed in the Church as an independent spiritual society and those who were prepared to acquiesce in its identification with the State. The custodians of the apostolic paradosis and the subjects or upholders of Caesaropapism were now face to face in open conflict.'[1]

N. At this particular juncture, the 'Caesaropapism' of the Byzantine emperors did not favour Rome, but more often its influence was strongly pro-papal, as for instance under the Emperors Marcian, Justinian, Paleologus. Temporary acknowledgements in the East of papal sovereignty (as contrasted with its simple traditional primacy) were due to imperial influence or pressure.

Just as the cautious and limited claims advanced by Pope St Julius in the previous century had been ignored by the East,[2] so now the downright assertions of sovereign authority by the later popes were repudiated in the East. The confident and arrogant claims made by the popes for themselves, supported by vague assertions of imaginary canons, went for nothing.

The aspect in which this deplorable schism was viewed in the East is illustrated by the relations of St Elias, patriarch of Jerusalem, with the other patriarchates. He was an orthodox Catholic who became patriarch in 494. He was in communion with Constantinople, but not with Alexandria or Antioch, which had anathematized the Council of Chalcedon. He was not in communion with Rome. For his constancy to the faith he was banished by a Monophysite emperor. He died in

[1] Jalland, *CP*, p. 319. [2] Supra, ch. xxvi (i).

exile in 518, out of communion with Rome. He was commemorated in the Roman martyrology on 4 July.

The biographer Cyril of Scythopolis (fl. 555) observes that 'The bishops of Rome dissented from those of Byzantium because the name of Acacius, a former bishop of Constantinople, had been inserted in the sacred diptychs, and Acacius had not followed the preciseness of the Romans. . . . Elias was only able to communicate with Euphemius, the Bishop of Byzantium; for, as has been said, the Westerns had separated themselves.'[1]

'It apparently did not occur to St Elias that it would be his duty at all hazards to get into communion with Rome.'[2]

[1] *Vit. S. Sabas*, cap. i. Cardinal Bellarmine describes this writer as a 'most accurate and trustworthy writer of saints' lives', and 'illustrious on account of his sanctity'. See Puller, p. 386.

[2] Puller, p. 387.

CHAPTER XLVI

Survey at A.D. 500

'The fifth is a melancholy century: a century of ruin and of tottering to a fall. The Roman Empire collapses in the West. . . . In the field of doctrine rival schools dash themselves into collision, parties wax hot and engage in strife. . . . Men whose opinions are at bottom the same anathematize each other for modes of expressing them. Rather than yield on the use of words, they set Alexandria in conflict with Constantinople, the East with the West. Christian unity is sacrificed to the unprofitable defence of personal feeling.'[1]

Amid the secular storms and floods, and the downfall of emperors, the Roman see stands firm, though it has its own tribulations. In doctrine, above all, its consistency is in contrast with the subtle variations of controversy in the East. Straightforward and stubborn loyalty to the faith of Nicaea unimpaired, and freedom from some refinements of the Eastern theologians, remain the glory of Rome.

The events and records of the century, as they bear upon our inquiry, are too copious to recapitulate. We may briefly recall the relations of St Augustine and the African Church with the contemporary popes; the Council of Ephesus, and the dominating influence of Pope Celestine; the impressive and commanding figure of Leo the Great, Chalcedon overshadowed by him, as it were; the uncompromising assertion by him and his successors of supreme authority, and its wide recognition in the West, followed by the great schism that implied a flat repudiation of it throughout the East.

The Roman see suffered from its own peculiar troubles. Rome's barbarian kings were Arians. Rome had Arian churches and an Arian bishop. The popes described themselves as 'Bishop of the Catholic Church of Rome' or 'Bishop of the Catholic Church', in order to distinguish themselves from the Arian hierarchy, and the style 'has survived to this day as the consecrated formula for certain official acts'.[2]

[1] Duchesne, *EH*, III, v. [2] Hughes, ii, 71.

Then when Pope Anastasius died, in 498, the deacon Symmachus and the archpriest Lawrence were each elected and consecrated to the see. King Theodoric, to whom both parties appealed, decided in favour of Symmachus. Nevertheless, the too-familiar riots and fatalities followed, and some ten years of local schism.[1]

The rulers of the West are heretic Arians; the emperor in the East is a heretic Monophysite. The Catholics of the East are in schism. 'The century ends with the pope in a curious isolation.'[2] The circumstance most unpropitious for the hopes of unity of the Church in East and West, under the Supreme Pontiff at Rome, was that 'the East was becoming accustomed to live in hostility to Rome'.[3]

A. The authority and supremacy of the Roman pontiff were fully recognized and acknowledged by the General Councils of Ephesus and Chalcedon, and (except for those Churches that had fallen away into heresy) by the consensus of the Church.

'There was much opposition in the East, as there was to so many sound doctrines. This was exaggerated (*a*) by national pride and unwillingness to submit to the West, (*b*) by too much subservience to the civil authorities.'

N. Notwithstanding the conspicuous grandeur and influence of the Roman see, enhanced by the prestige of St Leo the Great, and buttressed by Imperial Rescripts, the new and far-reaching claims of sovereign authority put forward by the fifth-century popes failed to gain the consent of the Church at large.

Throughout most of the century the Western patriarchate was submissive to its head (and in the decrees of the bishops of Rome they did not always distinguish their undisputed patriarchal authority from the universal authority they claimed);[4] but the totalitarian claims of the Roman bishop were rejected by the patriarchates of the East, and they only fostered antagonism, disunity, and schism.

[1] Funk, i, 195; Hughes, ii, 75.
[2] Hughes, ii, 72.
[3] Ibid., i, 330.
[4] Döllinger, *Hist.*, ii, 234.

CHAPTER XLVII

Relevant Evidence of Later Centuries

At this stage it is fitting to recall the purpose of the book, which is to present the great question of the truth of the Doctrine of the Papacy:

(*a*) in an objective statement of the facts of history, together with full quotation of the Saints and Fathers,

(*b*) separately studied, century by century and stage by stage in the history of the Church,

(*c*) followed wherever necessary by two *ex parte* statements of the conflicting inferences and arguments that have been drawn from the facts.

The Doctrine of the Papacy is based upon its 'accordance with the ancient and universal faith of the universal Church . . . faithfully adhering to the tradition received from the beginning of the Christian faith', as the *Dogmatic Constitution* of 1870 expressly declares.

In the light of that definition, the faith and tradition of the earliest centuries must be the primary matter for inquiry, the verdict on which should be of paramount importance, or even decisive. In the foregoing chapters, therefore, the records of the first five centuries have been examined in considerable detail, in an attempt to bring all available evidence under review. As the later centuries pass by, any evidence they afford of the ancient and primitive faith of the Church becomes steadily weaker.

Fourteen centuries and a half of eventful Church history remain. Within the reasonable limits of a volume they cannot be examined in the same detail. For the foregoing reasons, however, this is less needed. Yet some salient events must still be noticed, on two accounts:

(1) It is maintained (A) that any failures during the earlier centuries in the universal recognition of Roman authority and the Doctrine of the Papacy, and any instances of insubordination and schism, are shown

by later history to have been only temporary aberrations from the truth. Later declarations and councils, it is maintained, clearly demonstrate the universal assent of the whole Church, including the East, to the Doctrine of the Papacy. Some of these later declarations are quoted as important in the *Dogmatic Constitution* and the Encyclical 'Satis cognitum'. Contrariwise, it is maintained (N) that there never was genuine and universal assent to that Doctrine, even in the West, and moreover that nothing in later history could contradict or disturb the evidence of the early centuries which (it is maintained) shows plainly that the Doctrine of the Papacy was not part of the ancient faith of the Church.

(2) The history of these fourteen centuries presents some striking features which (although they throw no direct light on the early faith of the Church) have been painfully familiar in controversy concerning the papacy. The arguments that emerge from them may fairly be called 'prejudicial arguments', because, strictly speaking, they do not relate to the question, *What do Holy Scripture and the earliest tradition show to have been the pure and primitive faith of the Church?* Yet these arguments are often used; they sway the minds of many, and they certainly help to fortify the opinions of those whose opinions are already formed. In Chapter II these arguments were briefly referred to as 'self-evident truth', and the 'argument from results'. They are freely invoked by writers on both sides of the controversy.

Thus, the lamentable divisions and schisms of Christendom, when looked at from one point of view, seem clearly to show the monstrous evils that flow from rejection of the Vicar of Christ, and a consequent desertion of the unity of the Church, divinely committed to him. As seen from the opposite side, they seem to be the dreadful consequence of un-Scriptural and unprimitive assertions by the Roman bishops of a divine sovereignty, rightly rejected by half Christendom.

Then again, controversy battens on various unhappy features in the long history of the papacy, such as the doubtful and disputed elections of some popes, the papal schisms, the simoniacal elections to the papal throne, the dark pages in its records when horrible corruption and vice flourished at the very centre, and the cruelties of the Holy Office or Inquisition. There are also the eleven centuries of temporal power, during which the bishop who claimed to speak with the voice of the fisherman-apostle, and as Vicar of Christ Himself, 'entangled himself with secular business' (2 Tim. ii, 4), and was a great earthly potentate, embroiled in the wars and intrigues of a Machiavellian Europe.

Arguments based on historical features such as these are only prejudicial. If the Doctrine of the Papacy was indeed Scriptural, primitive, and universal, if it is true, then, however regrettable some of these things may be, they cannot make truth untrue. If the sovereign supremacy which the Doctrine asserts is of God's purpose and authority, we shall not believe that human frailty or sin have annulled His appointment. On the other hand, such blemishes as these make it appear to some minds 'self-evident' that the Doctrine of the Papacy is of man, not of God.

Mournful facts in papal history cannot therefore be simply ignored. They must be summarized; they need not be recounted exhaustively, nor should anyone wish to dwell upon lapses from Christian holiness, whether within or without the Holy Roman Church.

Several of these historical features must be given separate notice later, but one subject at least may be disposed of here, that of invalid elections to the papal chair. Instances have already been mentioned of disputed elections,[1] often decided by secular rulers; they have resulted in over forty antipopes. This arouses a suspicion that decision may sometimes have been wrong, the antipope rightfully pope. In certain instances there is much doubt; opinions have differed, for example, as to whether Christopher (903–4), Sylvester III (1045) and Benedict X (1058–9) should be counted as popes or antipopes. Such doubts have confused the numbering of the papal names; some names are given alternative numbers.

Simony has been another cause of invalidity; simoniacal elections were canonically invalid. Yet clerical simony was deplorably rife everywhere for centuries, and very many papal elections were undoubtedly tainted by it; it would serve no useful purpose to catalogue them.

The occurrence of invalid papal elections has sometimes been used in argument as if it invalidated the papacy itself and demolished the Doctrine of the Papacy; but does that follow? If a Divine Vicariate was indeed God's plan for His Church, that plan cannot be cancelled by the coming and going of false vicars.

Part Six, which follows here, relates to *The East until Separation from the West.* Even before the final schism, the East had been out of communion with Rome for periods totalling some two-fifths of the whole. That part is therefore chiefly concerned with events and declarations which nevertheless demonstrate (it is said) that the Doctrine of the Papacy was the true faith of the East as well as of the West.

Parts Seven and Eight, on the other hand, relate to the West where

[1] See also Funk, i, 195.

(in any view) the pope indisputably reigned supreme as patriarch. These parts are therefore more concerned with events which (it is said) show that the Doctrine of the Papacy was not known and believed even in the West, and, in addition, some features that have been supposed to discredit it. Consequently a word of warning is needed. Controversy, which names a few out of the long roll of popes, takes no account of the goodness and virtues of so many others, which are recorded in the many volumes of Mgr Mann, Dr Pastor, and other historians.[1] And a distinguished non-Roman scholar has declared that 'The Papacy, taking it all in all, was the greatest potentiality for good that existed at the time [the thirteenth century], or perhaps that has ever existed'.[2]

[1] Useful single volumes are *A History of the Popes*, by F. Hayward (1931), and *Dictionary of the Popes* by D. Attwater (1939).

[2] A. L. Smith, *Church and State, in the Middle Ages* (1913), p. 6. Yet in his view it took 'a downward path' and became 'a tyranny, an incubus and a byword', pp. 7, 57.

PART SIX

THE EAST UNTIL SEPARATION FROM THE WEST

CHAPTER XLVIII

The Formula of Pope Hormisdas, A.D. 519

Long before the final separation of the Latin and Greek Churches, the East had been out of communion with the Roman see for considerable periods of time. Thus in the 462 years between the first and seventh General Councils, the East was out of communion with the pope for 203 years.[1] These spells of schism are said to be the result of Eastern political intransigeance, and certain events and declarations are claimed as evidence that the papacy was acknowledged by the East and was its true belief. One notable event of this kind was the wide acceptance in A.D. 519 of the explicit Formula dictated by Pope Hormisdas.

The Acacian Schism had dragged on for thirty-five years, although a great part of the East, and especially Constantinople, held to the full faith of Chalcedon, but in 518, Justin I (originally a Balkan peasant) became emperor. The power behind the throne was his nephew, the great Justinian, who was a notable administrator and succeeded him in 527. They were orthodox Catholics, and their cherished aim for reasons both of religion and statesmanship was to restore normal relations with Rome. On 7 September 518,[2] Justin, Justinian, and the Oecumenical patriarch,[3] John II, wrote to Pope Hormisdas with this object. The latter had inscribed on his diptychs the names of St Leo and of Pope Hormisdas himself beside that of St Cyril, together with the four councils from Nicaea to Chalcedon.[4]

Next year the Roman legates came to Constantinople as invited; they brought with them the memorable Formula, written by Hormis-

[1] Duchesne, *CS*, pp. 109–10.
[2] A. A. Vasiliev, *Justin the First* (Harvard, 1950), p. 161.
[3] Ibid., p. 146, the first recorded use of this official style. [4] *PL*, lxiii, 429.

das, to be signed by the Eastern bishops who wished to restore communion with Rome; the *Dogmatic Constitution* quotes parts of it as follows:

> The first condition of salvation is to keep the rule of true faith. And inasmuch as the sentence of our Lord Jesus Christ cannot be passed over, in which He says: 'Thou art Peter, and upon this rock I will build My Church', these things which have been said have been proved by effects, for in the Apostolic See the Catholic religion has always been kept immaculate, and her well-known doctrine kept holy. . . . Therefore, desiring not to be in the least degree separated from the faith and doctrine of this See, we hope that we may deserve to be in the one communion which the Apostolic See preaches, in which See is the entire and true solidity of the Christian religion.[1]

The emperor insisted that the patriarch must sign this Formula; he did so unwillingly, addressing it to his 'brother and fellow-minister, Hormisdas', and, as 'a happy expedient to elude the direct recognition of the supremacy of Rome',[2] he embellished it with a remarkable preamble:

> As I have written to you, agreeing in the truth with thee, I too, loving peace, renounce all the heretics repudiated by thee; for I hold the most holy Churches of God, that is yours of Elder Rome and this of New Rome, are one; I define the See of the Apostle Peter and this of the Imperial City to be one See. I assent to all the Acts of the four General Councils, Nicaea, Constantinople, Ephesus, and Chalcedon, touching the faith and constitution of the Church. . . .[3]

The Formula was signed also by the other bishops who were at Constantinople; but things went less smoothly elsewhere. Although 'we do not hear of any difficulty whatever being raised on the score of papal pretensions',[4] there was general unwillingness to anathematize the Catholic bishops who had followed Acacius. There was much resistance, especially at Thessalonica and Ephesus. The emperor deposed the Monophysite patriarch at Antioch. His successor signed, but the monasteries were opposed, and the emperor dissolved them and used his army to enforce acceptance. Palestine was less hostile, but Egypt was so strongly opposed that the emperor refrained from insisting.[5] In 520 he wrote to Pope Hormisdas that 'a considerable part of the Eastern bishops could not be compelled, even by the use of fire and sword, to condemn the names of the bishops who died after Acacius'.[6]

[1] Cp. Labbe, iv, 1486–7; *PL*, lxiii, 444–5; Coll. Avell., no. 159, pp. 608–10; Denzinger, 171–2. See Vasiliev, op cit., pp. 167–8.

[2] Milman, i, 402.

[3] *PL*, lxiii, 443; Coll. Avell., p. 608.

[4] Chapman, *Studies*, p. 216.

[5] Hughes, i, 332.

[6] Coll. Avell., no. 196, 3, p. 655; Mansi, viii, 503–4.

The next patriarch of Constantinople replaced their names on his diptychs; both he and Justinian wrote to Pope Hormisdas of the difficulty of obtaining full acceptance of the Formula. Hormisdas urged the emperor to use force, but gave representative authority to the patriarch that those whom he should admit to communion with Constantinople should be reckoned as in communion with Rome. He included a concise form of belief to be required of them, which refers to the Holy Incarnation but not to the prerogatives of Rome.[1] It seems that restoration of communion may often have been effected on the basis of a Chalcedonian confession without insistence on the terms of the great Formula; but there are no certain records. A contemporary Roman scribe says that after the Acacian Schism the Council of Chalcedon 'was confirmed by the professions of faith of perhaps 2,500 bishops'.[2] Some writers assume that all such bishops signed the Formula.

A. The Formula of Hormisdas 'is perhaps the most symbolic expression of the belief of united East and West in the rightfulness of Papal prerogative'.[3]

N. 'The Formula was probably signed by about half the bishops of one out of the Eastern patriarchates; the patriarch himself refusing to sign it until he had prefixed a preamble which considerably blunted its point. . . . It was pressed upon the East by the emperor with threats of fire and sword; and yet, notwithstanding these threats, it was probably rejected by the majority of the Eastern bishops. Even if . . . it had been signed by them all, . . . it had not been synodically accepted in a free council, and therefore did not bind future generations. Each bishop who freely signed was personally bound by his own signature, but he could not bind his successors.'[4]

[1] Ep. lxxx; *PL*, lxiii, 515; Coll. Avell., no. 237, pp. 728–30.
[2] The deacon Rusticus, *contra Acephalos disputat.*, *PL*, lxvii, 1251. Hefele estimates the whole episcopate at over 6,000, Vasiliev, op. cit., p. 249.
[3] Ryder, p. 12.
[4] Puller, pp. 402–3.

CHAPTER XLIX

Cursing 'The Three Chapters', A.D. 538–55

In a story of ecclesiastical turmoil, which lasted for more than seventeen years, some see only the endeavours of a pope to maintain the decisions of Chalcedon and the prestige accorded to his office in spite of great personal indignities; others see only his vacillations and self-contradictions, and a general disdain for his doctrinal pronouncements.

The great Justinian married Theodora, a woman of base origin. Scandal blackens her former life, but as Empress he doted on her and raised her to equal power with himself; she revelled in dignity and influence. Her intrigues were momentous for the Church, for she favoured the Monophysite faction, unhindered by her Catholic but indulgent husband. She promised a Roman deacon, Vigilius, to use her influence to get him made pope on an understanding that he would support her schemes. At her instigation Pope Silverius was violently deposed and carried to the penal island of Palmeria, where he died. Vigilius was duly made pope. Notwithstanding his inauspicious enthronement, Vigilius eschewed the Monophysite school and disappointed Theodora's expectations.

Next it must be observed that the decisions of Chalcedon were venerated more universally in the West than in the East. Constantinople, however, was fiercely hostile to the Nestorian heresy. A certain bishop, Askidas, drew up a kind of indictment against three long-dead bishops. Theodore of Mopsuestia (†428) was accused, with some justice, as a precursor of that heresy. Certain writings also of Theodoret and Ibas had been of debatable orthodoxy. This made up the so-called 'Three Chapters', and they were cursed and anathematized in a decree published by Justinian in 544.[1]

[1] *PL*, lxix, 30.

Now Theodore had died without reproach in the bosom of the Church. Chalcedon had left his memory in peace, and had also absolved Theodoret and Ibas on their professions of orthodoxy. Consequently this cursing of the Three Chapters was widely regarded as a slur upon the Council of Chalcedon, the very banner of Catholicism.

Justinian coerced the Eastern patriarchs into signing the decree. The West was solid in disapproval. Pope Vigilius refused to sign, and Justinian had him brought to Constantinople. He was received with honour at first, but was kept there for eight years until shortly before he died, some of the time in prison or under arrest. When Vigilius suspended St Menas, the patriarch of Constantinople, from his communion (together with all other bishops who had signed the decree),[1] Menas struck his name out of the diptychs; but communion with Menas was resumed after a few months.

In 548, Pope Vigilius issued his *Judicatum* in which he himself anathematized the Three Chapters.[2] This aroused fresh opposition in the West, notably in Illyria and Dalmatia. At Carthage in 550 a council even 'withdrew Vigilius the Roman bishop from Catholic communion until he should do penance'.[3] Vigilius withdrew his *Judicatum*. After suffering much indignity he took sanctuary in the famous church of St Euphemia at Chalcedon. There, in 552, he published his Encyclical 'Damnatio', pronouncing deposition on Askidas, St Menas, and others. They came to him there and presented a confession of faith in terms described as 'more searching and humiliating than the Formula of Hormisdas',[4] and asking for forgiveness.

In the following year, on 5 May 553, the fifth General Council assembled at Constantinople by Justinian's command, in disregard of Pope Vigilius. Of the 156 bishops who attended, only twenty-five were Westerns.[5] Nine days later, Vigilius issued and sent to Justinian his *Constitutum* on the Three Chapters;[6] it was a carefully qualified anathematization of any writings that favoured Nestorianism. After using the technical word 'define', he closed thus:

> We ordain and decree that it be permitted to no one to write or bring forward or teach, anything contradictory to the contents of this *Constitutum* in regard to the Three Chapters, or, after this declaration, begin a new controversy about them. And if anything has been already done or spoken in regard of the Three Chapters in contradiction of this our ordinance, by

[1] Hefele, iv, 249. [2] Ibid., pp. 254–8; *PL*, lxix, 53.
[3] Victor Tunun., *Chronic.* ad an. 550, *PL*, lxviii, 958; Hefele, iv, 234.
[4] Chapman, *Studies*, p. 232; Hefele, iv, 285–6. [5] Chapman, *Studies*, p. 233.
[6] *PL*, lxix, 67; Hardouin, iii, 10; Hefele, iv, 316, 322–3.

any one whomsoever, this we declare void by authority of the Apostolic See.[1]

The *Constitutum* was addressed formally to the emperor, and may not have been brought officially to the knowledge of the council. At all events, the council, during eight sessions, fully debated the Three Chapters, and what had been decreed or pronounced concerning them. At its final session on 2 June it dealt with them at length in detailed condemnation, with many anathemas, including particular anathemas of Theodore, and of anyone who defends the writings of Theodoret or the letter of Ibas.[2] The pope's name was struck off the diptychs.

After an interval of some months, however, Vigilius gave his assent to the council, completely revoked his *Constitutum*, doctrine, anathemas, and all, and adopted the council's anathemas in its own words. He had been deceived by the devil, he said; there was no shame in confessing and recalling a previous error; Augustine had done this in his *Retractations*.[3]

Next year, Vigilius was allowed to leave Constantinople for Rome, but he died on the way there in Sicily. His deacon, who had attended him and had signed the *Constitutum*, now became Pope Pelagius I, by favour of Justinian, at the price of acknowledging the council; only two bishops could be found to consecrate him.[4]

A. The Easterns humbly acknowledged the pope. 'Each of the chief bishops of the East has to lick the very dust, before a Pope who has been insulted by the civil power, is in sanctuary for safety, has personally no good character, is not obviously in the right, and has already twice contradicted himself. Such is still the prestige in the East of the See of Peter, even in an unworthy representative.'[5]

'Whilst we cannot but regret in Vigilius a course of conduct at once impulsive and vacillating, we should remember that this quondam protegé of the Eutychian Empress Theodora, from the moment that he became the legitimate successor of St Peter, fought pertinaciously for the very shadow of Chalcedon, and for freedom from the uncanonical influence of the Imperial Court.'[6]

N. It was never in doubt or dispute that the Roman bishop was the first of the patriarchs, and was as such entitled to high respect in his office. But the claim to absolute religious subjection under a divinely

[1] *PL*, lxix, 114; Hefele, iv, 322.
[2] Hardouin, iii, 197; Hefele, iv, 326–42.
[3] Ibid., 213–44; Hefele, iv, 347–8.
[4] Hefele, iv, 352.
[5] Chapman, *Studies*, p. 232.
[6] Ryder, p. 70.

appointed Head, which ultimately matured, was not recognized. St Menas, for instance, who retaliated excommunication on the pope of 'Old Rome', could not have dreamed of doing so if he had known and held the Doctrine of the Papacy.

The doctrinal shifts of Pope Vigilius afford one example, out of many papal sayings and doings, hard to reconcile with the declared dogma that 'Blessed Peter lives presides and judges always in his successors the Bishops of the Holy See of Rome'. The fifth General Council contemptuously disregarded his doctrinal declarations.

CHAPTER L

Testimony of Greek Fathers

At least three Eastern saints and bishops, about the middle of the seventh century, made doctrinal statements that showed their belief in the apostolic authority of the bishops of the Roman see as successors and representatives of St Peter. Abbot Chapman has drawn attention to these.[1] St Maximus the Confessor, abbot and martyr, in a letter written perhaps about A.D. 648[2] observes that 'he who anathematizes the See of Rome anathematizes the Catholic Church'. The Church of the Romans is

> the Apostolic See, which from the incarnate Son of God Himself, and also by all holy synods, according to the holy canons and definitions, has received universal and supreme dominion, authority and power, of binding and loosing over all the Churches in the whole world.[3]

Stephen, bishop of Dor in Palestine, attending the Lateran Council of 649, presented a long written address to the pope, St Martin I; in the course of it he connects the 'canonical or apostolical authority' of 'the chair which rules and presides over all' with the three great Petrine texts, Matt. xvi, 19, John xxi, 17, and Luke xxii, 32.[4]

St Sophronius wrote, in his synodic epistle:

> Equally with the holy writings of the all-wise Cyril, I receive . . . the inspired letter of the great and saintly Leo . . . I accept all his letters and teachings as proceeding from the mouth of Peter the Coryphaeus. . . . I recognize the latter as definitions of Peter a former as those of Mark.[5]

It is interesting to notice that he does not confine to Rome the half-

[1] *Honorius*, pp. 18 sq., 21, 40.

[2] Its authenticity has been challenged, no original Greek is extent; see Denny, sects. 652–7.

[3] Mansi, x, 692; it is quoted in 'Satis cognitum'.

[4] Hardouin, iii, 711–14.

[5] Ibid., p. 1287.

poetical, half-mystical notion of the apostolic founder of a see speaking 'through the mouth of' its bishop.

Long before this period, doctrinal statements similar to those of St Maximus and Stephen were familiar at Rome and were not remarkable there. The significance of these declarations is that their authors were Easterns. In the East, although the primacy of the Roman patriarchate and see was never questioned or doubted, the supreme papal authority did not receive recognition as fully as in the West. Apparently none of the Greek Fathers of the first six centuries has been found to connect the position of the Roman pope with the great Petrine texts.[1] These three later saints or bishops, however, had had the advantage of close affiliations with Rome, and had resided there and elsewhere in the West; Bishop Stephen even held a papal commission with vicarial powers.[2]

[1] Chapman, *GCC*, p. 92. [2] *DCB*., iii, 884; iv, 719, 740.

CHAPTER LI

'Peter was speaking through Agatho', A.D. 680

Monothelitism was the last great Christological heresy. The Monophysite heresy had denied that our incarnate Lord continued to possess Two Natures, human and divine. This was a refinement of the former error; it denied that He continued to have Two Wills, human and divine, and asserted that He had only One Will. It gained strength in A.D. 634 when Sergius, patriarch of Jerusalem, discussed the theological problem in a letter to Pope Honorius and asked for his opinion. In the course of a careful theological exposition of these profundities, Honorius unfortunately declared that 'we confess One Will of our Lord Jesus Christ'.[1] It has been strongly argued that 'his meaning was far better than his expression, and that his real mind was confused rather than unorthodox';[2] but the damage was done, and 'without his unfortunate letters in all probability no Monothelite troubles would have disturbed the pages of history'.[3]

Although Monothelitism was definitely condemned by Pope St Martin I and his Lateran Synod in 649, it was still professed by Macarius, the patriarch of Antioch, and some others. Ultimately the emperor convened the sixth General Council, at Constantinople, in A.D. 680 for a 'peaceful Council' with Macarius and others to discover and accept the truth.[4] He asked Pope Agatho to send deputies, and Agatho sent with them a letter to the emperor. St Peter, the pope said, is a co-operator of the emperor in his pious toils, Christ is 'Fellow-ruler[5] of his Christian Empire'. This letter was intended as a counterpart of the celebrated Tome of St Leo;[6] in it the pope refuted Sergius and other 'innovators',

[1] Unam voluntatem fatemur Domini nostri Jesu Christi, Mansi, xi, 539; Denzinger, 251.

[2] Chapman, *Honorius*, p. 7.

[3] Ibid., p. 110.

[4] Mann, I, pt. ii, 37; Hefele, v, 138.

[5] *Corregnator.*

[6] Hefele, v, 142.

but he refrained from mentioning his own predecessor, Pope Honorius. He declared that through the protection of St Peter 'this apostolic Church of his has never been turned aside from the way of truth in any error', and cited St Luke xxii, 31–2—'confirm thy brethren'.[1]

The emperor presided at the council with the papal deputies in the place of honour on his left; it sat for ten months. The Monothelites, headed by Macarius, fought a long losing fight for their heresy. The patriarch and the other bishops fully considered Pope Agatho's letter, with the patristic passages adduced; after comparing them with the patriarchal archives, they declared their complete agreement with the pope's letter and the doctrine of the Two Wills, and they deposed Macarius.

The council proceeded to anathematize and cast out of Holy Church, together with Sergius, Cyrus, and others, 'Honorius who was pope of Old Rome, because in everything he followed the mind of Sergius and confirmed his impious dogmas',[2] and burned his letters as 'profane and soul-destroying'. It adopted a *Symbolum* or confession of faith, clearly defining the Two Wills. This received and embraced the exposition 'made to our most pious and faithful Emperor by the most holy and blessed Agatho, pope of Old Rome . . . and with the synodic epistles written by the blessed Cyril against the reprobate Nestorius'.[3]

At its final session the council delivered an 'acclamatory address' to the emperor, in which the following passage occurs; the two phrases in italics are quoted in the Encyclical 'Satis cognitum' as 'the voice of the Council':

> Through Christ thou reignest benignly, through you Christ loves to bestow peace on His Churches. He Himself has now incited your Serenity and moved you to zeal for the right faith, for the convoking of this oecumenical synod, that He might destroy the novelty of heresy arisen. . . .
>
> The spiritual contest was waged, and the defender of falsity was despoiled: he knew not that he should not obtain a crown of victory but be stripped of the crown of priesthood. *The chief priest of the apostles was fighting on our side; for we have had as ally his follower, the successor to his see*, elucidating by his letter the mystery of the Divine Sacrament. That ancient Roman state presented to thee a confession written by God, and the paper of dogmas has brought day(light) from the vespertinal West. *The paper and the ink were seen, and Peter was speaking through Agatho*, and at the same time thou, pious Emperor, with the all-powerful Fellow-ruler, wast decreeing. Simon (Magus) was falling backwards wallowing,

[1] Hardouin, iii, 1079–1115. [2] Ibid., pp. 1332 sq.; Mansi, xi, 555.
[3] Hardouin, iii, 1398 sq.; Denzinger, 289, 290.

and his image remains in ruins. The true faith rises again and harmony of the people is restored in its rightful grace.[1]

The ejaculations are reported in the acts as usual:

> To the new Constantine the Great, . . . to the new Justinian many years. We are slaves of the Emperor. To the orthodox Pope Agatho of Rome many years, to the orthodox Patriarch George many years. . . . Anathema to the heretic Sergius, to the heretic Cyrus, to the heretic Honorius, . . . and to all heretics and their friends.[2]

The acts were signed by all, and were confirmed in an edict by the emperor.[3]

A. The pervading theme throughout all the proceedings of the council was that it learned the true faith from St Peter and from the pope speaking with his authority, and accordingly declared it under apostolic guidance.

This great council accepted the Doctrine of Papal Infallibility.[4] 'Peter was speaking through Agatho.'

'The earlier council had not gained the assent of all the East, and Pope Agatho thought it best to have it confirmed by an oecumenical council. A Council obviously had a psychological value for winning the East, which the Pope's words alone had not.'

N. According to the Doctrine of the Papacy, the Monothelite heresy had been condemned thirty-one years before by the authoritative and supreme voice of Pope Martin I; but neither the new pope nor anyone else thought of this.

The new 'tome' of Pope Agatho was given approval after examination with the same care with which the doctrine of Macarius was examined and condemned.

In the exuberant language of the Easterns, St Peter was said to speak through Agatho, bishop of Rome, in the same sense in which St Mark, the traditional founder of Alexandria, had been said to speak through its bishop, Cyril.

But St Peter had not spoken through Honorius, bishop of Rome.

[1] Hardouin, iii, pp. 1418, 1422, 1423. [2] Hefele, v, 157, 173.
[3] Ibid., pp. 173–4, 178. [4] Sheehan, i, 188.

CHAPTER LII

Iconoclasm Condemned, A.D. 787

In the eighth century a controversy over Iconoclasm—'the breaking of images'—raged in the East, although it was never a living issue in the West.[1] Successive emperors took it up, and Constantine V, 'Copronymus', enforced it ferociously. Monks and others who withstood him were punished with death or the tearing out of eyes and tongues. One abbot, for example, who refused to trample on religious pictures, was tied in a sack and cast into the sea; another was first tortured and then burned alive. (Such amenities were not peculiar to the Orient; about forty years later, when Pope Constantine II was deposed, he and the chiefs of his party suffered the tearing out of eyes and tongue, of which some died.)[2]

In A.D. 754 this Copronymus had convened a synod of bishops (often called the Mock Council of Constantinople). The patriarchate of Constantinople was then vacant, and there was no representation of the other four patriarchates of Rome, Alexandria, Antioch, and Jerusalem. Although as many as 338 bishops attended, the synod had no real or conciliar authority; but it obediently anathematized the making of any religious pictures. Pope Hadrian I entirely rejected the Mock Council and its doings.

Copronymus was succeeded by a young son, whose mother Irene ruled as guardian. She wrote to Pope Hadrian I that they had resolved to summon an oecumenical synod, and she asked him to come to it or send his representatives. In a long and interesting reply, he insisted that the 'Mock Council' should be anathematized, and quoted the Sylvester-Constantine legend in defending the proper use of religious pictures; he sent two legates. In the list of names the first place is given to them as 'representing the Apostolic See of the pious and most holy arch-

[1] Martin, p. 108.
[2] Mann, I, pt. ii, 372; Duchesne, *BTS*, p. 76; the new pope, Stephen IV, is not blamed, and 'is represented as merely passive'.

bishop of Old Rome, Hadrian'. Then follow Tarasius, 'the pious, and most holy archbishop of the famous New Rome, John and Thomas, deputies of the Apostolic Sees of the Eastern dioceses', etc.[1] Tarasius conducted the proceedings.

The pope's letter to Irene was read to the council (which met at Nicaea) in a Greek version that differed significantly from the Latin, which spoke of 'the Chair of Peter . . . the chief of the apostles to whom power was given . . . his Vicar'. In the Greek version this read: 'the Church of the holy Peter and Paul the chief apostles . . . to whom power was given . . . their vicar'.[2] The legates also agreed to leave out the last part of the letter, in which the pope inveighed against the customary designation of the patriarch of Constantinople as 'Universal Patriarch',[3] and this style, so obnoxious to Rome, continued to be used at the council. Constantinople was always 'difficult'; it had been out of communion with Rome for a great part of the time since the accession of Constantine.[4]

The 'Mock Council' was condemned, 'for it had not the co-operation of the then pope of the Romans or the bishops about him, neither by his representatives nor by his encyclical letters as in the law of councils; nor had it the agreement of the patriarchs of the East, of Alexandria, Antioch, and the Holy City'. Its president, Theodosius of Ephesus, was anathematized.[5] Iconoclasm was condemned, and due reverence of religious images or pictures was declared to be lawful and commendable.

In this Iconoclastic Controversy, Constantinople showed its deplorable submissiveness to Imperial behests. This 'is common to orthodox and heterodox. It might be called Erastianism if such an idea had then come into being.'[6]

[1] Martin, pp. 90–3; Hefele, v, 370.
[2] Hefele, v, 349, 364.
[3] Ibid.; Hardouin, iv, 79–82, 94.
[4] Duchesne, *CS*, pp. 109–10.
[5] Mansi, xii, 1011–16; xiii, 399 (although he apologized abjectly).
[6] Martin, p. 3. In the West also the Church has been afflicted throughout its history by Erastian domination. Thus the Christian emperors exercised great control over the Roman Church. Afterwards, secular control was more political than doctrinal, but the Barbarian kings and the later Italian magnates were able to secure the appointment and deposing of the popes. Down to modern times the Holy Roman Emperors and the Catholic monarchs of Spain, Austria, and France have had great ecclesiastical power; this remained effective in the eighteenth century (see Mr Douglas Woodruff at pp. 10, 14 of his introduction to Lord Acton's *Essays on Church and State* (1952)). As recently as 1903 the election of Cardinal Rampolla by the Sacred College of Cardinals was successfully vetoed by Austria, and Cardinal Sarto was elected instead; as Pope Pius X he ended the veto for the future by the Bull 'Commissum Nobis', 20 January 1904. (*Enc. Brit.* 11th ed., vi 829; 1948 ed., vi, 203).

No Westerns but the two papal legates attended the council; 'the plain fact was that Western Europe had no concern in the matter at issue. The Pope's interest in the Council centred not on doctrine but on prerogative and temporalities.'[1] He had demanded the restoration to Rome of Southern Italy and Illyricum, which had been transferred to the see of Constantinople fifty-five years before by the Emperor Leo III. Because these just claims were not conceded by Irene, he sent her no formal confirmation; however he received the council and ordered the acts to be translated into Latin.[2]

A. The rejection by Pope Hadrian I of the acts of the 'Mock Council' of Constantinople exemplifies 'the office of the Roman pontiffs to ratify or to reject the decrees of Councils'.[3]

N. It was the seventh General Council, at Nicaea, that rejected the 'Mock Council' (which clearly had no general conciliar authority).

[1] Martin, p. 223.
[2] Mann, I, pt. ii, 452.
[3] Encyc. 'Satis cogn.'

CHAPTER LIII

The Photian Schism, A.D. 857–79

Photius became patriarch of Constantinople in the reign of Michael III, after the deposition, or resignation,[1] of the previous patriarch, Ignatius. Photius was a man of outstanding learning, and 'a saint and hero in the eyes of the Christian East'. The West, on the contrary, branded him as a great schismatic, fraudulent and unscrupulous, 'blinded by pride and lust for power'.[2] He sent the usual 'systatic letter' to Rome and Antioch, declaring his election and confession of faith.[3]

Pope Nicholas the Great dominated the West, where he made wicked kings tremble for their sins, and crushed their obsequious prelates. He sent two legates *a latere*[4] to Constantinople to inquire into the election of Photius. A synod held there in 861 acknowledged Photius as lawful patriarch, with the legates' consent (it is said they were bribed); but a Roman synod of 863 under Pope Nicholas declared Ignatius restored and Photius deposed and anathematized.

The Emperor Michael, unlike many of the Eastern emperors, was hostile to Rome, and he wrote to the pope a letter 'breathing contempt for pontifical authority, insulting the Pope's person and government'.[5] The pope wrote a devastating reply, a few passages from which will indicate the lofty stand he took; the third of these is quoted in the *Dogmatic Constitution* of 1870

> The privileges of this See are perpetual; they were planted and rooted by God Himself, . . . established by the very mouth of Jesus Christ Himself. . . .
>
> Of blessed Peter and Paul we were born the sons, and, although very

[1] Dvornik, pp. 42–8. [2] Ibid., pp. 1, 4; Mann, iii, 196, 217, 255–7.
[3] Every, p. 119.
[4] This is said to be the first use of the expression *a latere*, Roy, p. 54; but see the African bishops' letter to Pope Celestine I, supra, ch. xxxvii (v).
[5] Ibid., p. 55.

> inferior to them in merits, have been established as princes over all the earth, that is, over the Church, for the Church is the earth. . . .
>
> A judgement of the Apostolic See cannot be called in question by any one, nor is it lawful to any one to judge its judgements. . . .
>
> Neither the Council of Nicaea nor any other synod ever gave a single privilege to the Church of Rome. . . .
>
> It is plainly proved that the secular power can neither bind nor loose the Roman Pontiff, whom, as is well known, the pious Emperor Constantine, as we have said before, called God; and that God cannot be judged of men is manifest.[1]

A synod at Constantinople in 867, under Photius, in the presence of the emperor, excommunicated the pope;[2] but later in that year Michael was murdered and succeeded by his Armenian groom, Basil; he deposed Photius and reinstated Ignatius. Afterwards a Roman synod anathematized Photius for having dared to judge a pope, and Pope Hadrian II declared: 'We read that the Roman Pontiff has pronounced judgements on the prelates of all the Churches; we do not read that anybody has pronounced judgement on him.'[3] (This is quoted in the Encyclical 'Satis cognitum').

Later again in 869, the 'Anti-Photian Council' was held at Constantinople. In later times it was reckoned (in the West only) as the eighth General Council). It opened with the three papal legates and fourteen other bishops, but 107 were present before the end.[4] The legates insisted on assent to the Roman decisions. After seven sessions of debate, Photius refused to sign his own condemnation, and, on the legates' proposal, he was excommunicated 'because he was disobedient and resisted this holy and universal council'.[5] For some years after this a curious situation existed; there is evidence that Ignatius and Photius were on friendly terms, and the clergy 'with few exceptions, remained loyal to Photius'.[6] Ignatius died eight years later and Photius was restored. The new pope, John VIII, now decided to recognize him for reasons of policy, and 'to stave off as long as possible the inevitable schism between East and West'.[7] 'By this act of mercy and policy John VIII obtained the cession of Bulgaria to the Roman Patriarchate.'[8]

The wheel turned again. At the 'Photian Council', the fifth of Constantinople, in 879, at least 350 bishops attended, and the patriarchs of Alexandria, Antioch, and Jerusalem wrote repudiating their former

[1] Ep. lxxxvi; *PL*, cxix, 948–9, 954, 960–1; Roy, pp. 65–6, 154, 158; the statement about Constantine appears to be an 'amplification of a legend mentioned by Rufinus'.

[2] Mann, iii, 65–6.

[3] Mansi, xvi, 126; Dvornik, p. 142.

[4] Mann, iii, 201 sq.; Dvornik, p. 146.

[5] Dvornik, p. 149.

[6] Ibid. pp. 162–72.

[7] Mann, iii, 265.

[8] Chapman, *FEGC*, p. 82.

legates and disowning all proceedings against Photius. It anathematized the 'Anti-Photian Council', and the Roman legates here signed first, explicitly 'in accordance with the mandate, order and agreement' of the pope.[1] Some have supposed that the pope disowned his legates and condemned Photius afresh, but the evidence does not support this.[2] Pope Stephen VI sent to Photius his 'systatic letter'[3] and recognized him until he was imperially deposed a second time in 786, a few years before he died.

'The cleft was never completely healed after Photius.'[4] It has been usual in the West to attribute these lamentable events to the vicious ambition of Photius. Dr Dvornik's recent important work should be studied before passing judgement against him.[5]

There is a minor question as to whether the 'Anti-Photian Council' of 869 ought to be called the eighth General Council. It was not so reckoned by popes of the next three centuries,[6] and it has never been so reckoned in the East. It gained entry to the Western list of general councils because of the use of one of its canons in the Investiture Controversy[7] in the eleventh century; yet the Council of Florence in 1439 was also called the eighth General Council.[8]

A. 'Nationalist and political jealousy made it harder for Constantinople to accept papal primacy than any other part of the Church.'

The history of the Photian Schism supplies these two authoritative declarations of doctrine by Popes St Nicholas I and Hadrian II:

'A judgement of the Apostolic See cannot be called in question by any one nor is it lawful to any one to judge its judgement.'[9]

'We read that the Roman Pontiff has pronounced judgement on the prelates of all the Churches; we do not read that anybody has pronounced sentence on him.'[10]

[1] Mansi, xvii, 507; Dvornik, pp. 193–4.

[2] Mann, iii, 271–3; Dvornik, pp. 205–19; Jalland, *CP*, p. 386.

[3] Ibid., 357; Dvornik, pp. 205–19; Every, p. 142.

[4] Fortescue, *OEC*, p. 167. 'From Photius onwards the union is never cordial and is but occasional', Chapman, *FEGC*, p. 7.

[5] See the *Eastern Churches Quarterly*, vol. viii, no. 2, April-June 1949.

[6] Such as Marinus II (942–5) and Leo IX (1049–54); *PL*, cxxxiii, 874–5; cxliii, 772–3; Dvornik, pp. 314–19.

[7] Jalland, *CP*, pp. 387–8; Every, p. 131; Dvornik, pp. 319 sq. That was a long struggle from 1075 to 1122 between the German Kings Henry IV and V and the contemporary popes, regarding the right of appointing bishops, who had now become territorial magnates. The Diet of Worms in 1122 settled it by a compromise.

[8] Dr Dvornik examines this question at length.

[9] *Dogm. Const.* cap. iii.

[10] Encyc. 'Satis cogn.'

N. Assertions such as these by the later popes had become familiar. History shows that they had no genuine warrant in antiquity and the early Church. There is much that Pope Hadrian II 'did not read', for example, the history of his predecessors Popes Vigilius and Honorius.

The ancient customary primacy of the Roman bishop—*primus inter pares*—was never disputed. But Constantinople and the East constantly resisted his growing claims to a semi-divine sovereignty. They were repeatedly out of communion with Rome for long periods without any thought that they were 'cut off from the Church'.

From the sorry story of the Photian Schism stands out the fact that the modern Doctrine of the Papacy was always far from universal acceptance. Indeed, it was the overweening claims of the popes to sovereignty that ultimately divided East and West.

CHAPTER LIV

Separation of the Greek from the Latin Church, A.D. 1054

To date the separation of East and West exactly in 1054, and to attribute it simply to the Roman addition to the Creed of 'and from the Son', the *Filioque* clause, would be misleading. Since the conversion of Constantine, Constantinople had been only intermittently in communion with Rome; out of the 464 years before the Council of Nicaea (II) in the eighth century, they had been out of communion for 203,[1] and in the next century came the Photian Schism. As recently as 1009, too, the patriarch of Constantinople had struck off his diptychs a pope who pronounced it error to deny the *Filioque* doctrine.[2]

There was friction over territorial jurisdiction; both Rome and Constantinople claimed Bulgaria. Illyricum too and Southern Italy had been taken from Rome and transferred to Constantinople by the Emperor Leo III in 732. Pope Hadrian I in 787 protested against this robbery, and also against intrusion by Constantinople by consecrating bishops in his own metropolitan province.[3]

Then irreconcilable notions of the Roman primacy underlay all the disagreements. It was never doubtful that Rome was the first of the patriarchates and enjoyed a primacy or 'firstness' among them. Moreover its bishop had for many centuries been regarded as a particular successor of St Peter. But Rome interpreted its primacy in a sovereign and autocratic sense; although Easterns sometimes gave this lip-service, their actions continually belied it.

Constantinople was recalcitrant. In the Western view, this was caused

[1] Duchesne, *CS*, pp. 109–10.

[2] Mann, iv, 130; Every, p. 149.

[3] Every, p. 112.

by the pride and ambition of Eastern patriarchs; they sinned against the light; they rebelled against the pontiff whom they knew was their master. Actually there are indications that Rome's conception of its sovereignty was not fully grasped even by those of the Easterns who were well-affected towards Rome. In the Eastern understanding the Church was constituted in five patriarchates, Rome being only the first of the five. 'The five patriarchates are the heads of the Church . . . when two fall out they run to three; when three fall out they run to two; but when four have fallen, one which remains in Christ . . . calls back again the remaining body of the Church.' 'By the protection of our true God, the five patriarchates of the world hold the right view, and therefore whatsoever they judge, you must receive.'[1] After Rome had begun to use the *pallium* as a symbol of jurisdiction given by the pope to his own archbishops, the patriarch St Ignatius naïvely sent one as a mark of honour to Pope Leo IV (who politely declined the gift).[2]

Some of the open and declared differences that led up to the final breach do not now seem vital. Photius had numbered them in his indictment of Rome in the previous century. The Latins consecrate unleavened bread, *azymes*; they fast on Saturdays; they do not begin Lent on Quinquagesima Monday; their priests shave their beards; they despise married clergy, and thus show infection from the Manichaean heresy. Finally, they have changed and corrupted the Creed by adding to it the *Filioque*.[3] The same charges were brought out again in 1054.[4]

Something more must be said of the *Filioque* addition. The doctrine it expressed was widespread in the West. It was affirmed by a canon of the Council of Toledo in 589, and by a synod at Canterbury in 680.[5] When it was first included in the Creed is uncertain, but after two Frankish synods, shortly before and after 800, had adopted it, Pope St Leo III in 809 charitably forbade its introduction in order to avoid giving scandal to the Greeks, and he set up silver tablets in St Peter's engraved with the Creed without the addition.[6] Yet the *Filioque* remained in use, and after the bitter attacks of Photius, Pope Benedict VIII added it to the Creed. The Easterns said that Rome fell under the anathema of the Council of Ephesus (A.D. 431) against any departure from the Nicene Creed. They denied and resented the implied claim of a Western and Roman right to alter the oecumenical Creed without the consent of the East. In a later century, a peacefully minded Greek

[1] Bahanes, and the Emperor Basil at the Anti-Photian Council; Mansi, xvi, 140–1, 86–7.
[2] Every, p. 118. [3] Fortescue, *OEC*, p. 153. [4] Ibid., p. 178; Every, p. 166.
[5] Hardouin, iii, 1038; Mansi, xi, 175. [6] *Liber Pont.*, ii, 26; Funk, i, 295.

Franciscan unsuccessfully urged that the Latins should remove the addition, and that the Greeks should accept the reasons given by the Latins for inserting it; he added that those who fought for the opposing views had become somewhat deranged by over-scrutiny of the mysteries of God.[1]

It is right to notice that Rome did not call upon the Easterns to add the *Filioque* in their own use, and Pope Leo let it be known that, although the Latins preferred to use Azyme, they did not mean to disparage the Eastern use of leaven.[2] (It was alleged, however, that they had refused communion to bearded priests from the East.)

The actual events of 1054 can be told shortly. The Emperor Constantine IX, who wanted military help from the West, was anxious to keep on good terms with the Latins and was strongly against the schism.[3] Dr Fortescue considers that the patriarch, Michael Cerularius, 'must have been determined from the beginning on war with Rome on any or no pretext'.[4] At all events, Cerularius closed the Latin churches in Constantinople and told all the Latins there to stop being 'Azymites' and to use the Byzantine rite. Moreover, the Bulgarian archbishop wrote a stinging letter to the West, rubbing in the Eastern charges. It was meant for the eye of Pope Leo, who sent a reply which he addressed also to Cerularius; in it 'he most emphatically asserts the primacy of his see . . . quotes all the Petrine texts, and also makes much of the *Donatio Constantini*'.[5] He sent three legates to Constantinople, who 'made it plain to the haughty patriarch that they had come in the name of a superior to receive the submission of a subordinate'.[6] News arrived of the death of Pope Leo. The legates waited a little, and then while the papal see was still vacant drew up a Bull on their own responsibility excommunicating the patriarch and laid it on the altar of St Sophia.[7] This aroused such general indignation that the emperor had to permit a solemn anathema to be published against the Roman see.

All the East was involved. Cerularius desired the other Catholic Churches to join with Constantinople in breaking off communion with Rome. As to Alexandria and Jerusalem, enfeebled under Moslem rule, 'the assumption that they followed Constantinople into schism seems to rest more on evidence of their continued communion with Constantinople than any record of their breach with the West'.[8] Peter of Antioch would not at first strike off the pope's name, and perhaps he never did so. Dr Fortescue thus summarizes the general Eastern sequel:

[1] Mann, xv, 406–7. [2] Fortescue, *OEC*, p. 189. [3] Ibid., pp. 175–6.
[4] Ibid., p. 177. [5] Ibid., p. 180; Ep. c; *PL*, cxliii, 744–69.
[6] Mann, vi, 150. [7] Jalland, *CP*, p. 400. [8] Every, p. 158.

> The matter of the schism of the East is not so simple as many people think. Indeed it is very difficult to say when the Orthodox, outside Constantinople, became schismatics. . . . It is only because, eventually, the other Eastern Patriarchs and bishops took the side of Constantinople, remained in communion with the Œcumenical Patriarch, that they, too, shared his state of schism. But when did they do so? . . . The final test would be when they removed the name of the Pope from their diptychs. But we do not know when this happened.[1]

Whether immediately, or more deliberately, the whole Catholic East rejected the papal claims and abandoned communion with Rome. Strangely enough, on the Roman side, the excommunication stands on the Bull of the legates; it has never been given formal papal ratification.[2]

A. 'The story of the final schism in the eleventh century is a much worse case of Byzantine arrogance and intolerance than the story of Photius.'[3]

'The floodgates of racial hatred had been opened; and neither the wisdom of the learned nor the wishes of the moderate could stem the torrent . . . the die had been irretrievably cast, and it was the hand of Michael Cerularius which had finally thrown it.'[4]

'His love of power made him utterly unscrupulous as to the means he used to gain his ends . . . his ultimate object in throwing off all subjection to Rome, and in making himself the untrammelled ruler of the Greek Church, was the attainment of absolute power. It was with that object in view that he deliberately began a quarrel with the Pope.'[5]

Though the multitudes of people in the East gradually fell in with the view of their leaders, it cannot be said (any more than in England at the Reformation) that they had not previously believed in the Roman supremacy.

N. The hatred for the papal claims by the mass of the people in the East is notorious. It was chiefly through subservience of some leaders to imperial pressure that lip-service was occasionally paid to Rome.

In Eastern eyes, perhaps, the arrogance and intolerance seemed to be quite as much Roman as Byzantine. Moreover it is possible that Western writers have painted Michael Cerularius black unfairly. These are only side-issues. The schism was not a rebellion of one man, even supposing that he were ambitious. Thousands of bishops and priests, and millions of devout Christians who firmly held the Creed of Nicaea, rejected as

[1] Fortescue, *UOC*, pp. 189–90.
[2] Fortescue, *OEC*, p. 185; Jalland, *CP*, pp. 400–1; Every, p. 173.
[3] Ibid., p. 197. [4] Mann, vi, 162. [5] Ibid., p. 142.

firmly the 'subjection to the Roman Pontiff' which (it is claimed) 'for every human creature is altogether necessary to salvation';[1] they repudiated the sovereign jurisdiction to which all the faithful are bound to submit, according to 'the teaching of Catholic truth, from which no one can deviate without loss of faith and of salvation'.[2]

The schism demonstrates that the Eastern Catholics, in their millions, did not hold the modern Doctrine of the Papacy, and that it had never become 'the universal faith of the universal Church'.

[1] Pope Boniface VIII, Bull 'Unam Sanctam'. [2] *Dogm. Const.*, cap. iii.

CHAPTER LV

Reunion Attempted

(i) *Michael Paleologus*, A.D. 1274

Two Byzantine emperors strove for reunion of the East with Rome, but their efforts came to naught.

A century and a half after the great Schism, Constantinople had been given grievous cause for bitterness against the West. When the Fourth Crusade sailed from Venice to recover the Holy Sepulchre, it never reached the Holy Land. Instead, it attacked and conquered Constantinople, sacking the city in 1204 with frightful outrage and massacre.[1] Constantinople was put under a Latin emperor and a Latin patriarch; the Greeks were treated contemptuously as a conquered people, their churches were seized and their Orthodox worship was suppressed. The Greek rulers of Constantinople were a 'government in exile' beyond the Bosphorus until, after more than half a century, the Latin Empire at Constantinople weakened and was evicted. The Latin emperor Baldwin II fled; the Greek Paleologus became emperor as Michael VIII.

Notwithstanding these calamities, the popes never ceased trying to bring the Greeks back to unity with the Latin Church; while, on the other hand, the Greek emperors were equally anxious for this because of their political need. The Saracen Empire was spreading. Paleologus very soon wrote on the subject of ecclesiastical union[2] to Pope Urban IV, who at first supported Baldwin, but 'was more anxious for the reunion of the Greek Church than for the recapture of Constantinople';[3] he wrote to Paleologus in 1263 strongly urging the claims of Rome to submission of the East.[4] The next pope, Clement IV, continued these efforts, and in another long letter to Paleologus he proposed a Formula for his acceptance:

[1] Gibbon, vi, 30 (ch. lx); Milman, v, 347–53; *PL*, ccxv, 701; Kidd, *DI*, iii, 152.
[2] Mann, xv, 391 n. 1. [3] Ibid., pp. 181, 183. [4] Raynaldus, iii, 109.

> The Holy Roman Church has obtained the full primacy and principality over the universal Catholic Church, which it truly and humbly acknowledges to have received, with the fullness of power, from the Lord Himself in Blessed Peter, the prince or head of the Apostles, whose successor the Roman Pontiff is, and as the Apostolic See is bound before all others to defend the truth of faith, so also, if any questions should arise about faith, they must be determined by its judgement.[1]

These efforts seemed to be crowned with success, for Paleologus sent his Nuncio, the 'Logothete' George Acropolita, to the Council of Lyons in 1274 with a letter in which he accepted the Formula (which is now quoted in the *Dogmatic Constitution* and in the Encyclical 'Satis cognitum'). The Nuncio also presented a letter from prelates who supported the emperor, professing their submission to Rome. He and the other Greeks of the deputation made full submission to the pope. They also agreed to the addition of the *Filioque* to the Creed, and they sang it thrice 'with solemnity and devotion'.

The terms of the reunion, now apparently achieved, were (i) that the pope, along with the other four patriarchs, should be commemorated in the diptychs, (ii) that all should have the right of appeal to Rome, and (iii) that the pope should have the primacy in everything.[2]

The patriarch of Constantinople, Joseph, was recalcitrant and was deposed; the mass of the Greeks openly rebelled against the emperor. He took violent and cruel measures to enforce uniformity, but he was execrated as a heretic and an apostate.[3]

It became clear at Rome that many who had expressed adhesion to the union had given only verbal acceptance, and that only political expediency had influenced the emperor.[4] 'The union was really only a nuisance to be borne for political reasons.'[5] So in 1281 Pope Martin IV excommunicated and anathematized Paleologus, who died soon afterwards, execrated generally and even denied Christian burial. By the collapse of this precarious union 'the schism was aggravated, and the division rendered more profound'.[6]

A. The clear and definite confession of faith in the primacy and authority of the Apostolic See which has been quoted was solemnly declared, not only by the Greek emperor but by a representative body of Eastern archbishops and bishops, at the great Council of Lyons. The reunion of the Greeks with the Holy See was complete, as far as certain of their temporal and spiritual authorities were concerned.[7] It was after-

[1] Raynaldus, p. 230; Mann, xv, 401–2, 416.
[2] Mann, xv, 422 n. 7, 423.
[3] Ibid., p. 422; J. C. Robertson, *Hist. of the Christian Church* (1866), iii, 480.
[4] Mann, xv, 443.
[5] Fortescue, *OEC*, p. 205.
[6] Mann, xv, 446.
[7] Ibid., pp. 422–3.

wards broken only through their treacherous insincerity and shameless disregard of their solemn oaths.

N. 'It is plain (1) that the authority of the Easterns cannot be claimed for the Formula. It was signed by the Eastern emperor for political reasons, and its connexion with the Greeks was solely erastian. (2) The Greeks resisted any attempt to force them to act in accordance with it, repudiating the claims embodied in it, even at the cost of much danger to themselves. (3) The Formula itself is purely "Roman" in its origin, in no way representing the traditional attitude of the East towards Rome at the time when it was sent to the Emperor by Pope Clement IV.'[1]

(ii) *The Council of Florence*, A.D. 1439

The last hopeful effort to reunite the East and West proved to be 'almost an exact repetition of the union effort 165 years earlier by Michael VIII at the Council of Lyons'. 'Again the Eastern Empire is in the direst distress from the Turks, again the Emperor wants union with the Latins for purely political reasons—that they may come and fight for him—and again the union is hated and soon denounced by the Byzantines.' The emperor at Constantinople now was another Paleologus, John VII, a descendant of Michael VIII. His empire was in still more desperate straits. The Turkish hordes had already overwhelmed Macedonia, Thessaly, Thrace, Bulgaria, and Servia, as well as all Asia Minor.[2]

This time the emperor himself set sail with a distinguished team of negotiators consisting of his brother the patriarch, legates from the patriarchs of Alexandria, Antioch, and Jerusalem, and twenty-two other bishops. They landed at Venice in 1438 and attended the council over which the pope, Eugenius IV, was presiding. The main differences concerned the *Filioque*, Azyme bread at Mass, Purgatory, and the papal supremacy. On the first of these, agreement was reached after prolonged discussions. The Latins disavowed an erroneous sense that the Greeks had attached to the *Filioque*; the Greeks were not asked to adopt the clause in their own use. It was agreed too that the Eucharist is valid whether leavened or unleavened bread is used.

The worst obstacle was the papal supremacy, and at one juncture, negotiations seemed about to be broken off. But great pressure was brought to bear upon the Greeks;[3] the emperor steadily pressed for

[1] Denny, sect. 821. [2] Fortescue, *OEC*, pp. 208, 210, 220.
[3] Ibid., pp. 212, 334, 336; Creighton, ii, 348.

union; the pope undertook to supply him with 300 soldiers and two galleys for the defence of Constantinople and to preach a crusade and rouse the West to help the Greeks.

On 6 July 1439, the Union Decree, beginning 'Let the heavens rejoice and the earth be glad'—*Laetentur coeli*—was signed by 115 Latins and by the emperor and twenty-four Greeks, mostly metropolitans. The Latin version[1] (partly quoted in the *Dogmatic Constitution* and the Encyclical 'Satis cognitum') declares that:

> We define that the holy apostolic see and the Roman pontiff hold the primacy throughout the whole world, and that the same Roman pontiff is the successor of blessed Peter, the prince of the apostles, and the true vicar of Christ, the head of the whole Church, and the father and teacher of all Christians; and that full power was given to him in blessed Peter, by our Lord Jesus Christ, to feed, rule, and govern the universal Church, [as is also contained in the acts] of the oecumenical councils and in the sacred canons; renewing moreover, the order handed down in the canons of the other venerable patriarchs; that the patriarch of Constantinople be second after the most holy Roman pontiff, of Alexandria the third, of Antioch the fourth and Jerusalem fifth: saving all their rights and privileges.

(The Greek text of the clause in brackets ran differently: 'according to that manner that is determined in the acts', etc., as if the papal powers were measured by the councils and canons.)[2]

Only one of the Greeks, Archbishop Mark of Ephesus, refused to sign, although most of the others (according to the Greek historian, Syropulus) did so unwillingly, under cajolery and coercion; but as soon as the emperor and his followers returned to Constantinople all was in uproar against them. Mark became a hero. The emperor was powerless. The decree and its signatories were almost everywhere repudiated. The patriarchs of Alexandria, Antioch, and Jerusalem condemned the council as a council of robbers. At Constantinople, clergy and people were 'filled with fanatical hatred against the West'.[3]

For thirteen years the emperors did not dare to publish the Union Decree officially. In the very last extremity of the Greek Empire it was signed again in Constantinople in December 1452, amid general abhorrence,[4] but in May 1453, Sultan Mahomet II stormed Constantinople; massacre and destruction followed.[5] So ended the Greek Empire, and so failed the last near approach to a reconciliation of the East with Rome. (Yet before the Council of Florence had ended, it achieved the re-

[1] Labbe, i, 419; Mansi, xxxi, 1031–4; Denzinger, 694; Mirbt, no. 400, pp. 2334–.
[2] See Butler, ii, 117–18, referring to Janus, *Pope and Council*, p. 326.
[3] Funk, ii, 23. [4] Hughes, iii, 352. [5] Pears, p. 364.

conciliation of some Armenians, Chaldeans and Maronites of Lebanon,[1] and there are Uniat Churches in the East which remain to this day united with Rome.)

A. 'It was not till after the fall of Constantinople that the union was formally repudiated by the Byzantine Church. . . . During the thirty-three years then between 1439 and 1472, the Byzantine Church was, at any rate officially, in communion with the Holy See. But the people of the city, now as wildly fanatical and intolerant as the last remnant of a lost cause is (witness the Jews of Jerusalem during the siege), had said: rather the Sultan's turban than the Pope's tiara; and they have had their wish.'[2]

N. In qualifying the terms of the decree by the reference to the oecumenical councils (from which the Greeks specifically excluded the Anti-Photian Council of 869), and by the saving of 'all their rights and privileges', the Greeks strove desperately to limit the extent of their submission. Even so, had there been a true consent of the East, the admission of the papal claims would have been substantial. In fact, however, imperial pressure and the hopeless circumstances of the Greeks extorted a profession of agreement that was soon shown to be illusory, and was repudiated by the East at large.

[1] Funk, ii, 21; Fortescue, *OEC*, p. 220.

[2] Fortescue, *OEC*, p. 218.

PART SEVEN

THE WEST UNTIL SEPARATION OF THE EAST, A.D. 1054

CHAPTER LVI

Gregory the Great, A.D. 590-604

St Gregory I was a very great and good pope; his missionary zeal evangelized Saxon England. He fully maintained the authority of Rome as it was handed on from his predecessors; the Encyclical 'Satis cognitum' quotes several pronouncements made by him. The following passages are quoted by Mr Allnatt:

> I know not what bishop is not subject to the Apostolic See if any fault is found in bishops.[1]
>
> As to the Church of Constantinople, who doubts that it is subject to the Apostolic See? Because this is constantly declared both by the most pious Emperor and by our brother the Bishop of that city.[2]

In asserting his authority he cites 'the canons',[3] as the popes were now accustomed to do. Although he observes that St Paul 'was made the head of the nations because he obtained the primacy (*primatum*) of the whole Church',[4] he took remarkable exception to the title or epithet of 'universal', whether applied to himself or another, as a 'diabolical usurpation'.[5] The Greek equivalent of universal is 'oecumenical', and that style had by long custom been bestowed on the patriarchs of Constantinople.[6]

Pope Gregory wrote to John, its contemporary patriarch, 'By this abominable style the Church is split asunder, the hearts of all the

[1] Allnatt, p. 87; Lib. ix, Ep. lix; *PL*, lxxvii, 996.
[2] Ibid., Ep. lxxvii; *PL*, lxxvii, 957.
[3] Lib. v, Ep. xx; Lib. vi, Ep. xxiv; *PL*, lxxvii, 746, 814.
[4] Expos. in I Reg. Lib. iv, cap v, 28; *PL*, lxxix, 303.
[5] Lib. v, Ep. xliii; *PL*, lxxvii, 744.
[6] Hefele, iv, 117, 119, 198; Hardouin, ii, 1254, 1322, 1362; Novellae, iii, v, vi, vii, xvi, xliii; Corpus J. C., ii, 18 sq. But to the Easterns its meaning was more nearly 'cosmopolitan'. They gave the name both to Rome and Constantinople without conscious inconsistency, and St Cyprian could be called 'an oecumenical bishop' without suggesting any rivalry of jurisdictions (Newman *Development* (1845 ed.), p. 266, see also Hefele, v, 352 n.).

brethren are provoked to offence . . . you try to take from all that which you wish to usurp for yourself'.[1] To others he writes, 'Whoever wishes to be called universal priest exceeds Antichrist in his pride'.[2] 'This is done to the injury and splitting asunder of the whole Church; for if, as he thinks, one is universal, it remains that you are not bishops.'[3] 'If one patriarch is called universal, the name of patriarch is taken from the others.'[4] A letter from him to the emperor is quoted in 'Satis cognitum':

> It is evident to all who know the Gospel that the charge of the whole Church was committed to St Peter the Apostle and Prince of all the Apostles, by the voice of the Lord. . . . Behold he hath received the keys of the heavenly kingdom; the care of the whole Church is committed to him, the power of binding and loosing is conferred upon him: the care of the whole Church is confided to him, and yet he is not called Universal Apostle. And my most holy fellow-priest John endeavours to be called Universal Bishop! I am forced to cry out and say, 'O tempora!, O mores!'[5]

The patriarch of Alexandria rashly addressed Gregory himself as 'Universal Pope', and the pope's reply is quoted in the *Dogmatic Constitution*:

> I beg your holiness to do so no more, because whatever is given to another beyond reason is so much taken from yourself. It is not in appellations but in character that I wish to advance. Nor do I deem that an honour by which my brethren lose their honour For my honour is the honour of the Universal Church. Then am I truly honoured when to each the honour due to each one is not denied. For if your Holiness calls me Universal Pope, you deny that yourself are what you admit me to be—Universal. But this God forbid![6]

Nevertheless all these protests were ignored. John and his successors retained the style of Oecumenical Patriarch. Subsequent popes were addressed as 'Oecumenical Patriarch' or 'Archbishop of Old Rome and Oecumenical Pope'.[7] Pope Gregory VII (according to the *Dictatus Papae*) claimed that 'the Roman Pontiff alone is to be called Universal'.[8]

A. As is illustrated by many passages in the writings of St Gregory the Great, he uncompromisingly maintained the authority of the Apostolic See.

[1] Lib. v, Ep. xviii; *PL*, lxxvii, 738 sq.
[2] Lib. vii, Ep. xiii; *PL*, lxxvii, 891.
[3] Lib. ix, Ep. lxviii; *PL*, lxxvii, 1004.
[4] Lib. v, Ep. xliii; *PL*, lxxvii, 776.
[5] Lib. v, Ep. xx; *PL*, lxxvii, 746 sq.
[6] Lib. viii, Ep. xxx; *PL*, lxxvii, 993.
[7] Mansi, x, 914; xi, 195; Hardouin, iii, 1043; Chapman, *Honorius*, p. 31; Mann, I, pt. ii, 37; Hefele, v, 138.
[8] *PL*, cxlviii, 407.

'Although he rejected the name of universal bishop, he did not object to himself exercising authority throughout the world, he did not object to the *thing* involved.'

'His refusal of the title "universal bishop" is partly out of humility, partly thereby the more effectively to rebuke the patriarch of Constantinople. He prefers the title "*Servus servorum Dei*". This title is afterwards used by Popes.'

N. 'The "Petrine idea" had by this time become firmly rooted at Rome, and had been made use of with much insistence by previous popes. St Gregory is thus simply a witness to the Roman belief of his age, and consequently a witness of no value as to the truth of the Papal pretensions.'[1]

On the other hand, none of the Greek Fathers up to this time (i.e. for the first six centuries) connects the position of the Bishop of Rome with the promise to St Peter. As a rule it is only the popes themselves who directly cite Matt. xvi and John xxi as the grounds of their own jurisdiction.[2]

'According to the canons' had become a catch-phrase at Rome in connexion with the papal claims; St Gregory cannot have examined the canons for himself to verify their actual provisions.

In the fully developed Doctrine of the Papacy, the Roman pontiff is so completely the Superior and Master of all the bishops of the Church that 'Universal Patriarch' and 'Universal Bishop' fairly express the nature of the office claimed.[3] The expression 'Bishop of bishops' is occasionally openly used.[4] St Gregory prophesied better than he knew. The assumption by his successors of the position which he perceived to be involved in the claim of universality has proved how great was his foresight as to what must be its outcome, viz., 'the injury and splitting asunder of the whole Church'.[5]

[1] Denny, sect. 196. [2] Chapman, *GCC*, 92.

[3] Thus Pope Benedict XIV (1740–58) claimed to be 'the proper priest in the whole Church . . . able to withdraw any Church from the jurisdiction of any bishop', De *synod. diocesan.*, 10, 14 et 5, 7; Denny, sect. 1103.

[4] E.g. Humphrey, p. v, 'The Roman Pontiff is . . . Episcopus episcoporum, and has for his diocese—the world'.

[5] Denny, sect. 1131.

CHAPTER LVII

Local Schisms in the West (Sixth to Eighth Centuries)

'The Pope unites in himself several ecclesiastical dignities', as bishop of the diocese of Rome, metropolitan bishop, and patriarch of the West, in addition to his universal primacy.[1] Early Western provincial schisms were therefore rebellion against his undeniable patriarchal authority, apart from the papal primacy; moreover they were exceptions to the general obedience of the West.

Most of these schisms arose out of dissatisfaction with the condemnation of the 'Three Chapters' and the belief, however erroneous, that the popes who accepted this had betrayed the faith of Chalcedon. In A.D. 550 the Synod of Carthage even professed to excommunicate Pope Vigilius;[2] and three years later the provinces of Milan and Aquileia seceded from communion with Rome in the same state of mind.[3] Some thirty years afterwards, Pope Pelagius II still sends an apologia, defending the integrity of his faith, to the bishops of Istria, who had disputed it.[4] Even to Pope St Gregory I the bishops of Ireland wrote saying that the invasions and distresses by which Italy and Rome were scourged were a divine judgement on the agreement of the popes to overthrow (as they imagined) the faith of Chalcedon.[5]

The strange contradiction between the general reverence of the West for the office of the pope on the one hand, and on the other hand the tolerance of schismatic disloyalty to him, is shown in the letters of St Columbanus to successive popes, from Gregory I to Benedict IV. This great Irish missionary saint founded three monasteries in France, and Bobbio in Italy, where he died in A.D. 615. Among Mr Allnatt's quotations he includes this prayer from a missal attributed to St Columbanus:

[1] Hefele, i, 397.
[2] *PL*, lxviii, 958; Hefele, iv, 264.
[3] Ibid., p. 354.
[4] Ep. iii; *PL*, lxxii, 707–8.
[5] Baronius ad an. 592, pp. ix–xii; vol. viii, 26 sq.

O God, who on this day didst give to St Peter, after Thyself, the headship of the whole Church, we humbly pray Thee that, as Thou didst constitute him pastor for the safety of the flock, and that Thy sheep might be preserved from error, so now Thou mayest save us through his intercession.[1]

Always St Columbanus addresses the pope with affectionate veneration in a wealth of colourful language. He is in agony lest the chair of St Peter should suffer any dishonour. Yet he warns Pope Gregory, 'the grandest flower of all wilting Europe', that the Churches of Ireland will 'repudiate him as a heretic' if unhappily he should give a decision contrary to that which they supported (on the vexed question as to the right cycle for fixing the date of Easter).[2] He addresses Pope Benedict IV as 'the most beautiful head of all the Churches of Europe. . . . Because of the twin apostles of Christ ye are almost heavenly, and Rome is the head of all lands, saving the singular prerogative of the place of the Lord's resurrection.' But he earnestly entreats him to take warning from the corruption and fall of his predecessor, Vigilius. 'It is your fault if ye have swerved from the true belief, and *ye have made void your first faith* (1 Tim. v, 12): justly do your juniors oppose you and justly do they not communicate with you until the memory of the destroyer is blotted out.[3]

Another local schism began at Ravenna in 666 and lasted for fourteen years; it seems to have been caused by the recalcitrance of its archbishop. The schism of Milan lasted only for eighteen years, but Aquileia remained in schism for 147 years, until A.D. 700. 'Ten bishops of Como, who were never in communion with the pope, are venerated as saints by the Church of Como to this day.'[4]

After the seventh General Council, at Nicaea in 787,[5] had condemned iconoclasm, Pope Hadrian I accepted its acts, had them translated into Latin, and sent a copy to Charlemagne. Unfortunately, *proskynesis*—the reverent salutation given to images and pictures—was translated *adoratio*, without making it clear that it is distinct from the *latreia* (worship) paid to God alone. It was therefore supposed in the West that the Council of Nicaea had ordered the adoration of images, and it was condemned and rejected in the famous Caroline Books, and by the Council of Frankfort in 794, notwithstanding that the pope accepted it.[6]

[1] Allnatt, p. 87, source not stated. [2] *PL*, lxxx, 259–64. [3] *PL*, lxxx, 274–82.

[4] Puller, p. 405. The sanction of this by the Congregation of Rites seems benign rather than strictly principled.

[5] Supra, ch. lii.

[6] Mann, I, pt. ii, 442, 452, 456; Mansi, xiii, 909; Hefele, v, 399; Denny, para. 1044.

A. In the light of the full, loyal, and general recognition of the papal authority, occasional breaches of order in these disturbed times had no real importance or significance. Instances of disaffection in the West do not argue a denial of the pope's supremacy, for undeniably he was at least patriarch of the West.

'It would be a complete mistake to suppose that, because Columbanus wrote with more freedom than discretion, he regarded himself as one not subject to the Pope, or that he was a rebel against the papal authority. If he heard anything against the popes, against the *Chair of St Peter*, "he lamented over it", and if he cries out "to the mystic pilot", he only does so because the water has entered into the bark of the Church and the ship is in danger. And when he was told that the Pope had received heretics: "I declared in your name that the Roman Church defends no heretic against the Catholic faith."'[1]

'In all his letters, in spite of his scandal at what he regards as the imprudent silence of the Pope, he shows himself devoted to the Apostolic See. It cannot be a mere primacy of honour he recognizes, since he is so impatient for Rome to take some authoritative action in the matter of the Three Chapters.'

N. Those Westerns who broke away from the constitutional authority of the pope as their patriarch, and even repudiated his doctrine, were clearly unaware that 'for every human creature it is altogether necessary to salvation that he be subject to the Roman Pontiff'. The developed Doctrine of the Papacy was then unknown.

Even for St Columbanus, who associates the greatness of the Roman Church with the 'twin apostles Peter and Paul' (as in the primitive tradition handed on by St Irenaeus), the pope is 'head of all the Churches of Europe'; Rome is a glorious see, and its primacy (saving the prerogative of Jerusalem) is a primacy of honour, great honour, though not of jurisdiction. But if the pope is not very careful, he will lose that honour. In saying that the 'juniors' of the pope were right in opposing him and refusing communion with him, Columbanus shows that his affectionate respect for the Roman see was utterly unlike the developed Doctrine of the Papacy.

[1] Mann, I, pt. i, 275.

CHAPTER LVIII

Pope Honorius, A.D. 625-30

Pope Honorius was 'a pious and highly educated man',[1] yet he is unhappily famous because he was anathematized by council after council and pope after pope. It has already been narrated in Chapter LI how in a doctrinal letter to Sergius, the patriarch of Constantinople, he unluckily gave ostensible support to the Monothelite heresy, by employing its distinctive confession of the 'One Will'.[2]

In A.D. 680, the sixth General Council, at Constantinople, anathematized and cast out of Holy Church, together with Sergius, Cyrus, and others, 'Honorius who was pope of Old Rome, because he followed the mind of Sergius and confirmed his impious dogmas'.[3] Pope Leo II, when writing to the emperor approving of the council, wrote that 'we anathematize . . . Honorius also who did not illumine this apostolic Church with the teaching of apostolic tradition, but by profane treachery allowed the spotless faith to be polluted' (in the Latin version,[4] 'he sought to subvert it'). It is sometimes said that Pope Leo, at all events, meant to condemn 'no positive action, but a mere neglect of duty, grave enough in a Pope, but not amounting to the actual teaching of heresy'.[5]

Honorius was again expressly anathematized by the 7th General Council in 787 at Nicaea, and also by the 'Anti-Photian' Council at Constantinople in 869.[6]

Until the eleventh century, every pope on the day of his election made a solemn profession of faith, which included acceptance of 'the sixth holy Universal Council . . . which bound by eternal anathema the authors of the new heretical dogma, Sergius, etc., . . . together with

[1] Mann, I, pt. i, 344.
[2] Mansi, xi, 539; Denzinger, 251.
[3] Ibid., p. 555; Hardouin, iii, 1332.
[4] *PL*, xcvi, 408; see Hefele, v, 185.
[5] 'If Leo had meant this, he would have been mistaken', Chapman, *Honorius*, p. 114.
[6] Supra, chs. lii and liii.

Honorius because he added fuel to their wicked assertions'. This is recorded in the Book of the Popes, the *Liber Diurnus*;[1] that book was suppressed on the advice of Cardinal Baronius, and attempts were made to discredit the records of the condemnation of Honorius; but their genuineness is now admitted.[2]

It is maintained, however, that the unfortunate pronouncement of Pope Honorius is no concern of the papal infallibility as that was defined in 1870 (the subject of the last chapter of this book). Some theologians[3] who consider that he was teaching *ex cathedra* maintain that, when rightly understood, what he wrote was not heretical. Others[4] who regard it as heretical deny that he was teaching *ex cathedra.*

A. Pope Honorius was not really a heretic: he did not intend his words to have the meaning in which they were understood.[5]

'He did not actually define anything unorthodox, when understood in his own meaning, which he explains.'

'We judge the letters of Pope Honorius by the Vatican definition, and deny them to be *ex cathedra* because they do not define any doctrine and impose it upon the whole Church.'[6]

Moreover, they were addressed to the Patriarch Sergius, and not, therefore, addressed to the Universal Church, as the Definition requires.

N. The repeated condemnation of Pope Honorius for heresy by successive councils and popes is irreconcilable with the assertion[7] that 'the See of Holy Peter remains for ever free from all error'. That irreconcilability was seen by Cardinal Baronius and others, who made unavailing efforts to deny the facts, and to suppress the evidence of the Book of the Popes.

Whether the definition of the dogma of papal infallibility in 1870 successfully excludes Honorius from its scope, is a separate question.

The plain historical fact, that he was for centuries repeatedly anathematized for heresy without any attempt to propose a doctrine of infallibility that would exclude his lapse, shows that the Church in those days held no doctrine of papal infallibility, neither the doctrine of 1870 nor any other.

[1] Ed. Sickel, p. 100, ii, 9.

[2] Hefele, v, 193 sq.; Chapman, *Honorius*, p. 7; Acton, *Hist. Freedom*, p. 516; Denny, sects. 962–6.

[3] Bishop Hefele and others.

[4] Abbot Chapman and others.

[5] See Mann, I, pt. i, 334–44.

[6] Chapman, *Honorius*, p. 110.

[7] *Dogm. Const.*, cap. iv.

CHAPTER LIX

Territorial Dominion, A.D. 754

The Roman Church became wealthy at a very early date,[1] and by the end of the fourth century its riches and splendour were remarkable.[2] In later centuries, the papacy 'had become, perhaps, the greatest financial institution in Europe'.[3] Thus from very early times, 'the popes had that at least indirect temporal power which the possession and free use of wealth gives to its owners',[4] but the full temporal power of the Roman see as a monarchical state came later. Pope Gelasius (492–6) had indeed more than once condemned any assumption of secular government by the Church. Christ, he said, mindful of human frailty and desiring that His own should not be cut off by human pride, separated the secular and spiritual authorities; the emperors for eternal life needed the pontiffs; but they should make use of secular arrangements, so 'that he who wars for God may not entangle himself with secular business' (2 Tim. ii, 4).[5]

But after the Western Empire had faded out in the fifth century, the unstable Barbarian rule in Italy and the feeble grip of the Byzantine emperors left the popes high in civil power and responsibility over the city and province of Rome.

Lombard kings were spreading their conquests down through Italy. Pope Stephen III (752–7) begged for help from Constantinople in vain. So in 754 he journeyed to Champagne, to the palace of Pepin, whom soon after he anointed as King of the Franks. 'The outcome of that journey was the temporal sovereignty of the popes, the severance of Latin Christendom from Greek, the Frankish conquest of Italy, the Holy Roman Empire.'[6] By what is sometimes called the Donation of Pepin, the Frankish king granted a large part of northern Italy to the

[1] Mgr L. Duchesne, *Enc. Brit.*, 11th ed., xx, 689; 1918 ed., xvii, 197.
[2] Supra, ch. xxxi. [3] Maycock, p. 13. [4] Mann, I, pt. ii, 282.
[5] *Tomus de anathematis vinculo*, see also Ep. xii; *PL*, lix, 108–9, 42.
[6] CMH, ii, 581.

pope. His great influence over the Franks is illustrated by his impressive language to Pepin in a letter asking for help against the Lombards. It is supposed to be written by the apostle Peter and 'contains in this strange form the ingenious expression of the idea likely to prove most effective'.[1]

> Peter, called apostle by Jesus Christ, Son of the living God . . . and through me the whole Catholic and Apostolic Roman Church, head of all the Churches of God . . . and Stephen, leader of that gracious Church; grace, mercy, and peace . . .
>
> I, Peter, exhort you to defend this Roman city from the enemies' hands . . . and with us our Lady Mary Mother of God, ever Virgin, most solemnly adjures admonishes and commands you . . . so that I, Peter, casting over you my protection both in this life and at the Day of Judgement, may prepare bright shining tabernacles for you in the kingdom of God.[2]

The Donation of Charlemagne twenty years later confirmed that of his father Pepin and promised nearly two-thirds of Italy, with Corsica and Cyrenaica. Neither of the grants is extant; they do not seem ever to have taken full effect; yet they were the foundation of the papal states.

Thenceforward the territorial monarchy of the popes belongs to mundane history. By the thirteenth century, the papacy, with its armies and navies and vast revenues, had become a kind of supranational kingship.[3] It was for ever embroiled in the tortuous politics of Europe, its wars, and 'the sinuous writhings of its own diplomacy'.[4] The Vicar of Christ often appeared heavily disguised; Pope Julius II, for example, at war with France, to which five of his cardinals had deserted, besieged Mirandola with his armies in 1511. Accoutred in armour, and mixing with his soldiery, he delighted them with his coarse, blunt language, and by allowing them to sack the city when it fell.[5] All such things are a painful memory. 'The organizing of wars by the Popes for purposes hardly or not at all religious; their leading forth military expeditions to subdue to their authority rebellious cities or castles in the States of the Church; the ruthless use of the spiritual weapons of excommunication and interdict on issues often political and secular; the launching of crusades against cities, as at Venice in 1309, when no issue of heresy or religion was at stake: it all makes bewildering reading.'[6] The weapons of interdict and excommunication became familiar, and often failed to terrify or gain compliance, especially in Italy.

The temporal power of the popes as territorial sovereigns ended

[1] Duchesne, *BTS*, p. 44. [2] Ep. iii; *PL*, xcviii, 121–4. [3] Hughes, iii, 35.
[4] Ibid., p. 426. [5] Ibid., p. 420. [6] Butler, i, 8.

when the Italian troops entered Rome on 20 September 1870. By the concordat of 1929 with the Italian government, the Vatican City became again an independent state. On the loss by the papacy of its former large sovereign domains, an interesting comment is made in a well-known work of independent outlook:

> Once delivered from the cares of state, the Pope was able to devote all his time to questions of a spiritual nature. Standing high above the petty quarrels of the European politicians, the Papacy assumed a new dignity which proved of great benefit to the Church and made it an international power for social and religious progress which has shown a much more intelligent appreciation of modern economic problems than most protestant sects.[1]

A. Medieval conditions thrust secular power and territory on the popes. Although there were at times regrettable features in the administration of the pope as a temporal ruler, they were unrelated to his spiritual office as successor of St Peter and Vicar of Christ, and they afford no argument against it.

Pope Pius XI declared in 1929 that 'no earthly cupidity moves the Vicar of Christ, but only the consciousness of that which it is impossible to yield; because such a territorial sovereignty is a condition universally recognized as indispensable to every sovereign jurisdiction. . . . We are glad to see the material earth reduced to the minimum terms.'[2]

'The temporal power had at any rate the advantage of freeing the Pope from the undue influence of the State. The evils of the papacy being in the hands of an earthly king were shown during the Avignon captivity. This may be why the Eastern Church has never been able to assert its full independence in matters spiritual. Perhaps the best arrangement is the present one.'

N. The millennium of mammon, while the Roman popes were worldly potentates, embroiled in the intrigues and wars of Europe, and on occasion even leading the papal armies to battle, makes it difficult (for those who are not already convinced of the Doctrine of the Papacy) to see that the fisherman-apostle 'until this very time and constantly lives, presides, and exercises judgement in his successors the bishops of the Holy Roman See'.[3]

The 'supreme pastors' who often used interdict and excommunication as political levers, cared little for their thousands of innocent sheep, deprived of sacraments and left in peril of soul.

[1] H. van Loon, *The Story of Mankind*, ch. 56, 1949 ed., p. 397.
[2] Conway, p. 168.
[3] *Dogm. Const.*, cap. ii.

CHAPTER LX

The Donation of Constantine (Eighth Century)

The Sylvester-Constantine legend was popular before this remarkable document was written, probably at Rome in the third quarter of the eighth century.[1] The tale ran thus: Constantine the Great was stricken with leprosy; physicians were in vain. The priests of the Capitol prescribed a warm bath of infants' blood, but when a batch of babes was brought for slaughter, Constantine spared them in pity for their weeping mothers. That night two holy men came to him in his sleep. They told him that Sylvester, bishop of the city, was hiding from his own persecution in caverns on Mount Soracte (twenty-five miles north of Rome). If Sylvester were to dip him thrice in 'a pool of piety' the leprosy would be cured; Constantine in return should restore all churches in the world. Next day he identified his ghostly visitors (from portraits shown to him) as St Peter and St Paul. So he confessed, was baptized, and was instantly cured.

The ingenious and unknown author put this tale into the mouth of Constantine, and then makes him express humble adulation for the Church of Sylvester, at vast length and in fantastic language. Some more concrete passages of the Donation of Constantine are as follows:

> We decree that the sacrosanct Roman Church is to be reverently honoured as is our earthly authority, and the most consecrated see of blessed Peter is to be gloriously exalted more than our earthly and imperial throne—we rendering to it authority and the dignity of glory, and force, and imperial honour. We decree and ordain that the pontiff who for the time being presides over that same Roman Church shall hold supremacy

[1] CMH, ii, 586; *Cath. Enc.*, v, 119; Duchesne, *BTS*, p. 119. There had been a crop of apocryphal literature in the time of Pope Symmachus, round about A.D. 500, *Liber Pont.*, cxxii, cxxvi, cxxxiii, cxl; *PL*, vi, 1–9; viii, 822–40, 1387–95 (Gesta Liberii); Tellenbach, p. 140 n. 1; Hergenröther, p. 150; Jalland, *CP*, p. 207 n. 3.

> over the four principal sees of Antioch, Alexandria, Jerusalem, and Constantinople, and also over all Churches of God in the whole world. . . .
>
> We grant and yield up to our most blessed pontiff Sylvester, universal pope aforesaid, and to the pontiffs his successors, our imperial Lateran palace, and also the city of Rome, and all the provinces, etc., of all Italy and the regions of the West.[1]

Constantine concludes that it is right for him to vacate Rome and remove his merely earthly empire and kingdom to the East, where he will build a city in Byzantium. That is the only link with historical fact; Constantine did found Constantinople as 'New Rome' in A.D. 330, and he did restore confiscated property to the Church.

'Who was the author of the forgery, or when exactly it first saw the light are questions which cannot be completely answered.'[2] Its grants of palaces and territories suggest that it may have been concocted at a time when the popes were obtaining actual 'donations' from Pepin or Charlemagne; but this is only conjecture. What is certain is, that the Donation of Constantine gave a seal of venerable antiquity to the most exalted conceptions of papal dominion.

It was included among the False Decretals of the pseudo-Isidore[3] in 850, and throughout the Middle Ages it was regarded as genuine both by friends and opponents of the papal claims;[4] it was sometimes even embellished or improved upon.[5] In 1054 Pope Leo IX founded on the Donation to prove to the patriarch of Constantinople that his *imperium* was both earthly and heavenly. From that time onward, it gained in importance, and 'was more frequently used as evidence in the ecclesiastical and political conflicts between the papacy and the secular power'.[6] Its 'decrees' were added in to the great twelfth-century collection of canons, the *Decretum* of Gratian,[7] the text-book by which all churchmen were instructed. Its authenticity was doubted by no one before the fifteenth century,[8] and it still found defenders until after Cardinal Baronius had admitted it to be a forgery.

A. 'No one who has attentively followed the history of the growth of the temporal power of the popes can believe that the so-called "donation", produced, at the earliest, in the second half of the eighth century, had anything to do with the acquisition of sovereignty by the popes in that century.'[9]

[1] Labbe, i, 1530–9; Mansi, ii, 603.
[2] Mann, I, pt. ii, 467.
[3] See next chapter.
[4] *Enc. Brit.*, 11th ed., viii, 409; 1948 ed., vi, 524.
[5] As by Rufinus and by Pope Nicholas I in A.D. 854, supra, p. 297.
[6] *Cath. Enc.*, v, 120.
[7] Distinctio xcvi, c. xiv (cols. 470–2).
[8] *Cath. Enc.*, v, 121.
[9] Mann, I, pt. ii, 467–8.

N. The precise origin of the Donation of Constantine is only of antiquarian interest, and whether or not it procured more territory for the papacy matters little. Its fantastic but impressive testimony to an early sovereignty of the popes, and the (spurious) antiquity of their high claims of authority, gripped the credulous minds of churchmen in the West, and stifled any questionings of the discontented or doubtful.

CHAPTER LXI

The False Decretals, A.D. 850

Fabrication or forgery had produced the Clementine literature of the second and third centuries,[1] the 'Symmachian forgeries' at the end of the fifth, and the Donation of Constantine in the eighth century.[2] Everything was accepted with uncritical credulity. This 'most portentous of medieval forgeries',[3] consisting largely of imaginary epistles of early bishops of Rome from the first century onwards, was now put forth under the honoured name of St Isidore of Seville (†636).

It originated not in Rome but in the north of France. Churchmen there were being tyrannized over by unruly feudal and ecclesiastical magnates. They anxiously desired a right of appeal to the papal court, which it seemed only apostolic command could secure. It was not the primary purpose of the fabricator to extend by fraudulent means the authority of the Roman see.[4] Nor must it be supposed that he was conscious of doing anything wrong.[5] For at least two centuries there had been papal statements of doctrine similar to what he put into the mouths of the primitive bishops. Often 'the fraud consists in assigning the language of a later period to writers of an earlier age'. If the early saints had neglected to give such wholesome and necessary teaching, it was surely a pious task to supply their omission.

The famous *Epistle of Clement to James*[6] takes the lead, with four other imaginary epistles of Clement. The full 'papal' teaching of ninth-century Rome is foisted on the primitive bishops as apostolic doctrine received from the mouth of the Lord. A few examples will suffice:

St Anencletus (*circa* A.D. 79–91), in his 'third Epistle' addressed 'to all

[1] Supra, ch. xv. [2] Supra, ch. lx. [3] Lightfoot, *Clem.*, i, 102.
[4] Mr Davenport's monograph is informative. [5] Milman, iii, 192.
[6] Supra, ch. xv; Hinschius, pp. 30 sq.; *PL*, cxxx, 19 sq.

bishops', describes himself as having been ordained by blessed Peter, prince of the apostles, and is made to say that 'this sacrosanct and apostolic Roman Church did not obtain its primacy from the apostles but from the Lord Himself... for this apostolic see has been made the hinge and head by the Lord Himself, and no other'. Difficult suits are to be referred and terminated by the supreme tribunal of the holy see 'because it was so willed by the Lord', and is declared to have been so determined by Him.[1]

St Pius (*circa* 142–54), writing 'to all Churches', says that our Lord 'commanded that this holy apostolic see should be the head of all the Churches....'[2]

St Felix (269–74)—'Ever since the times of the apostles, who directed this in their instructions, it has been the custom that doubtful questions and greater affairs get their determination from this sacred see'.[3]

St Marcellus (269–74) tells the bishops of Antioch that 'his (St Peter's) see was first with you which was afterwards translated to Rome by the command of the Lord.... If your Antioch, which formerly was the first, yielded to the Roman See, much more there is no see which is not subject to its jurisdiction.'[4]

The Donation of Constantine reappears.[5]

St Athanasius and the bishops of Egypt are made to address St Marcus (A.D. 336) as Pope of the Universal Church, and his see as Mother and Head of all Churches. He replies that it is proved never to have erred from the path of apostolic tradition, nor to have succumbed to be depraved by heretical novelties.[6] They inform St Felix II (Antipope, 355–8) that 'the Lord Jesus Christ established your see, the sacred centre whither all resort, are strengthened, are refreshed'.[7]

The first General Council at Nicaea in 325 is made to proclaim that 'the holy Roman Church is exalted by no synodal decrees, but obtained the primacy by the evangelical voice of our Lord', and was given supreme jurisdiction in all cases of bishops 'by the ancient authority of the apostles and their successors'.[8]

The earliest genuine 'decretal' is an epistle of Pope Siricius in A.D. 385[9] and many genuine later epistles are included. 'The whole is compiled with an air of profound piety and reverence; a specious

[1] Hinschius, pp. 83–4; *PL*, cxxx, 77. [2] Ibid., p. 117; *PL*, cxxx, 111.
[3] Ibid., p. 204; *PL*, cxxx, 197. [4] Ibid., pp. 223–4; *PL*, cxxx, 218.
[5] Ibid., p. 252; *PL*, cxxx, 245–52. [6] Ibid., pp. 451, 454. [7] Ibid., p. 480.
[8] Ibid., pp. 255, 467; *PL*, cxxx, 251. [9] Supra, p. 182.

purity, and even occasional beauty, in the moral and religious tone.'[1] But in the edition of Hinschius there are about 378 pages of authentic matter and 375 of spurious.

The False Decretals quickly became known. They were referred to in the controversy of Archbishop Hinckmar of Rheims with Pope Nicholas I (858–67). Whether or not that pope gave them any positive countenance is disputed,[2] and is now of little importance, for they were accepted all through the West as venerable Scripture, and later on were widely used and appealed to by the popes from Gregory VII (1073–85) onwards.[3] They were embodied in the various collections of canons of the eleventh and succeeding centuries. Gratian's *Decretum* quotes 324 epistles of the first four centuries, of which 313 are spurious; it was the text-book of clerical instruction in Church Law, and it permeated and governed all education.[4]

The *Decretum* itself was a hotbed of error. For example, it falsely represents St Augustine as saying that 'the Decretal Epistles are reckoned among the Canonical Scriptures',[5] thus making him endorse even the False Decretals.

They became a touchstone in ecclesiastical questions. Thus, for example, we find Pope Paschal in 1105 quoting from spurious decretals of Victor and Zephyrinus to support his argument against King Henry I of England.[6] Even the Bull 'Pastor aeternus' of 1513 (quoted in the Encyclical 'Satis cognitum) was fortified by Pope Leo X with quotation from pseudo-Isidore.[7] Their effects were far-reaching: thus, the fifth canon of Nicaea had ordered provincial synods to be held twice yearly, but pseudo-Isidore said, not without leave of the pope;[8] and provincial synods fell into disuse.[9]

It only remains to be observed that the False Decretals held sway until after the Reformation. They were fully exposed by the Magdeburg Centuriators in 1559, and although gallant efforts were made to

[1] Milman, iii, 192.

[2] Ep. lxxv; *PL*, cxix, 901; 'If not expressly quoted, they are at least alluded to', Prof. L. Saltet, *Cath. Enc.*, v, 779; cf., Gratian, col. 79 (pars i, dist., xix, cap. i); Funk, i, 312; Milman, ii, 197; *Enc. Brit.*, 11th ed., xx, 689; 1948 ed., xvii, 196; Roy, pp. 2, 180–9; Rivington, *Dust*, pp. 9–13.

[3] Whitney, p. 68.

[4] See *Cath. Enc.*, v, 778.

[5] Gratian, col. 83, dist. xix, c. 5; cf. St Augustine, *De Doctrina Christiana*, lib. ii, c. 8; *PL*, xxxiv, 40.

[6] Ep. cclxxv; *PL*, clxiii, 379; cf. *PL*, cxxx, 123, 126.

[7] Hardouin, ix, 1829; ps.-Isid. Athan. Ep. *ad Felicem* P., Hinschius, p. 459.

[8] Julii Ep. ii; Hinschius, p. 459.

[9] Fleury *Quatrième Discours*, vol. XVI, pp. iv, v.

defend them, and the official edition of the *Corpus Juris* in 1580 upheld them as genuine,[1] no one upholds them now.

A. 'Long before these Decretals came into existence the Papal authority was fully accepted. . . . There was nothing in them to startle or suggest inquiry. . . . The Papal claim was taught and acted upon throughout the world more than two centuries before the fabrication. . . . It is, then, really throwing dust in people's eyes to insist, as so many Protestants do, on this episode in the Church's life as though it explained the growth of the Papacy.'[2]

'The spread of the spurious collection was of such easy accomplishment, only because it corresponded to the prevailing views and circumstances of the times.'[3]

The False Decretals 'added nothing to the substantial foundation of the canon law'.[4]

N. The False Decretals provided massive and unanswerable evidence, dating ostensibly from the times of the apostles and their early successors, for the divine and apostolic fixing of supreme authority in Rome, and for the conferring upon its bishop of supreme and sovereign jurisdiction by the apostles and by the Council of Nicaea.

For seven centuries, pseudo-Isidore stifled all misgivings, and silenced any scholars' doubts of the papal assertions and claims in the West. Even for the scholarly St Thomas More, who spent seven years in diligent examination of the sources of the power of the pope,[5] the False Decretals were established 'evidence'.

[1] *Cath. Enc.*, v, 773.
[2] Rivington, *Dust*, pp. 9, 11, 13, 14.
[3] Hergenröther, p. 158.
[4] Hughes, iii, 161.
[5] Cardinal Gasquet, *The Eve of the Reformation* (1919), p. 80.

CHAPTER LXII

Ubi Non Debuit Abominatio

In our times the Roman popes are recognized everywhere as bishops of lofty pastoral ideals, of purity of life and character, and there have been very many such in the past. Yet there have been periods when vice dishonoured and defiled the papal throne. It should be said again that this dismal fact of history does not bear directly upon the truth of the Doctrine of the Papacy; but it has supplied at least a prejudicial argument against acceptance of that Doctrine.

The tenth century had a bad prelude, following the death of Pope Formosus in 896, when 'nine Popes succeeded each other in eight years. Raised to the papal throne by factions, several of them suffered a violent death at the hands of factions.'[1]

The next pope but one, Stephen VII, held a Roman synod in 897, known as the Cadaverous Council, at which the nine-months-dead corpse of Pope Formosus was dug up, dressed in pontificals, tried by pope and synod, condemned, anathematized, mutilated, and thrown into the Tiber.[2] Stephen himself was strangled in a dungeon some months later. Some popes treated the ordinations of their predecessors as null, and repeated them.[3]

Cardinal Baronius in his *Annals* introduces the tenth century thus:

> A new age begins which, from its bitterness and barrenness of good has been called Iron, from the ugliness of its abounding wickedness, Leaden, and from the lack of writers, Dark. Pausing on this threshold we have thought it needful to warn the reader, lest the weak-minded be scandalized, and so that he may learn that divine power is watchful, and that desolation of the temple did not straightway follow such abomination.

[1] Mann, iv, 54.

[2] Ibid., p. 81.

[3] A. Robertson, p. 240, citing Cardinal Hergenröther, *Photius*, ii, 321 sq., *Die Reordinationen der alten Kirche*, esp. pp. 352, 365, 369. The distinction between irregularity of ordination and invalidity was only firmly established in the thirteenth century.

> ... Oh shame! Oh grief! How many monsters then, horrible to be seen, were thrust into that See which is to be reverenced by angels: how many were the evils and tragedies; with what filth did it befall her to be spattered who was without spot or wrinkle, with what stench to be corrupted, with what loathsome impurities to be polluted, and blackened with perpetual infamy.[1]

Theodora and her two daughters, women of notorious character, have given this period an ugly by-name. Pope John X, a warlike pontiff who led his troops bravely in battle, was imprisoned by Theodora's daughter, Marozia, in a dungeon where he died, of suffocation it is said. Pope John XI (931–6) was a son of Marozia.[2] For years after this, Alberic, another son of Marozia, and a typical Italian despot, ruled Rome and controlled papal elections. Pope John XII was Alberic's son[3] and is said to have been made pope at the age of eighteen. He is charged with having turned the Lateran into a brothel, and with other iniquities; at all events he was 'anything but what a Pope, the chief pastor of Christendom, should have been'.[4] Some other scandalous stories about particular popes in the time of Theodora and Marozia come from the chronicles of Bishop Liutprand, Bishop of Cremona (*circa* 900–70), who was 'frequently unfair' and a glutton for 'amorous' gossip which cannot be accepted as simple history.[5] Mgr Mann rejects them and, moreover, does not accept even Cardinal Baronius as authoritative on this period.[6]

For part of the following century, the eleventh, Rome was dominated by the 'noble' family of Tusculum, descended of Theodora and Marozia. Its citadel was the terror of the country around; its chiefs lorded it over Rome both temporally and spiritually.[7] Popes Benedict VIII and John XIX (1012–32) were sons of one count. On John's death, another count, 'by a lavish expenditure of money', procured the election of his youthful son as Benedict IX. He proved to be a peculiarly vicious young man, who varied sexual vice with murder and plunder. He was driven from Rome, and a certain bishop was set up as Pope Sylvester III. Benedict IX was restored soon after by the Tusculan family, but he tired of the papal throne and sold it 'for a considerable sum of money' to Gratian, who became Pope Gregory VI (1045–6).[8] St Peter Damian (†1072) attacked the evils of these dark times in his *Liber Gomorrhianus*, an 'outspoken denunciation of filthy vice', which is said to have been hidden away later as unsuitable for publicity.[9]

[1] Baronius, sub an. 900, x, 629.
[2] See T. F. Tout, *The Empire and the Papacy*, 4th ed. (1903), p. 35.
[3] Mann, iv, 163, 243. [4] Ibid., p. 241.
[5] *Cath. Enc.*, ix, 314; CMH iii, 160; Mann, iv, 137–141.
[6] Mann, iv, 138 n. [7] Ibid., v, 159. [8] Ibid. ,pp. 238–51. [9] Whitney, p. 103.

Dr Fortescue was moved to say that 'nearly all the popes for about a century were horrible people';[1] their reigns were usually brief; but it must not be overlooked that, even among the very numerous popes of this 'dark age', there were many of whom nothing but good is recorded.

A. 'The Church remains holy, no matter how many of her leaders prove faithless to the Gospel they preach, for these men are cut off from the Church's life by their sins, which can never be traced to her teaching or laws. Would you call an apple tree bad, because you discovered some rotten apples lying on the ground beneath it? No, you judge the tree by the ripening or ripe apples on its boughs. Wicked churchmen will one day have to render a strict account to Almighty God for their stewardship, for as Christ said: "Unto whomsoever much is given, of him will much be required" (Luke xii, 16).'[2]

Out of a long line of worthy popes, only a few were unworthy of their high office. 'But the proportion of unworthy Apostles was one out of twelve. No world dynasty can be compared from the standard of virtue with the illustrious dynasty of two hundred and sixty-two popes.[3]

'God permitted that there should be some bad Popes. . . . The failings of the Popes bring home to us this truth, that the Papacy stands not by the wisdom or prudence or strength of man, but by the might and protection of God.'[4]

The argument below is fallacious. 'Popes have to save their souls as others, have to go to confession. If a Pope sins, he is as much cut off from Christ as any other sinner, but the sinner Pope still remains external Head of the Church, although he is not united to Christ by grace, and if he dies unrepentant he is lost for ever.'

N. Many of those to whom it seems that Scripture, the records of the early Church, and the Fathers, utterly exclude the Doctrine of the Papacy, nevertheless keenly appreciate the greatness of the Roman Church and the profusion of saintliness that has been manifest within its communion. But when these merits are weighed as arguments in support of the developed papacy, they are met by contrary considerations (of which these 'dark ages' are only one instance). That 'blessed Peter, until this very time and continually lives, presides, and executes judgement in his successors the bishops of the Roman See'[5] seems hardly plausible.

[1] *OEC*, p. 166 n. 5. [2] Conway, p. 125. [3] Ibid., p. 126.
[4] St Robert (Cardinal) Bellarmine, Preface to *Controv. on the Pope*, Brodrick, i, 167.
[5] *Dogm. Const.*, cap. ii.

They do not forget that there have been great sinners among other bishops and clerics, but (in their understanding and belief) no individual bishop is a vital Head and life-centre of Christ's universal Church. A wicked bishop may be 'cut off from the Church's life by his sins', but not so, surely, if he were the necessary Head of the Body, 'constituting only one Head with Christ'.

The four notes or marks of the Church are its Unity, Holiness, Catholicity, and Apostolicity. In the Doctrine of the Papacy, the Roman pontiff is the divinely appointed and necessary centre of Unity in the Church. To Christians who have not felt able to accept that Doctrine (who indeed consider that a false development of the papacy brought about disunity rather than unity) there is a significant relationship between the two Notes of Unity and of Holiness. It seems to them that the Note of Unity can no more be attached to the papacy as its necessary centre than the Note of Holiness.

PART EIGHT

THE PAPACY AFTER SEPARATION OF THE EAST

CHAPTER LXIII

Centralization

The Holy Roman Church to day possesses a closely organized system of government. Through the Roman Curia and the various 'Congregations' the Supreme Pontiff exercises a sovereign control over all his bishops and the faithful everywhere throughout the Church. This is the outcome of a long process of development.

In the early centuries, Churches had chosen their own bishops, and bishops had governed their flocks in independence of one another. After sees became grouped under metropolitans, and patriarchates had come to be recognized, these were self-contained. Each Eastern patriarch presided in his own patriarchate much as did the Roman. Cardinal Newman saw papal power as something 'divinely bestowed, yet in the first instance more or less dormant, . . . as a mysterious privilege which was not understood, as an unfulfilled prophecy'.[1]

By the time of St Leo the Great, papal power was well understood, at all events in the West, but even there, for another six centuries, actual centralization made small progress, and in the East, constantly 'rebellious' and out of communion with Rome, it made none.

By the ninth century, authority was denied to any Western metropolitan until he obtained a *pallium*[2] from the pope, on payment of a large tribute.[3] Moreover, the popes began to appoint legates with wide powers; this shrank episcopal authority; provincial synods fell out of use.[4]

Severance of the East probably hastened the process of Roman

[1] *Development*, 1845 ed., pp. 166–9; 1878 ed., pp. 150–3.

[2] A stole-like garment bestowed by the emperors as a mark of favour; adopted by the popes, and still sometimes given thus to bishops who are not metropolitans, *Cath. Enc.*, xi, 428.

[3] Ibid., 'In order to counteract the aspirations of various autonomy-seeking metropolitans'.

[4] Fleury, *Quatrième Discours*, XVI, iv, v.

centralization; when St Gregory VII (Hildebrand), one of the greatest of medieval popes, began to reign in 1073, out of the five patriarchates only one, the Western, remained loyal. His lofty ambition was to free the Church from secular control; he also strove to enforce celibacy on the clergy, to put down concubinage, and to root out the all-pervading simony. He appointed more legates;[1] centralization made marked progress. He required an oath of obedience from metropolitans; it was later required from all bishops.[2] He established the final appeal to Rome.[3]

Pope Hadrian IV (1154–9) began to reserve to himself the conferring of ecclesiastical benefices away from Rome, and a decretal of Pope Clement IV in 1265 declared a papal right of disposal of ecclesiastical benefices which was universal in theory, though not altogether so in practice. During the twelfth century canonization of saints became centralized and reserved to the pope.[4]

When the Holy Office was set up in the thirteenth century, all archbishops, bishops, and others were commanded to obey the papal Inquisitors under pain of excommunication.

Today the long process of centralization is matured. The right of a local Church or chapter to elect its bishop 'has long been withdrawn and is no longer in force. . . . The choice of bishops belongs exclusively to the pope'.[5] Every bishop must report in person at Rome at set intervals of time. For his episcopal administration he must obtain an 'indult', a papal faculty or permission, periodically renewed;[6] he may, of course, be removed by the pope. The Supreme Pontiff's authority is 'immediate',[7] i.e., it can by-pass all intermediate authorities.

The change from the independent authority of the early bishop to his strictly subordinate modern status did not come about without protest. 'This dangerous man orders us about as if we were his bailiffs', said Archbishop Liemar of Pope Gregory VII.[8] At the Council of Trent in 1562, many bishops cried out against their growing subjection.[9] Even at the Vatican Council in 1870 some bishops protested that 'indults' ought not to be necessary for their ordinary authority;[10] an

[1] Döllinger, *Hist.*, iii, 178; Mann, vii, 50–1; Whitney, p. 44.
[2] Funk, i, 393; Whitney, pp. 56–7. [3] Funk, i, 392.
[4] Formally so decreed in 1234. E. W. Kemp, *Canonization and Authority in the Western Church* (1948), esp. ch. v; Fortescue, *OEC*, p. 103; formerly a bishop admitted names to his local liturgy or martyrology.
[5] *Cath. Enc.*, ii, 584; except in Oriental Uniat Churches, where an attempt to enforce this caused a schism, Butler, i, 223.
[6] *Cath. Enc.*, ii, 585, 588; vii, 789. [7] *Dogm. Const.*, cap. iii. [8] Whitney, p. 34.
[9] Acta Trid ii, 157, 164, 172–3, 183; Waterworth, cciii; see below, ch. lxx.
[10] Butler, i, 221, 268.

English bishop voiced a fear lest, having come as princes of the Church, they must go back 'satraps of a central autocrat'.[1]

Such grumblings may be natural, but they cannot be justified under the Doctrine of the Papacy and the sovereign rule of the Supreme Pontiff. The phrase 'vicar of Christ' can be used in widely different senses, but, in the tremendous sense in which it has been claimed for the pope alone since the thirteenth century ('Christ and His Vicar constitute only one Head'),[2] it implies a unique authority with no obvious limit. Since the popes as Christ's Vicars 'truly exercise for ever in the Church the same power which He exercised during His mortal life',[3] that authority cannot well be less than absolute.

Accordingly, the *Dogmatic Constitution* expressly declares that the pope as St Peter's successor today has a sovereignty of ordinary power, a true and proper jurisdiction, which is truly episcopal, to which all bishops and others of the faithful are bound to submit.

The Encyclical 'Satis cognitum' gives additional teaching. 'By the fact that the bishops succeed the Apostles they inherit their ordinary power', but 'whatever authority and office the Apostles received, they received in conjunction with Peter'. So, 'the authority of the Roman Pontiff is supreme, universal, independent; that of the bishops is limited and dependent'. They are subject, in implicit obedience, to the Supreme Pontiff, who appoints them, restricts their powers at his discretion, and can depose them. The Encyclical declares that 'bishops are not to be looked on as vicars of the Roman Pontiffs, for they exercise a power really their own'; yet they can only exercise that power in strict and complete subordination to the Pope.

A. The wisely planned organization through which the Supreme Pontiff governs the world-wide Church has gradually been developed and perfected to meet the changing conditions that the Church has encountered through the centuries. Although St Peter and his earliest successors did not need this organization, they were divinely and fully endowed with the same authority which in modern circumstances their successors now exercise in this mode.

'The *Sacramentum Unitatis* was acknowledged on all hands; the mode of fulfilling and the means of securing it would vary with the occasion; and the determination of its essence, its seat, and its laws would be a gradual consequence of a gradual necessity. . . . St Peter's prerogative would remain a dead letter, till the complication of ecclesiastical matters became the cause of ascertaining it.'[4]

[1] Butler, 267–8. [2] Supra, ch. vi. [3] Satis cogn.
[4] Newman, *Development*, 1845 ed., pp. 165–6; 1878 ed., pp. 149–50.

'Circumstances of their common life with our Lord, together with the very special prerogatives of the Apostolate, would naturally make Peter loath to exercise his authority unless absolutely necessary. Yet it is clear from the Petrine passages and his position in the New Testament that he was given the primacy.'

N. Seeing that the pope now has exclusive power to appoint and depose bishops and to control and limit their dependent authority, they are his subject vicars in reality and fact, although the name is deprecated. The modern jurisdiction of the Roman bishop over all other bishops, accurately defined by the *Dogmatic Constitution* as 'truly episcopal', is completer and more absolute than that of a bishop over his priests. By a wrongful 'development' the pope has in fact become 'bishop of bishops' and 'universal bishop', the name that Gregory the Great denounced and prophesied against.

All this sovereign authority is implicit in the modern Doctrine of the Papacy, as it is defined. Yet it is an utter innovation upon Holy Scripture and the primitive Church. Even an individual Petrine office (first suggested in the third century) could not raise the Roman bishop higher than St Peter himself. The modern doctrine therefore requires St Peter to have been actually Pontifex Maximus—Supreme Pontiff—and Vicar of Christ, Joint Head with Christ. If such titles were inserted where St Peter's name occurs in the New Testament, such as Acts viii, 14; xi, 2; Gal. ii, 6–14, it would be no more grotesque in wording than preposterous in fact. Not only was St Peter 'certainly not accustomed to order the apostles about',[1] but there is not the slightest suggestion that either he or anyone else supposed that he had an authority resembling what is claimed for the pope: but if not, the modern Doctrine of the Papacy cannot be maintained.

[1] Chapman, *GCC*, p. 62.

CHAPTER LXIV

Universal Temporal Power

The universal 'power in temporals' of the popes is wholly distinct from their sovereignty over the papal states,[1] and it is woven into the history of Europe through the Middle Ages.[2] Its 'theologically certain' foundation[3] is the authority of the pope, as Head of the Church, to censure and coerce all Christians on moral and spiritual grounds, by reason of sin, *ratione peccati*.

Many canonists of the eleventh to fourteenth centuries held that the 'sword' of the pope's temporal power is a 'direct' power and not only an 'indirect' power of intervention,[4] and indeed the popes themselves set forth their authority so broadly as to give this apparent support. Thus Pope Nicholas I (858–67) declared that 'by the Grace of God we have been constituted princes over the whole earth'.[5] The great pope Gregory VII (1073–85) declared that Christ appointed St Peter Lord of the kingdom of the world, so that the Roman see was judge also of temporal things;[6] Pope Hadrian IV would not crown Frederick I (Barbarossa) until the proud emperor did him groom's service. Pope Innocent III on his accession in 1198 preached that he was the superior of kings, and he applied to himself the Scripture (Jer. i, 10), 'I have this day set thee over the nations and over the kingdoms, to root out and to pull down . . .'. He was 'not the vicar of men but the

[1] Hull, pp. 1–12, 104–30.

[2] See, e.g., Mgr W. F. Barry, *The Papacy and Modern Times* 1303–1870 (1911) and T. B. Howells, *The Chair of Peter* (1935).

[3] Maritain, p. 21.

[4] C. H. McIlwain, *The Growth of Political Power in the West* (New York, 1932), pp. 206–88; R. W. and A. J. Carlyle, *History of Mediaeval Political Theory in the West*, vol. v (1928), pt. ii, esp. pp. 318–440.

[5] Epp. lxv, lxxxvi; *PL*, cxix, 882, 949. [6] Funk, i, 395.

vicar of God on earth'.[1] Pope Innocent IV in 1245 declared that Christ established in Rome a monarchy that is royal as well as priestly,[2] and Boniface VIII, in the great Bull 'Unam sanctam', declared:

> We learn from the words of the Gospel that in the Church and in her power are two swords, the spiritual and the temporal. For when the apostles said, 'Behold here are two swords', the Lord did not reply 'It is too much', but, 'It is enough'. Truly he who denies that the temporal sword is in the power of Peter misunderstands the words of the Lord, 'Put up thy sword into the sheath'. Both are in the power of the Church, the spiritual sword, and the material.[3]

Some of the canonists who held the theory of the 'direct' power went so far as to claim that the pope could say of himself, 'All power is given unto me in heaven and on earth';[4] but the theory of the 'direct' power is rejected by all modern theologians.[5] It is considered that the declarations of the popes recognize the authority of princes as a temporal power ordained by God distinct from that of the papacy, although subject to it *ratione peccati*. Innocent III said 'We do not intend to judge feudal affairs',[6] and Boniface VIII laid stress on *ratio peccati* as the basis of his temporal authority.[7]

In the exercise of papal power there were two elements that help to obscure the distinction between 'direct' and 'indirect' power. One was the Donation of Constantine which (as was implicitly believed) granted to the popes 'all the regions of the West'. Thus in 1154, Pope Hadrian IV made a grant of Ireland to King Henry II of England.[8] In 1493, Alexander VI, the Borgia pope, divided the world by a line (running north and south about 50 degrees west of Greenwich), and granted all new lands to the west and east of it to Spain and Portugal respectively. The theory of the so-called 'Translation of the Empire' also affected the exercise of papal authority.[9] Whether Innocent III's annulment of Magna Carta was based on his spiritual authority (which

[1] *Decretales*, I, vii, 3; 'non puri hominis, sed veri Dei vicem gerit in terris' Ullmann, *MP*, p. 118.

[2] Mirbt, no. 358, pp. 197–8.

[3] Mirbt, no. 372, p. 210, tr. Bettenson, p. 159; confirmed and renewed by Leo X, Bull 'Pastor Aeternus', 19 December 1516; Hardouin, ix, 1826.

[4] Ullmann, *MP*, p. 89.

[5] Maritain, p. 124.

[6] *Decretales*, II, i, 13; Ullmann, *MP*, p. 105.

[7] Denzinger, 468 n.

[8] Mann, ix, 324; C. W. C. Oman in *Enc. Brit.*, 11th ed., ix, 483; 1948 ed., xi, 602; CMH, vii, 534, 539–40.

[9] Innocent III taught that the coronation of Charlemagne on Christmas Day, 800, signified not only that the emperor received his crown at the hands of the pope, but also that the Eastern Empire was thereby transplanted (or translated) to the West. Ullmann, *MP*, p. 168, McIlwain, op. cit., p. 231; *PL*, ccxvi, 998, 1025, 1032; Gratian, *Dist.*, lxiii, c. 22.

included absolution from the performance of an oath), or on feudal grounds, is disputed.[1]

The universal temporal power was at all events wide and drastic, and warranted the summary deposing of monarchs. As M. Maritain observes, the subject matter of the indirect power 'is practically unlimited: any temporal arrangement, any kind of temporal activity may, if the *ratio peccati* is sufficiently seriously implicated, necessitate the exercise of the indirect power',[2] and it is for the pope alone to judge when and in what circumstances temporal matter calls for its exercise.[3]

Europe of today is very different from Europe of the Middle Ages, and in practice the exercise of the temporal power is necessarily constricted; but it would be unsafe to assert that there has been any change in doctrine. The power of deposing princes was strenuously maintained by Cardinal Bellarmine,[4] and devout Englishmen suffered martyrdom rather than abjure it.[5] Pope Pius IX in his Syllabus of 1864 condemned it as error to deny that the Church has power to exercise direct or indirect power.[6] He declared, however, that the power of deposing sovereigns, and absolving their subjects from their allegiance, had nothing to do with his infallibility.[7] M. Maritain insists that the 'modalities' of the present age, so different from those of the Middle Ages, imply no variation in the doctrine of the Church, although 'the contingent modalities of practice vary';[8] in the new era since the final liquidation of the Holy Roman Empire, the indirect power will be exercised 'in the form of *counsels* or *directions* which the nations will always expect from the supreme moral authority of the Church'; it will be 'merely moral influence over the things of the temporal order'.[9] This view is borne out by various encyclicals that have issued from the Vatican in the present century, dealing with social, moral, and political problems, in words the wisdom of which has often been recognized outside the Roman Church.

A. 'Every intervention of the Church in the temporal, even when she assumed the inheritance of the declining Empire in order to make Europe, has invariably proceeded from the indirect power only.'[10]

'It is the right of intervention which the spiritual power possesses

[1] The Bull of 24 August 1215 is printed in Rymer's *Foedera*, tom. i, pp. 203–5, Bémont, *Chartres des libertés anglaises*, pp. 41–4, and *Bullarium Romanum*, iii, 298–300. See Ullmann, *MP*, p. 71; McIlwain, op. cit., p. 231.
[2] Maritain, p. 21. [3] Ibid., pp. 24, 34. [4] Brodrick, ii, 193.
[5] Ibid., pp. 169–224. [6] No. 24, Denzinger, 1724. [7] Butler, ii, 21.
[8] Maritain, pp. vii, x. [9] Ibid., pp. xii, xvii. [10] Ibid., p. 123.

over temporal things themselves from the strict point of view of moral and spiritual interests.'[1]

'The Pope is the visible head of the mystical body, essentially supra-temporal, supra-political, supra-national, supra-cultural, of which Christ is the invisible head.'[2]

The exercise by the popes of their temporal power was beneficent; in ages of confusion the papacy provided a centre of unity in a distracted continent.

N. The claims of the popes, from Nicholas I in the ninth century onwards, to be princes of the earth and overlords of all monarchs, have no apostolic foundation; they contradicted the doctrine of earlier popes such as Gelasius I in the fifth century, who rejected secular power as a dangerous pitfall.[3] To base them on the two swords of St Luke xxii, 38 was ridiculous. They were wholly unapostolic and in contrast with the true character of the Church in guidance, monition, and spiritual control.

[1] Maritain, p. xii. [2] Ibid., p. xx.
[3] *Tomus de anathematis vinculo* and Ep. xii; *PL*, lix, 108–9, 42.

CHAPTER LXV

Forged Writings of St Cyril

St Cyril of Alexandria (†386) was so highly venerated as a doctor of the faith, both in East and West, that his epistles were bracketed with the decrees of Nicaea; the Council of Chalcedon added the Tome of St Leo, 'canonizing' all together.

In the thirteenth century an anonymous little book or *Libellus* appeared, purporting to contain the teaching of St Cyril from a work entitled the *Treasury*, in telling passages that upheld the Western attitude on the *Filioque* and the Roman interpretation of the papal sovereignty. A fictitious canon of Chalcedon of the same kind was included. They were all utterly spurious,[1] but, as usual, were accepted with innocent credulity. The *Libellus* does not seem to have reached the East, though Pope Urban IV quoted from it to Paleologus, the Emperor Michael VIII, on 28 July 1263,[2] in urging acceptance of the papal claims. The pope sent a copy to St Thomas Aquinas, who found it impressive, quoted it freely, and embodied its doctrine in his works. Aquinas quoted the following passage, evidently a favourite, in at least four different places:

> St Cyril, Bishop of Alexandria, says: Let us remain members of our head the Apostolic Throne of the Roman Pontiffs, from whom it is our duty to seek what we ought to believe and hold, venerating him, asking him before all men; since it is his duty alone to blame, correct, determine, dispose, loosen, and bind, in place of Him who set him up, and has given His own fullness to no one besides, but to him alone, to whom all bow the head by divine law, and whom the primates of the world obey as the Lord Jesus Christ Himself.[3]

[1] Bardenhewer, pp. 366–7; de Launoi, *Opp.*, ed. 1731, pp. 1–18, tom. v, pars i; *Epistolae* (Cantab., 1689), pp. 1–11.

[2] Raynaldus, iii, 109; cf. Aquinas, *Opusc.*, pp. 17–18.

[3] Lib. iv, *Sentent.*, Dist. xxiv, Q. III, Art. ii, *Opp.* xiii, 40; *Contra impugnantes Dei cultum*, cap. iii, iv, *Opp.* xix, 308, 313; *Contra errores Graecorum*, *Opusc.*, p. 17. In Matt. xvi, *Opp.* xiv, 251; *Summa*, Suppl. Q. XL, Art. vi, *Opp.* xxv, 116.

Aquinas also found in the supposed St Cyril that 'in all matters of doctrine Peter and his Church are in the place of God', and he quoted such sayings here and there.[1] He was followed confidently by the leading Western theologians[2] such as Cardinal John de Turrecremata, 'the Defender and Protector of the Faith' (1388–1468), and Bishop Melchior Cano (1509–60). The spurious St Cyril was good currency in debate; thus at the Council of Trent in 1562 an archbishop says, 'As rays to the sun and twigs to the tree, so are bishops to the Supreme Pontiff, as Cyril declares in his Treasury'.[3] They stood out in importance, because no other such teaching was to be found in the Greek Fathers of the first six centuries.[4] Bishop Cano observes that St Cyril (in these spurious passages) supplies evidence of papal authority 'much more plainly than any other authors'.[5] Devout theologians innocently relied on them, and when it was discovered at last that they were missing from the genuine *Treasury* of St Cyril, the reason of this seemed obvious to them. 'Wonder not,' says Cano, 'for the heretics have mutilated that book, and have erased all that related to the authority of the Roman Pontiffs.'[6] The pseudo-Cyrillines were still being relied on in controversy in the eighteenth century.

A. The reason why these writings attributed to St Cyril were accepted without question was just that they entirely accorded with well-known and settled doctrine. There is no evidence that they had any new or important effect on Western teaching.

'Too much should not be made of these unauthentic works; the period of the early Middle Ages is one in which they abound, and are by no means all supporting papal authority. Every writer of antiquity has numerous unauthentic works attributed to him. They are not all forgeries. Sometimes they were genuine early works which got attributed to the wrong author.'

N. The ultra-papal character of these spurious texts is striking. These were not errors of attribution, but deliberate fabrications. There was already ample support for the current Roman claims from Western writers, especially from the popes themselves, but there was a remarkable dearth of any such support to be found in the genuine writings of the Greek Fathers. The forger's object was to make good this defi-

[1] E.g., *C. err. Graec.*, cap. xxxiv–xxxviii, *Opusc.*, pp. 17–18.

[2] Bardenhewer, p. 367.

[3] Acta Trid., ii, 158; the real St Cyril addressed the pope as if an equal—'let us narrate our affairs to each other as brother to brothers, telling each other our actual plans', Mansi, iv, 1023.

[4] Chapman, *GCC*, p. 92. [5] *Opp.*, lib. vi, cap. v, p. 318. [6] Ibid.

ciency. With the authority of St Cyril's revered name, backed by that of St Thomas, his inventions could not fail to gain their intended effect.

Literary dishonesty was not looked on then as now, and there is no need to assess the degree of the forger's fault. The pregnant fact is, that the long procession of deliberate fabrications relating to papal authority, among which the False Decretals and spurious Cyrillines were most influential, completely deceived all Western Christendom for five centuries and more.

'This forgery, which gave St Thomas a wholly false idea of the tradition of the Greek Fathers, occurred at the critical period when the constitution of the Church was becoming incorporated for the first time into the framework of Dogmatic Theology, and is perhaps the most glaring and momentous of all.'[1]

[1] Robertson, p. 241.

CHAPTER LXVI

The Inquisition A.D. 1230

The Inquisition is one of the thorny subjects which (as has already been observed) afford neither direct proof nor disproof of the Doctrine of the Papacy. Lord Acton's unshaken devotion to the Holy Roman Church illustrates this, for no other historian of distinction has condemned the Inquisition in more scathing terms. Yet the subject has bulked large in controversy and cannot be ignored.

The death penalty for heresy was unknown in the early Church. 'To put a heretic to death', said St John Chrysostom, 'is an unpardonable crime.'[1] 'As late as the middle of the fourth century, and even later, all the Fathers and ecclesiastical writers who discuss the question of toleration are opposed to the use of force. To a man they reject absolutely the death penalty . . . faith must be absolutely free, and conscience a domain wherein violence must never enter.'[2] When Priscillian and his companions in Manichaean and Gnostic heresy were executed at Trèves in A.D. 385 by the Emperor Maximus, the bishops, and notably St Martin and St Ambrose, denounced the deed as atrocious and un-Christian.[3] In later centuries, however, there was much persecution of the Manichaeans.[4]

By the twelfth century the Catharan heresy had become rife in the south of France; it was also called Albigensian after the town of Albi in Languedoc. As puritans of a distorted kind its followers were called Cathari, 'the pure'. Their heresy was Manichaean, 'a strange amalgam of asceticism and laxity, of some lofty ideals with aberrations which were perverse and unhealthy'. They held marriage no better than adultery or incest,[5] and they would eat no food that was sexually begotten, so they were vegetarians; they refused to take any oath. One suspect, in order to clear himself, told the Inquisitors: 'I am not a

[1] Vacandard, p. 29; *Cath Enc.*, xii, 377.
[2] Ibid., pp. 7, 28.
[3] Maycock, p. 3; *Cath. Enc.*, viii, 27.
[4] Vacandard, pp. 11–13.
[5] CMH, vi, 706.

heretic, for I live with a wife and have children, I eat flesh and lie and swear, and am a faithful Christian.'[1]

For some time heretics had been hanged, burned, or lynched, without support from the bishops; but in 1224 the Emperor Frederick who, although 'virtually a Moslem free-thinker' himself,[2] was a zealous heresy-hunter, decreed that relapsed heretics were to be burned or, at least, to have their tongues torn out. In 1230, Pope Gregory IX adopted this law and set about enforcing it rigidly. Thenceforward the Inquisition was consolidated by a whole series of papal and imperial decrees.[3]

Mr Maycock gives a good account of 'the salutary operations of the Holy Office'. 'This medieval Inquisition', he says, 'was one of the most thoroughly successful tribunals in all history. It succeeded triumphantly in securing the extirpation of the anti-social poison of the Albigentes and, in so doing, preserved the moral unity of Europe for three hundred years.' It took about a century to do this.[4]

The Waldensians or Vaudois were very different from the Cathari. 'Their worship consisted chiefly of readings from the Scriptures and other sacred writings and of recitations of the Lord's Prayer. . . . They were distinguished by the simple piety of their lives and their strict adherence to the rules of poverty which they had set up for themselves.'[5] But they went on preaching when the bishops were opposed to them, in intolerable disobedience to the pope. So these evangelicals were persecuted and burned in large numbers; yet their cult was not wholly extirpated, and it survived into the Reformation.

In Spain, heretic-burning began in earnest after Pope Sixtus IV had authorized Ferdinand and Isabella to set up the Spanish Inquisition in 1478, and appointed Torquemada to be his representative and Grand Inquisitor. Jews in their thousands were forcibly 'converted',[6] and thus became qualified to be burned as heretics; at least 2,000 perished at the stake in twelve years.[7] There it became an instrument of national politics; at times the papacy made ineffectual efforts to check some of its proceedings.

At Rome, heretic-burning was less wholesale, but was still familiar in the seventeenth century. The victims there were usually strangled before incineration.[8] The Inquisition was active in Mexico, South America, and other countries.

[1] Guillemi Pelisso, *Chronicon.* ed. Molinier, p. 17; see Maycock, p. 139.
[2] Maycock, p. 91. [3] *Cath. Enc.*, viii, 34.
[4] Maycock, pp. 99–100. [5] Ibid., pp. 34–5.
[6] Often as alternative to death (Funk, ii, 39), although some thirteenth-century popes forbade forced baptism.
[7] Vacandard, p. 197. [8] Acton, *Letters*, pp. 113, 117.

Prison and torture[1] were routine affairs. There is, indeed, a startling resemblance between the cruelties and dungeon-secrecy of the Holy Office and the abominations of the Nazis and their Red rivals in this century.[2]

The Supreme Pontiffs were not, of course, directly responsible for all the cruelties of their Inquisitors, certainly not for the corruption of those who multiplied victims in order to get their property. The zeal of Inquisitors against Jews sometimes met with papal disapproval; some Jews even found asylum in Rome. But the popes occasionally honoured the burnings by their presence.

As regards Christian doctrine, the killing of heretics was supported by St Thomas Aquinas;[3] Pope Leo X declared it error to say that burning heretics is contrary to the will of the Holy Spirit.[4] Some modern theologians have continued to give it support.[5] There has been no authoritative pronouncement abandoning it as right doctrine. But the actual burnings have been discontinued for about three centuries, and the death penalty, not being mentioned in the 1917 revision of the *Codex Juris Canonici*,[6] is held as abrogated at the present day.

In justification of the Inquisition, it is urged that burnings often occurred before 1230, and were only systematized by the papal legislation. It has also been said that 'the Protestants were as bad'.[7] Thus the Calvinists of Geneva, it is said, burned 150 heretics. As against the 280 heretics burned in Mary Tudor's short reign, in the thirty-three years

[1] Torture, of course, was in common use and not peculiar to the Inquisition. Pope Nicholas I, indeed (858–67), had forbidden torture to obtain confession in criminal proceedings as contrary to law human and divine (Hardouin, v, 380), but Pope Innocent IV in 1252 formally permitted its use in Inquisitorial procedure.

[2] Suspicion or secret accusation was enough. There were some strange hypocrisies. A rule forbade torture for a victim on more than one occasion; it was regularly evaded on pretence of a 'continuation'. When torture had done its work, the victim was carried to another room and made to sign a statement that his confession was spontaneous and unforced (Maycock, p. 160). Canons forbade a cleric to be present; Pope Alexander IV in 1260 allowed Inquisitors to absolve one another of this irregularity (*Cath. Enc.*, viii, 32). Impenitent or relapsed heretics were passed out for 'secular' execution with the formula, 'We strongly beseech the secular court to avoid bloodshed or danger of death' (Maycock, p. 173), but the secular authorities had to carry out the burning under pain of excommunication and death to themselves. Abbé Vacandard calls this a 'legal fiction' (pp. 145–7, 179, 244).

[3] *Summa*, IIa, IIae, Q. XI, art. 3; vol. ii, 42.

[4] Bull 'Exsurge Domine', 15 June 1520 (classed as infallible in *Dict. de Théol. Catholique* (1923), vol. vii, col. 1703, Père E. Dublanchy), Denzinger, 773.

[5] References and quotations in G. G. Coulton, *The Death Penalty for Heresy* (1924), pp. 61–72, 88; C. J. Cadoux, *Roman Catholicism and Freedom* (1936), pp. 29–35, 55–61.

[6] *Normae Generales*, can. 6, n. 5.

[7] See Acton, *Hist. Freedom*, pp. 150–87.

after the pope had authorized the removal of Elizabeth and exposed her to conscientious assassination,[1] 210 devout persons, mostly priests, were hanged for treason (whether actual or only 'constructive') with the usual barbarities, including those who, like the saintly Edmund Campion, never meddled with treason. Later on, many other innocent persons suffered for their faith, notably after the imaginary 'Popish Plot' of the infamous Titus Oates. After the Reformation, moreover, witch-hunting became frenzied in Scotland and England, and thousands of persons were drowned or burned.

A. 'The Inquisition, in its establishment and procedure, pertained not to the sphere of belief but of discipline. The dogmatic teaching of the Church is in no way affected by the question whether the Inquisition was justified in its scope, or wise in its methods, or extreme in its practice. The Church established by Christ, as a perfect society, is empowered to make laws and inflict penalties for their violation. Heresy not only violates her law but strikes at her very life, unity of belief; and from the beginning the heretic had incurred all the penalties of the ecclesiastical courts.'[2]

'The ordinary, normal-minded person today, if suddenly dumped in the medieval environment, would probably have given his heartiest support to its establishment.'[3]

'That its processes, according to modern notions, were faulty; that, just like the secular courts of law, it often suffered from the abuses to which its procedure laid it open; that it was used to satisfy avarice and glut private enmities; that its officials were not always above suspicion in their methods; that its penalties were often arbitrary, unjust, cruel—these may be established facts; but the inference is not that the institution was unwarranted by the circumstances of the age or opposed to its mentality. The attachment of physical penalties to offences largely spiritual, the use of torture to elicit evidence, the defects of the legal methods, the harshness of the sentences, these characterized the tribunal, not because it was Catholic, but because it was medieval.'[4]

'The abuses of the Inquisition cannot be called a development of Catholic doctrine any more than the bad popes can be called a development of the Sermon on the Mount. In both cases we recognize a cor-

[1] See Acton, *Correspondence*, pp. 129–30; *Hist. Freedom*, p. 139. During Elizabeth's first twelve years, persecution consisted in a fine of 12d for non-attendance at church, G. M. Trevelyan, *Hist. of England*, p. 353 n. Afterwards, many 'recusants' were imprisoned or ruinously fined.

[2] *Cath. Enc.*, viii, 36.

[3] Maycock, pp. 101, 262.

[4] Conway, pp. 190–1, quoting Father Keating, *Does the Church Persecute?*, pp. 21–2.

ruption. . . . It was when the popes were corrupt that they gave whatever sanction they did to its abuses.'

N. The whole principle on which the Inquisition was based utterly contradicts the Christianity of the early Church and the teaching of the Fathers. Yet it was taught as doctrine by St Thomas, and by papal precept as well as long-settled papal practice (by Pope Leo X, for instance). It illustrates the Roman conception of development in operation. Just as the early primacy of the Roman bishop among his fellows was 'developed' by the popes into their later-asserted sovereignty, so the purer doctrine of the early Church—'thou shalt not kill the heretic'—was developed into 'thou shalt kill'.

The Inquisition cannot be passed off as a corruption of a few bad popes. It remained notorious, with all its cruelties and horrors, through some four hundred years[1] and the reigns of fifty-seven popes, two of whom were canonized.

Against the universal Church of Christ, the gates of hell shall never prevail. To the minds of many men it seems manifest that the gates of hell have often prevailed over the papacy; they cannot therefore recognize the papacy as the divinely appointed heart and centre of the Church, or as her unique fountain of truth. The sad history of much 'Protestant' sin and cruelty leaves that judgement unshaken, because they do not regard Calvin or any prince or prelate as 'Vicar of Christ'.

[1] Cf. Acton, *Letters*, p. 147; *Correspondence*, p. 108.

CHAPTER LVII

The Great Papal Schisms, A.D. 1378-1417

During the twelfth and thirteenth centuries, the popes were not settled in Rome; the papal court was set up in various Italian towns.[1]

Clement V, a Gascon, became pope in 1305 and settled at Avignon on the Rhône, just outside France proper; he was followed by six other non-Italian popes who reigned from Avignon until Pope Gregory XI removed to Rome shortly before he died in 1378. This period, sometimes called 'the Babylonian Exile', was bad in various ways. Among other things, the growth of ecclesiastical taxation and the rapacity of the Curia aroused vast discontent.[2] They paved the way for the Papal Schisms and even, perhaps, for the Western revolt of the sixteenth century.

The Roman populace violently demanded the election of an Italian. The cardinals elected an Italian (not himself a cardinal)[3] as Urban IV.[4] Soon afterwards they declared that they had only elected him in fear for their lives; if that was true, the election would have been canonically void.[5] Was it true? 'Until now the Church has not decided the matter by way of authority, and probably she never will.'[6] They declared Urban's election void, and then elected Cardinal Robert of Geneva[7] as Clement VII. He established his court at Avignon. There were now two dynasties or series of popes, at Rome and Avignon, each with his cardinals, under reciprocal excommunication.

[1] Hughes, iii, 155–6. [2] Ibid., p. 163.

[3] The last to be elected from outside the Sacred College of Cardinals, Funk, ii, 11.

[4] He turned out unbearable by his own cardinals (Salembier, pp. 51–2), and afterwards had them executed by torture (Hughes, iii, 240).

[5] Gratian, p. 380; *Dist.*, lxxix, c. ix; see Ullman, *GS*, p. 174.

[6] Salembier, pp. 25, 27.

[7] A resolute prelate who, as legate commanding the papal army, had recently punished Cesena by massacring 5,000 inhabitants, Creighton, i, 73.

In 1409, cardinals of the two camps came to an understanding, and twenty of them, with a multitude of prelates and other dignitaries, assembled in the Council of Pisa. It cited the two rival popes (by their family names) in vain, and then declared them both deposed as schismatics and heretics. The cardinals then elected another pope, Alexander V, who set up court at Bologna. Neither of the two other claimants would yield or resign; so now there were three rival claimants.

This Gordian knot was cut by the Council of Constance in 1417. It deposed the Bologna and Avignon popes. (The former submitted, but the latter was defiant and died six years later, still issuing comprehensive excommunications.) The Roman pope, Gregory XII, sent his formal abdication to the twenty-fourth session of the council, while still maintaining his legitimacy, and declaring that he now convoked the council and confirmed 'all things that are to be done by it'.[1]

The council resorted to a remarkable expedient. Of the three colleges of cardinals, all lying under reciprocal excommunication, only one could be legitimate and, on principle, two were composed of excommunicate schismatics, outside the Church. At the forty-ninth session all these cardinals met, together with thirty other prelates, and elected Martin V as pope. He presided at the remaining sessions, and declared it a General Council. Although the Avignon pope remained obdurate, 1417 is generally regarded as the end of this 'Great Schism of the West'.

This Council of Constance enacted certain decrees as to the relative authority of council and pope, and requires further attention.

A. The preservation of the Church in unimpaired strength and authority after all the perils and evils of the Great Schism proves its authority to be divine. 'What human institution could have withstood this trial?'[2]

N. For those who are unable to see the Doctrine of the Papacy in Scripture, the early Church, or the Fathers, the lamentable histories of Avignon and of the rival popes are among the many things which seem to them to mark the ineptness of the papal sovereignty as truly a centre of the unity of the Church.

[1] Mansi, xxvii, 734; done 'henceforward', Salembier, p. 348.
[2] Conway, p. 120, quoting de Maistre.

CHAPTER LXVIII

The Council of Constance, A.D. 1414-18

This council was convened by the Emperor Sigismund with the unwilling consent of the Bologna pope; it was intended to be a General Council of all prelates, princes, lords, and doctors of Christendom,[1] and it was attended by twenty-nine cardinals, three titular patriarchs, thirty-eight bishops, with a multitude of others, some 1,800 in all—'one of the largest ecclesiastical gatherings known to history'.[2]

At its fifth session, it enacted a remarkable decree:

> This holy synod of Constance, forming a General Council for the extirpation of schism, and for the reformation of the Church in its head and members . . . declares, first, that it is lawfully assembled in the Holy Spirit; constituting a General Council and representing the Catholic Church, it holds authority directly from Christ. Any one, of whatsoever status or rank, even if papal, is bound to obey it in what things pertain to faith, to the extirpation of the said schism, and to the reform of the Church in its head and members. Whosoever, of whatever condition, status or rank, even papal, contumaciously despises to obey the ordinances, precepts, acts, etc., of this sacred synod, or of any other general council lawfully assembled, shall be subjected to condign penance and be duly punished.[3]

(At the fifteenth session John Hus was condemned and burned as a heretic.)

At the thirty-ninth session (after its farewell acceptance by Gregory XII) the council made a long decree providing for the possibility of rival popes in the future. A General Council is to assemble, supersede both of them and pronounce judgement. This seems to carry an implication 'that the General Council as such is the pope's superior'.[4]

1 Pastor, i, 194.
2 Funk, ii, 16, 'In a certain sense a congress of the whole West'.
3 Mansi, xxvii, 590–1.
4 Hughes, iii, 298–9.

At the close of the council, the new pope, Martin V, approved and ratified 'all things determined, settled and declared conciliarly by the present council in matters of faith . . . and not otherwise or in any other manner'.[1]

The next pope, Eugenius IV, was elected in 1431 on his promising to hold a general council and, by its means, reform the whole Church.[2] This Council of Basle, with a small membership, opened in July. Pope Eugenius at once dissolved it by a Bull, which the council ignored, and it received such strong support that the pope resolved to yield to its demands.[3] He declared it a lawful General Council canonically conducted from its opening, and accepted it in terms that satisfied the somewhat contumacious assembly.[4] The council republished the famous decree of Constance. It is maintained that Pope Eugenius IV did not actually accept that decree of Basle. In any case, he seems to have deemed himself at liberty to repeal any canon at his own hand for, a few years later, he wrote:

> It is ridiculous to adduce the sacred canons and ask for observance of their provisions by Us whose is the issuing, publication and exposition of them; for the Pontiffs, who have power to establish and interpret laws, can suspend them, amend, alter entirely, or abolish them.[5]

In the meantime, however, Pope Eugenius had completely and triumphantly re-established his authority at the Council of Florence: he then vigorously denounced the obnoxious decrees of Constance and Basle.[6] They fell back into past history, although the principle involved in them lingered in Gallicanism, and only received its *coup de grâce* in 1870.

A. The Council of Constance, until it was validated by Pope Gregory XII at its fourteenth session, was an unlawful assembly, without any authority: its earlier proceedings were nullities. Pope Martin's subsequent ratification of its conciliar acts did not include its fifth session, for the council had not then become oecumenical.[7] 'He guarded himself against pronouncing a quite universal confirmation. His words ("con-

[1] Mansi, xxvii, 1199. [2] Pastor, i, 284.
[3] Ibid., p. 293; Hughes, iii, 327. [4] Hughes, *loc cit.*; Mansi, xxix, 78–9.
[5] Raynaldus, ix, 325 (1439, n. 37). See also ix, 474–5 (1446, n. 3, letter to his nuncios). He seems to have held a view contrary to that of Popes Zosimus and Celestine I, a thousand years earlier, 'The authority of this See cannot indeed assent or make alteration contrary to the statutes of the Fathers', Ep. v, *PL*, xx, 666; Ep. iii, *PL*, l, 426. But Pope John XXII in 'Quia quorundam', 10 November 1324, declared that a pope has power to reject his predecessors' decrees on questions of faith as erroneous.
[6] 'Moyses', 6 September 1439, Mansi, xxxi, 1718–19. [7] Salembier, p. 307.

ciliarly" and "in matters of faith") have a restrictive character.' 'He indicated by this that he excepted some decrees from the approbation but, in the interests of peace, did not wish to express himself more clearly.'[1] Any immediate blunt repudiation would probably have brought back schism.[2]

The decree of Basle as to the superiority of the General Council was not approved or confirmed by Pope Eugenius IV. 'He had to make a show of accepting the new unacceptable theories about the superiority of General Councils.'[3] 'He only recognized generally the *existence* of the Synod of Basle and made use of expressions which *implicite* might appear to include an approval of that thesis. In the same way as Martin V, in the interests of peace he was unwilling to express himself clearly on this controverted point, reserving this for a more favourable time.'[4]

N. Whether or not the decrees of Constance (and of Basle), which the popes detested, were technically confirmed according to the Doctrine of the Papacy, or whether Popes Martin and Eugenius contrived to avoid this, is a matter of debate for historians and canonists—although the decree of Constance at its thirty-ninth session seems to be beyond challenge.

For those who are not already persuaded of the Doctrine of the Papacy, what seems chiefly significant is, that the doctrine was not the faith of the great council of the West at Constance, which declared the pope to be subordinate to the council.

[1] Hefele, v, 408 (introd. to 2nd ed.). [2] Hughes, iii, 306.
[3] Ibid., p. 338. [4] Hefele, v, 410 (introd. to 2nd ed.).

CHAPTER LXIX

The Need for Disciplinary Reform

For long generations before the Reformation, there had been grave need within the Church to cleanse its organization from rampant evils. In the time of Constance and Basle there had been outcry for 'reformation of the Church in its head and members'; but abuses were left unchecked.

Simony, the buying and selling of benefices, had been forbidden again and again, century after century. Yet it was well known to be rife at the Vatican.[1] At Constance, bishops and other leading preachers each Sunday denounced the sins of episcopal simony, and the simony of the Roman Curia, as the chief cause of decay in Christian life.[2] Popes made it their first endeavour to endow their nephews with dukedoms and principalities and rich benefices;[3] many of them they made cardinals. Enormous papal taxation caused resentment everywhere;[4] the English House of Commons dared to petition 'against the pope and his cardinals', that 'the pope shears his flock but does not feed it'.[5] There was 'a stench of accretions of immense ecclesiastical wealth',[6] although the papal riches were dissipated to a great extent upon the papal wars.[7]

The system of papal provisions and reservations—the filling of benefices throughout the Western Church by papal nominees—had a good deal in its favour, as Mr Barraclough has shown. Although it was an utter innovation on ancient Church law and custom, it grew up gradually, by clerical habit rather than by papal initiative or 'usurpation', and it had been in practice for a century before it was formally

[1] Hughes, iii, 339; Pastor, v, 238. [2] Hughes, iii, 296.
[3] Ibid., p. 389; Funk, ii, 26–8; Pastor, v, 356.
[4] Hughes, iii, 158, 166; Funk, iii, 42–4.
[5] Hughes, iii, 310. [6] Ibid., pp. 158, 175, 359.
[7] Ibid., pp. 167, 434.

decreed in 1265.[1] It ran counter to vested interests and local nepotism; it tended to introduce new elements into chapters, to the benefit of cathedrals and collegiate churches.[2] There were tens of thousands of petitions for minor benefices, in disposing of which the popes inclined to recognize the merits of education and scholarship.[3] Yet 'papal provisions and papal finance were at the heart of the opposition which culminated in Protestantism'.[4] Dispensations to hold benefices in plurality were a fat source of revenue, and the intrusion of foreigners, chiefly Italian or French, into northern sees and benefices aroused angry discontent.[5] Thus a parishioner of Towcester in the diocese of Lincoln might (or might not) know that his rector also held two archdeaconries, one abbacy, and five canonries in France, two canonries and four churches in Rome, and a cardinal's hat.[6] The Medici who was pope when the storm of the Reformation broke had been made cardinal at the age of fourteen; he had held in his youth three canonries, six rectories, a priory, a precentorship, a provostship, and sixteen abbacies.[7] St Louis IX of France told Pope Innocent IV in 1247 that 'these foreigners do not reside; they are mere names, perhaps sham names, under cover of which churches and patrons are plundered. All that the Church of Rome gets is the scandal and the hatred.'[8] Sees were bestowed on children, or on men of utterly unsuitable antecedents, and these appointments were made by the popes. Church revenues were bestowed on laymen, cadets or bastards of great families, especially in Scotland.[9]

The lives of bishops and clergy were often notoriously scandalous,[10] and standards of morality among the priesthood were low everywhere. The Provincial Council of Paris in 1429 declared that the laity no longer regarded fornication as a mortal sin, because clerical concubinage was so common. It was even proposed at Constance and Basle to repeal the law of celibacy.[11] Immorality, luxury, and lasciviousness had become proverbial at the papal court at Avignon, and 'was, to say the least, condoned by the popes'.[12] St Catherine of Siena 'loudly complained that at the Papal Court, which ought to have been a Paradise of virtue, her nostrils were assailed by the odours of hell'.[13] Rodrigo Borgia, who became Pope Alexander VI (1492–1503) by means of 'the

[1] Barraclough, pp. 69–70, 155, 164, 168. [2] Ibid., pp. 56–7.
[3] Ibid., pp. 106, 109, 154, 160. [4] Ibid., viii, 70. [5] Barry, p. 41.
[6] Hughes, iii, 56. [7] Belloc, p. 46.
[8] A. L. Smith, *Church and State in the Middle Ages* (1913), p. 147.
[9] Belloc, p. 190. [10] Notably so in Scotland and Poland, Kidd, *CR*, p. 122.
[11] Hughes, iii, 328; Funk, ii, 76. [12] Ullmann, *GS*, p. 6.
[13] Pastor, i, 107–8.

rankest simony',[1] sired many bastards, some of whom he endowed with rich dukedoms at the expense of the Church. It was during his reign that Savonarola preached against the vices of the papal court and, because he would not be silenced, was tortured and hanged. 'The profligacy of the rulers of Naples, Milan, and Florence of that time was something almost unheard of. The fact that the lives of so many princes of the Church were no better than those of the temporal rulers gave little or no scandal to the Italians of the Renaissance.'[2]

How all this was regarded by the people is illustrated by Boccaccio's tale of the Jew Abraham of Paris, whose Christian friend had hoped for his conversion, but despaired of it when the Jew insisted on visiting Rome to see the Church at its papal centre. When Abraham returned, to his friend's amazement he sought baptism; he was now convinced, he said, that the Christian religion must be divine; otherwise it could not have survived the glaring wickedness of its chiefs. The popularity of this tale witnesses also to another striking fact, which Dr Pastor emphasizes,[3] viz., that the faithful were able to distinguish the venerable and sacred office of the pope from the person of wicked individual popes.

Yet all these evils brought about an indifference of Catholics to the cause of the Roman Church as such, and were perhaps a chief cause of its collapse in the West in the sixteenth century.[4] Attempts at Constance and Basle did little to better matters,[5] and the prolonged failure of the popes to set about reforms so urgently needed caused widespread discontent.[6]

Questions of faith not directly affecting the Doctrine of the Papacy are outside the scope of this book. Some of these went much beyond the abuses connected with indulgences that set the match to the Lutheran explosion. Many things led up to the Reformation. Cardinal Gasquet, in his study of *The Eve of the Reformation*,[7] will not 'draw a definite conclusion from the facts, or expound the causes of the ultimate triumph of the Reformation principles in England'. He is concerned to show that the mass of the people were not then estranged from the Roman Church; yet 'the time for a satisfactory synthesis is not yet come'.

A. The popular realization that the sacredness of the papal office was not impaired by the wickedness of some individual popes, was a true insight and understanding.

'Though we cannot approve sin, we must allow that the existence of

[1] Pastor, v, 385. [2] Ibid., p. 388. [3] E.g., at iv, 272.
[4] Hughes, iii, 174; see also Belloc, pp. 31, 36; Pastor, i, 142.
[5] Hughes, iii, 331. [6] Funk, ii, 78, 79. [7] Pp. 185 sq., 391.

sin does not prove the body in which sin exists to be in error, unless the sin follows from its teaching.'

It is unquestionable that worldliness, immorality, nepotism, and avarice marked many of the clergy in the sixteenth century, and that a reformation in the lives of many unworthy clerics and laymen was indeed called for.[1] Their personal sin was great.

Yet Reformation, in the sense of revolt from the Church established by Christ, and denying its doctrines, government, and worship, could not be of God. It was not in fact followed by an upsurge of virtuous living, but rather by social, moral, and religious deterioration.[2]

Within the Roman Church, the evils that provoked the great revolt have long ago been purged away.

N. A colossal system of corruption and vice centred on the papal chair, and had radiated from it for centuries. The 'Supreme Pontiffs', who retained absolute authority in the West, permitted it all and even promoted it. The explosion was inevitable, but few if any non-Roman Christians can rejoice over the manner of its occurrence, or be content with all its results. Explosion always does some injury, and it causes fragmentation.

There were innumerable persons of holy life within the Roman Church, as there are now. Moreover the Reformation certainly did not cause any sudden and universal mass-reform of conduct. These are evident facts to many who, nevertheless, see in Scripture a divine judgement on the peculiar claims of the popes: *Attendite a falsis prophetis . . . a fructibus eorum cognoscetis eos*; by their fruits you shall know them (Matt. vii, 16–17).

[1] Pastor, vii, 291–328; Conway, p. 91. [2] Conway, p. 91.

CHAPTER LXX

The Counter-Reformation

After the storm of the Reformation broke out in 1517, the Inquisition was roused to fresh severity in those countries that remained faithful; it was strengthened by Pope Paul III in 1542.[1] But the progress of the revolt, soon accompanied by doctrinal innovations, compelled him to summon a council.

The great Council of Trent met in 1545 and held many sessions during the next eighteen years. It examined and condemned the teachings of the Reformers, notably the Lutheran doctrine of Justification by Faith (Solfidianism). It explained and defined original sin, transubstantiation, and other important doctrines. It took in hand the task of disciplinary reform, and decreed against some evils that had caused scandal in the Church. It legislated against clerical concubinage,[2] reprehended the holding of pluralities 'even by cardinals',[3] ordered those appointed to cathedral churches, 'even cardinals', to be consecrated,[4] and prelates and other holders of benefices to reside in them.[5] There were renewed decrees against simony.[6] Commerce in indulgences was strongly condemned.

In the latter years of the council, there was a long angry dispute on the relationship of the episcopate to the pope. The Roman Curia, supported by the Italians, who outnumbered all the others by more than two to one,[7] maintained that bishops are not superior to priests inherently by their order, but only from a privilege allowed them by the pope, through whom alone they possess any jurisdiction;[8] 'the apostles

[1] *Cath. Enc.*, xii, 503–10; Ranke, i, 162 sq.; Paul IV punished serious heresies by burning, even without 'relapse', Fessler, p. 97.

[2] Sess. xxiv, cap. xiv; Waterworth, p. 270.

[3] Sess. vii, cap. ii; sess. xxiv, cap. xvii; Waterworth, pp. 59, 224.

[4] Sess. vii, cap. ix; sess. xxiii, cap. ii; Waterworth, pp. 62, 178.

[5] Sess. vi, cap. i; sess. xxiii, cap. i; Waterworth, pp. 49, 175.

[6] Sess. xxi, cap. i; sess. xxiv, cap. xiv, xviii; Waterworth, pp. 145, 221, 226.

[7] Waterworth, p. 311.

[8] Ibid., p. cciii; Acta Trid., ii, 197.

received jurisdiction from Peter, not directly from Christ'.[1] In support of this they invoked the False Decretals and the spurious St Cyril.[2] All the Spanish bishops, and some others, stood out for episcopal authority as of divine institution, even asserting that they were the apostles' successors and therefore vicars of Christ as much as the pope, even though he be the chief of them.[3] The dispute led to disgraceful scenes in the council, and fighting in the streets, with rival shouts of 'Hispania' and 'Italia' and much bloodshed.[4] Ultimately the canons declared that bishops are superior to priests in the divinely ordained hierarchy and that bishops 'who are assumed by authority of the Roman Pontiff' are legitimate and true.[5]

Although the reformatory decrees of the council were imperfectly obeyed at first, they prevailed in time, and many old abuses were purged. One marked advance was in the character and education of the clergy at large; they had commonly been men of mean quality and small education, too unlearned to preach. Seminaries were set up by decree, and this ultimately gave to the Church 'if not always a learned, at any rate a trained and disciplined clergy'.[6]

The powers of the Curia and the papal dispensing power (even as to pluralities and absenteeism) were left unimpaired. In the period following after the council there were some popes of high personal character and zealous for reform, although this led them to reinforce the Inquisition and extend the use of torture. But papal finance remained vast and unpopular, and the popes from 1585 to 1644 firmly re-established the bad old custom of nepotism and the 'founding of families', by endowing their nephews and other relations with Church property.[7] Long since then, of course, the Vatican has been purged of these old persistent abuses, and now we look upon 'a papacy politically weakened, but morally respected'.[8]

Nevertheless, reforms came too late to check the revolt, or reconcile to the papal obedience the mass of Western Christians who had cast it off, and who indeed were embittered by the severe measures taken against them. It is said that the true facts of the Massacre of St Bartholomew had been falsified to Pope Gregory XIII when he rejoiced over it,[9] but even Pope St Pius V urged the French king to pursue the Huguenots

[1] Acta Trid., ii, 190. [2] E.g., Acta Trid., ii, 157, 158, 197, 600.
[3] Ibid., pp. 157, 600. [4] Ibid., pp. 256, 606.
[5] Canons vi–viii, sess. xxiii, cap. iv; Waterworth, p. 174; see above, ch. lxiii. They did not refer to orthodox or other 'schismatic' orders, which are acknowledged as valid, although not 'legitimate'.
[6] Kidd, *CR*, p. 174. [7] Ranke, ii, 335–43. [8] Belloc, p. 53.
[9] See Conway, p. 198; Acton, *Correspondence*, pp. 132–5.

ruthlessly to the death.[1] He was a pope of earnest piety under whom men were hanged and quartered almost daily in Rome.[2] Yet there can be small doubt that the torturings, burnings, and other deaths conscientiously inflicted on the strayed sheep of the papal fold helped to engrain a hatred of Rome that is sometimes called Romophobia, and still lingers in some quarters. The no less earnest piety of recent popes has found more pastoral expression in a very different character of appeal to separated Christians.[3] Whether the history of the Church might have been greatly different if Pope Leo XIII and his successors had lived in the sixteenth century and spoken as they have spoken to this generation can only be conjectured. In the stark fact of history, the separation of those who had cast off the papal obedience widened into antagonism, followed by more doctrinal departures. In the course of two or three generations, further doctrinal divisions opened among them, especially in the Calvinist wing of the Reformation, from which are derived many Protestant denominations of today.

A. 'Reform was urgently needed in the Church; but it should have been a reform from within, as did seriously begin at Trent.'

The glories of the Counter-Reformation—the great revival of theology and spiritual life, the spread of missions—have been recognized as 'the finest flowering of the Church's sanctity'.

'The rejection of papal supremacy by the East was not for doctrinal reasons, but rather for national or political ones. The same was true in many cases at the Protestant Reformation.'

The fearful error and sin of the great revolt from the Church have been demonstrated by the instability of those groups that deserted the Rock of Peter, with their many sects and heresies, and frequent falling away from all Christian faith. 'Hundreds of religious bodies, all claiming to be Christian and all differing on vital and essential matters of belief, can be seen round about us today. The process of division is still going on, and it must continue where there is no authority to speak with a divine commission.'[4]

N. Alienated from Rome are millions of Christians who hold the Catholic Creeds. The steadfastness of the Orthodox East to the faith of Nicaea and Chalcedon, in separation from Rome for the last nine hundred years, is enough to show that separation from Rome does not involve lapse from the Catholic Faith.

[1] Letters of 28 March, 13 April 1569; Acton, *Hist. Freedom*, pp. 101, 139.
[2] Ibid., p. 138.
[3] E.g., Pope Leo XIII, 'Amantissima voluntatis', 14 April 1895.
[4] Cardinal Gasquet, *England's Breach with Rome* (1920), p. 13.

Yet these Christians of the Catholic Creeds mourn for the fact of separation and much that has since taken place, for the sin of schism opens the way to further evils. It seems to them that the primary and chief responsibility for the riving asunder of the Church rests on Rome:

(i) Because of Rome's false claims of papal sovereignty, rightly and inevitably rejected, first by the Orthodox East and afterwards in the North.

(ii) Because Rome's head and hierarchy displayed a depth of corruption peculiar to Rome and scarcely paralleled in the East or elsewhere in Christendom; it estranged millions of the genuinely devout; the cruelties of the Inquisition added to their repugnance; discovery that the papal claims were propped up on forgeries finally destroyed belief in the papal sovereignty.

CHAPTER LXXI

Gallicanism and the Society of Jesus

For more than five centuries before the definition in 1870 of the Doctrine of the Papacy, there had been a tendency or school of thought within the Western Church, 'a mentality among theologians and canonists and bishops', which subtly endangered the papal sovereignty, although it held firmly to 'the outward appearance and reverence, and the mass of the traditional Catholic beliefs'.[1] Thus William of Ockham, an English Franciscan (†1349), taught that the pope, although *caput* and *judex* of all Christendom, with the power of supervising preaching and divine worship, is no absolute sovereign in spiritual matters, and has no real primacy of jurisdiction.[2] Marsiglio of Padua, rector of the University of Paris, whose *Defensor pacis* appeared in 1324, maintained that Christ appointed no head of the Church and made no one His vicar, that the history of the papacy was one of gradual encroachments and usurpations.[3] Gerson (1363–1429), professor and chancellor of that university, one of the holiest men of his time, a man of really pious life, and marvellously void of ambition,[4] followed the same teachings; he was a leading figure at the Council of Constance. The famous decrees of that council (and of Basle) purported to subordinate the pope to the authority of general councils, and 'after Constance things are never the same'.[5] Yet these doctors and councils were all thoroughly Catholic 'in the sense of Catholic morals, tone, tradition and main doctrine',[6] in everything, that is to say, except the Doctrine of the Papacy.

The Gallican party or school of thought, dominant in France in the

[1] Hughes, iii, 316.
[2] Hull, p. 59; Pastor, i, 76.
[3] Hull, pp. 81–2. Others, such as Dietrich of Niem (†1418), thought similarly. See E. F. Jacob, *Essays in the Concilian Epoch* (1943), pp. 23–43.
[4] Hughes, iii, 227, 443. Some suppose him the author of the *De Imitatione Christi*; D. Barron, *Jean Charlier de Gerson*, (1936).
[5] Ibid., p. 282.
[6] Belloc, p. 154.

seventeenth century, retained these doctrines and held to the decrees of Constance. The Gallican Articles, which were adopted by the clergy of France and registered by royal command as laws of France, declared that the decrees of Constance, 'approved as they are by the Holy See and by the practice of the whole Church', remain in full force; the pope's decrees in questions of faith are not irreversible until confirmed by consent of the Church.[1]

The so-called Jansenist school of thought was contemporary in France, but had little in common with Gallicanism. It got its name from a bishop of Ypres (†1638) whose posthumous book was a study of St Augustine's teaching, with special reference to the doctrine of Grace. In 1654, the pope condemned certain 'Five Propositions of Cornelius Jansen', said to be extracted from that book. The 'Jansenists were ready enough to condemn the propositions, but stubbornly unwilling to profess that Jansen had taught them', and they maintained that papal infallibility did not extend to 'a judgement of fact', i.e., that the Five Propositions were actually taught in Jansen's book.[2] (This nice distinction raises a question that is not yet closed even by the *Dogmatic Constitution* on Infallibility.)[3]

Apart from the disciplinary questions in dispute, both Gallicans and Jansenists fervently held to the faith of the Holy Roman Church and the decrees of Trent; Gallicans heartily approved of the Revocation of the Edict of Nantes and the banishment of the Huguenots. Gallicanism was foredoomed by the self-contradiction of its principles, by an inherent fallacy. On the one hand it acknowledged the pope as Vicar of Christ by divine appointment in the individual and tremendous sense as 'constituting only one Head with Christ'. On the other hand it contended for legal or 'constitutional' limits upon the authority of Christ as wielded by His Vicar. These two positions were contradictory and irreconcilable in the end of the day. Non-Roman Christians may maintain (rightly or wrongly) that nothing in the New Testament or Tradition shows that our Lord made St Peter or any bishop His Vicar in this unique sense; but, if indeed He did so, the New Testament certainly sets out no provisos to control that divine vicariate, nothing to limit it as only a 'constitutional' sovereignty.

In resistance to Gallicanism, and all kindred doctrines and movements, the Society of Jesus played a notable part. This latest, and in some ways greatest, of the Religious Orders was established in 1540 as a *corps d'élite* in the army of the Church. Its zeal and activity enormously helped the Counter-Reformation, by good works, preach-

[1] Ranke, ii, 441. [2] Ibid., p. 447. [3] McNabb, p. 50.

ing, and especially by the work of teaching, not only the clergy but also the laity in those ranks and classes best placed to carry weight in the world. Its characteristic virtue and military rule has been from the beginning that of absolute and unflinching obedience to the Supreme Pontiff, and to the orders of its own General, 'as though Christ Himself were present in his person'.[1] The devoted labours of its members through four centuries are renowned; no missionaries have been more heroic, the French Jesuits especially. Yet it has aroused opposition and even hatred; many criticisms and charges have been made against it. It was driven out of some countries, banished from France in 1596 for seven years.

At the Council of Trent, and always, the Order has upheld absolute papal sovereignty against Gallicanism, Jansenism, and kindred tendencies, including the schism of Utrecht.[2] The Order was strangely 'abolished and annulled' in 1773 by a Brief of Pope Clement XIV, expressed as irreformable; 'it shall be, and for ever remain, valid, firm, and effective'.[3] But it was reinstated by Pope Pius VII in 1814,[4] and has remained vigorous in its labours and strong in influence.

It may be more than a coincidence that Febronianism[5] flourished during the forty years' eclipse of the Society of Jesus. Its doctrines 'advanced to a radicalism far outstripping Gallicanism',[6] and asserted that the Scriptural passages on which the papal claims are based have nothing to do with the papacy; that the primacy was placed at Rome by authority not of Christ but of the Church, which might transfer it elsewhere; that the primitive constitution of the Church has been distorted, largely through the False Decretals, and should be restored; that the pope is not infallible, and that decrees even of a general council gain binding force only after acceptance by the individual Churches. Febronianism had a tremendous success[7] in Germany and North Italy, and spread rapidly in Germany, but in the nineteenth century the 'integral and active Catholicism'[8] to which the curious epithet 'Ultramontane'[9] has been given prevailed, and Febronianism died out. The

[1] Ranke, i, 152–3.

[2] This began in 1702 and was never healed; it ultimately merged with those who seceded from Rome after 1870 and now form the Old Catholic Churches.

[3] 'Dominus ac Redemptor', 21 July 1773, *Continuazione degli annali d'Italia* di Muratori, tom. XIV, ii, p. 107; Ranke, ii, 497.

[4] Ranke, ii, 515.

[5] So called from the pen-name of Bishop von Hontheim in a book of 1763.

[6] *Cath. Enc.*, vi, 23–4. [7] Ibid. [8] Ibid., xv, 125.

[9] Dwelling 'beyond the mountains', *ultra montes*. Originally used of the Church north of the Alps—afterwards, in a reverse sense, for the *south* of the Alps, in Italy and at the Vatican, and 'extreme' fidelity to papal authority.

Vatican Council of 1870 identified the 'ultramontanism' of the Roman theological schools with Catholicism, and finally extinguished Gallican notions. Since then, ultramontanism 'has, for all in communion with the Holy See, been stamped as Catholicism'.[1]

[1] Butler, i, 38–9; but he distinguishes those whom he calls 'neo-ultramontanists' for their extreme views.

PART NINE

THE NINETEENTH, THE CENTURY OF DEFINITION

CHAPTER LXXII

Definition of the Immaculate Conception, 1854

(i) *History of the dogma*

This doctrine has no direct connexion with the universal belief of all orthodox Christians, that our Lord Jesus Christ was conceived by the Holy Ghost and born of the Virgin Mary. It declares with great preciseness that she herself was preserved from any taint whatever of human guilt, not merely that she never fell into sin, nor even that she was miraculously born sinless, but that from the very first moment of her being, at her conception, she was miraculously exempted from original sin and its guilt.

The doctrine of itself would present no difficulty to any orthodox Christian who believes, with Dr Pusey, that in all eternity the Most High foreordained her who was to be Theotokos, Genetrix Dei, the Mother of God,[1] and there are many who themselves believe the doctrine without holding it a necessary article of the Christian faith. In the Orthodox Eastern Church, never behindhand in giving reverence to the all-holy Theotokos,[2] most theologians reject the doctrine on theological grounds; a few have held it as a pious opinion; it has never been a dogma. Certain difficulties have been thought to stand in its way. It might seem to subordinate our Lord to His mother as second only to her in the grace of absolute sinlessness; and all, the Blessed Virgin included, must be saved through Him.[3] The New Testament tells little of the Virgin's life, but teaches that 'all have sinned',[4] and He alone is spoken of as sinless. Some centuries ago there were vehement disputes for and against the doctrine itself. Today there are none; it only enters controversy in relation to the *Dogmatic Constitution*.

From earliest time the Church has held the blessed Virgin Mary in loving reverence as greatest and holiest of saints. Orthodox Christians

[1] Pusey, p. 23.
[2] Fortescue, *OEC*, p. 108.
[3] St Thomas Aquinas, see p. 375.
[4] Rom. iii, 23; 1 Cor. xv, 22.

have honoured her as Theotokos, God-bearer, ever since the Council of Ephesus[1] confirmed the use of that title in asserting the perfect Godhead of our Lord. Yet Scripture has never been deemed sufficient alone to establish the particular dogma of her Immaculate Conception. Various texts in the Old Testament have been claimed as allusions to it, such as Ezekiel xliv, 2 and Canticles iv, 7; support has been claimed from Genesis iii, 15—'enmity between thy seed and her seed: it shall bruise thy head'. At some time after the fourth century the Vulgate text was altered to read, '*she* shall bruise thy head', and it has sometimes been argued that she, the Blessed Virgin, could never have bruised the Serpent's head if she had ever for an instant been subject to original sin.

St Clement of Alexandria in the second century says that 'the Word Himself alone is without sin'.[2]

Tertullian and Origen in the third century conceive the Lord's mother as subject at least to venial human faults. Tertullian considered that she, with His 'brethren', impatiently broke in on His work.[3] Origen thought that at the time of Christ's passion the 'sword' of doubt and disbelief pierced her soul, and that for her sins also Christ died.[4]

In the fifth century, St Basil's teaching agrees with that of Origen.[5] St Ephraem of Syria, who wrote nineteen long hymns on the Holy Nativity, finds no praise too high for her grace and sanctity. He calls her most holy, all-pure, all-immaculate, guileless; 'Jesus and Mary are alone completely beautiful and without stain, unlike other children'.[6] He does not refer to her conception or her birth. St Gregory Nazianzen speaks of her as 'fore-purified' before the conception of our Lord.[7] St John Chrysostom attributes to her ordinary human faults such as impatience or ambition;[8] yet his disciple St Proclus and later Eastern writers speak in a general way of her perfect sinlessness.

St Anselm, about A.D. 1100, taught explicitly that 'She was conceived in iniquity, and in sin did her mother conceive her; she was moreover born in original sin, since she also sinned in Adam, in whom all have sinned'.[9] But Eadmer, who had been his secretary, wrote a tractate[10]

[1] See ch. xxxviii. [2] See Pusey, p. 108.
[3] *De carne Christi*, vii; *PL*, ii, 767 (Matt. xii, 46–8; Luke viii, 20–1).
[4] *In Lucam*, Hom. xvii; *Opp.*, ii, 952.
[5] Ep. cclx, *ad Optimum*; *Opp. omn.* (Paris, 1730), iii, 400–1.
[6] *Carmina Nisib.*, 27 (27–8) 8; Pusey., pp. 301–4; *Cath. Enc.*, vii, 676.
[7] Pusey, p. 91.
[8] Hom. xlv, *in Matt.* (xiii, 10, 11); Hom. xxi, *in Joann.* (ii, 4); *Opp.*, viii, 122.
[9] *Cur Deus Homo*, II, xvi; *Opp.* (Paris, 1721), p. 92.
[10] Tractatus *de conceptione S. Mariae*, *PL*, clix, 302–18.

arguing for the belief that her conception was immaculate; that it was fitting and necessary that it should be so (thus anticipating the argument afterwards tersely expressed by Duns Scotus, *Potuit*, *decuit*, *ergo fecit*). The belief was widely held in England.

St Bernard (†1153) taught that she was conceived in sin, but sanctified and made sinless before birth.[1] St Thomas Aquinas (†1274), who was a Dominican, taught that the Blessed Virgin was sanctified before her birth, but not until after her conception, which necessarily carried with it original sin; moreover she would otherwise have needed no redemption through her Son, the Redeemer of all mankind.[2]

The belief was supported, however, by John Duns Scotus (†1309), a Franciscan. Of the possible modes of her sanctification, he said, 'which of them is true, God knows'; but he preferred that which is now accepted.[3] The Franciscans took up his view with enthusiasm, and for two centuries disputes raged between them and the Dominicans, who accused them of heresy for supporting the doctrine. Every year, at the Feast of the Conception, there were hostilities and disorders.

Cardinal John de Turrecremata, 'the Defender and Protector of the Faith', wrote an exhaustive treatise[4] condemning the belief shortly before 1439, when the Council of Basle (after it had been excommunicated by Pope Eugenius IV, and had declared him deposed) defined and declared the modern dogma.[5]

Controversy went on, and in 1483 Pope Sixtus IV, although he himself favoured the belief, forbade strife by a Bull 'Grave nimis',[6] in which he left it an open question whether the glorious Virgin Mary either was or was not conceived in original sin, 'for it has not yet been decided by the Roman Church and the Apostolic See', and sternly condemned any who should accuse of heresy those who asserted either opinion. When in 1546 the Council of Trent defined Original Sin, it added a proviso excluding the Blessed Virgin from its decree, and cautiously reaffirming the commands of the Bull 'Grave nimis'.[7]

Controversy grew hot again at the beginning of the seventeenth

[1] Ep. clxxiv; *Opp. omn.* (Paris, 1690), i, 170 (the holiness even of St Dominic seemed to his disciples to prove that he had received this same grace, Milman, vi, 11).

[2] *Opusculum* ix, tract. ii, cap. xl (*Opusculam* p. 186), or iii, cap. ccxxiv; *Opp.* xx, 129. *Summa*, pars. iii, Q. xxvii, arts. 1, 2; vol. iii, 98–9.

[3] *Sententiae*, Lib. iii, Dist. iii, Q.1 (Antwerp, 1620); ii, 29–30.

[4] Tractatus de veritate conceptionis beatissimae virginis pro facienda relatione coram patribus concilii. Basileae, 1438.

[5] Sess. 36, 17 September 1439; Mansi, xxix, 182–3.

[6] 5 September 1483; Denzinger, 735; Mirbt, p. 170; Kidd, *DI*, iii, 224.

[7] Sess. v; Denzinger, 792; Waterworth, p. 24.

century, and there were tumults in Spain, so in 1617 Pope Paul V reaffirmed 'Grave nimis'. Disorders went on, and King Philip III of Spain sent an embassy to ask the pope to decide the doctrinal question. Pope Paul in 1618 answered that 'God had not inspired, nor his conscience told him, anything beyond what he had already commanded in the Decree':[1]

> The Holy Paraclete, at whose indefectible prompting the Supreme Pontiffs bring forth the holy secrets of the mysteries of the Faith, has postponed this question to be revealed more fitly at some other time.[2]

Four years later, King Philip IV sent a still stronger embassy with the same petition to the next pope, Gregory XV. He answered in a Brief:[3]

> We, who have been placed by God over the Christian world in the chair of divine wisdom, ought to listen to the voice of the Holy Spirit, not weigh the matter by human reasonings. Wherefore, seeing that the Eternal Wisdom has not yet revealed to His Church the recesses of so great a mystery, faithful people are bound to rest quiet in the authority of God and of the Roman Pontiffs.

More than two centuries later, Pope Pius IX (1846–77) came to the throne. In the hurly-burly of the time, he had to flee from Rome for more than a year, taking refuge at Gaëta near Naples. It is said that he turned in his distress to the Blessed Virgin, to whom he always had a special devotion, and vowed that he would raise the pious opinion of her Immaculate Conception into a dogma which all must accept.[4] It was already an almost universal belief in the Roman Church. The Jesuit Order strongly supported it; Pius consulted a number of bishops who held the same view. On 8 December 1854, the Feast of the Conception, he proclaimed the dogma in the Bull 'Ineffabilis Deus':

> We declare, pronounce, and define the doctrine to have been revealed by God, and therefore to be firmly and constantly believed by all the faithful, which holds that the blessed Virgin Mary was preserved from all taint of original sin, in the first instant of her conception, by a singular grace and privilege of Almighty God, in consideration of Christ Jesus, the Saviour of the human race. (Any who should presume to think otherwise in their hearts are condemned as rebels from the unity of the Church.)[5]

When Pope Pius read the Bull to a large gathering of bishops, he told them plainly that they were not a council, and that the pronouncement of the dogma was solely his own act. It is therefore an important milestone in the recognition and acceptance of the Doctrine of Infalli-

[1] Wadding, p. 40. [2] Ibid., p. 425.
[3] 'Charissime in Christo', 4 June 1622; Wadding, p. 452. [4] Nielsen, ii, 188.
[5] Denzinger, 1621; Mirbt, no. 596, pp. 446–7; Bettenson, p. 378.

bility; doctrine had hitherto been expounded by the pope and council in conjunction. By this Bull, Pius IX 'did not indeed theoretically define, but practically claimed infallibility for the Pope'.[1] He defined the dogma *ex cathedra* for the acceptance of all the faithful. Since the *Dogmatic Constitution* of 1870, therefore, all within the Holy Roman Church are bound to believe it unquestioningly as if it had been an article of the Creed, 'with the same faith as they believe the mystery of the august Trinity'.[2]

A. The dogma of the Immaculate Conception, having been defined by the pope *ex cathedra* for the belief of all faithful Christians, is infallibly true, and requires no further assurance. Yet there is ample warrant for it in the grace and spotless holiness inseparable from her who is the Mother of God; in the message of the angel telling of God's especial grace conferred on her; in the constant reverence for her sanctity throughout the Church from earliest times, the settled belief in her holiness, and in the mature interpretation of the truth through the contemplation of the Church.

It was implied in the doctrine, taught from the early centuries, that as Christ was the Second Adam, so Mary was the Second Eve.

'It was a new definition in 1854, but not a new doctrine. The word "dogma" is ambiguous. It sometimes means a definition, sometimes a doctrine. The dogma of the consubstantiality of the Son was new at Nicaea, that of *theotokos* at Ephesus, that of the Two Natures at Chalcedon, but they were not new doctrines.'

N. Together with belief in the inspiration of positive truth by God, there must also be humble recognition of His reticence. No believer would deny, on abstract grounds, that God could have made the Blessed Virgin's conception absolutely holy, had He so willed. 'We only want the evidence that He has revealed that He did so.'[3] This doctrine is believed by some as a pious opinion; others, to whom it seems to subordinate our Lord to His mother as second only in perfect sinlessness, may doubt it.

Neither Scripture nor tradition includes this doctrine in the Deposit of Faith. It was not part of tradition, because it was never taught by anyone for more than a thousand years, the actual teaching of the Fathers was irreconcilable with it, and when at last it was proposed, the greatest doctors of the Church rejected it.

[1] Fr C. Schrader, S.J., quoted Nielsen, ii, 195.
[2] Pope Pius XI, Encyc. 'Mortalium animos', 6 January 1928. [3] Pusey, p. 58.

Popes Paul V and Gregory XV said that it was a mystery that God had not yet revealed to His Church.

It was never a dogma until 1854. Then it was made a new dogma, a thing that St Vincent of Lerins called 'accursed'.[1]

(ii) *Revelation and Tradition*

'Revelation was given in its entirety by our Lord and His Apostles. After the death of the last of the twelve, it could receive no increment.'[2] 'The Church is a living witness to a tradition from which nothing can be taken away, and to which nothing can be added. This is the fundamental principle.'[3] As Pope Pius IX himself taught in the *Dogmatic Constitution*, 'the Holy Ghost was not promised to the successors of Peter that by His revelation they might make known new doctrines, but that by His assistance they might holily keep and faithfully expound the revelation handed down through the Apostles, that is, the deposit of faith'.[4] It is now condemned as error to say 'that the Revelation was not completed in the life-time of the apostles'.[5]

So although in the Bull 'Ineffabilis Deus' he pronounced the doctrine of the Immaculate Conception to have been revealed by God, and notwithstanding the declarations by Popes Paul V and Gregory XV more than two hundred years before that it had not then been revealed, the Bull must not be misunderstood to announce a *new* revelation, for no new revelation can be added to the Deposit of Faith, i.e.,

> This supernatural revelation . . . contained in the written books and unwritten traditions which have come down to us, having been received by the Apostles from the mouth of Christ Himself, or from the Apostles themselves by the dictation of the Holy Spirit.[6]
>
> Any subsequent revelations which God may have been pleased to grant are private, and form no part of the Deposit of Faith. . . . The Deposit of Faith comprises all doctrines found in the Bible and in Tradition. . . . Tradition embraces all those truths which, although never committed to writing under Divine inspiration, have been handed down within the Church from age to age in various ways.[7]

Since the dogma of the Immaculate Conception is not sufficiently established by the Bible, the authority for it as revealed truth is Tradi-

[1] Supra, p. 43. [2] G. J. Joyce, S.J., in *Cath. Enc.*, xiii, 4.
[3] Chapman, *GCC*, p. 25. [4] *Dogm. Const.*, cap. iv.
[5] Pope Pius X, 'Lamentabili', 3 July 1907, Denzinger 2021.
[6] Constitution 'Dei Filius' on the Catholic Faith, 24 April 1870, cap. ii, tr. Butler, ii, 257; Denzinger, 1787.
[7] Sheehan, i, 179.

tion. At this point, however, a difficulty might be thought to arise; for none of the saints and doctors of the Church down to St Thomas Aquinas seems to give it explicit support, and apart from St Ephraem their actual teaching may seem difficult to reconcile with it. But the exposition by leading Roman theologians of what is meant by 'tradition' disposes of this difficulty.

Holy Scripture is, in a sense, part of tradition, but a decisive and regulative part, paramount in doctrine. Some unwritten teachings and customs have been retained and openly handed down from the earliest days of the Church; such are, the substitution of the Lord's Day, with its sacred celebration, for the Sabbath, baptism by affusion, and the baptism of infants. These examples are given by Professor J. Bainvel, and tradition in this sense has ample support from the Fathers. Thus St Basil the Great, writing of unwritten tradition, speaks of the sign of the Cross, the blessings at baptism and unction, the use of chrism, and the words of invocation at the Eucharist.[1] The authority of all unwritten tradition of this character comes from its having been consciously and openly handed down in the life and worship of the Church from the very earliest days—so early that there is no knowledge of a time when the Church did not possess it.

The dogma of the Immaculate Conception is based on tradition not in this sense but in an extended sense described as 'double', or 'profound'. A leading Jesuit theologian of the seventeenth century, Denys Petau or Petavius, argued that any doctrine which is generally taught by the Church as revealed must be taken as revealed, without further proof, because the testimony of Rome, as the only remaining apostolic Church, is equivalent to an unbroken chain of tradition.[2]

In the first half of the nineteenth century, another leading Jesuit theologian, Professor Giovanni Perrone of Rome, developed this further. He taught that tradition may be a secret tradition residing in the ministry of the Church and in the general consciousness of the faithful, until at length it makes its appearance before the public. So he maintained that neither Bible nor tradition (in the ordinary or primary sense) was necessary for the definition of the dogma of the Immaculate Conception.[3] This accorded with the constant wish of the Society of Jesus for a *de fide* definition of the doctrine, and with the views and wishes of Pope Pius IX, who found it possible to declare in the Bull

[1] *De Spiritu Sancto*, *Opp.* (Paris, 1620), tom. iii, pp. 54–5.
[2] Acton, *Hist. Freedom*, p. 514.
[3] De immaculato B.V. conceptu an dogmatico decreto definari possit (Rome, 1847); Nielsen, ii, 191.

'Ineffabilis Deus' that the doctrine had flourished from the most ancient times. Tradition in this developed and 'profound' sense ranks superior to any ancient recorded evidence; indeed when Cardinal Guidi spoke of the bishops as 'witnesses of tradition', Pope Pius replied, 'Witnesses of tradition? There's only one, that's me.'[1]

This doctrine of tradition has been systematically expounded by the theologian Professor J. Bainvel of Paris. Although, as he says, the word 'tradition' in the 'ecclesiastical sense' sometimes has the ordinary meaning of a 'doctrine, account or custom transmitted from one generation to another',[2] it has another and different meaning; 'the notion of tradition in the double meaning of the word'[3] is of greater theological importance:

> Traditional truth lives and develops in the Church, always the same, at once ancient and new; ancient, for the first Christians already beheld it to a certain extent; new, because we see it with our present ideas. Such is the nature of tradition in the double meaning of the word; it is Divine truth coming down to us in the mind of the Church. . . . What is believed has always been believed, but in time it is more commonly and thoroughly understood and explicitly expressed.[4]

Accordingly, the decree of Pope Pius IX 'defined what was actually the explicit faith of the faithful, what had always been implicitly in that faith. . . . In recognizing a new truth the Church thereby recognizes that it always possessed that truth.'[5] Thus the conscious belief of the Church today is sufficient proof of the mind of the Church in early times; even if the belief then were only subconscious or implicit which now is conscious and explicit, it *must* have been part of the Deposit of Faith, taught by the apostles.

This doctrine of tradition is in sharp contrast with the understanding of Christians outside the Roman Church, who recognize tradition only in the ordinary 'ecclesiastical sense' of beliefs or practices that are known to have been openly held and observed, and openly handed down. The divergence between the Roman and non-Roman conceptions of what 'tradition' means is fundamental, and does not only affect one particular dogma such as that of the Immaculate Conception. It goes deeper, and may even determine acceptance or rejection of the whole Doctrine of the Papacy.

Those who have been nurtured within the Holy Roman Church accept, loyally and without question, the statement of Pope Pius IX

[1] Butler, ii, 98. In another account, the pope expressed the same principle in the epigram, 'La tradizione son' io'—'I am tradition'. Quirinus, *Letters from Rome* (1870), p. 713.

[2] *Cath. Enc.*, xv, 6. [3] Ibid., p. 13. [4] Ibid. [5] Ibid.

in the *Dogmatic Constitution* that it is 'in accordance with the ancient and constant faith of the universal Church', and adheres to 'the tradition received from the beginning of the Christian faith'.[1] So for members of the Roman Church, Cardinal Manning's assertion is perfectly logical, that 'the appeal to antiquity is both a treason and a heresy'.[2] Converts also who are drawn into the Roman Church by its various compelling attractions[3] usually arrive at the same position untroubled by much 'appeal to antiquity'. Scholars of the Roman Church do indeed allow 'appeal to antiquity' in argument with non-Roman Christians whom they seek to convert, as is plain in the earlier chapters of this book. For themselves, they accept the papal claims because they believe in infallibility and in 'tradition' in the profound or double meaning.

Outside the Roman Church, however, are multitudes of orthodox Christians who, although warmly conscious of the strong appeal of much that it offers them, nevertheless feel bound to apply to its claim the test of truth. They cannot feel that the claim of the *Dogmatic Constitution* to agree with antiquity is demonstrated by its own assertion that it does so. Nor does acceptance by the Roman Church today of some additional belief as *de fide* demonstrate to them that it was really believed or taught by the apostles. In short, the 'double' meaning of tradition seems to them deceptive and illusory, and they feel bound to understand tradition in its ordinary 'ecclesiastical' sense, and learn from the Church's own primitive records what its tradition really was. For most non-Roman Christians, indeed, it is difficult to grasp what is meant by 'tradition' in the 'double' meaning. This is a parting of the ways so important that a lucid exposition recently given by Father Alexandre Durand, S.J., is valuable.[4] Tradition, he says, 'in its most profound sense has nearly the same meaning as Revelation'. Scripture is only 'a certain crystallization in written form of the revealed deposit': it could not enclose the whole of Revelation. Nor can 'a mere oral tradition . . . serve to fill what may be called the gap between the presentation of Catholic doctrine recorded in Scripture and that which might be put together from the works of modern theologians'. There is high authority, no doubt, for recognizing a process from *implicit* to *explicit* knowledge of the truths of faith.[5] Yet if such a progress be 'equated with a merely logical analysis or deduction', so that a particu-

[1] Preface and cap. iv. [2] *TMHG*, p. 241. [3] Supra, ch. i (ii)–(iv).

[4] 'The Development of Doctrine', in *The Month*, November 1950, iv, 300 sqq.

[5] Pope Pius IX, 'Inter gravissimas', 28 October 1870, quoted by Pope Pius XII, Encyc. 'Humani generis', 12 August 1950.

lar truth 'is said to be contained virtually in a more general and synthetic truth', this is merely analytical development and it 'is powerless to explain the growth of much of the Church's teaching'.[1] Tradition proclaims 'the fact that it is in the living consciousness of the Church that divine truth is handed down to us, is *handed on*'.

How is it handed on? Father Durand explains that tradition 'is a power of reflection whereby revealed truth is assimilated, investigated, catalogued and brought into conscious relation with every experience of life'. 'The conscious life of the Church is both Revelation and Tradition.' Christ has never ceased to teach His Church by the inspiration of the Holy Spirit, and 'it is precisely to the Church as hieratic, to the apostles and the bishops the successors, as perpetuating the authority and role of Christ Himself, that the gift and guarantee is given'. So, 'revelation is identical with the consciousness of the hieratic Church'.

Tradition, then, is brought into consciousness through the power of reflection of the hierarchy of the Holy Roman Church, and 'a dogma may be incorporated in the action and practice of the Church long before it finds conscious expression'. Thus, for the Roman Church, Father Durand demonstrates that 'the proliferation of particular dogmas adds nothing to the substance of Dogma, that is, of the revelation possessed by the Church from the beginning', that it is only 'a deeper appreciation of the one revelation that has all along remained substantially the same'.

A. 'The tradition of the Catholic faith is not its continued relation from individual to individual—from father to son, from generation to generation—but its continued existence in one individual mind throughout all generations of men, and from age to age.'[2]

'Its history is to be learned of itself. It is not therefore by criticisms on past history, but by acts of faith in the living voice of the Church at this hour, that we can know the faith.'[3]

'The visible Church itself is divine tradition.'[4]

'Tradition is a power of reflection whereby revealed truth is assimilated, investigated, catalogued, and brought into conscious relation with every experience of life.' . . . It is in the the living consciousness of the Church that divine truth is handed down to us, is *handed on*.'[5]

When Doctors of the Church have differed, 'only the Church can

[1] Fr Durand, loc. cit. [2] Humphrey, p. 46. [3] Manning, *VCD*, p. 119.
[4] Ibid., p. 124. [5] Fr Durand, loc. cit.

decide between them. This may be done (*a*) by universally teaching a doctrine, bishops as a whole approving, (*b*) through an oecumenical council, (*c*) through the Pope'.

The ultimate definition of traditional belief as an article of faith makes no change of doctrine, for 'if the promulgation of a dogma involves a change of doctrine, then the Christian faith was "changed" as long ago as A.D. 325, when the word "consubstantial" was first promulgated'.[1]

N. Tradition in the so-called 'double' or 'profound' meaning of the word is not tradition at all in any true sense. The attempts of its sincere and zealous supporters to justify this distorted interpretation lead them into sophistries, such as its 'continued existence in one individual mind throughout all generations'. To describe the myriad minds of faithful Christians from Pentecost until today as one individual mind is a fanciful figure of speech (indeed an individual mind might retain a belief but could not hand it down to itself). Those who assert that a dogma was believed in the early Church without any evidence whatever, and even in the face of plain evidence to the contrary, are seduced by this strained and fanciful notion into asserting the thing that is not.

In a manner resembling what modern psychology asserts of the individual human mind, truths are said to emerge into the conscious mind of the Roman Church, and these truths (it is claimed) must therefore have been always present in the unconscious mind.

The pretence of a secret tradition, preserved latent, underneath the open knowledge of the Church, was the specious plea of the Gnostic heretics, exposed by St Irenaeus, condemned and rejected by the whole Catholic Church at that time.[2]

The established doctrine that the Deposit of Faith was final, and that there can be no new Revelation, is subtly done away with by the developed Roman sense of 'tradition'. Without any new Revelation, the (Roman) Church gradually becomes inspired to discover that the original Revelation contained some dogma that was not formerly known or recognized. The dogma of the Immaculate Conception affords a striking illustration of this process, because when it was first proposed (after more than a thousand years), it was rejected by leading doctors of the Church, and two popes declared that it had not been revealed.

[1] Abbot B. C. Butler, O.S.B., *Tablet*, 10 May 1952, cxcix 377.
[2] Supra, ch. x.

In A.D. 325, the new Greek word *homoousios*[1] was used to repudiate the new Arian heresy as a false novelty and a change of doctrine.[2] This cannot warrant the addition of any distinct and novel 'tradition', so called, as an Article of Faith.

[1] Meaning 'of the same *ousia*, being or essence'. St Augustine said that the exact translation of *ousia* is the new Latin word *essentia* (*City of God*, XII, ii).

[2] Thus St Meletius and the Council of Antioch; Socrates, III, xxv; Sozomen, VI, iv.

CHAPTER LXXIII

The Vatican Council, 1870

Pope Pius IX had 'practically claimed infallibility' in 1854, when on the feast-day of the Blessed Virgin's conception, 8 December, he individually declared the dogma that it was Immaculate. Ten years later, on the same feast-day, he issued an encyclical[1] with a 'Syllabus' of eighty dogmatic truths, expressed as denials of the corresponding errors. Such 'errors' were:

> That Roman Pontiffs and oecumenical councils have exceeded the just bounds of their authority, usurped the rights of princes, and have even erred in defining matters of faith and morals.
>
> That the Church has not the power of applying coercion, nor any temporal power, direct or indirect.
>
> That in our age it is no longer expedient that the Catholic religion should be the sole religion of the state, and that all other forms of worship whatsoever should be barred.[2]

Some of the implied assertions caused a flutter in Europe and, says Abbot Butler, 'a storm of unprecedented fury in all quarters hostile to the Church and the Papacy'.[3]

Six years later, in 1869, again on the same significant day, 8 December, Pope Pius IX opened the great Council of the Vatican (the first council for three centuries), which sat until the following autumn. More than four months were spent in framing the Constitution 'Dei Filius' on the Catholic Faith (God the Creator, Revelation, Faith, and Reason). The pope decreed this on 24 April 1870. The council then began its main task of framing the *Dogmatic Constitution* on the Church. The first three of its four chapters define (1) the institution of the primacy in St Peter, (2) the perpetuity of the primacy in the Roman

[1] 'Quanta cura', 8 December 1864; Denzinger, 1688.

[2] Syllabus of Errors, nos. 23, 24, 77; Denzinger, 1723, 1724, 1777.

[3] Butler, i, 68. References in this chapter are all to Abbot Butler unless otherwise stated.

pontiffs, and (3) its power and nature.[1] Except on one matter, included in Chapter III, the doctrine they define had been proclaimed again and again from the papal throne for centuries past, and was familiar throughout the whole Roman Church. These three chapters 'got through easily'.[2]

The anxious task of the council was the fourth chapter, and the wording of the definition of papal infallibility. It was known long beforehand that this was to be proposed as a dogma, and it had caused tense feeling. 'For those in communion with the Holy See, the fourth chapter, on the Infallibility, was the most crucial and the most controversial issue.'[3] Yet in Abbot Butler's penetrating judgement, the doctrine of the Primacy, as defined in Chapter III, is really more important and fundamental 'for others, Orthodox, Anglicans, and Western Protestants of all kinds', and presents a much greater obstacle to a united Christendom in communion with Rome.[4] The Abbot's verdict is perhaps supported by the fact that this chapter confirms to the pope the tremendous title of 'true Vicar of Christ' in the unique sense applied to him alone; nothing that has ever been claimed for papal authority goes beyond, or could go beyond, what that may be thought to imply.[5] No one dreamed of questioning the title itself, but doubts were expressed as to certain of its implications, in particular that the Roman pontiff has a superiority of ordinary power and jurisdiction over all other Churches which is 'truly episcopal and immediate'. The subjection of the bishops to the pope had given trouble at the Council of Trent,[6] and now some voices were raised in the Vatican Council against acknowledging his jurisdiction as 'episcopal, ordinary, and immediate'. But when the Bishop of Nice objected to these words, and recalled that St Gregory the Great had rejected the title of 'universal bishop', the presiding Cardinals declared that this doctrine was 'inadmissible', and ruled him out of order.[7] These words were therefore kept in the definition.

Papal infallibility, however, was the great and absorbing question; it caused the heated atmosphere, both inside and out, in which the council was held. Even before the opening day, Bishop Ullathorne wrote:

> Things are daily growing hotter and hotter, thanks in great measure to the constant straining after extremes on the orthodox side. A great deal of controversy is raging round the question of proposing the infallibility, and there will be warm work at Rome.[8]

A considerable majority of the bishops and other members of the council, probably three-quarters, were heartily in favour of affirming

[1] Supra, ch. i. [2] II, 90. [3] II, 78. [4] II, 71, 77, 78, 209.
[5] Supra, pp. 76, 79, 339, 367. [6] Supra, ch. lxx. [7] II, 80. [8] I, 58, 148.

the pope's infallibility. The extremists or 'neo-ultramontanes' wanted it to be asserted with little or no limitation as to occasion or subject-matter, 'a fanatical extending of the papal prerogatives beyond the fact'.[1] Prominent among these was Archbishop Manning, afterwards Cardinal. They were vehemently supported by another convert, W. G. Ward, editor of the *Dublin Review*, and by other influential publications in France and Italy. Indeed the 'exuberance of quite untheological devotion' to Pope Pius led some of them to substitute 'Pius' for the name of God, or the Holy Ghost, in the hymns of the Church; one bishop declared to the council that it is the pope who 'sitteth on the throne surrounded by the four and twenty elders' of the Apocalypse.[2]

A substantial minority were opposed to the defining of papal infallibility, although most of them protested that they personally believed it. The usual objection was that it would be inexpedient or inopportune: because of this the minority were described as the 'inopportunists'. They dreaded lest the definition should 'create a fresh barrier against the return of the Oriental Churches and the Protestant Bodies to Catholic Unity'.[3] It was also objected that a 'personal, separate, absolute' infallibility of the pope was being formulated, and it was proposed, unsuccessfully, to link together the Pope and the Church by some phrase such as 'using the counsel and help of the Church'.[4] Some were influenced by historical difficulties[5] in the way of proving the dogma to unbelievers; a few[6] dared even to argue subversively against the doctrine itself.

The minority was numerous at first, but afterwards it dwindled, for reasons that will appear. At the 'trial ballot', only 88 out of 601 voted against the definition. Rather than oppose the majority and the pope himself, they slipped away from Rome on the day before the final vote and the declaration. Before they entrained, fifty-five of them wrote most respectfully to the pope that their filial piety and reverence would not allow them to say 'non placet' in his presence.[7] On 18 July 1870, the council voted approval of the definition as worded, by 533 to 2, and the pope declared the *Dogmatic Constitution*. The two dissentients at once declared that they now accepted it. All the 'minority' bishops ultimately professed their acceptance, as they were bound to do, although some perhaps did so unhappily.[8] Certain leading Church historians and

[1] I, 144. [2] I, 76–7. [3] I, 124; II, 48. [4] II, 144–5. [5] I, 124, 213.
[6] Especially Hefele, Verot, Bonnaz, and Kenrick. [7] II, 158–9.
[8] Acceptance only of the Definition was required, not any particular interpretation of it (Chapman, *FEGC*, p. 94). It is said that the clause '*ea infallibilite qua* divinus Redemptor Ecclesiam . . . instructam esse *voluit*' soothed some uneasy consciences.

others, especially in Germany, found themselves unable to believe and accept the Infallibility, and there was a secession, still represented by the Old Catholic Churches.

The arguments that are advanced for and against the newly defined dogma of Infallibility will be outlined in the remaining chapter. Meanwhile some criticisms of the Vatican Council must be noticed. It has been said that its composition and its proceedings were so unfair and unfree as to impair its validity as a council. That is an old debate now, and may be recounted shortly. It probably has little influence nowadays upon acceptance or non-acceptance of the Doctrine of the Papacy.

(a) *Composition of the Council*

Out of some 750 members who attended, 64 were not bishops, and 34 were merely titular bishops. Among the others, the Italians, who were almost all 'infallibilists', preponderated, because every little town in Italy is a bishop's see, in contrast with Northern Europe. There were, for example, only 19 bishops in all Germany, most of whom were 'inopportunists', as were also all the 15 bishops of Hungary;[1] the three 'minority' bishops of Paris, Cambrai, and Cologne represented seven times as many Catholics as the 62 bishops of the Papal States.[2]

(b) *Procedure*

The pope himself laid down the procedure of the council;[3] and vested in himself the right of proposing all matters for discussion. A 'Deputation on Faith' of twenty-four members prepared the 'scheme' for discussion and was given absolute control, even over amendments that might be suggested. Manning, by means of 'a determined intrigue', contrived that this Deputation should be composed of 'infallibilists'.[4] It had tight control: out of two hundred amendments put in by bishops, it allowed only two to be heard, and simply ruled out the rest.[5] All this was innovation, and it was thought prudent to keep secret from 'the opposition' the former order of business observed at Trent. Father Theiner, prefect of the Vatican archives, was summarily deposed because he had let it become known.[6] On the whole, the 'inopportunists' got their hearing, although two of them were shouted down,[7] and over forty intending speakers were silenced by the single application of the closure.[8] Among them was Archbishop Kenrick of St Louis who had prepared a strong argument against the dogma.[9] The presidents were not conciliatory towards the minority, to whom the dominant party

[1] I, 262–4. [2] Salmon, p. 323. [3] In his decree 'Multiplices inter', i, 158.
[4] I, 168–71. [5] II, 197–8. [6] *Cath. Enc.*, xiv, 566. [7] I, 229, 272.
[8] II, 55. [9] Afterwards printed, Mansi, lii, 453–81.

seemed 'an insolent and aggressive faction',[1] which would force through approval.

(c) *Papal influence*

There was much devotion and reverential fear for the aged 'Pio Nono', who had gained unusual respect and affection. It was notorious that he was eager for the definition. He referred to 'inopportunist' speakers as his enemies; he would send for such an offender and give him a painful quarter of an hour. The mere fact that some hundreds of bishops were entertained at his expense might be unworthy of mention, except that it gave point to his *bon mot*: 'I do not know if the Pope will come out of this council fallible or infallible, but this is certain, that he will be *fallito* (bankrupt).'[2] But 'at the final stages he exerted his personal influence to the utmost'.[3]

He declared the *Dogmatic Constitution* during a tremendous thunderstorm. The old custom of signature of the Acta by each bishop ('ego definiens subscripsi') was omitted. The very next day the Franco Prussian War broke out, and many more members of the council left Rome. It did little more business, and in October it was 'suspended'. It was never closed and, technically, it might be reopened at any time.

Whether or not the *Dogmatic Constitution* is truly part of the Catholic Faith is our fundamental question. So far as concerns its first three chapters, on the Roman Primacy, any review of the arguments A and N would amount to a recapitulation of this book. Its fourth chapter, which defines Papal Infallibility, calls for further study in our remaining pages. So far as concerns the authority of the Vatican Council as a council of the Church, the conflicting views, A and N, can be outlined here:

A. The Vatican Council was an oecumenical council of the whole Catholic Church. Its impressive membership of bishops from all parts of the world made it, indeed, the greatest council ever held. Its approval of the *Dogmatic Constitution* carried unchallengeable authority.

'Nor can we say that the fact that some people think a definition inopportune is a proof that they regard the doctrine as indefinable. Newman always said he accepted infallibility but thought it inopportune to define it when it was defined; some theologians today thought it inopportune to define the Assumption, while agreeing that it was part of the faith, others, like Manning, thought that if it was part of Revela-

[1] Dom D. Pontifex, *The Vatican Council* (1931), pp. 16, 22; cp. Butler, i, 213.
[2] I, 170 n. [3] I, 198.

tion it must be opportune. But we cannot conclude that everyone felt the same about it.'

'The Vatican Council has at least been accepted throughout the Church as an infallible Council, and that is the most important criterion.'

N. If the Vatican Council were truly a general council of the whole Church, its approval of the pope's individual and council-less infallibility would purport to be an abdication of the old authority of general councils. But only those who already hold the Doctrine of the Papacy can regard as oecumenical the Western council of the pope that agreed to his decree of his own infallibility. Moreover no general council was under a moral subjection as was the Pope's council of 1870; nor could the large number of bishops make it authoritative. At Nicaea in A.D. 325, for example, the greatest council of any since the first Council at Jerusalem, there were only 318 bishops, nearly all of them Easterns.

When it is recalled that the dogma was asserted to be part of the Deposit of Faith, held and believed by the whole Church for eighteen centuries, the suggestion that it could be 'inopportune' to declare it is almost fantastic. Dr Salmon's comments on this strange contention are supported by an unusual ally, Cardinal Manning, who says: 'Can it be permitted to us to think that what God has thought it opportune to reveal, it is not opportune for us to declare?'[1] Dr Salmon remarks that 'All this controversy about opportunism shows distrust in the infallibility of their guide . . . the fact that Popes and Councils have often found it inopportune to make dogmatic definitions is proof enough how little their own Church believed in their power to do so'.[2] The unhappy argument of the 'inopportunists' is significant. They loyally smothered doubts that weighed on the minds of many of them.

[1] *VCD*, p. 39. [2] Salmon, p. 184.

CHAPTER LXXIV

Papal Infallibility

(i) *As defined and expounded*

A. Proofs advanced in support of the doctrine.
B. The Definition in the *Dogmatic Constitution.*
C. Some misconceptions put aside.
D. The conditions of infallible teaching within the Definition.
E. What *ex cathedra* definitions are recognized.

A. PROOFS OF THE DOCTRINE

(a) *Catholic consent*

The doctrine was defined in 1870 by the pope as Head of the Church, with the consent of a great General Council, and it is therefore infallibly true. No further proofs are needed for any member of the Holy Roman Church although her scholars study them; proofs are given for the enlightenment of others.

(b) *Antecedent probability or necessity*

'If the faith that was demanded of our Lord's contemporaries was to be demanded of Christians of all time, if that faith was absolute certitude, though not absolute knowledge, if only objective certainty, i.e., Infallibility, can beget subjective certitude, then it would seem that the charisma of Infallibility must abide with the Church to rule its faith until the end of the world'.[1]

If the Church could err in exacting the assent of faith for her doctrine, it would follow that God has bound men on pain of damnation to believe what is false. 'If there be no organ of infallibility on earth, it follows that Christ's office as teacher ceased when He left the world.'[2]

'If the Spirit guides the Church and leads it into all truth, He could

[1] McNabb, p. 17. [2] Sheehan, i, 139.

not allow the Church's principal member to lead others astray in the name of Christ.'

'The absolute need of a spiritual supremacy is at present the strongest of arguments in favour of the fact of its supply. . . . If Christianity is both social and dogmatic and intended for all ages, it must humanly speaking have an infallible expounder.'[1]

(c) *Holy Scripture*

The whole of Scripture accords with the doctrine, and numerous passages conduce to support and prove it.[2] The following outstanding passages are mentioned by Archbishop Sheehan:[3]

Matt. xvi, 15–19 (The Rock, and the Keys.
Matt. vii, 25 (The house founded on a rock).
John xxi, 15–17 (Feed My sheep).
Luke xxii, 31–2 ('Confirm thy brethren').

(d) *Tradition*

The whole tradition of the Church from the beginning accords with the doctrine, and many declarations and actings set it forth or imply it. Archbishop Sheehan[4] selects the following for mention:

(1) The testimony of St Irenaeus to the pre-eminence and authority of the Church of Rome.[5]

(2) The condemnation, *circa* A.D. 200, by St Zephyrinus, Bishop of Rome, of the Montanists, 'who thenceforward are regarded as outcasts from the Church'.[6]

(3) The letter of Pope Julius I to the Eusebian bishops at Antioch, A.D. 341.[7]

(4) 'Peter has spoken by Leo', in the acclamations at the Council of Chalcedon, A.D. 451.[8]

(5) 'Peter was speaking through Agatho', etc., at the sixth General Council, at Constantinople, A.D. 680.[9]

(6) The Union Decree of the Council of Florence, A.D. 1439.[10]

To all the supposed historical objections that have been advanced against the doctrine (which have been studied and answered by scholars), the Holy Roman Church has a comprehensive answer in its teaching with regard to Tradition.[11] The Church is the divinely appointed guardian and interpreter of tradition.[12] What the Church

[1] Newman, *Development* (1878 ed.), p. 90 [2] See e.g., Conway, pp. 95–6, 169.
[3] I, 181, 186. [4] P. 183. [5] Supra, ch. x.
[6] This is a little obscure; they were condemned and excommunicated in the East long before (Abbot Chapman in *Cath. Enc.*, x, 522).
[7] Supra, ch. xxvi (i). [8] Ibid., ch. xli (iii). [9] Ibid., ch. li.
[10] Ibid., ch. lv (ii). [11] Ibid., ch. lxii (ii). [12] Sheehan, i, 179.

now defines explicitly was always the faith of the Church implicitly.[1] It is not by criticisms on past history, but by acts of faith in the living voice of the Church at the present day, that we can know the true tradition and faith.[2]

B. THE DEFINITION OF PAPAL INFALLIBILITY, 1870

The introductory part of Chapter IV of the *Dogmatic Constitution*, after referring to the Formula of Pope Hormisdas,[3] the Council of Constantinople in 869,[4] the Council of Lyons in 1274,[5] and the Council of Florence in 1439,[6] recalls that, as a matter of history, the Roman pontiffs have sometimes assembled councils, or particular synods, and have sometimes used 'other helps which Divine Providence supplied'. That is only introductory, however, and was deliberately[7] kept out of the Definition, which is in the following terms:

> Therefore, faithfully adhering to the tradition received from the beginning of the Christian faith, for the glory of God our Saviour, the exaltation of the Catholic Religion, and the salvation of Christian peoples, the Sacred Council approving, We teach and define that it is a dogma divinely revealed: that the Roman Pontiff, when he speaks *ex cathedra*, that is when in discharge of the office of Pastor and Doctor of all Christians, by virtue of his supreme Apostolical authority he defines a doctrine regarding faith or morals to be held by the Universal Church, by the divine assistance promised to him in blessed Peter, is possessed of that infallibility with which the divine Redeemer willed that His Church should be endowed for defining doctrine regarding faith or morals: and that therefore such definitions of the Roman Pontiff are irreformable of themselves, and not from consent of the Church.
>
> But if any one—which may God avert—presume to contradict this Our definition; let him be anathema.[8]

C. SOME MISCONCEPTIONS PUT ASIDE

(a) *Impeccability*

'The Pope is infallible in doctrine, but not impeccable in conduct. He must work out his salvation "in fear and trembling" like other men.'[9]

(b) *Inspiration*

The infallible utterances of the pope are not inspired.[10] Therefore

[1] Prof. J. Bainvel, *Cath. Enc.*, xv, 13.
[2] Manning, *VCD*, p. 119. [3] Supra, ch. xlviii. [4] Ibid., ch. liii.
[5] Ibid., ch. lv (i). [6] Ibid., ch. lv (ii). [7] Butler, ii, 144–5.
[8] *Dogm. Const.*, cap. iv, tr. Butler, ii, 295. [9] Sheehan, i, 189. [10] Ibid, p. 190.

they cannot be compared with the Gospel.[1] 'God is the author of inspired utterances. He is not the author of Papal definitions, but He guarantees them against error.'[2] The infallibility of the pope comes from divine assistance, not inspiration, and confers 'inerrancy, or the power of not being misled'.[3]

(c) *Omniscience*

The doctrine does not declare that any individual pope will be enabled to give some particular teaching to the Church at any particular time; a thousand years may pass without any exercise by a pope of his individual infallibility. This answers the objection, sometimes urged, that there have been times and occasions when the reigning pope 'could' or 'ought to' have given infallible teaching on some question of faith or morals. He will do so only when he sees fit occasion; we are not authorized to say that the occasion is determined by inspiration.

(d) *Revelation*

The *Dogmatic Constitution* in Chapter IV declares clearly that:

> The Holy Spirit was not promised to the successors of Peter that by His revelation they might make known new doctrine, but that by His assistance they might inviolably keep and faithfully expound the revelation or deposit of faith delivered through the Apostles.[4]

It is emphatically denied that the *Dogmatic Constitution* (or any other infallible teaching) contains any new revelation, or goes beyond the Deposit of Faith, i.e., the original 'supernatural revelation . . . received by the Apostles from the mouth of Christ Himself, or from the Apostles themselves, by the dictation of the Holy Spirit'.[5] This is constantly emphasized by theologians.[6]

(e) *Tradition, and the mind of the Church*

It is clearly taught that the infallible decision of the pope (or of pope and council) expounds only what has been the original Deposit of Faith, retained ever since by Tradition in the Mind of the Church, the *sensus fidelium*. 'The *ex cathedra* judgement of the Pope needs the Mind of the Church as its necessary preliminary material.'[7] But that is the source or doctrinal quality of infallible teaching, and cannot be

[1] Fessler, pp. 80–1. [2] Sheehan, i, 190.
[3] McNabb, pp. 33, 38. [4] Tr. Butler, ii, 293.
[5] Pope Pius IX, Constitution 'Dei Filius' on the Catholic Faith, 24 April 1870, cap. ii; tr. Butler, ii, 257.
[6] Supra, ch. ii (iv) and ch. lxii (ii). [7] McNabb, p. 93.

appealed to as a criterion or test of its infallibility; the truth of Tradition is determined by the Mind of the Church, irrespective of its expression in any ecclesiastical records.[1] Moreover, the pope is the sole and final authority of the Mind of the Church. It was regarded, indeed, as unthinkable that a pope should ever neglect to seek suitable counsel,[2] but the infallibility of his decision cannot be judged or questioned by reference to the counsel he has sought or obtained, or the reasoning that has influenced him. So as to emphasize this, Father Humphrey pictures what is, of course, an extreme improbability: 'Suppose among the papers of a deceased Pontiff is found a note of authorities and the train of reasoning which led him to the theological conclusion which he has embodied in a definition; and that all these authorities are transparently false, and all his syllogisms fallacious and unsound; it in no way affects the infallibility of the definition.'[3]

D. THE CONDITIONS OF INFALLIBLE TEACHING

The Definition prescribes four marks or conditions of an infallible definition; apart from these, infallibility is not asserted. If careful attention be given to them, they will be seen to meet objections to the dogma that have been based on supposedly erroneous decisions of former popes; no questionable papal judgement or decree possessed these marks of infallibility.

'*ex cathedra*'

'The Pope is infallible only when he speaks officially as supreme pastor of the universal Church. He is not infallible as supreme legislator, supreme judge, or supreme ruler. He is not infallible as a simple priest, local bishop of Rome, Archbishop of the Roman Province, Primate of Italy, or Patriarch of the West.'[4] Nor is he infallible when he teaches as a 'private doctor'. 'When Roman Pontiffs publish books about anything, they only express their own opinion, like other learned men; they do not declare the faith of the Church.'[5]

'*doctrine regarding faith or morals*'

Papal infallibility does not extend to decisions on matters of fact that do not involve faith or morals, or even to decisions on ecclesiastical discipline.[6]

'*when the Roman Pontiff defines*'

'Nothing is to be understood to have been declared or defined dog-

[1] Supra, ch. lxii (ii). [2] Butler, ii, 146. [3] Humphrey, p. ix.
[4] Conway, p. 169; Fessler, pp. 42–3. [5] Cano, VI, viii, p. 335.
[6] Fessler, pp. 65–75, 96–119.

matically unless it manifestly appears to have been so defined.'[1] 'The Pope is said to "define" a doctrine when he makes it clear that the doctrine must be believed with a firm, interior assent of faith.'[2] The usual phrase, 'we define', is not necessary;[3] nor, when used, is it always decisive.[4]

'to be held by the Universal Church'

The pope is infallible only when addressing the whole Church, and not merely part of it. Thus 'an instruction to the English or Armenian Churches might be true, but would not be infallible'.[5]

E. WHAT 'EX CATHEDRA' DECISIONS ARE RECOGNIZED

As to which papal utterances bear the true marks of infallibility in accordance with the Definition, theologians have not been unanimous. In some instances it still remains a matter of opinion whether the pope was speaking *ex cathedra*, and whether (taking words in their context) he intended to define a doctrine of faith or morals for the acceptance of the whole Church. Bishop Fessler discerned 'only a few' instances of infallibility;[6] in the opinion of some others, instances must be more numerous; but no list of *ex cathedra* decisions is available for guidance. Instances as to which an opinion of infallibility seems to be most general are:

(*a*) In the Bull 'Unam Sanctam' of Pope Boniface VIII in 1302, the last seventeen words only—'For every human creature it is altogether necessary to salvation that he be subject to the Roman Pontiff', although Bishop Fessler[7] would attribute infallibility to more of this Bull.

(*b*) The Dogma of the Immaculate Conception of the Blessed Virgin, declared by Pope Pius IX in 1854.

(*c*) The decrees of Pope Pius IX in 1870, including the *Dogmatic Constitution* and Papal Infallibility itself.

(*d*) The Dogma of the Corporeal Assumption of the Blessed Virgin, declared by Pope Pius XII on 1 November 1950.[8]

Some theologians would include other instances of infallible papal decisions, for example the Bull 'Unigenitus' of Pope Clement XI in 1713.[9]

[1] Codex J.C., Can. 1323, para. 3. [2] Sheehan, i, 185. [3] McNabb, p. 69.
[4] Butler, ii, 225–6. [5] McNabb, p. 69.
[6] P. 53; he did not specify them. Some theologians apparently would admit only the two Bulls concerning the Blessed Virgin; Fr W. R. Carson, *Reunion Essays* (1903), p. 251.
[7] Pp. 69–70. [8] See Appendix at the end of this chapter.
[9] Condemning 'Jansenist' teaching attributed to a book by Père Pasquier Quesnel; Denzinger, 1351 sq.

Contradictory opinions and arguments have been put forward as to the infallible or non-infallible character of various papal pronouncements, such as the Tome of Leo the Great;[1] the Syllabus of Pope Pius IX in 1864;[2] the Bull 'Apostolicae curae' of Pope Leo XIII in 1896 concerning Anglican Orders; the Syllabus of Pope Pius X in 1907;[3] and, more generally, all 'lesser definitions on faith or morals'[4] and decrees of canonization.[5]

True Christians must believe every infallible papal definition 'with a firm, interior assent of faith',[6] i.e., 'with the same faith as they believe the incarnation of our Lord'.[7] Yet any uncertainty as to the infallible character of a papal utterance occasions little difficulty in practice. 'The Pope possesses a twofold teaching authority, viz., supreme or infallible, and ordinary. When he employs his ordinary authority he is not infallible and does not, of course, bind us to an assent of faith. Still, it is the common and safe opinion that we must give his teaching an interior, religious assent.'[8] 'Utterances of the ordinary magisterium of the Church are accepted as true expressions of Catholic doctrine. . . . Such adhesion to teaching not infallible is not the firm assent of faith, but a prudent assent based on a moral conviction that such teaching will be right.'[9] A position advanced in an encyclical *ipso facto* claims assent.[10] Therefore, 'the question whether this or that solemn utterance of the Pope, freely expressed, comes within the scope of the Vatican definition of Infallibility is for Catholics largely a question of technical interest'.[11]

(ii) *Objections to the dogma*

A. The claim of 'Catholic consent'
B. Holy Scripture.
C. Tradition.
D. Heretical popes.
E. Papal blunders.
F. Papal silence.
G. Utility of the dogma.

[1] Supra, ch. xli (iii). [2] *Cath. Enc.*, xiv, 368; supra, ch. lxxiv.
[3] Ibid., xiv, 370. [4] McNabb, pp. 46–7, 50. [5] *Cath. Enc.*, ii, 366–7.
[6] Sheehan, i, 185. [7] Encyc. 'Mortalium animos' of Pope Pius XI, 1928.
[8] Sheehan, i, 190.
[9] Butler, ii, 226; Maritain, p. 29; Leo XIII, 'Sapientiae christianae', 10 January 1890.
[10] Pope Pius XII, Encyc. 'Humani generis', 12 August 1950.
[11] Fr J. A. Phillips, S.J., *Upon this Rock* (1949), p. 21.

A. THE CLAIM OF 'CATHOLIC CONSENT'

This claim, however valid for those who have accepted the Doctrine of the Papacy, is worthless for all others. It rests on an argument in a circle, i.e., that according to the Doctrine of the Papacy the Vatican Council was a General Council of the whole Church, and that it agreed to the dogma. Outside the Roman Church, however, no one regards the Vatican Council as a council of the whole Church; that standing could be claimed only for the early general councils. Even so, their doctrinal statements only acquired final authority from the after-consent of the universal Church. 'Neither the decrees of popes, nor even those of councils, acquire irrefragible authority save by virtue of the consent of the Universal Church'; this could formerly be taught by a Roman theologian,[1] but not of course since 1870.

B. HOLY SCRIPTURE

Scripture gives no support for the doctrine of papal infallibility. Neither the apostles, including St Peter himself, nor the early Fathers disclose any knowledge of it whatever.

The well-known passages from St Luke xxii and St John xxi have nothing to do with it. St Peter, after his forgiveness and restoration, did indeed strengthen his brethren and feed the sheep; the first of the apostles was also the first great evangelist. But numberless other apostles and evangelists, priests and bishops, have strengthened their brethren and fed the sheep; among them remarkably few of the bishops of Rome can be recognized.

In saying that 'He will teach you all truth', our Lord was speaking of the Holy Spirit, not of St Peter or any individual bishop. Nor is it St Peter or any individual bishop whom He will especially teach, but 'you'—first all the apostles, and then the whole Church. 'All truth' was to be taught. He taught all truth necessary for salvation, the Deposit of Faith.[2] Much truth remains hidden in the unrevealed mysteries of God. The promised teaching does not include any manifest additions to the Deposit of Faith, such as the new dogmas concerning the Blessed Virgin; these dogmas were not necessary for salvation before 1854 and 1950, and they could not then be made necessary.

[1] Abp. de Barral of Tours, *Défense des Libertés de l'Eglise Gallicane* (Paris, 1817), p. 284.

[2] 'He revealed that which it concerned us to know, but what was beyond our grasp He kept secret. Let us be content with these things and stick to them, nor let us over-step age-long bounds and the divine tradition.' St John of Damascus, *De fide orthodoxa*, lib. i, cap. i; *Opp.* (Paris, 1712), i, 124.

C. TRADITION

The Deposit of Faith and the actual tradition of the Church contained no doctrine of papal infallibility; this is perfectly clear in the Church's own annals and records. It is enough here to recall a few examples; others may come to mind.

St Irenaeus, in the five books of his great theological work on the Church, the faith, and heresies from the faith (A.D. 185), gives no hint or indication of any Petrine office, infallible or not.

St Vincent of Lerins, in his directions for the distinguishing of true doctrine from all heresies, never suggests that the bishop of Rome possesses any unique function of the kind.

The repeated condemnation for heresy of Pope Honorius (†638) by successive councils and popes, without any attempt to rescue or distinguish some doctrine of papal infallibility, shows that there was then no doctrine whatever of that kind known to Catholics.

The great Council of Constance (1414–18), 'in a certain sense a council of the whole West',[1] declared that the pope's decisions on doctrine are subject to the judgement of a general council,[2] and thus flatly denied the modern dogma. This continued to be the teaching of leading theologians such as St Antonino of Florence (†1459), Francis Veron (†1645), and Bossuet (†1704).

Until 1870, papal infallibility was freely and vigorously repudiated within the Roman Church. Thus in 1789 the 'Protestation of the English Catholics', signed by all the vicars-general and 'all the Catholic clergy and laity in England of any note', and laid by them before Parliament, declared among other things in the most solemn terms that 'We acknowledge no infallibility in the pope'.[3]

In 1822 Bishop Baines, vicar-apostolic in England, wrote that 'Bellarmine, and some other divines, chiefly Italians, have believed the Pope infallible, when proposing *ex cathedra* an article of faith. But in England or Ireland I do not believe that any Catholic maintains the infallibility of the Pope.'[4]

In 1826 the 'Declaration of the Archbishops and Bishops of the Roman Catholic Church in Ireland' was issued over the signature of

[1] Funk, ii, 16.

[2] Supra, ch. lxx; it is answered (A) that any supposed papal ratification of this was illusory, and it is therefore worthless.

[3] Charles Butler, *Historical Memoirs respecting the English Catholics* (1819), ii, 113–18.

[4] *A Defence of the Christian Religion* (Bath, 1822), p. 230; see W. E. Gladstone, *Vaticanism* (1875), p. 48.

thirty bishops, stating that 'The Catholics of Ireland declare on oath their belief that it is not an article of the Catholic faith, neither are they required to believe, that the pope is infallible'.[1]

During the nineteenth century, 'Keenan's Controversial Catechism' was widely used throughout England, Scotland, and Ireland, with the imprimatur of two vicars-apostolic and two other bishops. The various editions down to 1870 taught thus: 'Q. Must not Catholics believe the Pope in himself to be infallible? A. This is a Protestant invention: it is no article of the Catholic faith: no decision of his can oblige under pain of heresy, unless it be received and enforced by the teaching body, that is by the bishops of the Church.' All this was quietly dropped out of the next edition in 1870.[2]

Since 1870, members of the Roman Church are told that the new dogma is 'in accordance with the ancient and constant faith of the universal Church', and part of 'the tradition received from the beginning of the Christian faith'.[3] The actual records of Catholic belief in the past are unknown to the great majority of members of the Roman Church; yet they are known to scholars among them. Non-Roman Christians sometimes find it difficult to understand how sincere and intelligent men can accept the proposition that the dogma always was the universal faith of the Church; but they are enabled to do so by the extraordinary and distorted meaning given to Tradition.[4] What the (Roman) Church believes today *must* have been held by the apostles; therefore any doctrine the pope may declare *must* be part of the original Deposit of Faith. All the ecclesiastical records that contradict it go for nothing. What, in the opinion of today, ought to be true, *must* be true.

In the famous and forthright saying of Cardinal Manning, 'the Dogma must conquer History';[5] for the Roman Church and its members, it has done so. As was said of the Vatican Council which accepted the new dogma, 'The sentiment on which infallibility is founded could not be reached by argument, the weapon of human reason, but resided in conclusions transcending evidence. . . . No appeal to revelation or tradition, to reason or to conscience, appeared to have any bearing whatever on the issue.'[6]

[1] Bp. J. W. Doyle, *Essay on the Catholic Claims* (1826), p. 300. It is answered (A) that papal infallibility truly was not an Article of Faith in 1826.

[2] Salmon, pp. 26, 192.

[3] *Dogm. Const.*, preface and cap. iv.

[4] Supra, ch. lxxii (ii).

[5] *Dublin Review*, July 1930, p. 5.

[6] Acton, *Hist. Freedom*, pp. 512–13.

D. HERETICAL POPES

It has been authoritatively declared that the election of a heretical pope may be quashed.[1]

The Council of Pisa in 1409 deposed two popes as heretics.[2] Pope Hadrian VI, indeed, declared it to be certain that the pope may err, even in matters pertaining to the faith, by asserting heresy through his determination or decretal, 'for several Roman Pontiffs have been heretics'.[3] He declared this publicly, but in a book, and therefore as a 'private doctor' and not *ex cathedra*, so that his own infallibility (as that is now defined) was not compromised. But his statement gets some support from earlier papal history. The excommunication of Pope Formosus by his successor Pope Stephen VII at the Cadaverous Council in 897[4] did not necessarily imply heresy, but Pope Honorius was anathematized for heresy again and again by popes and councils for several generations.

Since the defining of papal infallibility in 1870, it is taught as doctrine that even a pope who himself held heretical doctrine could not teach it to the whole Church in an utterance of his supreme teaching office. It must be believed as an act of faith that divine assistance would restrain him from doing so.[5]

E. PAPAL BLUNDERS

Defenders of the decree of papal infallibility, as defined in the *Dogmatic Constitution*, are concerned to show that its careful wording shuts out the more notorious papal blunders of the past. If so, however disastrous these may have been, they are assumed to have no doctrinal importance, and to cast no doubt on the dogma.

The Definition was drawn up with great care; the extremer 'infallibilists' were sagaciously overruled.[6] The members of the Deputation of Faith, who put forth its wording, were well aware of difficulties in the papal annals which would stultify any definition that was not carefully confined within narrow limits. Accordingly the privilege or charisma of infallibility was enclosed within the four walls of the Definition—(1) '*ex cathedra*', (2) 'faith or morals', (3) 'defines', (4) 'to the whole Church'. These limitations give invaluable protection to the Definition in controversy; there is little or nothing that any pope

[1] Pope Paul IV, Bull 'Cum ex apostolis'; Fessler, p. 75. [2] Supra, ch. lxvii.
[3] Bossuet, *Defensio*, 'Amsterdam' 1745 (Praevia dissertatio, para. xxviii), i, 21.
[4] Supra, p. 331 [5] Fessler, p. 75. [6] Butler, ii, 144–5.

has ever said or done which cannot plausibly be said to lie outside them. A less convenient result is that the technical infallibility of almost all papal pronouncements is open to question and remains a matter of opinion; only an indefinite, but certainly small, remnant of 'infallible' pronouncements is left.

These limitations of the Definition must therefore be set against the blunders of the popes, of which a few examples follow. In each instance the usual exculpations of infallibility as defined will be noted. But to the minds of non-Roman Christians, such technical defences, even if they should be thought to rescue the Definition from clear contradiction, leave no basis for a theory of really beneficent, effective inerrancy; that is ruled out by what so many popes have actually and harmfully said and done (as well as by their silence when need was great).

In 1590, Pope Sixtus V issued an edition of the Vulgate Bible, prepared under his supervision, revised and corrected by his own hand. He prefixed a Constitution in which he affirmed the plenary authority of this edition for all time. 'By the fullness of Apostolic power, we decree and declare that this edition, approved by the authority delivered unto us by the Lord, is to be received and held as true, lawful, authentic, and unquestioned, in all public and private discussion, reading, preaching, and explanations.' Anyone who should disobey the Constitution, or alter the version in the smallest particle, would incur the indignation of God and of St Peter and St Paul, and would come under the greatest excommunication. But it was a botched version after all, and a later pope had to replace it by another; blame was politely cast upon the printers.[1] Cardinal Hergenröther, however, considers that the Biblical blunders 'refer not to matters of faith', and observes that Pope Sixtus had not promulgated a Bull on the subject; so that the infallibility of the Definition of Infallibility is thought not to be compromised.[2]

In 1279, Pope Nicholas III issued a Bull 'Exiit qui seminat';[3] he declared the Franciscan rule of poverty to be divinely inspired; Christ both taught by word and established by example that renunciation of property, individual or common, for the sake of God, is holy. It is meritorious, lawful, and possible also because, he said, the actual use (*usus*) can be separated from ownership (*dominium*). This exposition of

[1] Brodrick, i, 276–309; Salmon, pp. 225–8.

[2] Hergenröther, p. 91. His Bull 'Aeternus Ille' bore 'an official attestation that it had been promulgated on 10 April 1590'; but 'it still remains extremely doubtful whether all the formalities required for an official promulgation were fulfilled'. Brodrick i, 305, 307.

[3] *Bullarium Franciscanum* (Rome, 1759), iii, 404 s; Robertson, p. 301 n. 1.

the rule of St Francis was to be permanent and to be strictly interpreted under pain of excommunication. But forty-four years later, Pope John XXII issued his Bull 'Cum inter nonnullos'.[1] He flatly denied that a state of poverty which excludes proprietorship is meritorious or holy; it was heretical to assert that our Lord taught such a kind of poverty either by word or example. In 'Quia quorundam', 10 November 1324, he said this was not inconsistent with previous papal decrees, but he declared it useless to appeal to them because, he said, a pope has power to reject as erroneous and invalid the decrees of his predecessors in questions of faith.[2] Probably John XXII really meant to deny a universal command of holy poverty applying to all men—which Nicholas III had not asserted. Cardinal Hergenröther[3] considers that the opposition between the two popes 'lies not in the sphere of dogma, but in different philosophic and juridical views' with regard to *usus* and *dominium*, which he proceeds to discuss; neither pope 'wished to pronounce a definition in this matter'. Whether or not this scholastic defence shields the Definition of Infallibility, the actual pronouncements of John XXII were calamitous. The unfortunate Franciscans, fortified by Pope Nicholas in their fanatical devotion to holy poverty, became Pope John's disobedient and fanatical heretics, and numbers of them were burned at the stake.[4]

The fearsome annals of the Inquisition are not felt to embarrass the Definition of Infallibility. For one thing, although the rack and the stake are in disuse, it is not clear that the principles on which the Inquisition in full vigour was justified have ever been authoritatively disowned; so that some defenders of the Definition may still maintain them. Others, however, would probably deny that any pope committed himself to an *ex cathedra* definition of these principles, although Pope Leo X, for example, perhaps came near it in 1520 when he condemned it as error to say that burning heretics is contrary to the will of the Spirit.[5] Rome taught for four centuries and more that heretics ought to be put to death.[6] But it is said that no doctrine is involved. Centuries of imprisonings, torturings, and burnings, by express author-

[1] Ibid., v, 518; Denzinger, 494.

[2] Bossuet, *Defensio* (Praevia dissertatio, xlvi), vol. i, 42–3; Robertson, p. 304; see Raynaldus ad an. 1324 (v, 276–82); D. L. Douie, *Heresy of the Fraticelli* (1932), pp. 153–208.

[3] P. 87.

[4] *Cath. Enc.*, vi, 248; sometimes in presence of the pope.

[5] Bull 'Exsurge Domine', 1520, Denzinger, 773 (classed as infallible in *Dict. de Théol. Catholique*).

[6] Acton, *Correspondence*, p. 108.

ity of the popes, are brushed aside as mere matters of discipline, not of doctrine.[1] Papal infallibility takes no account of such affairs; it is answered simply that 'papal infallibility is not papal impeccability'.

The case of Galileo has sometimes been misunderstood. For one in the grip of the Holy Office, he was treated with most unusual gentleness. He was a devout Catholic and a friend of cardinals. His imprisonment was mild, and the threatened torture was not inflicted when he submitted. He was a firm believer in the truth of Scripture, but he had seen the Copernican discovery to be true. He rashly endeavoured to make out that there was nothing in the Bible that forbade him to believe that the earth moved. The inquisitors, acting under the pope's authority and in his presence, obliged Galileo to profess belief in what is now admitted to be false. If he had afterwards repeated his sin, he would have been liable to be burned, as he knew well. During the remaining years of his life he never fully recovered his liberty, and of course his tongue was tied. All books teaching the mobility of the earth remained on the Index until 1831. It is now recognized that Popes Paul V and Urban VIII were mistaken about the truth of the Copernican theory. But in defence of the Infallibility as defined it is said that 'a careful study of the decrees they issued proves clearly that they were not infallible pronouncements. There is no question in either of them of any *ex cathedra* teaching, or of any intention to propose a doctrine to be held by the universal Church. . . . It is true that the reasons which prompted the Pope and Cardinals to pass the decree were doctrinal, but these reasons never formed part of the decree itself.'[2] 'This was an order imposed, not on the whole Church, but on a single man. . . . Urban VIII acted as Pope, but not as supreme teacher.'[3]

Infallibility must surely extend to the right declaring of the Sacraments. It must be 'able to determine by what rites, and consequently by which men in general, these sacraments can in point of fact be conferred'.[4] Pope Nicholas I was asked by the Bulgarians if baptism by a Jew, or a pagan, was valid. He replied in the affirmative in a dogmatic instruction,[5] adding that the baptism would be valid whether given in the Name of the Three Persons of the Trinity or in that of Christ alone. That is now generally regarded as erroneous, so that numbers of Bulgarians, if they trusted to the teaching of Nicholas I and were mis-

[1] *Cath. Enc.*, viii, 36.

[2] Conway, p. 179; Galileo's science was crude, but his Scriptural exegesis remarkably superior; on this paradox see Brodrick, ii, 349–51, 360.

[3] S. F. Smith, S.J., *Papal Supremacy and Infallibility* (1917), p. 16.

[4] J. A. Phillips, S.J., *Upon this Rock* (1949), p. 20.

[5] Labbe, viii, 548; Denzinger, 335.

led by it, may have died without valid baptism. St Athanasius pronounced baptism in the single Name to be ineffective and null.[1] Some theologians, however, think that it was at one time admitted by the Church.

Pope Eugenius IV issued a decree of instruction to the Armenians on the faith and sacraments.[2] He said that the matter of ordination to the priesthood was the tendering of the sacred vessels (the *porrectio intrumentorum*). That was erroneous.[3] He omitted to mention the laying on of hands, which is the true essential.[4] If the Armenians omitted the laying on of hands, in reliance on the pope's instruction, they may have had unordained priests administering invalid sacraments. It is answered that they must have been otherwise too well informed to trust to this.[5] Most Roman theologians deny the infallibility of Eugenius' decree; some, however, think it was infallible and therefore impregnably true.

Pope Nicholas, it is said, spoke only *obiter*, incidentally; perhaps only as a 'private doctor'.[6] It has even been said[7] that a question of the validity of baptism is a matter of discipline only, not of doctrine. Another answer is available, that these were only fallible teachings given to Bulgarians and Armenians, not infallible teaching given to the whole Church.[8] Thus it is strenuously denied that any papal blunder of the past can throw any doubt whatever upon the Definition of Infallibility. Every supposed instance is met by an answer, sometimes by several different answers. In fact there is a triplet of answers, any single one of which, if accepted, safeguards the Definition. (i) Rightly understood, the teaching was not erroneous. (ii) Any erroneous teaching was not given *ex cathedra*. (iii) If given *ex cathedra*, it was infallibly true, so that any supposed evidence of error must be illusory and wrong.

The unfortunate lapse of Pope Honorius may be briefly recalled. It has caused more anxiety to the defenders of the Definition than other difficulties because he asserted the Monothelite heresy in its express terms, 'One Will', and because he was anathematized as a heretic for generations by popes and councils. For the honour of the Definition, scholars have laboured to exonerate him; it has been a difficult and deli-

[1] Ep. i *ad Serapion.* 30, *Opp.* i, p. 678.

[2] *Decretum de Unione Armeniorum*, Raynaldus ad an. 1439, xv, (ix, 299); Denzinger, 701.

[3] In 1655, Morinus showed that *porrectio* was unknown for the first thousand years, Gore and Turner, *Church and Ministry* (1936), p. 57 n.

[4] Sheehan ii, 239; Pope Pius XII, 'Sacramentum ordinis' of 1947.

[5] Hergenröther, p. 90. [6] Ibid., p. 87.

[7] H. E. Hall, *The Petrine Office* (Catholic Truth Society, 1917), p. 16.

[8] McNabb, p. 69.

cate task. One eminent scholar for example, Bishop Hefele (with support from others), holds that Honorius intended to teach the whole Church *ex cathedra*,[1] but he argues that the teaching was not positively heretical. Contrariwise, another eminent scholar, Abbot Chapman, admits that Honorius taught heresy, but derides the idea that he did so *ex cathedra*.[2] There the matter may be left.

F. PAPAL SILENCE

Non-Roman Christians are urged to perceive the absolute need of the Church for an infallible voice, the 'living Divine Teacher'.[3] Christianity, said Newman, 'must, humanly speaking, have an infallible expounder'.[4] But orthodox Christians outside the Roman communion possess the Catholic Faith, expressed in the Catholic Creeds, and they can see nothing in Scripture, or the exposition of the Fathers, to show that God has indeed seen fit to ordain for His Church a teacher of additional dogmas. Moreover it seems to them that the actual existence in the Church of a 'living Divine Teacher' could not have remained obscure throughout the centuries, that he could not have remained dumb in times of desperate need. Yet that is what they see in the history and records of the Church. Throughout the greatest doctrinal crises for the Church, it did not occur to any one that there was a living Divine Teacher at Rome, with a voice of final authority.

> There was never, perhaps, a time of confusion in the Christian Church equal to the second century. . . . The various forms of Gnosticism were so seductive that Tertullian witnessed in his day the spectacle of 'one and another—the most faithful, the wisest, the most experienced in the Church going over to the wrong side'.[5] The points under discussion were the most fundamental conceivable, the questions of the creation of the world, the unity of God, and the reality of the Incarnation. If ever a clear rule of faith, a papal voice, a centre to Christendom was needed, it was then. But not only had the Church at that time to struggle through her difficulties without an infallible teacher, she had not even yet formulated her creeds or settled her canon.[6]

Again, when the great Arian heresy menaced the Church, when 'the whole world groaned and wondered to find itself Arian', it was not the pope of Rome but the pope of Alexandria, St Athanasius, who with

[1] Hefele, v, 61, quoting Honorius, '. . . quantum *ad dogma ecclesiasticum pertinet . . . definire debemus*'.
[2] Chapman, *Honorius*, pp. 9, 16, 17, 114.
[3] Cardinal Vaughan, in Rivington, *PC*, pp. xi, xii, xv.
[4] *Development* (1878 ed.), p. 90. [5] *De praescr.*, p. 3.
[6] Bp. C. Gore, *Roman Catholic Claims*, p. 51.

his council 'snatched the world from the jaws of Satan', whom St Gregory Nazianzen looks upon as 'entrusted with charge over the whole world'.[1] Newman and others may be perhaps harsh in condemning Pope Liberius as a 'renegade', considering the pressure put on him; but throughout that epoch of doctrinal peril, even before Liberius proved to be a broken reed, the 'living Divine Teacher' was silent and impotent.

After such monumental dumbnesses of the infallible teacher, the doctrinal feebleness of later popes is a minor matter. Thus when the preaching of Pope John XXII threw doubt on the usual doctrine of the Beatific Vision (that perfected saints may attain to it without passing through Purgatory), he was sharply challenged by the prelates and clergy of France, with royal support; whereupon he made a humble and apologetic reply.[2] He said that he was not well-read and had not meant to say anything contrary to Scripture or faith: if so he withdrew it; a submission, it has been said, 'as humble and apologetic as if he were a young student at Paris in danger of losing his bachelor's degree for heresy'.[3]

The great Cardinal Bellarmine's real trust in his infallible guide appears from his autobiography. A book by a Jesuit author was accused of semi-Pelagianism by the Dominicans, who wished Pope Clement VIII to condemn it. 'You are no theologian', said Bellarmine to him, 'and you must not think that by your own study you can come to understand so very obscure a question.' 'I mean to decide the question,' said the pope. 'Your Holiness will not decide it', retorted the Cardinal.[4]

The dogma of the Immaculate Conception[5] has a remarkable history. It is now declared to be an article of the original Deposit of Faith, which must be believed on pain of loss of salvation, equally with the mystery of the Holy Trinity. After John Duns Scotus supported it, violent disputes rent the Church. Pope after pope refused to decide the question of faith. Popes Paul V and Gregory XV said that it had not yet been revealed.[6] After two more centuries of papal ignorance and silence, Pope Pius IX declared that it was part of the original and revealed Deposit of Faith and the constant and universal belief of the Church. Popes Paul V and Gregory XV, indeed, had said that a

[1] St Jerome, supra, ch. xxvi; St Greg. Naz., *Or.*, xxi, *PG*, xxxv, 1008.
[2] Raynaldus ad an. 1334, xxvii (vi, 12); cf. Hergenröther, p. 89.
[3] H. Rashdall, *Universities of Europe* (2nd ed.), 1936, i, 552–3.
[4] Cap. xlv, Brodrick, i, 479–80; *Selbstbiographie des Cardinals Bellarmin* (Bonn, 1887), p. 260; Salmon, p. 185; see Cardinal Gasquet, *Lord Acton and his Circle* (1906), p. 52 n.
[5] Supra, ch. lxxii.
[6] Wadding, pp. 40, 425, 452.

further revelation by the Holy Ghost must be waited for, but the *Dogmatic Constitution* ruled out that view.

The doctrinal teaching of the pope is not inspired; it is guaranteed against error.[1] This now-settled doctrine emphasizes the extraordinary ineffectiveness of the popes as infallible teachers:

> If the pronouncing a decision on a controversy was solely the result of a divinely communicated impulse, and a thing in which the Pope's natural powers had no part, it were surely idle to blame him for silence and non-interference. He could say that he could only speak such words as God might be pleased to put into his mouth, and that he was bound to be silent until a Divine inspiration was communicated to him. But if the initiative rests with himself; that is to say, if the order of proceeding is, that he must first use his natural powers and ordinary means of informing his judgement, and then has a guarantee that when he publishes the result of his investigations in an *ex cathedra* decision, he will be divinely secured from error, what but want of faith in the reality of this guarantee can account for his not so using his natural powers, when a decision is urgently needed for the appeasing of controversies within his Church?[2]

G. UTILITY OF THE DOGMA

The antecedent probability or necessity that the Church should have an infallible teacher is usually put in the forefront of argument for the truth of the dogma.[3]

Non-Roman Christians rest their belief in God's dispositions upon what He has actually revealed, not on a human opinion of what He ought to do or to have done. Moreover, when they look back on the past of the Church they can see nothing to confirm this supposed 'probability'. It seems to them that if God in His wisdom had indeed appointed an infallible voice for the Church on earth, it would have been both manifest and effective. Instead of this, they see the supposed infallible guide impotent and dumb in times of crisis for the Church, yet ready enough with non-infallible dictation, sometimes of a kind very embarrassing to his loyal subjects, who are anxiously concerned to show that he has not compromised the infallibility of the Definition. Non-Roman Christians are told that there have not been many instances of the exercise of independent papal infallibility. They know that the Roman Church has learned from it (1) the necessity of being subject to the Pope, and (2) the *Dogmatic Constitution* with the dogma of Infallibility itself. It has now learned also (3) the new dogmas concerning

[1] Sheehan, i, 190; McNabb, pp. 33, 38.

[2] Salmon, p. 257.

[3] E.g., McNabb, pp. 9–31.

the Blessed Virgin. But devout saints have lived and died without any need to know these as new Articles of the Christian Faith.

Within the Roman Church, however, the utility of the dogma may be to foster a 'prudent, interior, religious assent' to anything that is currently believed and generally taught, to exhale 'an atmosphere of infallibility';[1] but authority is discreetly silent regarding much past ill-teaching and error that the Definition was designed to shut out of absolute Infallibility. This quasi-infallibility also has its embarrassments. For example, the faithful for centuries were bound to give 'interior, religious assent' to the doctrine that heretics ought to be put to death, and that it is in accordance with the will of the Holy Spirit to burn them.[2] Authority, indeed, has not as yet recanted that as doctrine.

There is a line of thought and argument peculiar to Rome and developed since the twelfth century; it underlies every characteristically Roman doctrine. It was tersely expressed by Duns Scotus as *Potuit, decuit, ergo fecit.* 'He (God) had the power; it was fitting that He should do so; therefore He did it.' Eadmer before him had reasoned thus in affirming the Immaculate Conception. As is shown in the recent Bull defining the Corporeal Assumption, devout saints from the eighth century onwards have felt it so fitting, so necessary, that God—who of course had absolute power—should ordain this in special honour for the Blessed Virgin, that He *must* have ordained it so. In regard to the whole Doctrine of the Papacy, the Roman mind is permeated and dominated by the same method of reasoning; it comes to light often in theological argument, and even in papal declarations. Thus to Newman's mind infallibility is demonstrated: 'The absolute need of a spiritual supremacy is at present the strongest of arguments in favour of its supply.... Christianity... must, humanly speaking, have an infallible expounder.' Thus taught Pope Leo XIII in 1896 in the great Encyclical 'Satis cognitum'—'Since Christ willed that His kingdom should be visible, He was obliged, when He ascended into Heaven, to designate a vicegerent on earth.... Because He was about to withdraw His visible presence from the Church, it was necessary that He should appoint someone in His place, to have charge of the universal Church.'

Potuit, decuit, ergo fecit. The logic is unanswerable, the argument is conclusive if only we are empowered to say *decuit*, to determine what particular choice or ordinance was fitting or necessary for God.

The devout Roman mind is confident that the Roman Church is so

[1] W. Ward, *William George Ward and the Catholic Revival* (1912), p. 189.

[2] Pope Leo X, Bull 'Exsurge Domine', 16 May 1520; Denzinger, p. 224; classed as infallible by Père E. Dublanchy, *Dict. de Théol Catholique* (1923).

empowered. And when the Roman Church in general has reached the stage of persuasion that God should, or must, have ordained this or that, the argument is clinched by 'tradition', in its modern 'double meaning', which 'proves' that a newly defined dogma must have been part of the original Deposit of Faith delivered by the Apostles.

The devout non-Roman mind cannot feel that even the whole Roman Church is empowered to decide on the choice God ought to have made. It firmly believes all it is able to perceive that God has actually revealed to us of His will and ordinance. It cannot accept the voice of the Roman Church or its hierarchy as equivalent to actual Apostolic Tradition and Divine Revelation.

That tremendous cleavage of thought divides Christendom.

APPENDIX

Definition of the Corporeal Assumption, 1950

Holy Scripture is reticent concerning the life of the Blessed Virgin, and silent as to its close. (According to Orthodox traditional belief, it was her desire not to be spoken of.) Christians have always thought of her as in heaven. For some thirteen centuries, her Falling-asleep, Assumption, Birthday, or Passing-away (as it was variously called) has been a festival of the Church. 'Assumption' is the day of death of any saint whose soul is received into heaven, and has been used of other saints and martyrs without implying a translation of their earthly bodies.[1] That the Blessed Virgin attained to the full glory of the Resurrection of the Body has been believed throughout all the Orthodox Eastern Church, and widely among other orthodox Christians.[2] It is not stated in Scripture and, as Pope Benedict

[1] Du Cange, *Glossarium*, i, 443; Cabrol, *Dictionnaire d'Archéologie et de Liturgie*, i, 2997.

[2] In whose general belief, however, the Resurrection of the Body does not necessarily involve a resuscitation of the actual physical particles that compose the human body at the moment of death.

XIV declared,[1] the passages adduced as proofs of it can be otherwise explained. The early Fathers were entirely silent in the matter.[2] In the fourth century, there were current various apocryphal stories of the disappearance of the venerable body, not many days after death, to the accompaniment of angelic singing. One such writing was condemned as apocryphal by Pope Gelasius I.[3] Although it is said[4] that the belief in the Corporeal Assumption was founded on one of these writings, the Bull does not refer to them, and they may be ignored. The Roman Breviary until 1570 provided for the Feast a lection that referred to the belief as uncertain.[5] Pope Benedict XIV (1740–58), although he pronounced the belief to be a venerable and pious opinion which it would be temerarious to oppose, declared that the tradition of it was not of the kind sufficient for the raising of the opinion to the rank of the Articles of Faith.[6] It has not hitherto contributed to the separation from Rome of other Christians.

The new Dogma is therefore based on Tradition in the 'double' or 'profound' sense,[7] and in the Bull 'Munificentissimus Deus' of 1 November 1950, His Holiness Pope Pius XII shows very clearly how a pious opinion, not certain or *de fide*, becomes definable as an Article of Faith; he thus illuminates the developed sense of Tradition, and its potency in the formation of dogma.

Since the definition in 1854 of the Immaculate Conception, there had been innumerable petitions for a definition of the Assumption, the two privileges of the Blessed Virgin being intimately related by the connexion between original sin and death. His Holiness had ascertained from all the bishops a remarkable unanimity of the whole Church on the definability of the Bodily Assumption as a Dogma of Faith; this showed that the ordinary teaching authority and the belief of the faithful were in accord, and thereby proved with infallible certainty that it is a truth revealed by God and is contained in the Deposit of Faith. There were proofs and traces of this common faith from early times. Thus the Feast of the Assumption was given gradually greater and greater prominence by the Holy See. Many saints, from St John Damascene (†749) to St Alphonso Liguori (†1787) declared that a mortal dissolu-

[1] *De festis*, II, viii, 18; *Opp.* (Venice, 1767), ix, 190.

[2] Ibid., sect 15 (ix, 189), 'the most ancient Fathers of the primitive Church'.

[3] *PL*, lix, 162; see James, pp. 194–227; he said nothing concerning the belief itself.

[4] *Cath. Enc.*, ii, 6.

[5] 'In what manner, or at what time, or by whom that most holy body was carried away, or whether translated, or whether it rose again, we know not.' See *PL*, xxx, 123.

[6] *De festis*, loc. cit.

[7] See above, ch. lxxii (ii).

tion of that supremely holy body was unthinkable; believing in the Corporeal Assumption, they found allusions to it in many Scriptural passages, recognizing for example Our Lady as the Ark in the psalm: 'Arise, O Lord, into thy resting place: thou and the ark which thou hast sanctified',[1] and as 'the Woman arrayed with the sun' in the Apocalypse.[2]

His Holiness therefore deemed that the time appointed by God had arrived for the definition of this truth, and with full solemnities he defined: 'that it is a dogma divinely revealed that the Immaculate Mother of God, Mary Ever Virgin, when the course of her life was finished, was taken up body and soul into Heaven'.

This is therefore now an Article of Faith in the Roman Church, to be believed with the same absolute faith as the Resurrection of our Lord.[3]

But whether or not the Blessed Virgin actually died[4] has been left by the Bull a completely open question, which is now under earnest discussion.[5] 'The definition of the Assumption is the starting-point for a steady increase in number of those who hold that Our Blessed Lady did not die.'[6] If that comes to be the general belief, a future Definition may declare that it is part of the original Apostolic Tradition, and add it to the Faith.[7]

[1] Vulgate and Douai version of Ps. cxxxi (cxxxii), 8, quoted in the Bull.

[2] xii, 1–6; some Roman theologians regard this as the best or only Scriptural support. Other passages referred to are: Gen. iii, 15; Ps. xliv, 10, 14–16 (xlv, 9, 13–15); Cant. iv, 8; vi, 9 (10); viii, 5; Is. lx, 13; Luke i, 28; Rom. v, vi; 1 Cor. xv, 21–6, 54–7; Eph. v, 27; 1 Tim. i, 17; iii, 15.

[3] It has been suggested that, 'in a way, the Assumption of Mary focuses the issue raised by the Resurrection more sharply than even the Resurrection itself', Walter J. Ong, in *The Month*, December 1951, at p. 367.

[4] As the fourth-century apocryphal stories asserted.

[5] Most Rev. G. M. Roschini, O.S.M., 'Did Our Lady Die?' in *Irish Eccles. Record*, Aug. 1953, vol. LXX.

[6] Ibid., p. 88.

[7] See above, ch. LXII (ii).

I. Index of Persons, Places and Councils

II. Subject Index

INDEX